Queen Victoria's Archbishops of Canterbury

— MICHAEL CHANDLER —

Sacristy Press

Sacristy Press
PO Box 612, Durham, DH1 9HT

www.sacristy.co.uk

First published in 2019 by Sacristy Press, Durham

Copyright © Michael Chandler 2019
The moral rights of the author have been asserted.

All rights reserved, no part of this publication may be reproduced or transmitted in any form or by any means, electronic, mechanical photocopying, documentary, film or in any other format without prior written permission of the publisher.

Scripture quotations, unless otherwise stated, are from the New Revised Standard Version Bible: Anglicized Edition, copyright © 1989, 1995 National Council of the Churches of Christ in the United States of America. Used by permission. All rights reserved worldwide.

Every reasonable effort has been made to trace the copyright holders of material reproduced in this book, but if any have been inadvertently overlooked the publisher would be glad to hear from them.

Sacristy Limited, registered in England & Wales, number 7565667

British Library Cataloguing-in-Publication Data
A catalogue record for the book is available from the British Library

Paperback ISBN 978-1-78959-056-2
Hardback ISBN 978-1-78959-059-3

To Janet and our family

Foreword

"Never since the Reformation has there been such a crisis of danger to the church," wrote Bishop Bagot of Oxford, "and the peace and unity of the Church may, and I fear does, much depend upon the course of so humble an individual as myself—who took this diocese solely from its smallness, quietness and the little anxiety it need give one."

He was writing about the rise of Tractarianism in the midst of his "small, quiet" diocese. It was just one of the crises to hit the Victorian Church of England. If Bishop Bagot was disturbed, it was even more the case that the Archbishop of Canterbury had cause for discomfort. Archbishops were the top of the tree and had to navigate complex power games with the Crown, Parliament, and a Church full of both passion and apathy.

This crisis was but one of many that faced Victorian archbishops. What this colourful period needs is a skilled interpreter, and this is what it has been given in this fine book by Michael Chandler. Michael is a master of his subject, deeply immersed in nineteenth-century ecclesiastical life. He has written widely on the Oxford Movement and its key characters, vividly explaining and exploring the issues of the time. Here again he proves to be an amiable and trustworthy guide.

The six archiepiscopal subjects of his book are as varied as they are fascinating. William Howley was a natural conservative and the last archbishop to wear a wig. He had to face the challenge of the Roman Catholic Relief Bill of 1829 and the Reform Bill of 1832, both of which he opposed. John Bird Sumner is sometimes thought of as the first modern evangelical to be Archbishop of Canterbury. More progressive and practical than his predecessor he was more a pastor than a politician, and was described by Samuel Wilberforce as "good, gentle, loving and weak". Charles Longley arrived from having been the Archbishop of York and had come via one version of the usual route: Winchester, Oxford, headmaster of Harrow, Bishop of Ripon, Bishop of Durham. His abiding legacy was the first Lambeth Conference, dominated as it was by the crisis over Bishop Colenso of Natal.

Archbishop Archibald Tait had suffered the calamitous loss of five of his six daughters to scarlet fever while Dean of Carlisle. He had to manage the Anglo-Catholic revival and the vexed question of ritualism, making the mistake of trying to stamp it out with a Private Members Bill. The autocratic Edward White Benson came next and is known for the introduction of the service of nine lessons and carols and the unfortunate trial of the saintly Bishop of Lincoln, Edward King. That left Frederick Temple to see out the century, taking on the role of archbishop at seventy-six and with failing sight. He was austere on the surface but compassionate within, and deeply concerned about unity in the still fractious Church of England.

Michael Chandler introduces us to each of these archbishops with fluent insights, telling anecdotes and well-chosen quotes. To place each archbishop in historical context requires a clear grasp of nineteenth century social upheavals and political machinations. Michael achieves this with distinction, deftly handling the rich cast of characters and the tasks they faced against the background of dynamic social change. The analysis is acute and the pace relentless.

Four of these considerable archiepiscopal figures had previously been headmasters of England's famous public schools. Harold Macmillan was a Governor of Eton when he said, "It's good to have a clergyman as a school headmaster. If he's a failure, you can always make him a bishop."

This career path has dried up since the Victorian archbishops. In any case, I doubt they would have approved of Macmillan's observation. What I am hope they would have approved of is this fascinating and very welcome account of the ministries at Canterbury of six able men, struggling to make sense of one of the most difficult roles in the Church of God.

+John Pritchard
Bishop of Oxford, 2007–2014

Contents

Foreword iv
Introduction 1

Chapter 1. William Howley (1828–1848) 21
Chapter 2. John Bird Sumner (1848–1862) 77
Chapter 3. Charles Thomas Longley (1862–1868). 127
Chapter 4. Archibald Campbell Tait (1868–1882). 181
Chapter 5. Edward White Benson (1883–1896) 237
Chapter 6. Frederick Temple (1896–1902) 291

Conclusion 351
Bibliography 356
Notes 361

Introduction

"The steam of the first locomotive passed Rugby", and the sight symbolized "the death blow of the feudal system," said the Reverend Dr Thomas Arnold, Headmaster of Rugby School. The railway reached Rugby in September 1838, just a few months before Queen Victoria ascended the throne. Arnold died in 1842, but his observation was recalled many years afterwards by E. W. Benson, later the Queen's penultimate Archbishop of Canterbury.[1] As this anecdote illustrates, by the start of the Queen's reign the social fabric of Britain was changing, even though much English life continued to be largely rural and agricultural. Some, like Thomas Arnold, perceived what was developing, but relatively few foresaw the magnitude of the upheavals that were occurring, and even fewer were able to make a difference.

The Church of England was one of the country's most significant institutions, but its leaders were slow to recognize what was happening and were unprepared to make the changes which nineteenth-century life would demand. This was not due to obduracy, but as Canon Henry Scott Holland, writing later with colourful dismay, described it, the Church of England at the time when Queen Victoria came to the throne was "snug and smug among the hedgerows . . . tied up in Elizabethan red tape, smothered under the convention of Establishment, fat with dignities and very scant of breath."[2] Historically, its parishes had developed in an almost exclusively rural economy, so they struggled to meet the challenges of urban developments which had begun before the new reign. Matthew Arnold (1822–1888), the eldest son of Thomas Arnold, a prolific author and a lay theologian, described the situation in 1877 in words that could have been written in his father's time. He said that the Church of England was "an institution devoted above all to the landed gentry, but also to the propertied and satisfied classes generally: favouring immobility, preaching submission, and reserving transformation in general for the other side

1

of the grave."[3] Yet the Church of England proved able to reinvent itself, and Scott Holland went on to refer to the remarkable way in which the apparently somnolent Church had under its calm exterior the potential for dynamic adaptation at home and also for growth across the world of the British Empire. The Church, he said, "has thrown feelers out far and wide. It has overleaped the paddock fence. It has flung out its frontier line. It has set sail on every wind that blows; and planted its feet on every shore that ocean washes." Holland's stirring words tend to conceal that the witness in the colonies was erratic as the empire expanded, although the beginning of the organization of the Anglican Communion was to be a very significant achievement later in the reign.

Similarly, the witness in England was also not the outcome of any considered policy or policies. It was a pragmatic process by which the Church perceived and responded to some of the needs of the developing society and, at the same time, made its own adjustments to its witness and the proclamation of the Christian gospel in changing circumstances. The Church of England was presented with urban challenges in Britain to which its ancient and rural parochial structure could only respond in piecemeal ways. There was often a lack of provision for effective spiritual or pastoral ministry in the changing circumstances. When this was recognized, it was often followed by bafflement as to what ought to be done within a system that seemed unable to adapt. Parochial clergy were generally ill-equipped to address the new problems. They were recruited exclusively from the educated classes, but they received no professional training in the early decades of the century and were often helpless in circumstances beyond their experience and control. Alongside this sense of bewilderment, a factor which added to the inflexibility of the system was the long-accepted practice of ecclesiastical pluralism, whereby successful clergy held a portfolio of lucrative appointments, employing less fortunate clergy as curates to do the work for only a modest stipend. Pluralists had strong reasons for maintaining existing practices, yet the absence of the actual office holder could militate against properly effective ministry in such places. In the circumstances, the clergy of the Church of England were fortunate not to experience the anti-clericalism that developed in France after the Revolution of 1789. The Church woke only gradually to the changing demands of nineteenth-century life, because its mindset was largely unable to perceive the profundity of those demands. It would be a mistake, however, to draw conclusions entirely unfavourable to the Church. There were conscientious clergy and bishops, and committed laity, battling against the odds in an ecclesiastical environment which was unimaginable only a few decades earlier, but the Church needed to renew its spiritual life if it was to recover anything like its authority and standing among the English people.

Archbishops and bishops lead the Church of England and are recruited from the ranks of other clergy. Consequently, the leadership of the Church was every bit as out of touch as the parish clergy. For over a thousand years, bishops had been courtiers and administrators at governmental level, in England and across Europe. This role still cast its shadow across the nineteenth-century Church of England. It had made inevitable a remoteness from the anxieties and needs of ordinary people; bishops and archbishops had been largely distanced from the worship and occasional offices of parochial life. Early nineteenth-century episcopal life and work was as remote from the concerns of the dwellers in the new urbanized industrial areas as the lives of the medieval "prince bishops" had been from the rustic population of earlier centuries. In nineteenth-century England that was to change as bishops became more intimately involved in the life and work of their dioceses, in addition to their continuing political role in the House of Lords. Men like Samuel Wilberforce, who served successively as Bishop of Oxford and then of Winchester, and Charles James Blomfield of Chester and then of London, were particularly fine examples of bishops who raised the diocesan work of the episcopate to new levels of involvement and efficiency. The archbishops of Canterbury and York continued to be significant national figures and also became more involved in their dioceses in the long reign of Queen Victoria, and they also found that their work expanded because of the development of the wider Anglican Communion.

A deep conservatism was entrenched in the decades before Queen Victoria came to the throne. The ruling classes had been much alarmed by the revolution in France at the end of the eighteenth century. Some had initially welcomed the French Revolution, particularly the first generation of those whose names are linked to the Romantic period in English literature. Most often cited are William Blake, Samuel Taylor

Coleridge, and William Wordsworth, whose well-known initial reaction is frequently quoted, "bliss was it in that dawn to be alive." But this enthusiasm was soon left behind, having been by no means widespread, as the Revolution's idealism gave way to the Terror, which cost many thousands of lives, the rise of Napoleon, long years of war, and the fear of a French invasion. There developed, in the British establishment, a determination that nothing like the French Revolution should be allowed to happen here. That reactionary mindset made the prospect of political and social reform an object of dread to many. As a result, the country and its institutions remained ill-equipped to deal with change in any practical way, and the bishops and clergy could hardly be blamed for sharing that view.

Change, which would have an impact on Church life as in all other areas, was a major and unavoidable consequence in Britain of the ongoing development of manufacturing industries, with the subsequent urbanization and a growth in population. Industrialism was behind the inexorable shift from an agrarian to an urban economy with subsequent and widespread social consequences, not least for the ancient parochial arrangements of the Church of England. This process is baldly evident in the decennial census returns which had begun in 1801. That census revealed that the population stood at 15.8 million. Forty years later the first census held in the reign of Queen Victoria took place. It recorded the population of the United Kingdom at 26.8 million in 1841. By the end of the Queen's reign, the 1901 census recorded a total population of 41.6 million, nearly triple the figure of a hundred years before.[4] Significantly, the census of 1851 revealed that more than half the population had become located in urban areas. A decade later this change was recognized as irreversible, and the 1881 census revealed that more than two thirds of the population were urban dwellers. This was driven by the development of manufacturing industries which required large numbers of workers and led to newly urbanized areas that were often overcrowded and insanitary. The unplanned industrialization of the nation lay behind William Blake's telling phrase of "dark satanic mills", which burned itself into the national consciousness. The chronicle of the Archbishops of Canterbury in Queen Victoria's reign illustrates the reaction of the Church of England as it roused itself to face the challenges of its changing environment.

In England, bishops continued to be important men at the level of national life, and archbishops even more so, even as the increasing claims of their diocesan and pastoral responsibilities developed. The response was unplanned and unavoidably erratic, but it shows how the largely somnolent Church of England was capable of reinventing itself. Matthew Arnold's gloomy view of the Church of the eighteenth century has already been noticed, but it would be a mistake to impute from his words that the Church was culpably negligent. A large part of its incompetence was no one's fault and was due to the burden of the history of the Church as an institution.

Gradually, more effective parish clergy began to be recruited for the densely populated industrial areas and devoted themselves to pastoral work in demanding or unpleasant circumstances. Effective parish priests were able to create communities in such localities, but their heroic efforts only scratched the surface. The work was urgent, hard, and seemed overwhelming. Few could do it well, but that did not detract at all from the fact that many clergy were conscientious and worked hard at their ministry in overcrowded slums. Some were notably successful in an urban ministry, and two examples can illustrate this. One was Walter Hook, Vicar of Coventry from 1828 and, later, of Leeds from 1837 to 1859; he had been nurtured in the old High-Church mode. In one part of his parish in Leeds, many thousands were crowded in one squalid and disease-ridden area; often the diseases were cholera or typhus. Hook's energy and insight made him redoubtable and, although not unique, earned him an honoured place in the history of the Church of England. He created new parishes equipped with churches and schools and also vicarages. Another notable example was the evangelical Charles Simeon (1759–1836), who combined a college fellowship with his energetic parochial work as Vicar of Holy Trinity in Cambridge. As will be seen, he had a significant influence on J. B. Sumner, who became the second Archbishop of Canterbury of Queen Victoria's reign. Simeon served the university and the city of Cambridge for fifty years and ministered to generations of undergraduates. His influence was thereby spread across the country and was a significant element in Victorian evangelicalism. Later, Simeon's influence was further spread by the purchase of the right to appoint clergy to parishes, known as advowsons; a plan with which his trustees continued after his death. The process enabled the appointment of evangelical incumbents, and the Simeon Trustees eventually became a significant force within the parochial system; his funeral in 1836 was attended by many hundreds of mourners from across the country, his parish and the university.

Prior to the accession of Queen Victoria, the Evangelical Revival had for decades been influencing English life. Many earnest Christian believers of a protestant cast of mind had looked outside the Church of England for spiritual solace to nonconformity. Those who accepted the Calvinistic doctrine of predestination followed leaders such as George Whitefield; others, less rigorous doctrinally, accepted the Arminian teaching of John Wesley and his followers. However, a third strand of the Evangelical Revival consisted of those who sought to revitalize the Church of England from within, of whom Charles Simeon and Archbishop John Sumner may be considered as representative. Across the Evangelical Revival, there developed an increased devotion to scripture and an increasing emphasis on its inerrancy. With that phenomenon came an emphasis on the importance of the doctrine of atonement for the salvation of the individual sinful soul. Evangelical clergy often preached powerfully in ways which appealed to the emotions as much as to the intellect, and the gradual spread of evangelical convictions in the Church led to a recognizable grouping, which eventually became an influential party. Like their nonconformist compatriots, the evangelical party within the Church of England emphasized the forgiveness of sins, salvation through a personal relationship with Christ, and taught that a true relationship with God in Christ was established as the result of the conversion of the individual. This was combined with belief in the regeneration of the believer's soul under the purifying and guiding action of the Holy Spirit. The emphasis on the personal religious experience of the individual believer meant that this school of thought sat relatively lightly to form and order within the Church. By such "Church evangelicals" the clergy, not excepting bishops and archbishops, were perceived as functionaries who were useful for the proper ordering of the life of the institution, but not as essential to the nature of the Church. The two dominical sacraments were important to the evangelicals, but principally as commemorative acts. As such, the Church was not perceived as a divinely founded institution or organization, and church buildings were convenient as places of assembly for prayer and praise, and to hear the Scriptures expounded.

Notwithstanding the evangelical tendency to concentrate on the religious experience of the individual believer, an outstanding example of evangelical effort is to be seen in the combined work of a number of men who became known as the "Clapham Sect". The name was coined by the unsympathetic clerical wit Sydney Smith as a result of their custom to worship at the parish church in Clapham because of the proximity of the homes of more than a few of them. Inspired by their personal experience of evangelical conversion and salvation they were a collection of mostly wealthy laymen who cooperated informally. Smith's designation became widely used because of its convenience, even though it suggests that they were more of a religious society with agreed goals rather than simply a number of like-minded individuals linked by personal friendships, although they founded a number of societies which were lastingly influential. Their endeavours were motivated by a sense of moral responsibility, which led to dedicated service to charitable causes. The most prominent individual who was at the centre of the Sect and whose name is still, and rightly, remembered was William Wilberforce (1759–1833), the Member of Parliament who succeeded in banning slavery and, ultimately, the trade in slaves throughout the range of Britain's influence. The Clapham Sect was most active in the decades before the beginning of the reign of Queen Victoria, but its influence was long lasting.

From 1792 to 1813, the Rector of Clapham had been John Venn. He had a keen sense of the wider implications of the Christian faith and is remembered as one of the founders of the Society for Missions to Africa and the East. Later, this developed into the Church Missionary Society which was a dynamic force throughout the mid-nineteenth century and beyond, and was largely run by his son, who became its long-serving secretary in 1841. In political terms, the Clapham men tended to be conservative in their convictions about social order. This dedication was motivated by their individual awareness of the believer's moral obligations arising from his personal belief in Christ as each person's saviour. Among the societies it promoted, the Sect was associated with the founding of the British and Foreign Bible Society. It was also concerned about moral standards, about the welfare of the poor, and the provision of Sunday schools. Its members were well-connected and consequently exercised a wide influence on public life. The Clapham Sect was the most important manifestation of evangelical solidarity.

Another important group, but with a markedly different theological emphasis, developed around a parish a few miles to the south of Clapham and also a little later. The so-called "Hackney Phalanx" was centred on the parish of Hackney, where the rector was John James Watson. They drew their inspiration from the old-fashioned sort of high churchmanship that had prevailed before the Evangelical Revival. The term was first encountered in the biography of one of its principal associates, Joshua Watson (1771–1855), brother of the rector. They were brought together not only by family links, but also (like the Clapham Sect) by friendship and shared interests. They believed the Church to be uniquely the source of that grace which can only be found through the sacraments, and that the episcopate is the Church's necessary form of governance; it was altogether a higher doctrine of the Church. One of their most profound convictions was that the Church of England was unique in rejecting the excesses of medieval Roman Catholicism and the later excesses of Protestantism. Joshua Watson was a wealthy man who retired early, aged forty-three, from his business as a wine merchant and devoted his life to the Church of England, which he loved and believed to be "divinely appointed". He was an example of the finest type of devout layman, accustomed to call Sunday "the day of the Eucharist". Joshua Watson was a man who was both influential and philanthropic. He even bought a periodical, *The British Critic*, in 1812 to gain publicity for the views of the Phalanx. This may have strengthened the idea that the Hackney men were more of an organization than simply another like-minded group who sought to cooperate. The so-called Phalanx was more than a forum where high churchmen met informally and discussed the future work of the Church. In 1811 it founded the National Society for the Education of the Poor in the Principles of the Established Church, and later was behind the Church Building Society. The Phalanx included, among others, H. H. Norris, who was John James Watson's curate and later colleague in a newly-founded parish of South Hackney, and William Stevens (1732-1807), the treasurer to Queen Anne's Bounty, who was another devout and self-effacing layman, the original "Nobody" of Nobody's Club, a high church dining group, which later became known as Nobody's Friends. Also involved were Charles Manners-Sutton and Ralph Churton, who wrote a biography of Joshua Watson and who ended his career as Archdeacon of St David's. Another was William Van Mildert (1765-1836), who became Bishop of Durham in 1826. William Howley, when Bishop of London, appreciated their Tory cast of mind and shared some of their views on social and theological issues, although he did not embrace all their enthusiasms. Several of them lived to see Howley succeed Manners-Sutton as Archbishop of Canterbury.

———

Enthusiasts of all opinions realized that the urban population in many places exceeded the seating capacity of the parish churches, and a desire grew to build new churches and expand existing ones. Walter Hook, in his parochial ministry, was exceptionally good at this, but it needed organizing on a scale greater than that of any particular parish. The Church Building Society has already been mentioned. It was founded in 1818, in large part inspired by Watson and his fellow workers. In that year, the government gave one million pounds as a thank offering for the victory of Waterloo; in addition, in 1824, a further half million pounds was given; the monies were exclusively for the established Church. These were the largest donations among many; donors included the king and many wealthy individuals. The expenditure was overseen by a permanent body of commissioners. By 1830, 130 new churches had been built, a number which rose to 612 by 1857. A less worthy but occasionally acknowledged part of the motivation of the new society was to prevent parishioners from attending nonconformist chapels because of the established Church's lack of pew accommodation, especially as the trading classes became wealthier. But the motives of the society were not about maintaining privilege and cannot fairly be dismissed as such. It was an effective body, and eventually six million pounds was spent on building new churches.

The initiatives which have been described so far took place against the background of the ongoing life of the Church of England and did not disturb the manner in which the established Church operated. In fact, these gradual adaptations to the circumstances of the nineteenth century were sustained by the way the Church was governed, a result of one of the most remarkable aspects of the English Reformation. This was the survival of the traditional orders of ministry in the Church: bishops, priests, and deacons. This phenomenon was regarded by high churchmen as providential, and it was certainly convenient.

Some background can be given in brief form. Until the Reformation, archbishops and bishops had been appointed by the Pope. However, from about the time of the Norman Conquest, the English monarch had enjoyed considerable freedom of choice in nominating to Rome individuals whom he found congenial. Although there were occasions of disagreement, usually the monarch successfully secured the appointment of his nominee. From the fourteenth century, English law had repeatedly sought to assert the rights of the Crown against the claims of the papacy. The legislation went under the general title of Praemunire, and it eventually gave King Henry VIII the opportunity to act against Cardinal Wolsey in 1529, just a few years before the final break with Rome. Unsurprisingly, the English Reformation strengthened the Crown's position. Archbishops and bishops were appointed exclusively by the sovereign under the Appointment of Bishops Act of 1533, which removed all domestic and foreign constraints from the English monarch, although even Henry VIII did sometimes consult advisors. The theory of the relationship of the Church and the State was formally described in the preamble to the Statute by which King Henry abolished the right of clergy to appeal to Rome in matters of clerical discipline. The preamble to the first Statute declared, "England is an Empire . . . governed by one supreme head and king . . . ." As such it has "all sorts and degrees of people divided in terms and by names of spirituality and temporality."[5] Thus England was an independent, self-contained nation which had two intimately interconnected aspects, each of which managed its own affairs under the supremacy of the Crown. One was the State, the civil authority;

and the other was the spiritual body, the Church. Consequently, Church and State were seen to be coextensive, consisting of the same persons; its drawback was that many regarded the Church of England as a department of the State. This phenomenon, naturally attractive to politicians, was known as Erastianism. This situation was scarcely modified over several centuries, despite the growth of nonconformity and also a developing sense of toleration after the religious upheavals of the sixteenth and seventeenth centuries. The sixteenth-century Elizabethan Settlement, reinforced after the restoration of the monarchy in 1660, identified the House of Commons with the "lay voice" of the Church of England and the Convocations of Canterbury and York with the "clerical voice". This, when stated so baldly, is an oversimplification of the subtleties of a situation which was further complicated when Convocation collapsed into abeyance in the eighteenth century, and its meetings became the briefest of formalities. The revival of Convocation in the middle of the nineteenth century, which will be noticed below under the relevant archbishops, is an indication of the Church's growth in self-confidence and reveals a weakening of Erastianism.

Another relevant historical factor was the later seventeenth century requirement for all Members of Parliament to be communicant members of the Church of England; a similar obligation was laid upon all holders of civic office. Whether this ideal was ever achieved in more than notional terms cannot be known; some individuals rejected the claims and authority of the Church of England from the start, and others only conformed because of this obligation and to avoid the penalties attached to contumacy. Consequently, by the late eighteenth century Erastianism was dominant, and the Church had largely come to be seen as subservient to the State. Archbishops and bishops tended to be regarded as part of the mechanism of the State and were appointed for their political usefulness to the governing interest, and their diocesan responsibilities were secondary to such considerations. As a result of bishops having seats in the House of Lords, prime ministers tried to ensure that they appointed to the episcopate men on whose support they could rely. Sometimes the outcome was very unsatisfactory. Perhaps the individual who illustrates this most vividly, although he was not entirely unique, was the long-lived Benjamin Hoadly (1676–1761). Remembered principally for a controversy brought about by his liberal theology expressed in a sermon preached before the king and later published, Hoadly was Bishop of Bangor. He spent most of his time in London, and it is thought that he never visited Bangor; however, he was promoted and ended his days as Bishop of Winchester. Such indifference by a bishop to his diocese became unthinkable. By the end of Queen Victoria's reign, bishops were known to their clergy and much more involved in the life of their dioceses than had been the case even in the 1830s.

The appointment of archbishops and bishops was a valuable element of patronage which the prime minister had acquired and which he could use to strengthen his government. The arrangement achieved its final form because the first Hanoverian monarch, King George I, did not speak English and knew almost nothing about the Church of England. The political usefulness of the episcopate in the House of Lords meant that prime ministers were anxious to retain the right to nominate the Church's leaders; they also preferred to be free of any obligation to consult beforehand. This obviously applied most acutely with regard to the archbishops of Canterbury and York. They were chosen by the prime minister from the existing episcopate (although in theory the prime minister was not restricted to those already in episcopal orders). It was not until quite late in the nineteenth century that prime ministers allowed political motives to dominate the exercise of such useful patronage. Queen Victoria's first prime minister, the cynical and worldly but theologically informed Lord Melbourne, wrote that " . . . I feel myself bound to recommend for promotion clergymen whose general views on political matters coincide with my own . . . ."[6] This sentence neatly summarizes the situation, although Melbourne, who read the Early Fathers for pleasure, added that he always sought candidates whose "doctrines are . . . in unison with those of the Established Church." This element in the selection process (if, indeed, it can be called a process) became less dominant as Victoria's reign progressed, although Disraeli saw no reason to stop exploiting a system that served the needs of his government. However, it was largely abandoned by the 1870s and came to be remembered with distaste in the later decades of the nineteenth century. Credit for the change is generally given to Gladstone, who as a loyal, well-informed, and widely-read churchman tried conscientiously to make appointments according to the needs of the Church.

The prime ministerial right and duty to nominate a preferred individual for an episcopal or archiepiscopal appointment came with the full expectation that the proposed name would be accepted by the sovereign. However, the monarch never lost the liberty to suggest alternative candidates and retained the power to veto nominees. Both sides usually tried to avoid confrontation, but occasionally the sovereign tried to rebel. A successful instance occurred when George III hastily offered the Archbishopric of Canterbury to Charles Manners-Sutton in 1805, before the Prime Minister, William Pitt the Younger, could nominate his former tutor, George Pretyman Tomline, the Bishop of Lincoln. Pitt was not pleased and quarrelled with the king, but had to accept the situation, and it never happened again. As will become clear, Queen Victoria was not afraid to argue. She readily expressed her opinion, and as she got older, she argued more often; sometimes she prevailed, not least in the appointment of Archibald Campbell Tait to Canterbury in 1868. However, she never confronted any of her prime ministers in the way that her grandfather had out-manoeuvred Pitt.

An energetic prime minister might need the active support of the Archbishop of Canterbury and his episcopal colleagues in the Lords in times of political conflict or difficulty: in calmer days that influence would be less important. Despite the continuing appeal of Erastianism for prime ministers, by the beginning of the reign of Queen Victoria no one could pretend that Parliament was the lay expression of the Church of England; the old conviction that Parliament and the Church of England were simply two sides of the same coin was untenable. Yet even before the decline of the practice of overtly political appointments, the influence wielded in the House of Lords, and elsewhere, by the individual archbishops and bishops obviously varied according to the personalities involved, so a prime minister was, at best, taking a calculated risk with every appointment. So the skills and personality of the man chosen to be archbishop became more important than his political usefulness, particularly when religious toleration showed that a person could be a member of a religious body other than the Church of England, or indeed to have no religious affiliation, without being a threat to the established order or regarded as disloyal to the country.

Parliament recognized the need to address anomalies from previous generations, including some which affected the Church of England. Several were dealt with before the Queen's reign commenced. First of all were the civil difficulties caused by the continuance on the statute book of the Corporation Act of 1661 and the Test Act of 1673, which can be briefly summarized. The former had been passed by the so-called Cavalier Parliament following the restoration of King Charles II in 1660 and had been designed to exclude non-Anglicans from public life. It required members of municipal corporations to be communicant members of the Church of England and to take an oath that they would not rebel against the monarchy. The Test Act had tightened the screw by requiring all office holders under the Crown to take an oath of supremacy and allegiance to the king, to receive Holy Communion according to the rites and ceremonies of the Church of England, and to sign a declaration against transubstantiation. Unsuccessful attempts at repealing both Acts had been made in 1787, 1788, and 1790, and by the reign of King William IV it had become apparent that this anomalous legislation was urgently overdue for repeal. They were eventually repealed in 1828 and 1829 respectively. Three important contemporary legislative issues which affected the Church of England must also be noticed. They were the Act for Roman Catholic Emancipation in 1829, the Great Reform Act of 1832, and the Irish Church Temporalities Act of 1833.

The contentious issue of Roman Catholic emancipation had been developing for more than twenty years. The Act of Union with Ireland, passed in 1800, had brought the population of the island of Ireland under the rule of Parliament. That population numbered around seven million, of whom about two-thirds were Roman Catholic. The Act created a significant number of constituencies with new Members of Parliament representing them. Many Irish Roman Catholics gained the right to vote as a result of the Act, and in some constituencies they formed the majority of the electorate, but Roman Catholics were excluded from sitting as Members of Parliament. It was inevitable that eventually one of their number would stand for election and be successful, and it happened in 1828. The Prime Minister, the Duke of Wellington, realized that action was essential if the situation was to be peacefully resolved. Faced by the facts he decided that Roman Catholic emancipation posed less of a threat than the prospect of civil war in Ireland. His plan was very unpopular in England, and Wellington himself was not keen on the idea except as a necessity. A Private Member's Bill for emancipation had been proposed by Sir Francis Burdett in 1825 but had failed. Wellington's Bill was eventually carried and came into law in 1829. In a real sense, the repeal of the Test and Corporation Acts, together with the Roman Catholic Emancipation Act, effectively marked the end of what has been called "the confessional state".

A second issue arose after Whigs replaced Wellington's administration in 1830 at the general election necessitated by the death of King George IV. The bishops in the Lords, and many other clergy and laity, became anxious about the Church's future when the Whigs took office with the intention to reform Parliament and improve representation in the House of Commons. Most obvious and most necessary was the need to alter the property conditions of the franchise and the distribution of seats. There was a significant number of "rotten boroughs", which returned Members of Parliament at the whim of local aristocrats and landowners. Other boroughs had few electors to return, in some cases, more than one Member of Parliament. Yet others, particularly the newly developed industrial towns, were underrepresented and some had no representation at all. The new government with Lord Grey as Prime Minister introduced a Bill in 1831. When it reached the House of Lords there was trouble, and it was rejected by forty-one votes. The majority of the bishops voted against the Bill and made up more than half of those opposed. The press was not slow to point out that without episcopal opposition the Bill would have passed. Nationally, the Bill was generally popular, so its loss generated much public anger, even among those classes which would not have benefited if it had passed. There were pamphlets and protests and heckling at a meeting chaired by Archbishop Howley. There was even rioting in several towns; the house of the Bishop of Bristol was burned to the ground, and a number of bishops, including Howley, feared further violence. Despite the rejection of the Bill, the proposals for parliamentary reform had caught the mood of the nation, and there was no way that it would be allowed to fade away. Grey was an astute man, and in 1832 he decided to bring it back again. His confidence was well-placed. The House of Lords did not have the stomach to continue the fight, and quite a few of the bishops had also reconsidered. The Bill passed the Lords in April. Twelve of the bishops voted in favour, although sixteen continued their opposition, but they were among the minority. The Bill passed into law and became known to history as the Great Reform Act of 1832. It was one of the most important political upheavals of nineteenth-century Britain. A constitutional crisis had been averted, but many churchmen were left fearful that the Church of England might be the next target of the Whigs' reforming zeal.

In 1833, the Whigs did turn their attention to the Church, but decided to tackle the anomalies of the Church in Ireland, where it had few adherents in relation to an over-large hierarchy and was a minority of the population. The planned legislation was known as the Irish Church Temporalities Bill. There was an outcry, although there was a general recognition that the existing arrangements did need reform. They decided to abolish two archbishoprics and reduce the number of other Irish bishoprics. In addition, parishes were to be amalgamated and others, which had very few or even no parishioners who were not Roman Catholic, were abolished, as was the levying of the so-called "Church rate". No decision was made about redistribution of the revenues which the reforms would release, although there was no lack of suggestions, some of which were unacceptable to members of the Church, but revenue was a secondary matter to them. Objections were based on two anxieties, which might be described as political and theological respectively. First, if the government was able to make such sweeping changes to the Church in Ireland, there existed the possibility that it might turn its hand next to the Church in England. Members of the Church began to fear the possibility of disestablishment and disendowment. The second fear arose from the conviction that if the Church was to be reformed, it should be the Church that initiated and carried through the process; that the government had no right to interfere with the governance of a divine society. Conservative churchmen were vociferous with pamphlets, sermons, and meetings. One sermon which dealt with the issue and became historically famous came from an unexpected quarter. In Oxford, it was the custom, as in other places, for judges to attend a church service before the assizes. The preacher in St Mary's Church, Oxford, for the Assize Service on 14 July 1833 was the learned and devout John Keble. He used the opportunity to attack the Bill, although he did so with characteristic courtesy, expressing himself in such a way that a modern reader of his sermon can hardly detect any vehemence.

The Irish Church Temporalities Act did become law and the reforms were carried out, and men with a high doctrine of the Church, such as Keble, were more fearful that the government might force through unwelcome reforms in England. The very idea that the secular authorities had no right to interfere with the Church flew absolutely in the face of the comfortable Erastianism that had prevailed for so long; as did those who believed the authority and the motivation for church reform could come only from within the Church. At about the time that Keble was preparing his Assize Sermon, a small group of similar-minded clergy were meeting to discuss the situation at Hadleigh in Essex. They decided to produce pamphlets setting out their convictions. In addition, John Henry Newman, the Vicar of St Mary's, Oxford, had been reflecting on his calling whilst abroad. He was fired-up and took upon himself the task of writing about the situation. He called his pamphlets *The Tracts for the Times* and set to work immediately. His first *Tracts* came out in September 1833, and he inspired others to write more, until a total of ninety were published. Later, he was to claim that Keble's sermon was the original inspiration behind the Oxford Movement, but that was too modest an assertion.

In its influence upon the Church of England, the dedication of its clergy, and its position in English life, the Oxford Movement was to exceed the Evangelical Revival of fifty years before. But the *Tracts for the Times* became contentious as enthusiasts for the Oxford Movement believed that they were rediscovering neglected doctrinal truths. Gradually, the Tractarians' influence spread beyond Oxford and within a generation had led to fundamental changes in many parishes, including a greater concern and interest in the building, equipping and decoration of churches. Liturgical worship was taken very seriously by the Tractarian party, and their teaching about the Eucharist meant that it became central to the devotional lives of many. Together these developments led to an increased concern with the ritual practised at church services.

Ritualism was, in many respects, an unintended (and unanticipated) consequence of the original Tractarian doctrinal teaching and not an intrinsic part of the thinking of the originators of the Oxford Movement. But it was inevitable that some enthusiasts for the catholic insights of the Tractarians would see the external expression of their convictions in the ritual practices and liturgical vestments of Roman Catholicism and would seek to adopt those practices in their own liturgical worship. Such individuals were also motivated by the idea that ancient ritualistic practices and liturgical garb (or what they believed to be ancient ritualistic practices and garb) ought to be re-adopted as expressions of ancient doctrinal convictions. The imprecision of the Ornaments Rubric of the Book of Common Prayer allowed them to allege that the Church of England was in default and acting illegally, because it had abandoned its earlier "fuller" ritual and vestments, and that a return to more elaborate ritual would be no more than correcting error. In addition, some clergy definitely desired to imitate Roman Catholic sacramental practices. This allowed naivety in some cases to be compounded by provocation in others when a distinct "Romanizing" element developed among the new brand of high churchmen and excited vociferous opposition. There was also a resurgence of spiritual direction including the neglected, but not forbidden, discipline of sacramental confession among Anglicans, which was strongly opposed by evangelicals and others of protestant convictions.

Ritualism and confession became highly contentious in the 1850s and later. It became a factor with which every Archbishop of Canterbury after William Howley had to deal in the reign of Queen Victoria. None of them did so with marked success, and their problems will be considered in due course. However, the insights of the Tractarians gave the Church of England a degree of self-awareness and knowledge which assisted it to reach beyond the confines of the British Isles as the British Empire spread. The separate growth of the Church in North America later had a permanent influence upon the whole Anglican Church as the wider Communion developed.

—

The six Archbishops of Canterbury who served during the reign of Queen Victoria were devout men of differing abilities and very different personalities. Their backgrounds varied, but they did have things in common. Two of them were educated at Cambridge and the others at Oxford, and all of them had college fellowships (although Benson never went into residence). Four served as headmasters of great schools. Each one had proved himself capable earlier in his career as a diocesan bishop, and (to varying degrees) in the House of Lords. However, their skills and perceptions did not always translate easily into serving in the unique and increasingly complex role of the Archbishop of Canterbury. They found themselves called to lead the Church in a rapidly changing England with increasing population, and with industrialism and urbanization growing rapidly in ways that could not be foreseen. The Church also underwent upheavals through revival, the growth of biblical criticism, and doctrinal disputes, alongside an immense change in understanding the origins of the natural world. In addition, the Church of England began to recognize that, largely as a result of the growth of the Empire, it had responsibilities across the globe in the development and the expansion of the Anglican Communion.

Nothing could have prepared the successive archbishops for the changing circumstances with which they had to deal, yet their historical reputations rest largely, and properly, on the ways in which they led the Church in response to the profoundly changing situation in which it was called to minister. The Church of 1837, when the new Queen ascended the throne, was more like the Church of (say) a hundred and fifty years before than the Church in 1901, when the Queen died. By the close of her reign the Church, as the institution of which Victoria had become Supreme Governor in 1837, was leaner and fitter with its clergy better trained and equipped to continue its ministry and mission into the twentieth century. This was illustrated in a diary entry of Archbishop Benson's (11 July 1884), when he had dinner with the Queen:

> I told her that the Bishops of to-day were not like the Bishops of fifty years ago or fifty-five. Then they did such governing as they did through the superior clergy or by missives. Now meetings, lectures, temperance gatherings, constant openings of mission

rooms and churches, above all schools, familiarize them with the people as well as the people with them. They have all this time been teaching them, going in and out among them, addressing them, educating and elevating them in every way.[7]

What Benson said was true not only of the ministry of the bishops in general, including the archbishops. It was especially true of the ministry of their leader, the Archbishop of Canterbury. The following chapters describe the successive holders of the office of archbishop and how they met the challenges.

CHAPTER 1

William Howley (1828–1848)

When the child who was to become Queen Victoria was born at Kensington Palace, on 24 May 1819, William Howley was fifty-three years old and had been Bishop of London since 1813. The Archbishop of Canterbury was Charles Manners-Sutton, and he baptized the infant at Kensington Palace just a month after she was born, "assisted", it was said, by the Bishop of London. Howley's presence at the service was the start of an involvement with the future monarch that was to last for the rest of his life. As the archbishop waited to be told the names of the infant, there was a fierce disagreement between her parents and the Prince Regent, who was the infant's uncle and later King George IV. Her mother wanted her daughter to have her name Victoria, but the Regent declared that she should have only one name: Alexandrina, after the Tsar who was a godfather. The baby's father, the Duke of Kent, requested that a second name should be added. He wanted Elizabeth, which the Regent dismissed, before suggesting Georgina, which was, in turn, rejected. He brusquely insisted on the mother's name of Victoria and stipulated that it should follow that of Alexandrina. At this point, the bickering ended, and the child was baptized Alexandrina Victoria. For several years, she was known in her family circle as "Drina", although her mother continued to be understandably eager to give prominence to the second name.

When the princess came to the throne in 1837, shortly after her eighteenth birthday, William Howley had already succeeded Manners-Sutton as Archbishop of Canterbury (in 1828). Howley had been liked by King William IV, whom he had crowned king on 8 September 1831, and he was among those present in the early hours of 20 June when the monarch died at Windsor. He died with Howley's name on his lips.[8] Howley at once set out for London with the Lord Chamberlain, the

Marquis of Conyngham, to inform the princess that she had become queen. Montague Fowler, in *Some Notable Archbishops of Canterbury*, rightly thought that "the following narrative will be of interest", although he did not give his source. Howley and Conyngham, he recorded,

> left Windsor for Kensington Palace, where the Princess Victoria had been residing, to inform her of the king's death. It was two hours after midnight when they started, and they did not reach Kensington until five o'clock in the morning. They knocked, they rang, they thumped for a considerable time, before they could rouse the porter at the gate; they were again kept waiting in the courtyard, then turned into one of the lower rooms, where they seemed forgotten by everybody. They rang the bell, and desired that the attendant of the Princess Victoria might be sent to inform her Royal Highness that they requested an audience on business of importance. After another delay, and another ringing to inquire the cause, the attendant was summoned, who stated that the princess was in such a sweet sleep that she could not venture to disturb her. They said, "We are come on business of State to the queen, and even her sleep must give way to that." It did; and to prove that she did not keep them waiting, in a few minutes she came into the room in a loose white nightgown and shawl, her nightcap thrown off, and her hair falling about her shoulders, her feet in slippers, tears in her eyes, but perfectly collected and dignified.[9]

Fifty years later that historic meeting was the subject of a painting by H. T. Wells, *Queen Victoria receiving news of her accession to the throne, 20 June 1837*. Howley and Conyngham are shown kneeling in the presence of the new monarch, who was dressed as Fowler described. A print of the painting formed the frontispiece of the first volume of the Queen's published letters, which were edited in 1907 by Viscount Esher and A. C. Benson, a son of her fifth archbishop. The new monarch was not allowed to waste any time in coming to terms with her accession. Less than three hours after hearing the news the Queen wrote to her uncle Leopold, the king of the Belgians, "The melancholy news was brought to me by the

Lord Conyngham and the Archbishop of Canterbury at six. I expect Lord Melbourne almost immediately and hold a Council at eleven."[10]

Although the business of monarchy began at once, Queen Victoria's coronation took a year to arrange. Her predecessor, King William IV, had insisted on a relatively simple ceremony in 1830 with a comparatively modest budget of £50,000. He had wanted a deliberate contrast to the extravagance of that of King George IV in 1821, which was accompanied by great expense and pageantry. Howley, as Bishop of London, had been present in 1821 and had officiated in 1830 as Archbishop of Canterbury at the coronation of William IV. The crowning of Queen Victoria was therefore the third coronation with which Howley was involved. It was planned as an occasion of great splendour. Preparatory events began in May 1838 with balls, levees, and a concert, and the eventual cost of her coronation was £200,000.

The event itself took place on 28 June 1838 in Westminster Abbey, a month after the Queen's nineteenth birthday and close to the first anniversary of her accession. Despite the planning, the ceremony was not rehearsed. Archbishop Howley was seventy-three years old, and his involvement was not a success. It was noticed that his voice was "tremulous", and he committed blunders. Before the ceremony the Queen seems to have been anxious about Howley, whom she knew well. He had confirmed her three years before in the Chapel Royal, and although Howley's unfortunate bungling at the coronation and at the wedding of the Queen lay in the future, the princess had grounds for her anxiety. At her confirmation, Howley had preached a sermon which was much later described as "formidable", and he had been discomforted, as she had, by another wrangle. The King had complained that the retinue accompanying Victoria's mother was too large, and he ordered its reduction. Her concern was perhaps understandable; when she showed the crown to Lord Melbourne, before the coronation, she instructed him to make sure the archbishop "put it on firmly".[11] Whether Howley received the instruction is not known, but "with a ray of sunshine falling on her head she was crowned by the Archbishop of Canterbury Queen of England."[12] Afterwards the Queen complained about the weight of the crown, but her woes were not over. When Howley asked for the orb to be passed to him, so that he could give it to the Queen, he failed to notice that it had already been placed in her hand; having received the orb, she complained that it was also "very heavy". With regard to Howley, she recorded that "he (as usual) was so confused and puzzled and knew nothing . . . ."[13] The archbishop was required to place the ring on the Queen's hand. He forced the ruby ring on to her finger, not noticing that it had incorrectly been made to fit the next and smaller digit. She managed to remove it, after bathing it in cold water, but the process was very painful. The Bishop of Durham traditionally stands next to the throne, but he (Maltby) appeared not to know what was going on, and at one point the Queen asked the sub-dean of the abbey what to do as she was aware that the senior clergy were at a loss. However, a much more public element of farce, which gave rise to ironic applause, came about when the aged Lord Rolle, in paying homage with the other peers, caught his foot in his robes on the steps of the throne and rolled to the bottom.[14] More than one of those present would have echoed Howley's wry comment made subsequently that a rehearsal would have been wise.

Remarkably, Howley was almost to make a similar mistake with the ring when he conducted the Queen's marriage service to Prince Albert on 10 February 1840. On that occasion, Howley tried to get Prince Albert to put the ring on the appropriate finger, but of the wrong hand. As he was obliged to do, Howley read the full text of the service in the Book of Common Prayer but received criticism for doing so.

> The Archbishop of Canterbury did not spare us one word of the ceremony, which is very disagreeable, and when one looked at all the young things who were listening, most distressing, however he mumbles a good deal.[15]

The Queen had wanted the marriage ceremony to be held privately in Buckingham Palace, but Howley, supported by Bishop Blomfield, persuaded her that it should be in the Chapel Royal, St James's. In the circumstances, it is hardly surprising that the young Queen disliked the elderly archbishop in her early years on the throne. She did come to appreciate his wisdom later and developed a genuine regard for him.

—

Archbishop William Howley was his parents' only son and was born on 12 February 1766; he had one sister whose name was Mary. His father, also called William, was Vicar of Bishop's Sutton and Ropley near Winchester, in Hampshire, to which Howley succeeded after his father's death in 1796. The young Howley was educated at Winchester College. Later, his growing distinction was recognized when he was elected a Fellow, or governor, of the school in 1794. A younger contemporary at Winchester, who later became a canon of St Paul's Cathedral, was Sydney Smith, who spoke of the school "with horror of the wretchedness of the years he spent there: the whole system was ... one of abuse, neglect and vice", although other pupils did not share Smith's dislike of the school.[16]

Howley continued his education from 1793 at New College, Oxford, of which he was later to become a Fellow and tutor, and where an uncle, Samuel Gauntlett, was Warden from 1794 to 1822. As an undergraduate at Oxford, he won two prizes for English verse in successive years and had the conventional expertise with the classical languages. He enjoyed a considerable knowledge of Hebrew, which "gave him that keen appreciation of the Divine beauty of the inspired compositions of the prophets and psalmists, which contributed to make those sacred strains of holy prayer and praise his resource and his comfort to the last." All his life "his Greek Testament was the constant companion of his journeyings ...."[17] Unusually for the time, he also "made himself familiar with most of the languages of modern Europe, in particular the German, Italian and Spanish." As was often the case with men in Howley's position, he took work as a private tutor. One of his pupils was the Duke of Orange, later King William II of Holland. In 1792, he became domestic chaplain to the Marquess of Abercorn, and was also private tutor to the Marquess' son.

Little is known of his personal ambitions, although his critics later felt that he exploited to the full his royal connections and the patronage of Abercorn. No biography of Howley appeared until 2015, when *Archbishop Howley, 1828–1848* by James Garrard was published with useful extracts from some of his most important writing and speeches. That long biographical neglect was probably due to an underestimation of his importance by the generation that followed him. This is a cause of regret, because Howley was an important transitional figure between the Church of the Hanoverian period and the Victorian. Howley was not an insignificant figure, and he did not lack moral courage. Like many of his generation, he had been appalled at the revolutionary events in France and this, with his family background and his cautious personality, rooted him completely within the Tory mindset and made him distrust any prospect of change. G. F. A. Best, in *Temporal Pillars*, described it well:

> Men like ... Howley, who had been taught to refuse on principle to consider on their merits ideas or alleged facts that lay outside their rules, clearly had great difficulty in responding to new ideas and facts that beat their way through the barriers of set responses and defences, and imperatively demanded recognition on their own terms. They paid the penalty of seeming stupid for having done and said the correct thing for so long that it became nature to them.[18]

However, when the time came for him to face Sir Robert Peel's initiative for church reform in the mid-1830s, he did not shrink from involvement. The future archbishop was a courteous, likeable, shy, and scholarly man, but he had a poor speaking voice, an unassuming presence, and a mild manner. Owen Chadwick offered an insightful analysis of Howley:

> The Archbishop of Canterbury was a wise person. He had the merit that he looked and sounded like a pushover; everyone thought they could bend him to their wills. Inside he had quite a backbone of steel.[19]

That he was often mistakenly dismissed as insignificant surely accounts for the lack of interest by biographers, and there was no surviving child to undertake the not uncommon task of Victorian biographical piety. It is apparent that Howley had more strength of character than his demeanour suggested. There was a tough-mindedness about him which sprang from his personal piety but was often not apparent to many with whom he had to deal. His friend, colleague, and sometime chaplain at Canterbury, Benjamin Harrison (1808–1887), the Archdeacon of Maidstone, delivered a *Charge* to the clergy of his archdeaconry in May 1848, shortly after Howley's death; the published version was headed "The Remembrance of a Departed Guide and Ruler in the Church of God". Harrison believed the firmness of character of their late "chief Pastor" and "immediate spiritual Ruler" was based upon his personal faith:

> He was one ... who "set God always before" him, and therefore it was that he was "not greatly moved";—not to be moved from what he saw to be right;—not easily "shaken in mind", or "troubled", by opposition or difficulty, though he had much, at different times, in these various ways, to try him.[20]

William Howley was ordained deacon by the Bishop of Chester in 1789 in Christ Church Cathedral, Oxford, and was ordained priest exactly one year later by the Bishop of Oxford. Although he was well connected from his years at Oxford, it seemed likely that his career would be that of a parish priest, when in 1802 he was appointed to the prosperous living of Andover, for which he received about four hundred pounds per annum. Out of this stipend he paid a curate the relatively handsome sum of one hundred pounds per year.[21] Howley remained Vicar of Andover until 1811, when he accepted another living which, like Andover, was in the gift of Winchester College. This was Bradford Peverell, near Dorchester in Dorset, but he held it for only a short time. He had a clear, if very conventional, understanding of the role of a parish clergyman which he later described. He was to be

> in the midst of his Parishioners, like an Angel of God with a message of grace to each individual, administering commendation or censure, rebuke or encouragement, admonition or comfort, and adapting his language and manner, with parental consideration and tenderness, to every man's particular condition.[22]

From May 1804, Howley held his parochial appointments in plurality with a canonry at Christ Church, Oxford. The Crown was the patron of the canonry, and Howley's biographer, James Garrard, thought that Howley's relationship with Lord Abercorn helped his nomination, for Abercorn was close to the Prime Minister, Pitt the Younger. His role as a canon is described by Garrard in general terms:

The Dean and Chapter administered Christ Church's huge estates and regulated its internal economy. They exercised a large ecclesiastical patronage by electing Students and by appointing to parishes in the College's gift. The canons were by long tradition accorded the status of Heads of Houses and as such did not teach undergraduates. They were not formally concerned with educational policy.[23]

Howley was awarded his DD in 1805, and he married in that year at the age of thirty-nine. His wife was Mary Frances Belli. She was twenty-two years old; her father was John Belli of Southampton, a wealthy man. John Belli was associated with the East India Company and had served as private secretary to Warren Hastings when the latter was Governor General of India. The Howleys went on to have two sons and three daughters, but their lives as parents were marred by tragedy as four of the children died relatively young; the eldest and surviving son died in 1832 at the age of twenty-two. Benjamin Harrison noted the "depth" of the archbishop's "personal piety . . . in the fortitude and resignation with which he bore domestic bereavements of more than ordinary severity."[24]

After five years (in 1809), he became Regius Professor of Divinity at Oxford, although he was initially unsure whether he should accept the position. The nomination to the professorship also came from the Prime Minister, Spencer Perceval, who felt that Howley was well-qualified for the post, even though he had published little and despite the candidate's own self-doubt. At the time of Howley's appointment the Regius Professor of Divinity was expected to offer a course of lectures at which attendance was compulsory for undergraduates who hoped to be ordained into the Church's ministry. Garrard estimated that such individuals numbered about half of the Oxford undergraduate population at that time. Howley was keen to make the best use of the time available to him for lecturing, there being no other ways in which the students were prepared for ordination. He was concerned about the number and accessibility of the divinity lectures and was determined to change the pattern, perhaps because of his own experience of them as an undergraduate. In those days the lectures had been delivered late in the evening and by candlelight; it is recorded that many students slept through them.

Little from Howley's personal papers survived destruction, perhaps (as was rumoured) at the instigation of his widow; other material may have been lost after the death of Benjamin Harrison, whose wife is known to have burned much of her late husband's correspondence; it is likely that some Howley material was among Harrison's material. But Howley's library was extensive and remains accessible at Canterbury Cathedral. The basis of his collection of books was a working library of classics, patristics, church history and related studies. Howley had collected them, in part, for use at Addington, the country house acquired by his predecessor, Manners-Sutton, as a residence for the Archbishops of Canterbury. Addington remained in the possession of the archiepiscopate until it was sold in 1898 by Frederick Temple to assist in the financing of a house for himself and his successors in the precincts of Canterbury Cathedral. On Howley's death, his library was brought to Canterbury, because he had bequeathed it to Benjamin Harrison for the use of the clergy of the diocese. Harrison, in turn, left Howley's books to the cathedral library together with his own extensive collection of volumes. In 2004, a useful article, "William Howley and his books" by Margaret Sparks, appeared in the *Chronicle of the Friends of Canterbury Cathedral*.

> [Howley] started with editions of Vergil, Ovid, Lucretius, Cicero, and the appropriate Greek authors. From there he progressed, as was natural at the time, to the study of the Church Fathers, Augustine, Ambrose and Jerome in Latin, John Chrysostom and Basil the Great in Greek, and Ephraem the Syrian in Syriac— and of course many others. His interest in Church History was not just for the early church, but continued into sixteenth and seventeenth-century France, some Protestant but mostly Catholic. The seventeenth and eighteenth centuries in Europe were times of great scholarly enterprises, especially among the Benedictines and Jesuits. Howley collected their editions of the Fathers, of Canon Law, of the records of the Councils of the Church, many of them in rows of folio volumes. There are reference books necessary for a library—lexicons for Greek, Latin, Hebrew and Syriac, two volumes on the art of verifying dates in ancient documents, and Angelo Mai's publications of ancient texts from

the Vatican Library. A personal interest is shown in three volumes of German historical records, all published 1718–30, and perhaps more unusual, a Greek calendar of saints' lives (1728) with text in Greek and Latin and many engravings.[25]

Sparks added the pertinent comment that Howley's "library would do credit to an institution: as the collection of one man it is remarkable." It is a source of regret to those who would study William Howley's life and work that such a learned and devout man published so little. Over the course of his life, his publications consisted largely of episcopal *Charges* and occasional sermons. The extracts from key documents, given in Garrard's biography of Howley, are particularly valuable.

Howley knew that he was likely to be made a bishop and was ambitious enough to wonder privately which see he might be given. He had good grounds for such self-indulgent musing but expected no more than a conventional diocese such as Oxford or Rochester;[26] many people thought he might get "a minor bishopric". He had been told by Lord Aberdeen that Spencer Perceval, the prime minister who was assassinated in 1812, had been undecided whether to appoint Howley to the next available bishopric or whether he should appoint the aristocratic Edward Legge, who had been Dean of Windsor since 1805. In the event, both had to wait and Howley was the first to be elevated. Legge became Bishop of Oxford in 1815.

Lord Liverpool eventually became prime minister in succession to Spencer Perceval, and Howley was interviewed by him as a possible candidate for episcopal office. Liverpool wanted to raise the level of academic distinction of the episcopal bench and, at least, maintained it when he nominated Howley for the bishopric of London. The man he followed as bishop, John Randolph, had been Bishop of Oxford and then of Bangor. He had also been a predecessor of Howley as Regius Professor of Divinity at Christ Church, and it was his lectures Howley had attended as an undergraduate. Whether Howley had remained awake is unknown. Randolph had died after only four years as Bishop of London. He had suffered some ill health, but his death came suddenly as the result of an apoplectic seizure, which occurred while he was riding his horse.

Howley was consecrated Bishop of London by Archbishop Manners-Sutton at Lambeth Palace on 10 October 1813, a few days after being made a member of the Privy Council. The Bishops of Gloucester, Salisbury, and Oxford shared in Howley's consecration.[27] A sermon was preached at the consecration by W. S. Goddard, who had been headmaster of Winchester from 1796 to 1809; he was appointed to a prebendary at St Paul's Cathedral in January of the following year. An unusual aspect to the consecration service was the presence in the congregation of Queen Charlotte, the consort of King George III, and two of the princesses; none of them had attended such a service before. Garrard noted that Howley was, in fact, the fourth man to be offered the See of London, and that some astonishment was expressed at his appointment because of his diffident personality and his apparent lack of worldliness. He was a likeable man, later described as "gentle among the gentle" by W. E. Gladstone and "mild among the mild". His demeanour, voice, and small stature led many to underestimate his strength of character and his skill in assessing difficult issues. Many years later the *Times* obituary for Howley remarked that it was unusual for someone without episcopal experience to be appointed to the Diocese of London. It also described the situation on which he entered:

> The ecclesiastical management of the Diocese of London is not amongst the easiest tasks confided to episcopal hands. It contains three or four millions of the most mixed and miscellaneous populations in the empire, for this diocese comprehends not only the city and Westminster, but the whole of Middlesex and Essex with parts of Hertfordshire. The clergy appointed to minister to the spiritual necessities of this mighty multitude are pre-eminent among their reverend brethren for learning, ability, and zeal, as well as some of the faults and errors closely allied to these excellent properties. To lead, superintend, and control a body so circumstanced and constituted demands qualities that may not be extraordinary in their separate excellence though in their combination they are alike valuable and rare. Fifteen years of

successful administration in the see of London attested at once to the prudence and piety the mild firmness and regulated energy of bishop Howley.[28]

Howley's early years in London witnessed the conclusion of the war with France, and once the optimism of victory had passed, the bishop was uneasy. He was aware that the peace might be a challenge to the nation and, consequently, to the Church of England, and he was worried. In a *Charge* of 1818, he spoke as follows:

> Now all is changed, it is our lot to have fallen on days of innovation and trouble: the political character of the age has produced an alteration in the circumstances of the country and an agitation in the public mind, affecting the Church as well as the State.[29]

By 1822, his *Charge* of that year shows that his mind was more at rest, "the immediate danger is now passed". Howley had immediately found himself caught up in the ordinary work of a diocesan bishop, "the spiritual necessities of [the] mighty multitude", with its routine of clergy discipline, correspondence, and confirmations. An interesting pastoral detail, in the light of events much later during Howley's primacy, was that he confirmed Edward Bouverie Pusey in the Chapel Royal, St James's, about a year before Pusey left Eton.

In the early days of his London episcopate a good deal of Howley's correspondence was to do with requests for patronage. There was no arrangement within the Church of England to control or limit the number of men being ordained, and no mechanism existed to create such a policy. This resulted in more men being ordained than there were curacies available, and the bishops could do nothing about the situation. Howley complained that even in the Diocese of London he had relatively little patronage at his disposal. Problems caused by non-residence of clergy also exercised his mind. It was a nationwide concern, particularly acute in rural areas, but by no means unknown in towns and cities. It was a matter of sufficient seriousness for a committee of the Privy Council to be established, of which Howley was a member along with Archbishop Manners-Sutton of Canterbury and the Chancellor of the Exchequer. The problem was exacerbated by the accepted custom of many clergy holding more than one post. Although some clergy found pluralism lucrative, a good deal of non-residence was due to necessity when a lack of adequate endowment or tithe meant that individual parishes could not provide an income sufficient to support a resident clergyman. Other instances of absenteeism occurred when a clergyman lived near his parish but outside its boundaries, because suitable accommodation was unavailable within the parish. Howley used the phrase "virtual residence" to describe such circumstances. Back in 1800, the man who was to be Howley's successor as Regius Professor and later his rival for the archbishopric, William Van Mildert (1765-1836), had endured such a prosecution for non-residence when he was Rector of St Mary-le-Bow in central London, but resided just outside the parish. At the time when Howley was addressing the problem, Van Mildert's case was cited as a relevant illustration of that situation.

It was acceptable practice at the time for fortunate clergy to accumulate appointments, which enabled them to live as wealthy men, and these circumstances sometimes led to the abuse of the system. One such was Howley's brother-in-law, the Reverend A. C. Belli, whom the bishop appointed Precentor of St Paul's Cathedral in 1819, when he was twenty-seven years old. He remained Precentor until his death at the age of ninety-four in 1886 but appeared in the cathedral very rarely. Sydney Smith, himself a pluralist canon of St Paul's, said that a more correct title for the office held by Belli should have been "the absenter". History provides other examples of similar individuals, some of whom amassed fortunes from their combined preferments, and, as has been noted, Howley, before he became a bishop, had personally benefitted from a plurality of appointments. Howley used his own patronage to obtain clergy whom he wanted for his diocese, however small the degree of patronage he had at his disposal. A notable example was Charles James Blomfield (1786-1857), a rising star among the clergy, an able priest with a high reputation as a preacher. He enjoyed the patronage of Lord Bristol, who brought him to the attention of Lord Liverpool shortly after Howley was appointed to the See of London. Howley appointed Blomfield as one of his chaplains. The two became friends and close allies. Howley later appointed him to the wealthy living of St Botolph-without-Bishopsgate, and then in January 1822 appointed him as Archdeacon of Colchester, which was then in the Diocese of London. Howley's high opinion of Blomfield was shared by others, and in 1824 he was appointed Bishop of Chester. His successor in Chester after he moved to London in 1828 on Howley's translation to the archbishopric was J. B. Sumner, who was to follow Howley to Canterbury.

In parochial terms, the usual practice was that curates were employed to cover the ministry in the places where the incumbent did not reside, and their pay was his responsibility. Howley was regarded as making good provision for such curates, but many incumbents were less generous than Howley had been in his days as a pluralist. Cases of clerical poverty were widespread, partly because the large numbers of available unbeneficed clergy inevitably drove down the level of pay. Consequently, there were examples of non-residence which were scandalous where absent incumbents retained the income associated with the posts, paid mere pittances to curates to do the work, and cared little for the welfare of the people to whom they owed a pastoral ministry. Not infrequently such pluralists could find only desperate or problematic men to serve for meagre stipends.

From 1813, an Act of Parliament sought to protect curates from the worst excesses of low pay. However, the arrangements were supposed to be under the supervision of diocesan bishops and reviewed regularly, but often were overlooked. The legislation set an upper limit to the stipend of curates of no more than two hundred and fifty pounds per annum, although few achieved such sums. It was to his credit that under Howley incumbents found that they were required to pay more fairly. In addition, Howley asserted his authority by requiring morning and evening services in churches on Sundays: "double duty". This desirable ambition hit at pluralists who were not conscientious in making appropriate arrangements for parochial duties to be undertaken. As Bishop of London, and later as Archbishop of Canterbury, Howley was only partially successful in limiting the harm done by a system that was open to abuse but difficult to control. However, even when parochial duties were properly covered, often the technicalities of obtaining episcopal permission lapsed. The situation gave ammunition to the Church's critics, which they were not reluctant to use, especially when scandalous examples of neglect or the excessive appropriation of funds were uncovered. John Wade's *Extraordinary Black Book* (1831) is remembered as a hard-hitting polemic against the system.

An earlier Act of Parliament, in 1803, had endeavoured to control and contain the situation, but was limited in its effectiveness, and later amendments were not successful in improving things. Clergy could be prosecuted if they failed to renew licences for non-residence, and the Act encouraged informants.[30] When prosecutions did occur, incumbents sometimes found themselves heavily penalized financially. The author of more than one scandal was a man named William Wright, whom Bishop Randolph had employed as his secretary, and who served in a similar capacity for several other bishops. Wright was entitled to a fee when licences for non-residence were issued but felt aggrieved at the financial loss which resulted from the inadequate enforcement of the practice for licences. Garrard noted that Wright took advantage of Randolph's failing health to manipulate the system for his own advantage and records a particularly outrageous case where a conscientious incumbent was prosecuted for having an unlicensed curate. The failure to issue a licence was because Wright deliberately delayed doing so, and then imposed a fine against the incumbent for non-compliance. By 1814, Howley had replaced Wright with a new secretary. Bishop Howley spoke about the matters of non-residence and pluralities in his first *Charge* to the Diocese of London in that year. He said that amendments to the Act of 1803 had not fully "answered the purpose of protecting the clergy from vexatious attacks", although that had been the intention. Howley had initiated an investigation into alleged abuses and

> the result of the inquiries ... I am happy to state, has been peculiarly creditable to the clergy of this diocese. In the numerous cases referred to my decision, the fault has, almost without exception, been found to consist, not in the wilful dereliction or criminal neglect of duty, but in the disregard of those precautions, which are necessary to legalize virtual residence, or to confirm the claim of justifiable absence to the indulgence allowed by law. Among the objects of attack, it is bare justice to say, are

many individuals irreprehensible in character, and exemplary in conduct.[31]

The efforts of Howley and those who worked with him did achieve a reduction in the number of non-resident clergy. Howley's biographer noted that "nationally between 1810 and 1815 approximately 1,000 fewer clergy became non-resident, and there was an increase of residence of 800."[32]

In the same *Charge*, Howley reminded his hearers once again that curates should receive adequate remuneration. Howley expressed his views about recent legislation for the

> farther support and maintenance of Stipendiary Curates, which ... requires every incumbent not duly residing on his benefice to nominate, within a specified time, a proper Curate, to be licensed by the Bishop ... The primary object of the Bill is to secure a more adequate provision for the maintenance of stipendiary Curates; and if its enactments may, in certain respects, be considered as pressing too hard on benefices of inferior value, they afford little complaint to the wealthier incumbent.[33]

Howley remained emphatic that clergy should reside in their benefices but accepted that it was not always possible. Where curates were employed, he was consistent in his view that "ample provision for the care and instruction of the parish" must be made. He insisted that curates should not be required to work in more than one parish, but recognized that difficulties did occur and he had, with "the utmost reluctance", occasionally committed the care of "three churches to the same hand", but he reserved the right to revoke such arrangements if further enquiries revealed that the situation was not as he had been led to believe.

For Howley the matter of clergy deployment was but one of the pastoral and administrative issues with which he had to deal on becoming Bishop of London. He was concerned with several of the issues to which the Hackney Phalanx devoted its efforts, and he found the churchmanship and the politics of the Phalanx to his liking, when he came to London. Howley, like the Phalanx, was committed to the Church's work in elementary education. In 1811, Joshua Watson had founded the National Society for the Education of the Poor in the Principles of the Established Church. As the society's full title makes clear, it was unashamedly an Anglican venture. The teachers in the schools it supported were required to teach the liturgy of the Church of England and to inculcate the Prayer Book Catechism; often such teaching was carried out by the local incumbent, or under his specific direction. Howley's involvement in the national society as Bishop of London came to be of great importance to him. He attended the society's business meetings regularly, mentioned it in his episcopal *Charges*, and supported its fundraising work in his diocese. When he became archbishop, he continued to support the society. Nevertheless, he continued to oppose the non-denominational teaching of Christianity favoured by nonconformists and secular educationalists, and two decades later, in 1839, he opposed Lord John Russell's scheme for national education. Another element of the Phalanx's work of which Howley approved was the desire to reinvigorate the Society for the Promotion of Christian Knowledge, which had been founded in 1698, yet was at a low ebb by the early nineteenth century. A significant part of the society's work was the provision of Bibles for the Anglican Church overseas, and Howley went so far as to assert that there should be an official connection with the society for that purpose. He also supported Archbishop Manners-Sutton in an unsuccessful attempt to revive the Association for the Relief of the Manufacturing Poor, which had been established in 1812.

Howley was introduced into the House of Lords within weeks of his consecration to the bishopric of London. He took his seat on 4 November 1813 and was conscientious in his attendance for the rest of his life. He did not hesitate to involve himself in debates where he felt he could make a relevant contribution, although his poor voice was a hindrance.

Soon, however, his personal wisdom was recognized by the more discerning of his peers, and he earned their respect. He was concerned with a particularly sensitive matter which came before the House of Lords at the time of George IV's accession to the throne in January 1820. The background can be explained briefly. As Prince of Wales, the future George IV had reluctantly married Princess Caroline Amelia Elizabeth of Brunswick-Wolfenbüttel in 1795. The relationship was not a success, and the two lived separately from the year after the marriage. However, they had one child, a daughter, Charlotte, who would eventually have inherited the throne. However, Victoria became the heir apparent as a result of Charlotte's death, which happened in 1817 after she gave birth to a stillborn son, having married Prince Leopold of Saxe-Coburg in 1816. In the years after the separation of Charlotte's parents, the Prince of Wales treated his wife badly, and Caroline behaved in an increasingly indiscreet manner; an official investigation of her behaviour had been ordered in 1806. By the time George ascended the throne following the death of his father, the marriage was defunct. The new king told Lord Liverpool, the prime minister, that he wanted a divorce from Caroline. This required the assent of Parliament. A Bill was introduced in the Lords in July 1820 to deprive the queen of the "Title, Privileges, and Exemptions of Queen Consort of this Realm and to dissolve the marriage between His Majesty and the said Caroline Amelia Elizabeth". The grounds for the divorce was adultery committed by the queen when she was Princess of Wales. A modern biographer of Lord Melbourne, Philip Ziegler, described Queen Caroline's life as one of "flamboyant indiscretion".[34] She had taken a lover during a trip to Italy and other places on the Continent, compounding "the fact of adultery . . . with indecent and suspicious behaviour". The allegations were supported by "certain proof", and in the Lords her behaviour was described at length and in considerable detail, causing what Lord Erskine in the debate described as a "great sensation".[35]

Howley spoke in the debate in the Lords, broadly in support of the king's position, earning the monarch's gratitude. Howley's speech was not at all inflammatory, but it was unfortunate that a personal remark of his made around the same time was misreported, and he suffered damage to his reputation as a result. He had said, perhaps unwisely and probably incorrectly, that the king could do no wrong "morally or politically"; but he was alleged to have said that the king could do no wrong "morally or physically". Everyone knew that the king was not a man of blameless rectitude. If Howley had indeed spoken as reported, he would have deserved the abuse that he received. Critics leapt upon the bishop's reported words, especially as public sympathy was with the queen, and there was a good deal of agitation in support of her. Howley was not guilty of the double standard of which he was accused, but he suffered obloquy as a result of the incorrect reporting of his words. Probably the fiercest attack came in a pamphlet from the reformist and radical pen of William Hone (1780–1842); Hone's vigorous condemnation of Howley as the Bishop of London was as "cringing [and] promotion-seeking". Whether Hone's vitriol reached Howley is not known, but he was strong enough not to be disturbed unduly by such rancour. In due course the monarch's divorce Bill passed into law and wrangling ensued concerning the former queen's future. In the immediate period afterwards, she was forbidden to attend the king's coronation on 20 July and was turned away when she attempted to get into Westminster Abbey for the service. The sorry affair only ended with her relatively sudden death in August 1821; her body was taken to Brunswick for burial.

—

When Howley began his episcopal ministry in London, it was a time when the population of the manufacturing towns and cities was still growing rapidly. The capital shared in that growth. In 1801, around a million people lived in or close to London, and within thirty years that number had almost doubled. Howley presided over the Diocese of London for the second half of that period. Concerned churchmen, including Robert Peel, wanted to extend the parochial ministry of the Church and were acutely aware that the church accommodation was insufficient. This was an anxiety shared by the new bishop and his friends and collaborators, particularly those associated with the Hackney Phalanx. It was estimated that, in the worst case, only ten percent of the population could be accommodated in the parish churches of the most populous areas. A clear need to increase the number of church buildings, and to extend and enlarge many existing churches, was recognized. The reality of the need was also fuelled by the increase in the number of dissenting places of worship, which were regarded as being in competition with the work of the established Church, although the Roman Catholics, until freed from restrictions by emancipation, were not involved. The problem was made worse by the fact that it was legally difficult to establish new Church of England parishes, and so to build new churches, because of due regard for the interests, often financial, of the clergy affected. In contrast, nonconformists were not restricted by anything other than the costs of building and equipping chapels. Joshua Watson drew this to Howley's attention formally in 1818. Eventually, money was raised for the provision, and to a lesser extent the endowment, of churches by individuals and by diocesan efforts, and church building became something of a fashion.

One man who committed his own resources to building projects was John Bowdler (1746–1823), one of the Hackney collaborators; like his younger contemporary Joshua Watson, he was a layman. He used his influence and his wealth to raise money for the building of new churches in densely populated areas. He wanted specific seating to be available to the poor, free of pew rents, and believed that the government should provide funds for the extension of existing churches and the building of new ones. Bowdler's concern was not exclusive to London. He recognized the need in other towns; but London was, of course, Howley's main concern for the fifteen years from 1813. Bowdler, with Watson, began his campaign in 1815 by lobbying Howley and, the following year, the government. Also, Bowdler, again with Watson, was instrumental in the founding of the Church Building Society, which was formally launched in February 1818.[36] As noticed in the previous chapter, the target was one million pounds, and the society secured donations from many wealthy individuals, including the king. Lord Liverpool, when prime minister, was instrumental in persuading the government to give one million pounds for new Anglican churches. As has been noted, this very large sum was designated as a thank offering for the victory of the Battle of Waterloo; the churches built by the fund were sometimes known by the sobriquet, "Waterloo churches". In 1824, Lord Liverpool obtained another half million pounds for the cause. Those sums were the most significant part of the six million pounds raised and spent on new church building by 1833. By the early 1850s, only a few years after Howley had been succeeded as archbishop by J. B. Sumner, more than 2,500 new Anglican churches had been built across England, and the process was to continue during much of the reign of Queen Victoria. Howley consecrated those built within the boundaries of his diocese, including the substantial rural areas of the diocese as well as the densely populated areas of the capital itself. Unfortunately, relatively few of them were adequately endowed, and many were poorly built, facts which were to lead often to dire consequences in later decades.

—

Back in 1634, an Order in Council had entrusted to the Bishop of London the ecclesiastical care of the country's overseas territories. Consequently, Howley had a formal responsibility for the small but growing number of overseas dioceses. This involvement with the Anglican Church outside the British Isles will be considered here in order to avoid an artificial division by his appointment to Canterbury in 1828. The situation was sometimes a source of frustration because communications were so slow. Since the early eighteenth century, the Society for the Propagation of the Gospel in Foreign Parts (SPG) and the Church Missionary Society (CMS) had both been active, but even by the end of Howley's time as Bishop of London, there were only five colonial bishoprics; these were Nova Scotia, Quebec, Calcutta, Jamaica, and Barbados.[37] When he was Archbishop of Canterbury, the numbers grew steadily. Howley wanted to help, but in the early days there was little he could do much beyond trying to use his influence on the government when relevant issues arose. This he did when he was asked to get the East India Company to provide religious instruction to its trainees before they left the shores of England. Also, Howley consented to ordain men for the colonies, and was prepared to accept individuals whom he did not regard as adequately qualified to serve in the English Church. For his own diocese, he insisted that only graduates should be ordained to the ministry, and so incurred criticism for seeming to have a double standard.[38] A useful and practical contribution to the overseas dioceses was his effort to ensure that Bibles and Prayer Books should be available, together with a number of other books for teaching. He also tried to keep in touch with bishops abroad, even when no longer responsible for them. He was encouraged by Joshua Watson, as Archbishop Manners-Sutton had been, to work towards an increase in the number of colonial bishoprics. This led to the founding of the Colonial Bishoprics Fund in 1841, which although under the official leadership of the two archbishops, had the indefatigable Bishop Blomfield as its main episcopal driver. Thanks, in part, to Blomfield's energetic personality, the number of colonial bishoprics did increase during the 1840s with the approval and encouragement of Archbishop Howley. Also, in 1841, Howley and six diocesan bishops, including Blomfield of London and Harcourt of York, became vice-presidents of CMS. Howley's relationship with the society was not always an easy one, and its leaders frequently expressed a fear that he might resign, with possibly calamitous results, particularly over issues with the society's work in India.

Also in 1841, there occurred a curiously Erastian development, which was to have wider implications than its originators expected, and to which both William Howley and Blomfield gave cautious support. This was the establishment, by an Act of Parliament passed on 5 October 1841, of a bishopric in Jerusalem. The proposal was to prove controversial, but at first it excited little opposition. The idea owed its origin to the political circumstances in the Middle East, particularly in the desire of the British government and the government of Prussia to limit French influence in the area. A proposal was conceived by the King of Prussia, Frederic William IV, whom the Tractarian Pusey believed to be in all probability an episcopalian "in heart".[39] He sent the Chevalier Bunsen to England in June 1841 to get agreement for an episcopal ministry in Jerusalem to care for the Protestant and Anglican communities in the area. Harrison recorded, in his 1848 *Charge,* that Howley took a "deep interest" in the proposal, but he was not naive. Rather, as Harrison noted, he thought that the scheme would provide "opportunities of friendly communication with the ancient Churches of the East [and] at once make known among them the apostolical constitution of our Church". In addition, it would "without offence or suspicion, lay the foundations of a more perfectly apostolical order in the countries of Europe" and assist King Frederic in achieving his unspoken ambition of introducing episcopal orders into Lutheranism. Although he seems not to have voiced an opinion about it, Howley was also under some pressure from evangelicals such as Lord Ashley (later Shaftesbury) who believed that the conversion of Palestine to Christianity would bring about the return of Christ in glory.

Howley was involved in the practicalities of the proposal. He had a long meeting with Bunsen, with Blomfield and Harrison present, to sort out the details, but none of the other English bishops knew what was going on. It was agreed that the Jerusalem bishop would, in the words of Blomfield's modern biographer,

> be empowered to ordain any Germans who would subscribe to the Thirty-Nine Articles and the Confession of Augsburg, minister to the protestants only and have oversight of the English congregations in Syria and Palestine.[40]

The bishop would be consecrated according to the rites of the Church of England, but nominations would be alternated between the governments of Britain and Prussia; the Archbishop of Canterbury, who would consecrate the candidates, was to possess the right of veto of Prussian nominees. These arrangements were a cause of dismay among many. The prospect of episcopal orders being conferred on Lutheran ministers was one that horrified those who believed Lutheranism to be heretical. John Henry Newman was significant among such, and the proposal was a body-blow to him; later he claimed that it fatally undermined his belief in the catholicity of the Church of England. Notwithstanding Newman's objections, it was only slowly that the opposition mounted and became articulate. Pusey, who knew Bunsen personally as a friend of his brother, had initially believed that it was indeed a good way of introducing apostolic episcopacy into Prussian Lutheranism, but he withdrew his support and opposed the plan.

It was not just the Anglo Catholics who opposed the scheme. The small number of Protestants in Jerusalem had no episcopal ministry available to them, and little thought was given to the size of the community to whom the bishop would minister and, indeed, whether a bishopric was the best way of caring for them. Later, surprise was expressed at the discovery that there was no congregation of Jewish converts to Protestantism in the city. The Turkish authorities feared that the appointee would set about the conversion of other Christians, and also Muslims, to the Protestantism that the scheme enshrined. An undertaking had to be given that such activity would not be part of the new bishop's work. Regretfully, the bishops who served in the post did not always respect that undertaking. Howley had to give similar reassurance to anxious individuals; he wrote to A. P. Percival on 27 October 1841:

> If the Bishop sent to Jerusalem invades the rights of the Greek prelates, requires obedience from their flocks, or seizes on their churches or possessions, as the Latins in different places are said to have done or attempted to do, that indeed would be a most culpable intrusion. But I cannot see that any such charge will attach to him, if he confines his attention to the clergy and members of his own Church.[41]

Later, Howley was keen to make the same point, in more official and formal terms, in a commendatory letter "to the Right Reverend our Brothers in Christ, the Prelates and Bishops of the Ancient and Apostolic Churches in Syria and the countries adjacent . . . ." He wrote when the first bishop had been consecrated, and he was by then aware of, and concerned about, the small numbers of persons for whom the bishop was responsible, by referring to the bishop's "authority to exercise spiritual jurisdiction over the Clergy and congregations of our Church, which are now, *or which hereafter may be*, established in the countries above mentioned".[42]

The first person chosen to be Bishop in Jerusalem (the preposition was important) was Michael Solomon Alexander (1799–1845), and his tenure of the see was short but comparatively successful. Howley consecrated him in November 1841 in the chapel of Lambeth Palace, assisted by Blomfield, with the newly consecrated Selwyn of New Zealand and the Bishop of Rochester. Alexander was a convert from Judaism and had been ordained an Anglican in Dublin in 1827. Having served as a missionary in Danzig (modern Gdansk), he had been Professor of Hebrew at King's College since 1832. He had translated the New Testament and the Book of Common Prayer into Hebrew. In Palestine, the number of German Protestants increased in the area, whereas the number of Anglicans did not, and tensions developed. Some of Alexander's successors were guilty of proselytizing among the local Orthodox congregations, thereby undermining the reassurances that Archbishop Howley had sought to give. Alexander's immediate successor in the see was also consecrated by Howley at Lambeth. He was Samuel Gobat, nominated by the King of Prussia. Gobat was ordained to the priesthood of the Church of England a few days before his consecration in July 1846, and he held office until his death in 1879. He encouraged the CMS to base its work in the Middle East at Jerusalem and in his later years formally involved the society in the work of his diocese. Despite the genuine commitment of the two men the scheme never really thrived and later had a chequered history before finally lapsing in 1886 during the archiepiscopate of Edward White Benson.

With the growth of the colonial Church Archbishop Howley showed a continuing commitment and enjoyed a more conventional relationship. In his *Charge* of 1840, Howley characteristically remarked that "he is no true servant of Christ if he can be indifferent to the fate of the Heathen world, or to the spiritual interests of our countrymen who are widely dispersed through the British dominions in every quarter of the globe."[43] In the same year that the Colonial Bishoprics Fund was established, George Augustus Selwyn was consecrated Bishop of New Zealand in the chapel at Lambeth Palace by Howley himself, and so was able to share in the consecration of Bishop Alexander. Other consecrations of colonial bishops by Howley as archbishop, in chronological order, were Calcutta (1829 and 1832), Madras (1835 and 1837), Montreal and Australia (both in 1836), Bombay (1837), Newfoundland (1839 and 1844), and Toronto (1839), in addition to the appointments to Jerusalem (1841 and again in 1846), Fredericton and also Colombo (1845), and Cape Town, Adelaide, Melbourne, and Newcastle (in 1847). The consecrations for the colonial Church were only a few among the consecrations over which Howley presided as archbishop, but they are listed above to illustrate his continued involvement with the Church overseas.

The first Bishop of Cape Town was Robert Gray, the Tractarian son of the Bishop of Bristol, whose palace had been destroyed in 1831. Howley encouraged Gray to accept Cape Town. Under Gray came the famous Colenso controversy, which many came to see as a factor behind the need for the Lambeth Conference of 1867 initiated by Archbishop Longley, although it was not quite as important a factor as some contemporaries alleged. The faithful Harrison noted that among Howley's activities in the last months of his life, when already failing, he found the energy "to perform a service which those about him had, a little while before ... feared would be almost too much for his strength, the consecration of the four Colonial Bishops [mentioned above] who were set apart for their holy work, in the Abbey Church of Westminster, on St Peter's Day", 1847.[44]

The focus of the Church's foreign expansion was linked at this time with the growth of the British Empire, but Howley managed to have a wider perspective. The Episcopal Church in North America had a quite distinct character from the Anglicanism of the British colonies. No episcopal ministry had been established before American independence in 1776, although the SPG had campaigned from 1701 for bishops to be appointed. After independence no bishop could be consecrated for America from the Church of England until an Act of Parliament permitted the archbishops of Canterbury and York to consecrate bishops for foreign states without requiring the candidates to take the oath of allegiance to the Crown. Despite the constitutional impossibility American churchmen had wanted links with the Church of England. In the 1820s, several American bishops had visited Archbishop Manners-Sutton at Lambeth Palace. Archbishop Howley was one of very few people in England who had some knowledge of the American Church and tried to keep himself well informed.[45]

—

The Duke of Wellington was prime minister when Archbishop Manners-Sutton died at Lambeth Palace in the morning of 21 July 1828. Among senior bishops the most obvious candidate for the primacy was Howley, whom many already expected would become Manners-Sutton's successor; another was his near contemporary William Van Mildert, who had been Bishop of Durham since 1826. The Duke of Wellington, when considering the vacancy, was aware that there were no other satisfactory candidates for the primacy. He was an early example of a prime minister who chose bishops on merit and did not restrict himself to men who would support his government. He had already recognized that the need for Roman Catholic emancipation was becoming politically necessary and knew that it would have to be determined in the near future whoever was appointed to the archbishopric. He also knew that both the Bishop of Durham and the Bishop of London were opposed to it. Indeed, Van Mildert was to clash bitterly over the proposed Bill in the House of Lords with Charles Lloyd, his friend, who was Bishop of Oxford, and who was not at all opposed to the proposal. Wellington was aware that the king's regard for Howley was by no means limited to appreciation for the support he had received over his divorce. The king liked Howey and his conservative cast of mind exhibited in his Tory principles. King George IV shared the antipathy towards the idea of Roman Catholic emancipation and was pleased to think that Howley would oppose Wellington's plans.

Howley's Tory politics had been apparent in the debates concerning the repeal of the Test and Corporation Acts which were both noticed in the previous chapter. They dated back to the seventeenth century and had become obsolete. Many individuals with nonconformist convictions had held public office in the preceding century and a half and had been protected from the legal consequences of so doing by the annual passing of an Indemnity Act. At a basic level the proposed repeal of both Acts had been no more than a legislative "tidying up", similar to unsuccessful attempts in the late eighteenth century. Attempts at repeal had been considered before, in the archiepiscopate of John Moore in 1787; another occasion had occurred the following year, and yet another in 1790.

As the life of Manners-Sutton was drawing to its close after over twenty years as Archbishop of Canterbury, the king had given thought as to who should follow the aged primate and was pleased when Wellington nominated William Howley. The prime minister, fully aware of Howley's opinion regarding Roman Catholic emancipation, hoped that, with his mild manner, Howley could be bullied out of his opposition. Wellington was to be proved wrong, at least initially. However Wellington may have expressed himself when approaching Howley about the archbishopric, the king's official communication to the Dean and Chapter of Canterbury, even within its formal phraseology, shows the monarch's high opinion of Howley. It was received in Canterbury on 5 August, little more than a fortnight after the death of Manners-Sutton.

> We, of our Princely Disposition and Zeal being desirous to prefer to the same See a Person meet thereunto and considering the virtue, learning, wisdom, gravity and other good Gifts wherewith the Right Reverend Father in God Doctor William Howley, now Bishop of London, is endued We have been pleased to name and recommend him unto You to be Elected and Chosen into the said Archbishoprick of Canterbury. Wherefore We require You upon receipt hereof to proceed to your Election according to the Laws of this Our Realm and Our Conge d'Elire herewith . . .
>
> . . . Given under Our Signet at Our Palace of Westminster the sixth day of August in the Ninth Year of Our Reign.[46]

On the same day, the King's Order was published in the *London Gazette*, and events continued to move rapidly. The election of William Howley as the eighty-eighth archbishop took place in the audit room of Canterbury Cathedral on 8 August 1828, and his enthronement was arranged for Tuesday 28 August. This was conducted by proxies, as had been the case with Howley's two predecessors in the archbishopric. The use of proxies was by no means unusual; nevertheless, Howley was criticized for it. Sydney Smith, Howley's erstwhile school fellow, described it as "an act of the most extraordinary indolence ever recorded in history". One reason for the practice, Garrard noted, was economy.[47] The new archbishop was represented by a Canterbury clergyman, William Welfitt, and the Archdeacon of Canterbury by another. Both of them were appointed formally by a process which involved the production of legal documents which declared their authority to act. The document for Howley's proxy bore the archbishop's seal, and the archdeacon's also bore a seal, so the ceremony was not quite as spontaneous, as Sydney Smith hinted, when he wrote: "a proxy was sent down in the Canterbury Fly . . . the archbishop [being] detained in town by business or pleasure." The "Inthronisation", as it was designated on the order of service, took place when the archdeacon's proxy led the archbishop's proxy through the cathedral to the "Marble Chair behind the Altar" in which he placed Welfitt and read the prescribed prayers before leading him back to the dean's stall, from which Welfitt gave a blessing at the end of the service. The ceremony concluded with a procession to the chapter house where the members of the Cathedral Foundation swore canonical obedience to the archbishop; Welfitt, on the primate's behalf, promised to "maintain the Rights and Liberties of this Church, and to observe the customs thereof...."

Howley's decision to be enthroned in Canterbury by proxy seems to add anecdotal force to Thomas Mozley's later assertion that Howley became archbishop at a time when the Church of England seemed to be "folding its robes to die with what dignity it could". That the Church of the Hanoverian period was in decline has often been accepted as beyond question, but that assertion is an oversimplification, as the previous chapter noted. The Church did have its vitality, but it was, however, a vigour that was exemplified by such a man as Howley: intelligent, quiet, and dignified, reserved and undemonstrative, cool, and unexcitable.

The new archbishop was sixty-two years old when he became primate, a shy man with considerable ability; he was always courteous and likeable, but not ineffectual. Many misread his character, which sometimes led to misconceptions. He was to serve faithfully through twenty turbulent years as archbishop. It is clear that he was a "high and dry" churchman, an old-fashioned high churchman of the "Church and King" school. Self-confessedly, he wrote in 1840 to Bishop Bagot: "I am really afraid of innovations, not knowing to what they may possibly lead, and we have sufficient means of grace if we would only make the best of them."[48] Politically he remained by instinct an unswerving Tory. The record of his public life is, in that sense, predictable, although even he could not ignore, far less prevent, the changes that were already occurring within society as they impinged on the Church of England.

The appointment meant that London needed a new bishop. Howley was pleased when Blomfield followed him there, seeming to be more pleased at Blomfield's preferment than his own elevation, according to his own secretary. It is likely that Howley recommended Blomfield to the prime minister for London, as it was probably at Howley's suggestion that in 1824 Blomfield had been appointed Bishop of Chester. The forceful Blomfield was a good foil for Howley. From the time of his move to the capital, Blomfield worked closely with the wise but cautious Howley for the remainder of the latter's life. They successfully negotiated their way through the reforming zeal of the time and achieved much for the Church of England. The assertion that Blomfield dominated the partnership is not as accurate as was thought at the time and subsequently; yet it is fair to suggest that each of them, working alone, would not have been so effective on behalf of the Church.

An interesting, but little noted, episode in Howley's work was his involvement in what became known as the *Bridgewater Treatises*. The Eighth Earl of Bridgewater was Francis Henry Egerton (1756–1829), an eccentric pluralist clergyman, who lived in Paris for his health. He provided in his will, written in 1825, for the publication of the proof of "the power, wisdom and goodness of God, as manifested in the Creation; illustrating such work by all reasonable arguments, as for instance the variety and formation of God's Creatures in the animal, vegetable, and mineral Kingdoms." The legacy was the handsome sum of £8,000, and it was left to the President of the Royal Society to select the author or authors to write the treatises which the money was to reward. The president (Davies Gilbert) invited Archbishop Howley and Bishop Blomfield, among others, to assist him.

Bridgewater died thirty years before the publication of Darwin's *Origin of Species* in 1859, and Howley a decade before, but the matters which Darwin addressed had been part of the intellectual landscape for many years. "Natural philosophers", as those with scientific interests were known from the eighteenth century, had long been enquiring into the origins of the Earth and development of living creatures. The Christian doctrine of God as the creator is an article of faith for believers, along with the belief that the Scriptures are part of revelation. Nevertheless, many Victorian believers wondered about the veracity of the accounts of creation in the book of Genesis, and geologists had long been puzzling about the evident antiquity of the rocks of which the Earth is constituted. Others, though, believed that the whole faith edifice was threatened if any concessions were made to the speculations of the natural philosophers.

The intention of Bridgewater's legacy was to demonstrate that the findings of science were compatible with Christian orthodoxy. This accounts for the inclusion of the two bishops in Davies Gilbert's group. Howley and his fellow judges did not see the scheme as intended to reward a single individual but rather several scholars of eminence, although the finished works were largely undistinguished. Davies Gilbert's group concentrated on identifying established scholars, and it took them nearly a year and a half to decide on a series of eight authors. The number was obviously selected because of the amount of the bequest, but the choice of contributors was eventually rather hurried and open to criticism. About half the authors were members of the Royal Society; several of the authors were clergy, and most were (at least) acquainted with one another. Critics were severe, accusing the selection committee of providing commissions for their friends. Others pointed out that important subjects were not covered by the series. The idea, as it was refined by the committee, was to present in an accessible format the work of leading authorities on various aspects of scientific insight. Each author chose his own subject. The most eminent Anglican was William Buckland, Professor of Mineralogy at Oxford at the time of the publication, who became Dean of Westminster in 1845. He had long been fascinated by geology and wrote one of the best books in the series, although he was to be criticized for making concessions to the scientific position that conservative opinion regarded as dangerous. The *Bridgewater Treatises* were published between 1833 and 1840. The books varied: an inevitable consequence of the imprecise nature of the original brief and, perhaps, of the non-scientific background of the two bishops and others who helped to select the writers, and also because the authors did not work together as a group. One critic referred to the series as "The Bilgewater Treatises"! Nevertheless, they were popular, and in some cases volumes went into extra editions over several decades. It is estimated that more than 60,000 were produced by the 1850s. Few thought it odd that the Archbishop of Canterbury was involved in such a scheme, which is a tribute to Howley's reputation for fair-mindedness.

—

As noticed earlier, the contentious issue of the repeal of the Test and Corporation Acts had been dealt with before Howley became Archbishop of Canterbury, but the anticipated and, by some, feared emancipation of Roman Catholics was shortly to come before the Houses of Parliament, and Howley's involvement will now be examined in more detail. Since the religious settlement under Queen Elizabeth I and the "revolution" of 1688, Roman Catholics had endured political distrust and religious discrimination. An attempt to relax some of the restrictions under which they lived had sparked the Gordon Riots of 1780, and in the 1820s there still remained a profound unease in the hearts and minds of many English people. Part of this was an old and deep-seated fear that Roman Catholics could not be loyal to the English monarch, because they professed a higher spiritual loyalty to the Pope. The fear was greater than the reality. Many Roman Catholics were entirely loyal subjects of the Crown, and many Irish Roman Catholics had fought for Britain in the Napoleonic Wars, and others had sought to contribute to the life of the nation. It is necessary to remember that the political fact of the Act of Union had meant that Irish Roman Catholics had come under the direct rule of Parliament; a fact that significantly altered the political equilibrium. In practical terms, it was only a matter of time before an Irish Roman Catholic was elected as a Member of Parliament, yet Roman Catholics were prohibited from sitting in the Commons. It came as no surprise when Daniel O'Connell was elected in July 1828 (the same month that Manners-Sutton died). Wellington had come to believe that Roman Catholic emancipation was necessary. Those who opposed it were not all obscurantists or bigots with long memories of persecutions under Mary Tudor, the treachery of Guy Fawkes and his compatriots, nor even the fiasco of the reign of King James II. They were, in most cases, men of conservative views, and some of them were vehement in their defence of the Church of England. Howley's biographer states that opposition in the Commons was limited to a minority, or only to a small majority, and that a neutral view had been held by the government from as early as 1812.

In the Lords, particularly among the bishops, the situation was very different. The Duke of Wellington already knew that Howley would not support the Bill, because he had spoken against the concept as Bishop of London. As expected, when the Bill came before Parliament "within eight months of his elevation to the chair of St Austin", the new archbishop opposed it in the House of Lords with the same hostility he had expressed as Bishop of London.[49] He unsuccessfully proposed a wrecking amendment. If Howley's stance disappointed Wellington, it should not have surprised him. The new archbishop knew his own mind and had the courage to act according to its convictions; he was not a man to be bullied by a forceful prime minister. Wellington also knew that Blomfield was opposed to the measure. He, too, spoke in the Lords in opposition to the Emancipation Bill. Aware of the political niceties, Blomfield nevertheless acknowledged that his speech was not consistent with gratitude for his new preferment, and he did say that he would accept the result of the vote.

Howley's personal stance is well-described in the *Charge* delivered by Archdeacon Harrison shortly after Howley had died.

> In regard to ... the Roman Catholic emancipation Act, it is to be observed, that the Archbishop gave on that occasion the same determined opposition to the Roman Catholic claims, which he had uniformly given, since first he took his seat in the House of Lords as Bishop of London ... he protested against the policy of the Minister from whom he had received his appointment.

"Our Primate said, that, at his consecration he had sworn to stand by the Church of England." Harrison continued by quoting an unidentified journalist who declared that the archbishop's "post as an ecclesiastical leader required ... that he should exalt his 'mitred front in courts and parliaments,' indifferent to the power of Minister or Monarch. Respectful of both, but fearless of either."[50]

Howley had been willing, his friend Harrison continued,

> in the spirit of that true loyalty which Christianity teaches, and which the Church of England has ever exhibited, to lend, to the utmost of his power, the support of religion to the fabric of civil government: but when calumny and suspicion have done their worst, they have failed to prove that Caesar, or Caesar's throne, have ever obtained from his lips, or at his hands, the homage or the obedience which were God's.

Wellington, with Sir Robert Peel who had also originally opposed emancipation, spent time with Howley, Blomfield, and Van Mildert, seeking their support, but with no success. Wellington and Peel also spent a good deal of time talking to King George IV; one session lasted six hours. Eventually, they were successful in trying to persuade him that his signature on the Act of Parliament removing civil disabilities from Roman Catholics was necessary, even though he feared that it was a violation of his coronation oath. The king was persuaded or coerced into signing the Act, even though he had told Manners-Sutton and Howley, back in 1827, that he would never give his consent to legislation that opened the way for Roman Catholics to attain political power. Howley had spoken of the king's determination at a clergy banquet; it is inconceivable that he was being indiscreet; the king must have wanted to have his view made public. It was political reality which forced the king to sign the Act; he was faced with the prospect of Wellington's resignation and knew there was no alternative politician able to form a government, but he wept as he signed. He had previously said he understood his coronation oath in the same way as had his father before him: that Roman Catholic claims were utterly inadmissible. The king did not have to endure the consequences of the new Act for long. He died on 26 June 1830 and was succeeded by his brother William. Archbishop Howley officiated at the coronation of King William IV, "the Sailor King", which took place on 8 September the following year. A sign of the changing times was the presence at the coronation of a robed Roman Catholic bishop.[51]

The Roman Catholic Emancipation Act was a remarkable achievement by Wellington's administration, but its passage had weakened the Tory party. Wellington's government was subsequently vulnerable and was ousted in 1830 in the general election which was required following the death of George IV. The Whigs, led by Earl Grey, came to power and their reformist plans confirmed Sir Robert Peel's earlier gloomy prediction that the process was irresistible when they turned their attention to the House of Commons. It had been long recognized that political reform was needed, and the Reform Act of 1832 was one of the most important political events of the nineteenth century. The concept was popular in the country as a whole, although not among Tories. A revolution in France in 1830 had added to the fears of conservative individuals. But, in 1831, Grey's government introduced a Bill for Parliamentary Reform. Grey sought to abolish the so-called "rotten boroughs", where the election of Members of the House of Commons was in the hands of all-powerful local landowners, or where the place was too small to merit the representation it enjoyed. Among the latter were Old Sarum, where seven voters returned two Members, and Dunwich in Suffolk, where the number of voters was only twelve, again for two Members. Equally unsatisfactory at the other end of the scale, the newly grown great towns of Birmingham, Leeds, and Manchester had no parliamentary representation at all. So, it was planned to remove MPs from fifty-six rotten boroughs in England and Wales, reduce another thirty-one boroughs to only one MP, and also create sixty-seven new constituencies in urban areas. It was also proposed to widen the franchise by broadening the property qualification for voters to include small landowners, tenant farmers, shopkeepers, and householders who paid a yearly rental of ten pounds.

The idea was opposed by most, but not all, of the clergy: "in every village we had the black-coated recruiting-sergeant against us", a Whig observed of the Tory clergy. Grey's Bill also faced fierce opposition from most of the bishops. There was no specific ecclesiastical or theological interest in the bishops' rejection of the Bill, but some feared that its passage might begin a process which could lead to changes being forced upon the established Church. Archbishop Howley spoke and voted against the Bill. His speech was made in the evening of 7 October and was deliberately brief. It was very late when he rose to speak; he had hoped for the opportunity to speak earlier. He explained that he had "greatly desired to have entered into a full statement of the reason which imposed upon him the painful necessity of opposing a measure which came before the House with the strong recommendation of his Majesty's Government, and which had been carried by a majority of the House of Commons." He knew he did not have time for that, but first he paid tribute to the country's "happy Constitution", which he said he admired whilst accepting that there was always need for correction. His opposition to the Bill, he explained, was not due to a fundamental belief in its imperfection. On the contrary, "to a Reform synonymous with the extermination of abuses, and the restoration of the excellencies of the Constitution, he professed himself a sincere friend." Howley professed himself pleased that others who had spoken in opposition to Grey's Bill had

> declared that their opposition was directed, not against the principle of the Bill, or the general principle of the Reform, and they had expressed their willingness to accede to a measure of gradual, temperate, and safe Reform. In that sentiment he entirely concurred with them. He could not help indulging a hope, that the result of this discussion might be a union of men of all parties, having the same great object in view—the good of the country, and that, thus uniting, they would prepare some measure for the consideration of Parliament, so cautiously worded as to tranquillize the fears of those who dreaded agitation, and, at the same time, sufficiently efficient to satisfy the friends of the Constitution, who, while they desired to have its excellencies preserved and its blemishes removed, were unwilling to try an experiment so extensive as that which was now proposed.[52]

Howley concluded by saying that, if the Bill were not passed, he did not think that there would be violence, as some had predicted, but if disturbances did ensue, he "would be content to bear his share in the general calamity". His opposition was based on the conviction that the Bill was "mischievous" and might be "extremely dangerous" to the constitution. Archbishop Howley's mild tones clearly revealed his Tory views, but his speech was not the expression of a man whose mind was closed to the prospect, and even the desirability, for Parliamentary reform. Rather it shows his extreme caution as a man of conviction, who could see all sides of a problem. He was one who believed that reforms should be identified by people from all segments of political opinion, and not from any specific political group. While it is possible to dismiss his words as coming from someone ineluctably conservative, it was nevertheless the speech of a wise man.

When the Bill was defeated in the Lords on 8 October, it was lost by 199 to 158 votes. Twenty-one of the votes against the Bill were those of bishops. The enemies of the Church did not fail to notice that the episcopal vote was more than half of the majority, and they were aware of the opposition from ordinary clergy in parishes across the country. The popularity of the Church of England, already low among the general populace, plummeted. There were riots in a number of towns, so Howley was proved wrong on that point. They included Derby and Nottingham, but the worst riots were in Bristol where the Bishop's Palace was among the buildings sacked and burned. The bishop was fortunate to be away from home at the time. In Durham, Van Mildert was burned in effigy. Archbishop Howley did not escape the wrath; he was threatened by a mob at Addington, and was "assailed and grossly insulted", and so had the opportunity to share in that "general calamity" which he had not believed to be likely. He was confronted with hostile elements in the audience when taking the chair at an SPG meeting in Croydon and was dismayed. In Lambeth, he heard a rumour that his palace was to be attacked, and he asked, to no avail, for an armed guard; but there was no attack. At Canterbury, he was "hissed" as his carriage passed through the streets, and a story persisted that a dead cat was thrown into the carriage and struck his chaplain. The archbishop dismissed his complaint by telling him to be grateful that the cat was dead, although a wit remarked later that there was no record of how long it had been dead! James Garrard, Howley's modern biographer, believed that the whole story was apocryphal, but its existence reveals something of Howley's calm and detachment.[53] The archbishop postponed a Visitation *Charge* for some months because of the political situation.

A general election followed, which the Whigs won conclusively. When Grey agreed to form a government, he extracted from the king a commitment to create up to fifty new Whig peers if the House of Lords were to reject a new Bill. Word got out, and the threat proved to be sufficient to bring the House to heel when Grey brought back his somewhat amended Bill the following year. Again, the bishops mostly voted with the majority, this time in support of the Bill, aware that they had taken much of the blame for the earlier failure. So the new Bill was successful and received royal assent in 1832 and is known to history as the Great Reform Act, or First Reform Act. More formally, though, it was the Representation of the People Act, 1832. The eventual changes were a landmark in British constitutional history, but were not as drastic as many Tories feared, nor were they as radical as others hoped, and within a generation the Act of 1832 had become a spent force.

Howley's change of heart with regard to the Great Reform Act did not mean that he was won over in any comprehensive way to the cause of reform. On concluding that the need for reform was unanswerable he had supported it with his usual caution. He always judged proposals on what he deemed to be their merits, but he opposed a Bill designed to remove civil disabilities from Jewish citizens in 1833. Six years later he went on to oppose a very mild scheme for national education promoted by Lord John Russell, because many clergy feared the loss of the Church's hold over elementary education. Howley's leadership of the opponents was quiet but very firm, and his diplomacy enabled a compromise to be reached in 1840. Part of Russell's original proposal had involved government inspection of the schools of the National Society, and the eventual deal gave the archbishops the right of veto regarding the appointment of the inspectors. Howley continued to support the National Society in its work for elementary education according to the principles of the Church of England.

It was equally consistent of Howley to oppose the Irish Church Temporalities Bill of 1833, although Archbishop Whately of Dublin incorrectly thought that Howley had been consulted beforehand by the government and had agreed in principle to the Bill's provisions. Whately was wrong; and Howley described those provisions, speaking in a *Charge* of 1832 in anticipation of the Bill coming before Parliament, as "organized for the subversion of the Irish branch of our Church by the general spoliation of its property". The Irish Church Temporalities Bill was the touchstone of John Keble's famous Assize Sermon in St Mary's Church, Oxford, in July 1833 which, due to an imprecise but frequently quoted comment by John Henry Newman, that he "kept the date", has commonly been marked as the starting date of the Oxford Movement.

—

The particular combination of circumstances which produced the Oxford Movement had been developing for some years before John Keble's sermon. Newman, the Vicar of St Mary's, Oxford, felt called to some "great work" in defence of the Church of England, and decided that the best way forward was the production of pamphlets: the famous *Tracts for the Times*. He wrote the largest number, twenty-four of the eventual ninety that were published. The series generated a controversy that engulfed the Church of

England, and Oxford University, between 1833 and 1845. The *Tracts* were to change permanently the Church's understanding of itself, its role, and spirituality. Howley, as a high churchman, had a degree of sympathy with the Tractarians' thinking to begin with, although he believed their views were somewhat excessive.[54] He was an old-fashioned high churchman, well informed theologically as a former Regius Professor of Divinity, and as his remarkable library attests. He was well able to understand the original appeal by the Tractarians to Catholic antiquity, even though his sympathy was by no means entirely engaged by them.

Garrard pointed out that Howley's chaplains were always of the same cast of mind as the archbishop. At least two of them, who became personal friends and advisors, are also associated with the Oxford Movement. Benjamin Harrison, the author of the insightful *Charge* of 1848 which memorialized Howley, was the author of four of the *Tracts for the Times*. Earlier he had been an assistant of E. B. Pusey at Oxford, and the Tractarians hoped at first that having in effect a "friend at court" would help the nascent Movement. However, as he gained experience of the wider Church, Harrison gradually and inevitably cooled from his earlier enthusiasm and proved to be less useful to his Oxford friends. Another chaplain was Hugh James Rose (1795–1838), who was associated with the Hackney Phalanx. His comparatively early death was thought by his contemporaries to have robbed the Oxford Movement of a possible leader, particularly after Newman's conversion to Rome. Rose died in Florence in 1838, where he had gone with his wife for his health; they had spent their last night in England at the home of Harrison. Rose had been the host of a small conference held at his home in Hadleigh, coincidentally also in July 1833, and was a moving light behind setting up an Association of Friends of the Church with William Palmer of Worcester College, Oxford. The association, which had parallels in other parts of the country, sought to "maintain pure and inviolate the doctrines, services and the discipline of the Church . . . ", and to provide church people with the "opportunity of exchanging sentiments, and cooperating together on a large scale".[55] For the association, Palmer drew up an address to be presented to the archbishop by the clergy; it attracted a good deal of publicity, and a similar document was composed for signature by lay people. The Clergy Address, which deplored the tendency away from the doctrine and discipline of the Church of England and the growing ignorance of its spiritual claims, was signed by 7,000 clergy; the latter petition by 23,000 "heads of families". The former was presented to Howley in the library at Lambeth on 5 February 1834. He received it courteously and said that "he anticipated good effects from this public declaration of the sentiments of the clergy". Furthermore, he "regarded it as a direct contradiction of misrepresentation and falsehood of different kinds which have been widely circulated, as an avowal of your unshaken adherence to our National Church, its faith, and its formularies, and as a testimony of your veneration for the episcopal office, and your cordial respect for your bishops."[56]

Throughout the controversy surrounding the *Tracts for the Times*, Howley kept in close contact with Bishop Richard Bagot of Oxford, although the initiative was principally Bagot's and was partly due to timidity on his part. Howley at Lambeth was aware of the potential difficulties and exerted a steady and gentle pressure on Bagot to contain the situation. At first, Bagot held Newman in high regard, but the feeling cooled as the *Tracts* multiplied and Newman became increasingly intransigent. The relationship was ruptured by Newman when he produced his famous *Tract 90* in 1841 with the title *Remarks on certain Passages in the Thirty-nine Articles*. It was a tract too far, and clearly an exercise in special pleading from the pen of a man who was disillusioned with the Church of England. The story of its publication is well known, and it convulsed Oxford and the whole Church. As the controversy developed, Howley hoped that Bagot would get the increasingly disillusioned and reclusive Newman to end the series and to withdraw *Tract 90*. But the harassed and anxious Bagot only achieved the cessation of the series, and sensibly Howley did not rely entirely on Bagot's efforts. He invited Dr Pusey to visit him at Addington Palace at the height of the agitation over *Tract 90*. Pusey wrote guardedly afterwards to reassure Newman: characteristically, the archbishop's "manner and all that he has said has been very kind". He was keen that the situation should not be made worse by further precipitate action by the Tractarians. Pusey's biographer, Henry Parry Liddon, writing forty years later, observed that the letter contained "a welcome picture of that most learned as well as the most equitable of the Primates of the present century".[57]

The Movement in its earliest stages was theological rather than pastoral or liturgical. This was something which Dr Pusey wanted to emphasize, for he was never completely reconciled to some of its more elaborate ritualistic manifestations. In 1836, the Tractarians were involved in a major row over the teaching of Renn Dickson Hampden, which will be considered below. In striking a blow against Hampden's liberalism, Pusey saw an opportunity to assert the intellectual credentials of the Oxford Movement and of the Church of England. To this end, he initiated a plan to publish in English each year a volume of *The Library of the Fathers*. This would be, he wrote to Keble, a "Library of the Catholic Fathers of the Holy Church Universal anterior to the division of East and West, translated by Members of the Anglican Church". The idea was an effort to remind Anglicans of their heritage and thus to legitimize the Movement. He approached Archbishop Howley with the request that he would permit the series of volumes to be dedicated to him. The archbishop was able to see beyond the immediate controversy to the good that such a *Library* would bring. He liked the idea of the scheme and replied in a letter dated 11 October 1836:

> In respect to the undertaking in which you are about to engage, the reasons which in general induce me to decline dedications have no weight. On the contrary, I should not feel myself justified in foregoing the opportunity of expressing my approbation of your design.
>
> It is highly desirable to direct the attention of the clergy to the writings of the pastors and teachers who enjoyed the highest reputation in the early ages of Christianity. Those writers at present are known to few even of the clergy, except by quotations or references on controversial questions, which convey very imperfect notions of their character or opinions.
>
> I remain my dear Sir, your faithful servant,
> W. Cantuar.[58]

The first volume to appear, in 1838, was an edition of the *Confessions of St Augustine*, edited by Pusey himself, although he shared the editorship of the series with Keble and Newman. However, most of the work fell on the shoulders of their colleague Charles Marriott, and he found the strain too great in addition to his other duties. The infrequent appearance of further volumes, eventually spread over many years, meant that the effectiveness of the series was not as powerful as was hoped.

The history of the expansion of the Oxford Movement from the university into the parishes of the nation has been described often. The *Tracts for the Times* had a surprisingly wide circulation and came to be widely read. They generated much publicity for the ideas they propounded, even as controversy developed around them. In addition, as men graduated and were dispersed in curacies across the country, they took with them the Oxford Movement's theological insights and its perception of ministry, out from the university into the wider Church of England. Parallel with that original intellectual process, there developed the phenomenon known by its opponents as "ritualism". This latter had hardly begun by the end of Howley's life, but it was to become a significant issue for later archbishops of Canterbury.

Howley's concern with the controversy surrounding Renn Dickson Hampden has been mentioned. It began in January 1836 with the death of the Regius Professor of Divinity at Oxford, Edward Burton, and projected the archbishop into unexpected difficulties. Because the vacancy was that of a Regius Professorship, the Prime Minister, Lord Melbourne, had the duty of nominating Burton's successor to the Crown. He sought advice, including from Archbishop Howley, who was, it will be remembered, a previous holder of the post. Howley offered a list of eight names. Dr Pusey was at the head; also on the list were Pusey's friends and collaborators, John Keble and John Henry Newman, the intellectual leaders of the Tractarians. The names which the archbishop submitted to Melbourne were disclosed to Newman by H. J. Rose, Howley's chaplain. After further enquiries, Melbourne made his choice and sent to the king the name of Renn Dickson Hampden (1793–1868), a learned man whose style was obscure and whose manner was unattractive. Before doing so, he mentioned his choice to Howley, who raised no objections, even though Hampden had not been among the archbishop's suggested candidates. Hampden was already a distinguished man; recently appointed the Principal of St Mary's Hall, Oxford, and a former Fellow of Oriel College, he had been Professor of Moral Theology since 1834. It is not likely that either the prime minister or the archbishop expected an outcry. Opposition to Hampden quickly gathered, and a pamphlet war ensued. The cause of the row was a series of lectures which Hampden had delivered in 1832. In those days given annually, the Bampton Lectures were an important Oxford institution which had been founded in the eighteenth century to expound and defend the Christian faith. Hampden's lectures had revealed his theological position as that of a broad churchman of the kind that the Tractarians dismissed as "rationalistic". They also revealed that he had been considerably influenced by a liberal Oxford theologian named Blanco White, a fact which added nothing to Hampden's reputation. White was a controversial figure with mixed Irish and Spanish ancestry; before becoming an Anglican, he had been a Roman Catholic priest, and he ended his days as a Unitarian.

Hampden, it was wittily said, "stood before you like a milestone and brayed at you like a jackass." His lectures had been published with the cumbersome title *The Scholastic Philosophy, considered in its relations to Christian Theology*. They had attracted little attention at the time. This changed when he was nominated to the Regius Professorship. The Tractarians and many who thought like them, and some who did not, were united in the view that Hampden's theological opinions disqualified him from holding this new post. Pusey wrote accordingly to Lord Melbourne without success. He also wrote to Howley's chaplain, Harrison, his former assistant, in the hope that he could persuade Howley to join in the protest. Howley did try to get the prime minister to change his mind, but to no avail. Indeed, King William IV also spoke to Melbourne, who was displeased at his intervention. The king claimed that he had given his approval under the impression that Melbourne's nomination had the approval of the archbishop. Newman and Pusey were among those who wrote pamphlets critical of Hampden. Melbourne hesitated but stuck to his guns, and the appointment went ahead, but he warned Hampden to be cautious. Hampden produced a careful inaugural lecture, but his enemies kept up the pressure and invented various schemes to reduce Hampden's influence in Oxford. The correspondence between Howley and Hampden concerning the professorship was subsequently published and ran to several editions. In future, Melbourne was very cautious in his ecclesiastical appointments. The battle lapsed from Howley's concerns, but Hampden's career proved troublesome once again at the very end of the archbishop's life.

—

At the end of 1834, by which time Howley had served more than six years as Archbishop of Canterbury, King William IV dismissed Lord Melbourne, and on the advice of the Duke of Wellington invited Sir Robert Peel to form an administration, even though he could not command a majority in the House of Commons. The monarch chose Peel with the intention of protecting the Church, particularly after the upheaval of the Irish Church Act of 1833. Everyone knew that Peel's government was likely to prove a temporary phenomenon, and so it proved, but in its mere 135 days it set in train events which permanently altered the Church of England. Peel took office on 9 December 1834, knowing that the Church could not escape the prevalent reforming momentum in the life of the nation, as Howley feared. He was keen to initiate moderate reforms as a means of saving the Church from the possibility of more aggressive Whig intervention at a later date. Peel saw that he could only protect the Church by making concessions. It was surprising to many that a Tory prime minister could come to power with the intention of introducing even a modest reform policy, and the fears of churchmen who had been discountenanced by the Whigs' 1833 Act for the Irish Church were still alive. It is clear that Keble, Newman, and Pusey, and their followers at Oxford, were very concerned about further possible reforms, and the Archbishop of Canterbury and his colleagues shared that concern, albeit for different reasons. Peel also knew that the reforms of the Church in Ireland, having begun, would have to continue. For England, Peel had the modest ambition to increase the numbers of clergy resident in their parishes and to reduce the financial exploitation of pluralities. Other motives were the easing of two of the "disabilities" irksome to dissenters: the church rate, which compelled dissenting ratepayers to contribute to the maintenance of the parish church, which they abjured, and the obligation for all marriages to be solemnized in those same parish churches according to the rites of the Church of England.

In the event, the outcome of the reforms initiated by his government were much more wide-ranging and made a great and permanent difference to the life of the Church of England. However, as he took office, his plans for the reform of the Church were not known. This was partly due to his circumspect and aloof nature, but also because he had no clear idea of what action he should take.[59] Peel did recognize that if any reform was to have a chance of success, he would need the support (or at least to avoid the direct opposition) of churchmen. It was clear to him that with the involvement of lay people, as well as clergy, there would be more likelihood of accurately identifying the areas most urgently in need of attention. Similarly, it would make it easier for the Church as a whole to accept what was implemented. He was aware, though, of the inherent danger that clergymen with vested interests might seek to neutralize the process if their preferments were threatened. This danger was averted by the careful choice of personnel to serve on the various commissions and, in the early weeks, by Peel's own ability to grasp details. This way of thinking commended itself to the conservative and cautious mind of Archbishop Howley.

Accordingly, Peel had a long meeting with Howley on 4 January 1835. Blomfield, the Bishop of London, was there, and was to be a key figure in the events that unfolded; also present was Peel's colleague and friend, Henry Goulburn, who was to serve as his Chancellor of the Exchequer. The meeting went as Peel had hoped, and the next day he wrote to the king and proposed a commission should be appointed. Its brief would be to review both Crown and episcopal patronage with the intention of improving the pastoral efficiency of the Church of England. The clergy members were recruited by Howley, who proved to be a very conscientious chair, while Peel chose the laypeople. Naturally, Archbishop Vernon Harcourt of York was a member, so were Bishops Kaye (Lincoln) and Monk (Gloucester), together with the indefatigable Blomfield. Peel's ministerial choices were Lord Lyndhurst (the Lord Chancellor), Goulburn, Charles Wynn (Chancellor of the Duchy of Lancaster), and three others who were not part of the government: Jenner (the Dean of the Court of Arches), Lord Harrowby, and Henry Hobhouse. Their names were published on 4 February; they constituted the Ecclesiastical Duties and Revenue Commission, but, as Geoffrey F. A. Best in *Temporal Pillars* observed, it was this commission which in 1836 effectively "metamorphosed" into the Ecclesiastical Commissioners. With the members chosen in this way, with Howley's help and concurrence, Peel successfully ensured that reforms would not be imposed on the Church by the government, but rather they would be implemented by the government after being commended to it by the commissioners. It was hoped that the process which Peel adopted with Howley's agreement would go some way towards reducing opposition to its eventual proposals, at least from within the Church; it was not entirely successful in this aim.

Howley was a reluctant reformer in the early 1830s, but he saw the necessity to be thorough in carrying through the commission's task. In this he had the inestimable support of Blomfield, whose powerful personality seemed to dominate the proceedings; someone sneered that he was "an ecclesiastical Peel"; Sydney Smith, from 1831 a canon of St Paul's Cathedral, remarked in a letter that "Charles James of London will become the Church of England here on earth."[60] Archbishop Harcourt of York famously said of the commission's meetings, as Blomfield's biographer son recorded, "till Blomfield comes, we all sit and mend our pens and talk about the weather." Critics of Archbishop Howley made ammunition from such observations, declaring that he was too weak to constrain Blomfield, or to have his own view. The truth was more subtle, the archbishop was not perturbed by Blomfield's powerful presence; the two men shared almost identical views as to the need for reform and the way of achieving it. A benefit to Howley arose when the commissioners' proposals were unpopular in that Blomfield was blamed, but merely avoiding opprobrium would not have consciously motivated the archbishop. It is unlikely that the other members, bishops and laymen, all of them able and self-assured people well accustomed to public life, would have accepted Blomfield's domineering if it had not had the tacit support of the Archbishop of Canterbury, and if he had not been so obviously competent. It is significant that both men devoted their time wholeheartedly to the work of the commission. Sometimes it met two or three times a week. Of its 103 meetings, Howley attended ninety-five and Blomfield ninety-three.[61] This showed a remarkable level of commitment by both men, especially by Howley, who was seventy years of age in 1836, twenty years Blomfield's senior.

Peel's government resigned on 8 April 1835, and Lord Melbourne once again took over. With the loss of Peel and his political colleagues, the remaining lay members, Harrowby, Jenner, and Hobhouse, along with the bishops, asked Howley to act as intermediary. Archbishop Howley, reluctant originally to embrace reform, knew that it was necessary to get the new prime minister to authorize the continuation of the work of the commissioners, if the initiative was to remain with the Church. Melbourne agreed, and in late May they resumed their work. During the first year of his new ministry, the commission concentrated on consolidating its position and gathering information. It surfaced with a series of reports early in 1836 of a reforming nature, in which it addressed, most importantly, residence and the problems posed by pluralities, and considered the patronage exercised by the episcopate and deans and chapters.

If Blomfield's energy was significantly responsible for the speed at which the commission worked, he was aided by the tendency of Melbourne's Whig nominees to be absent from the meetings. The commissioners hoped that their three proposed statutes would quickly be passed into law, but the process took much longer than anticipated. In effect, the recommendations made by the commissioners did become law through three Acts of Parliament. In 1836, the Established Church Act was passed; this was followed by the Pluralities Act of 1838; the third was the Dean and Chapter Act of 1840. Included in the latter was the widening of the membership of the commission to include all diocesan bishops. Howley, however, was angered when Lord John Russell introduced, on behalf of the government but without having consulted him, a Tithe Commutation Bill in 1836. This was contrary to an understanding he had reached with Melbourne that government would not introduce ecclesiastical legislation without prior reference, but the change met with general approval in the country.

The uneven distribution of the Church's financial resources was to be addressed across the board. At the parochial level a great deal was done to improve the circumstances of the poorest clergy. To assist in the redistribution, not only episcopal estates were appropriated, but so were those of cathedrals; indeed, the latter were almost the commissioners' only resource. Deans and chapters proved to be among the most reluctant in accepting reforms which were the expropriation of a proportion of their assets. Howley's old school fellow, Sydney Smith, at St Paul's, said of him,

> fifty-three years ago he knocked me down with a chess-board for checkmating him—and now he is attempting to take away my patronage. I believe these are the only two acts of violence committed in his life.

Howley emphatically denied the story of the chessboard, but Smith was unapologetic. He also remarked that when Howley was enthroned at Canterbury by proxy, he had promised to protect the resources of the cathedral, and by implication (Smith implied), the resources of all the cathedrals of England. Howley's apparent indifference to that obligation, acknowledged on his behalf by his proxy, was not the sort of thing to escape criticism from Smith's sharp pen, although he acknowledged Howley's "gentleness, kindness, and amiable and high-principled courtesy to his clergy".

Restrictions were placed upon the holding of multiple benefices, and a minimum level of pay for curates was recommended. The requirement for incumbents to be resident in their parishes to a greater degree was a much-needed reform. An unexpected consequence of the enforcement of residence by incumbents and the increased costs of curates was a drop in the number of curates acting for absent incumbents. There was 3,078 of them in 1838, but by the early 1860s that number had dropped to just below a thousand. Improved residence was a desirable change, but it increased the difficulties faced by curates seeking posts, notwithstanding the increase in the number of parishes in densely populated industrial areas.[62]

The wide discrepancies in episcopal incomes were also addressed. The commission proposed that bishops in poor dioceses, such as Chester, should receive more; bishops in rich dioceses, such as Ely, were to receive less and thus subsidize their poorer brethren. The aim was to provide bishops with not less than £4,500 per annum and not more than £5,000, with certain exceptions. Changes in population density were recognized, a rearrangement of diocesan boundaries was undertaken, and two new dioceses were proposed. A couple of dioceses were amalgamated in order that the bishops of the newly formed dioceses would have seats in the House of Lords without increasing episcopal representation. This was partly pragmatism; it sought to avoid the radical question of why, if some bishops did not sit in the Lords, should any of the others? The relatively new conurbation of Manchester became a diocese in its own right, although not until 1847. The urban development as a result of the industrialization of Yorkshire was recognized with the establishment of the Diocese of Ripon. That happened in 1836, and its first bishop was Charles Thomas Longley, who, in 1862, became Queen Victoria's third Archbishop of Canterbury on the death of Howley's successor, J. B. Sumner.

The Archbishop of Canterbury's own stipend was to be "pegged" for future appointments at £15,000 per annum, that of the Archbishop of York and the Bishop of London at £10,000, the Bishop of Durham's at £8,000.[63] The current bishops, along with all clergy, were exempt from a reduction in their income for the changes only came into force at the next vacancy. In each case, the new figures represented a substantial reduction. For example, Johnson, the modern biographer of Bishop Blomfield, said that Howley's Canterbury stipend was £28,000, whereas his successor, J. B. Sumner, received the new rate: a reduction of nearly half.[64] Provision was also made for the adequate housing of bishops, so that the cost of improvements did not fall at the feet of any individual bishop. Howley, however, had already spent considerable sums on London House in St James's Square, when he was Bishop of London. When he became Archbishop of Canterbury, he saw that the palace at Lambeth needed repair and extension. He engaged an architect, Edward Blore, to report on the situation and, later, to plan the alterations. Eventually, there was considerable redevelopment at Lambeth. In all, Howley's work on the archbishop's estates and property cost around £60,000, which Howley financed by a mortgage authorized by a private Act of Parliament and from his own resources. By the time of his death, the loan had been repaid to the extent, Harrison's *Charge* noted, that "there is no deduction, on this score, from the amount to which the income of the See has been reduced."

The modern history of Lambeth Palace records that in 1829 over half of the old medieval and Tudor buildings at Lambeth were demolished.

In their place was built a great "perpendicular Gothic" block of three storeys with a grand entrance.[65] The new domestic buildings were known as "Mrs Howley's lodgings". The chapel was restored "according," said Harrison in his *Charge*, "to its original symmetry of structure, and ... adorning with a simplicity of taste, and chasteness of beauty, which make it now the gem of the whole building."[66] Howley also had much work done in terms of alterations and additions at Addington Palace, which Manners-Sutton had acquired as a rural archiepiscopal residence a few miles from Croydon in Surrey. Howley's changes included a chapel and a library. He also restored the chancel of the parish church at Addington and the interior of the church. At Canterbury, where there was no archiepiscopal residence to improve, Howley gave the cathedral the Gothic-style archiepiscopal throne, which still stands on the south side of the choir. Not far away on the north side his monument and effigy are close to the high altar.

Archbishop Howley may have been slow to convert to the concept of church reform, but from 1835 he led the process. Best tellingly observed:

> He may still have seemed "the meek archbishop" in private, but one would not gather that he was anything of the kind from *Hansard's* reports of his speeches in the House of Lords. Melbourne's speeches in the Commissioners' defence would be as long, and to Blomfield would inevitably fall the hatchet-work of debate; but whenever Howley was there, he had to lead for the prelates, and he always did it well. It is inconceivable that he did not believe in the Commissioners and their work, that he was only assuming a politic pose. Between 1832, when the majority of the bishops were huddling together at Lambeth and praying for a counter-revolution, and 1836, when he appeared as the inflexible supporter of quasi-revolutionary measures, Howley had apparently undergone a change of heart.
>
> The Howley who came so regularly to the Commissioners' meeting and spoke so well on their behalf was not just a puppet pulled by Blomfield's strings. He believed in what he was doing.
>
> The result was infinitely creditable to him.[67]

Best concludes, without in any sense diminishing the achievement of Archbishop Howley, that in the mid-1830s, "to the institution of some body (sic) or other like the Ecclesiastical Commissioners, there was no serious alternative." It is to Howley's lasting credit that in recognition of this, he gave it his quiet and efficient blessing and gave Blomfield, as the man most able to deliver the reforms, the capacity to do so.

—

By the late 1840s it was known that Professor Hampden was hoping for a bishopric, and Lord John Russell, prime minister from 1846 to 1852, was considering him as a possibility for the proposed new diocese of Manchester, but that was not to be. However, in the winter of 1847 and 1848, in the final months of Howley's life, the matter of Hampden's episcopal ambitions did become an issue. It happened when a bridge collapsed and the Archbishop of York fell into a pond in the grounds of his palace. Vernon Harcourt had been archbishop for almost forty years and had achieved the age of ninety-one. "I think we have frightened the frogs," he said laconically to his chaplain, but there were greater consequences, for the aged archbishop died a month later, on 5 November 1847. Harcourt's demise at such a great age could not have been entirely unanticipated, although Howley "experienced a severe shock in the tidings he received, without previous intelligence of his illness of the death of his aged and highly-esteemed brother in the primacy of England."[68]

Russell decided to appoint Thomas Musgrave of Hereford as Harcourt's successor after overtures were rejected by Bishop Maltby of Durham, who was in his seventy-eighth year. There was a need to find a new Bishop of Hereford, and Russell offered that see to Hampden, aware that the appointment might prove contentious. Archbishop Howley had warned him that there might be what he called an "explosion" of protest. He repeated and reinforced his warning a fortnight later, when he perceived the full force and vigour of the protests. Many, and not just the Anglo Catholics, still believed that Hampden's theological opinions should exclude him as a candidate for the episcopate. It caused great offence across the Church that the prime minister had chosen for a bishopric a clergyman who had been defined as heretical by his own university following the row over his Bampton Lectures. Oxford had excluded Hampden from the group which chose the university's select preachers, and from the committee which enquired into heresy. A proposal to remove the inhibitions in 1842 had been lost. Some diocesan bishops, of which Phillpotts of Exeter was the most emphatic, forbade their ordinands from attending Hampden's lectures.

Those who protested about Hampden's unsuitability were also protesting, at least by inference, about the prime ministerial liberty to nominate whomever he wished to the Queen. So they were in effect questioning the royal prerogative, as they had been with regard to Hampden's Regius Professorship. The controversy over Hampden's appointment to Hereford moved from the question of his orthodoxy and developed into a constitutional quarrel about the absolute freedom of the prime minister to nominate whomever he wished, and the convention that the choice would not be questioned. The Tractarians had borne the blame for the opposition to Hampden's nomination as Regius Professor in 1836, although they were not the only ones opposed to him. This time opposition came from a wide spectrum of churchmen, and the situation was much more than a dispute among academics.

Russell should have expected trouble; he knew about the quarrel of 1836, and he had been warned by Archbishop Howley. Characteristically, Howley did not publicly protest at the time of Hampden's nomination to the bishopric; such a move would have been unthinkable for the Archbishop of Canterbury. He cautiously confirmed that Hampden had written nothing controversial since his Oxford appointment. In addition, however, he did express privately his doubts about Hampden's discretion and his judgement.[69] Russell, knowing Howley's characteristic diffidence, should have anticipated from this that the nomination would indeed be controversial: if a man of Howley's caution expressed reservations, then there was undoubtedly ground for wider concern. In the event, the opposition was greater than anyone expected. Across the country, there were meetings of protest, attended by clergy and by laypeople. In Exeter, the formidable Bishop Phillpotts reacted with predictable outrage at the prospect of Hampden's promotion. Bishop Samuel Wilberforce of Oxford, who was still ambivalent towards the Tractarians, was nevertheless vehemently opposed to Hampden's preferment. The bishops sent a letter of protest to the prime minister, and thirteen of them out of twenty-five signed it. Howley (having been consulted privately by the prime minister) was not a signatory, and could not have been; neither were the men destined to be his two successors at Canterbury, Sumner, at that time Bishop of Chester, and Bishop Longley of Ripon, although the latter had allowed the publication of a private letter of protest. It was reported that the Queen was annoyed by the bishops' protests. In addition, many other letters poured in to the prime minister, and the press joined in the campaign. However, not all the volubility was generated by Hampden's opponents; fifteen heads of Oxford colleges wrote in his support, as did the aged Maltby.

Despite the objections, Russell persisted with the nomination. Even if he had wanted to change his mind, it would have been constitutionally difficult to do so. The next step in the process was the necessity for Hampden to be elected by the Dean and Chapter of Hereford. This was arranged despite the dean, John Merewether, declaring that he would not vote for the nominee. Indeed, he informed Russell of his position in long letters, one of around 3,000 words. This brought from Russell the laconic response, "I have the honour to receive your letter . . . in which you intimate to me your intention of violating the law." There was, for a time, a fear that the Dean and Chapter of Hereford would indeed break the law and not elect the Crown's candidate. Even though twelve prebendaries absented themselves, and Dean Merewether did vote against Hampden, the election was successfully concluded.

English law also requires that episcopal elections are formally confirmed as valid. The ancient ceremony for Hampden took place in the church of St Mary-le-Bow in central London on 11 January 1848, the traditional location for such events. Despite the formal nature of the occasion which was concerned with the validity of the election and the identity of the candidate and no other issues, protesters endeavoured to express objections. They were ruled out of order but continued their efforts afterwards by appealing to the Queen's Bench. When the case was heard, a ruling in favour of the Crown was made, and Hampden's consecration could go ahead.

Howley was the unwitting cause of further delay. The archbishop's health had been in decline for some time, and he was in the grip of his final illness. His death on 11 February 1848, the day before his eighty-second birthday, meant that Lord John Russell had to find a new Archbishop of Canterbury, and get him in post before Hampden could be consecrated to the Bishopric of Hereford. Perhaps Howley was fortunate to be removed from the scene, as he had told Lord Aberdeen that he "would rather go to the Tower" than consecrate Hampden. Howley's successor, John Bird Sumner, was able eventually to proceed with the consecration of Hampden to the Bishopric of Hereford. Hampden went off to his diocese, which he administered faithfully and uncontroversially until his death in April 1868. As the years passed, he became a strong advocate of Anglican orthodoxy and worked quietly in his diocese.

—

Despite his personal modesty, Archbishop William Howley was aware of the dignity of his office, and he lived in considerable state in Lambeth Palace. No one left the room when he dined until he rose to go, and he was conducted across the courtyard at Lambeth Palace at night by footmen carrying lighted flambeaux, when he returned to "Mrs Howley's lodgings", the domestic quarters. To reach the House of Lords he was conveyed across the River Thames by barge, and he also had a fine coach. Howley knew that, following the Ecclesiastical Commission reforms, his successors would not be able to maintain the pomp which surrounded the life of the Archbishop of Canterbury, and so he did what he could to reduce the demands made upon the archiepiscopal purse whilst maintaining the dignity of the office. He took advantage of an illness in the early 1840s to abandon some of the more extravagant customs that bore upon the archbishop's daily life.

As has been noted often, Archbishop Howley was a reserved man, described sometimes as "cold", and seemed to lack a forcible presence. All these factors were exacerbated by his reputation as a poor public speaker and because he published little. Howley's poor performance in public often gave rise to the view that he was a weak man, although it is clear that he was not. In his long episcopal and archiepiscopal ministry, William Howley led a Church which gradually perceived that it was facing immense changes in the society to which it ministered. In his quiet way, he prepared it well for its demanding future and for its increased activity in the second half of the nineteenth century. Like his contemporaries, he could not see the outcome of the growth of the population and the development of industrialization. He was an immensely conservatively-minded man, brought up in the certainties of the previous century's Anglicanism, but he left the Church able to face the uncertain future. A trivial anecdote may be taken as symbolic of his awareness of a changing world. He gave up wearing his episcopal wig, except in church where he retained the habit all his life, as a custom that was outdated when he learned that Blomfield had received permission from King William IV to dispense with his.

Howley "lingered at death's door to the wonderment of his doctors and the frustration of the speculators with his pulse beating only five strokes a minute."[70] On the day he died, Queen Victoria (despite Howley's ineptitude with her rings) wrote fondly in her diary:

> After having been out walking, we received the news of the death of the excellent Archbishop of Canterbury, at which I am truly sorry. He was in his 83rd year, so that one could not expect him to recover from this illness. He was so mild & gentle. There was no important event in my life in which he was not interested & did not officiate.[71]

CHAPTER 2

John Bird Sumner (1848–1862)

When John Bird Sumner, the Bishop of Chester, became the Archbishop of Canterbury in succession to William Howley, he was immediately thrust into the centre of the controversy surrounding the appointment of Renn Dickson Hampden to the Bishopric of Hereford. Although the appointment process had been completed, the consecration of Hampden had been delayed by Howley's final illness and demise. When the end came, it left the prime minister with the urgent problem of finding a replacement. His choice was unusually limited, for he could only choose from among those bishops who would be willing to consecrate Hampden.

When Russell chose John Bird Sumner (1780–1862), he had just passed his sixty-eighth birthday and had been Bishop of Chester for twenty years, where he had exercised a notable ministry. Sumner was a man with a simple and straightforward personal faith. His holiness of life was evident to those with whom he came in contact, his pastoral zeal was well known, and in his earlier years he had been a prolific author of theological works. Unfortunately, despite his earlier writings and perhaps because of his age, he lacked the breadth and the rigour necessary to meet the expectations implicit in his selection for the primacy in 1848. Some of his contemporaries believed him to be a weak character. Much more recently Edward Carpenter, in the chapter on Sumner in his *Cantuar*, was consistently critical of the new archbishop, and that criticism, on balance, is justified. An obituary in *The Times* captured, perhaps unwittingly, the ambivalence of his contemporaries towards him. In the opening paragraph, it referred to Sumner's "good but not striking qualities". Then it moved on to his "holiness of life and the strength of his example. In this view the late archbishop must be regarded as one of the best Prelates that ever lived." However, the tone changed again when the obituarist considered Sumner's public ministry: it praised his discretion, which "is of more avail than enterprise", and ended by observing that "in these difficult circumstances, it cannot be said that he was a great leader."[72] Carpenter summed him up as "not always perceptive in distinguishing between good and bad advice. He had neither the capacity nor the inclination to offer real leadership, lacking the essential flair."[73] Sumner had no biographer in the nineteenth century, but in 1995 a sympathetic study by Nigel Scotland appeared, *The Life and Work of John Bird Sumner*.[74]

John Bird Sumner was born on 25 February 1780 at Kenilworth, where his father was the vicar. The biographer of Charles Richard Sumner, the archbishop's younger brother, described their father as "a quiet, earnest country clergyman of small means". Their mother, Hannah Bird, was a first cousin of William Wilberforce. John Bird Sumner was the oldest son of his parents. He was educated at Eton from 1791 to 1798, and then went to Cambridge. He achieved academic distinction and was elected a Fellow of King's College in 1801. At Cambridge, he encountered Charles Simeon (1756–1836), the most influential Church-evangelical of the period, and he had great influence on both Sumner brothers. Simeon also held a fellowship at King's College and, in plurality with his fellowship, was Vicar of Holy Trinity, Cambridge. Under Simeon's influence the Protestantism of the two Sumner brothers was turned into committed evangelicalism, a quality which commended J. B. Sumner to Lord John Russell in 1848.

Charles Simeon described himself as a "moderate Calvinist", as did many of his contemporaries, and was part of the Clapham Sect. Although this informal association was never as influential as the high church Hackney Phalanx, which had influenced Sumner's two immediate predecessors at Canterbury, it included a number of significant figures of whom the most important was William Wilberforce. In addition to Wilberforce's famous opposition to slavery, the Clapham Sect was concerned with factory working conditions, prison reform and even the ending of the Royal Navy's practice of press gangs. Simeon's appointment as Vicar of Holy Trinity, Cambridge, back in 1782, had been made in the teeth of opposition from influential parishioners, who had not wanted an avowed evangelical; on at least one occasion he was locked out of the church. He persevered, stayed for the rest of his life, won many souls for

Christ, and by the end had developed into the greatest spiritual force in Cambridge. He was at the height of his powers by the time the Sumner brothers were at Cambridge. Simeon did not neglect the poor of the town, and his approach to pastoral care was an inspiration to many who participated in it, not least J. B. Sumner, who devoted some of his spare time to the work of the parish. With an emphasis on the spiritual care of his people, Simeon had divided his parish into areas for visiting, a practice which Sumner was to follow when he became an incumbent. In his later years as a bishop, he recommended the appointment of "district visitors" to his parish clergy. At Holy Trinity, Charles Simeon's preaching attracted very large numbers, and it has been said that his impact "on generations of ordinands was such that his influence on the Church of England at large extended to the remote corners of the country and 'was greater than that of any primate."[75] Although Sumner was no slavish follower of Simeon, the ministry of Simeon was a permanent source of inspiration to him. Sumner encountered destitution while visiting in the parish of Holy Trinity before his ordination. He returned to his old school as an assistant master in 1802. As a school master, it is surprising that he "had no direct religious influence upon the boys" at Eton, but, in addition to his school work, he ministered in a local chapel of ease, a small church under the care of a local incumbent, and "spent his leisure visiting the sick and poor in Windsor and Eton, and was greatly respected."[76] From his own experience he learned of the horrible conditions under which many of the poor lived and carried this concern and practice into his own parochial and episcopal ministry. He consistently sought to ameliorate the poverty which spoiled the lives of much of the population, particularly in the great towns of the Diocese of Chester and especially before it was divided by the creation of new dioceses. A prominent element of his work as a bishop was his commitment to the education of the poor; this arose from his early experience.

In 1803, he was ordained deacon by the Bishop of Salisbury, and was ordained priest two years later. Also in 1803, on 31 March, he had married Marianne Robertson; they went on to have two sons and eight daughters. Sumner's wife had been born in 1781 and was a daughter of George Robertson of Edinburgh, a captain in the Navy. Her family had lived at Kenilworth during the incumbency of Sumner's father. Sumner's marriage meant that he had to surrender his Cambridge Fellowship, but he continued his career as a school master. After fifteen years, Sumner was held in such high regard that he was appointed a Fellow of Eton in 1817. He remained at the college for only one more year, and more than fifty years afterwards it was recalled that his sermons had been appreciated by his pupils, which seems to contradict H. P. Liddon's view. He left Eton when he was appointed to the profitable living of Mapledurham, in Oxfordshire, in 1818: a still picturesque village by the Thames close to Reading. At Mapledurham he conscientiously developed his ministry along the familiar lines and had time to pursue his academic interests. He established a reputation as an author whose publications were representative of the evangelical party of the Church of England. This judgement is rather generous, as Sumner's books were seen to reflect a rather conservative evangelical scholarship by the time he became archbishop, and his biblical fundamentalism was naive. Two examples of that fundamentalism, both from much later in his career, give a wider insight into Sumner's thinking than the issues which occasioned his utterance. When the House of Lords, on 25 February 1851, debated a Bill which sought to legalize marriage with the sister of a deceased wife, he claimed scriptural authority for his opposition to the proposal, "he considered that the question at issue had been decided for them, being already settled by the law of God . . . It is no slight advantage that they should be told by authors which could not err, where the conjugal relationship might and might not exist." The second example also concerned marriage law, specifically the Divorce Act of 1857, and is to be found in his *Charge* to the clergy of the Canterbury diocese in that year. Concerning the indissolubility of marriage, with the exception of adultery, Sumner said:

> To doubt or deny the inspiration of Scripture, so as to suppose that it can contain anything inconsistent with the purpose and mind of God, is to attribute to the Almighty a want of foresight (I speak it with reverence) which we should hardly expect to find even in man's weak and fallible nature.[77]

At Mapledurham, he published *Evidences of Christianity derived from its Nature and Reception* and *Sermons on the Christian Faith and Character*, which proved to be very popular. The former was read within three years of its publication by Charles Darwin, who found it impressive, and who, at that time, was considering offering himself for ordination.[78] Sumner's book appeared more than forty years before Darwin published his greatest work.

Sumner had published his first book back in 1815, *Apostolic Preaching considered in an Examination of St. Paul's Epistles*. It was well regarded by many contemporaries and went through many editions. An historical curiosity is that Newman later claimed that this volume was one of the most significant pieces of writing in turning him away from evangelical doctrine.[79] This is to be understood as a reference to Newman's gradual abandonment of his early Calvinism. It seems likely that Newman was repulsed by what Sumner wrote, rather than that Sumner was inconsistent. However, inconsistency was a charge particularly levelled later by Bishop Henry Phillpotts of Exeter when Sumner's support for C. G. Gorham, which will be examined below, became contentious. However, the book was popular. It was eventually translated into French and published in Paris in 1856, more than forty years after its publication in England.

Sumner's second book, *A Treatise on the Records of Creation, and on the Moral Attributes of the Creator* (1816), won recognition on its publication, and Sumner was awarded for it a Burnett prize of four hundred pounds. With this book and his volume on the epistles of St Paul, according to his *Times* obituary, Sumner established his reputation. The same writer also claimed that this book vindicated the Mosaic account of the creation and accepted the conclusions of geological science as then understood. This enigmatic phrase enabled the obituarist to be loyal to his subject and to get round the contemporary confusion surrounding geology and Genesis at a time when a geologist like William Buckland was seen as consistent with the insights of eighteenth-century divinity. Buckland, in his two-volume *Bridgewater Treatise* of 1836, *Geology and Mineralogy Considered with Reference to Natural Theology*, had no serious difficulty reconciling the discoveries of geology and the work of a divine creator as revealed in the Old Testament, even though he did not believe that the creative process was completed in a week. Long before Sumner wrote, thoughtful divines were already trying to encompass the accounts of creation in Genesis with the growing body of knowledge about the age of the world and the development of animal life. Sumner's only biographer, Nigel Scotland, offers no evidence as to how, later in his life, he reacted to the developing discoveries around evolution; nor how he saw his way to reconciling the insights of geologists with the Mosaic cosmology. He merely observed, without explanation, that with regard to the "challenge posed by the publication of Charles Darwin's *Origin of Species* in 1859 Sumner was better equipped than most of his contemporaries."[80] It should be noted, however, that Sumner's most substantial works were published before the debates about the origin and age of the physical world became a source of conflict and before popular books such as the *Bridgewater Treatises* brought those debates before general readers. Popular works by other authors included Charles Lyell's *Principles of Geology* (1830) and Robert Chambers's anonymously published *Vestiges of the Natural History of Creation* (1844). It is noteworthy, however, that Lyell later felt that Sumner's book demonstrated that revelation and geology were not necessarily "discordant forces". Other pieces of theological writing by Sumner were a series of *Practical Expositions* of the four Gospels published between 1835 and 1847, and books on the Acts of the Apostles and the Epistles which appeared over a twenty-year period. Volumes of sermons appeared intermittently throughout Sumner's career. According to his biographer, Sumner's books were well-received by evangelicals, and he has some claim to be the most prolific author to have served as Archbishop of Canterbury. Sumner's reputation as a religious author did not survive. His work was soon out of date as a consequence of the growth of subsequent scholarship, biblical as well as scientific. Nevertheless, it was important at the time, and he was made DD in 1828, the year of his appointment to Chester.

In 1826, he had the good fortune to be appointed to a residentiary canonry at Durham through the patronage of the Bishop of Durham, Shute Barrington, who died in the same year. Sumner retained a canonry at Durham until his appointment as Archbishop of Canterbury in 1848, although over the years he moved to three different stalls at Durham when vacancies occurred, each one better rewarded financially, but he was by no means just a careerist seeking a fortune. Sumner turned down the Bishopric of Sodor and Man in 1827, but in 1828 the prime minister, the Duke of Wellington, appointed him Bishop of Chester, the twenty-ninth bishop since the diocese had been founded in 1541. He followed Blomfield, whose translation to the Diocese of London was to render such great service to Archbishop Howley. Sumner was consecrated in the chapel at Bishopthorpe, the home of the Archbishop of York, on 14 September 1828. He was forty-eight years old. The consecrating bishops were Archbishop Harcourt, together with Sumner's brother Charles, newly translated to Winchester, and Bethell of Gloucester. However, tragedy struck very early in his new ministry. Marianne Sumner died in March 1829. Characteristically, in his bereavement, he devoted himself single-mindedly to his work. As he told William Wilberforce in a letter, he resolved "to forget my own loss and the destitution of my family".

Sumner's appointment as Bishop of Chester compelled him to become active within the wider life of the Church of England. He took his seat in the House of Lords in February 1829, and readily took part in the work of the House, as was expected of all diocesan bishops. Only a few months into the Chester episcopate, the Duke of Wellington as prime minister proceeded with plans to remove almost all civil disabilities from Roman Catholics. Wellington was right in recognizing it as a political necessity, but as was noticed in previous chapters the proposed legislation was unpopular at virtually every level of society in England. W. E. Gladstone, then an undergraduate at Oxford, said that even college servants were alarmed and critical. At the other end of the social scale, the Duke of Cumberland, the brother of the king, speaking in the Lords, expressed anxiety. Some members of the Commons used incendiary language, and some of the less sophisticated blamed the Bill for the bad weather of that summer.[81]

Sumner's behaviour was anomalous, when the Bill came to the Lords. He made his maiden speech in April, when the Bill was introduced, and to the surprise of those who knew the man's evangelical proclivity, the new Bishop Sumner voted in favour of the legislation, as did his brother, although the latter later regretted doing so. The entry by W. P. Courtney in the *Dictionary of National Biography* (1898) noted that it was known that Sumner was opposed to any concessions to Roman Catholics, and it was generally thought that he had been appointed because of his firm opinions on the matter.[82] If that is correct, it must mean that Wellington changed Sumner's mind in favour of emancipation between choosing him for his bishopric and introducing the Bill the following year. In voting as he did, Sumner was no less consistent than the Duke of Wellington, but he felt it necessary to justify his vote in a letter to the duke, claiming that "the safety of the whole measure depends very much upon the presumption that the papal cause is a declining cause, and will become so more and more". Whether Wellington was impressed is doubtful; he had, after all, secured his Bill, and the consistency or otherwise of a recently appointed bishop would hardly have bothered him. Perhaps the anomaly can be explained in terms of Sumner's Erastianism having been fuelled by a sense of obligation towards what he thought Wellington expected of him; a feeling which he allowed to override his protestant convictions at an early point in his episcopal ministry.

Certainly, Sumner's vote for the Bill revealed an inconsistency less than a year after his consecration. Bishop Sumner's friends believed in the moderate nature of his evangelical convictions, but such supposed moderation cannot adequately explain his vote; particularly when his almost visceral fear of "Romanism" led to his at times excessive condemnation of the Tractarians a few years later. The assertion that his support was due to a recognition that a large number of Roman Catholics lived in his diocese does nothing to explain his action, even though there was to be a great influx of Irish Roman Catholics into Lancashire, particularly Liverpool and the other great towns of the diocese, during the middle years of the nineteenth century. Courtney also noted that Bishop Sumner had felt compelled to address a circular letter to the clergy of his diocese explaining his vote. When the Emancipation Act was signed by a reluctant and tearful King George IV in the summer of 1829, fearful that he had broken his coronation oath, it was an indication of the gradual change in Church-State relations which the union with Ireland had made inevitable.

It was a couple of years later that parliamentary reform, which was looked at in the previous chapter, became an issue. Here it is to be noted that Sumner initially opposed the Great Reform Bill which was introduced into Parliament in 1831 and was part of the majority of opposing bishops on the first vote. When the new version of the Bill came before the Lords in 1832, Sumner again voted with the majority of bishops which, this time, supported the legislation. With the Reform Act of 1832 on the statute book, Sumner had again demonstrated his Erastian reliability.

Sumner's personal concern for the welfare of the poor was an enduring and genuine element in his ministry, to the extent that on some occasions he had sought to ameliorate the distress of poverty from his own resources, when he encountered it through his parochial visiting scheme as a parish clergyman. As a bishop, he was able to bring his experience to governmental level to address more widely the problem of poverty, and it was appropriate that he was called upon to assist in shaping the Poor Law. The regulations to alleviate the lot of the poor were the tangled outcome of successive attempts at legislation, some of which dated back to the time of Queen Elizabeth I. A significant part of the problem was the so-called Speenhamland system, which had been established in 1795, to subsidize the wages of poverty-stricken agricultural workers. In the event, it enabled employers to pay inadequate wages in the expectation of subsidies from civic funds. This arrangement needed addressing, as the crushing poverty was apparent to all observers. A Royal Commission was set up in 1832 by the Whig government, partly motivated by the fear of unrest, and partly by a desire to reduce the cost of poor relief. Sumner was an effective member of the commission which met with Bishop Blomfield in the chair, who worked with his characteristic thoroughness and never missed a meeting. Blomfield steered the subsequent legislation through the Lords. His modern biographer, M. Johnson, observed: "the presence of two bishops [Blomfield and Sumner] on the Commission was meant to be a guarantee that the interests of the poor would be humanely represented", and together they were effective.[83] Blomfield was regarded as an expert and, since his time as Sumner's predecessor at Chester, had been a trusted adviser to the government on such matters.[84] A lay member of the commission, N. W. Senior, appreciated their efforts. Writing much later to Blomfield's son and first biographer, he said, "I do not believe that we could have agreed on our report if the courage and authority of your father and of the late Bishop Sumner had not supported us."[85]

The Poor Law Amendment Act of 1834 was, as its title suggests, a tidying-up of what had gone before, although it did not entirely reflect the recommendations of the commission. The Act established a national system for the management of workhouses run by guardians elected by the ratepayers of parishes and grouped into Poor Law Unions. The management of each workhouse was under the day-to-day supervision of a master and a matron. The need to reduce expenditure made a distinction between the "deserving" and the "undeserving" poor in an attempt to eliminate idleness and immorality and to make what they provided less attractive than seeking work. Conditions in existing workhouses were often deplorable; the new Act did not ameliorate them, and in some places made them worse. Sumner hardened his approach when he learned "that many poor would rather take parish relief than go in search of honest labour". Sumner's 1995 biographer regretted that "a Christian like Sumner should have had a hand in its creation",[86] but he was a man of his time even in his efforts to alleviate the suffering that poverty caused. The workhouse scheme of the Poor Law Act of 1834 is remembered as inhumane. This was due to the inherent contradiction of the commissioners' report. It tried to ensure that no idle person would choose its charity, but that aim was achieved at the cost of imposing hardship for those whose circumstances compelled them to be there.[87] An attempt was made to centralize the administration of the Poor Law with the formation of a commission of three, in the hope of gaining uniformity across the country and with it a fairer system. That aim also proved unachievable.

During the Chester episcopate, Sumner continued to write and publish. In addition to various *Charges*, an insight into his mature theological views came in 1843, when he wrote *The Doctrine of Justification Briefly Stated*, which followed the *solifidian* teaching which originated in Martin Luther's translation of the Letter to the Romans and his belief that it is "by faith alone" that believers are saved. Sumner's book was a re-statement of the doctrine of the Protestant Reformers and took little account of subsequent scholarship and theological reflection. In fact, *The Doctrine of Justification* was written, in part at least, as an attack on the Oxford

Movement. Sumner profoundly disliked Tractarianism and vehemently denounced it, believing it was undermining the Protestantism of the Church of England. As Richard Church wrote in his influential history of the Oxford Movement, "the first who condemned the movement was the Bishop of Chester, J. Bird Sumner; in a later *Charge* he came to describe it as the work of Satan."[88] Sumner's book, which upset other followers of the Tractarians as well as Dean Church, indicates that Sumner was simply being consistent when later as Archbishop of Canterbury, dealing with the Gorham case, he declared that the rejection of baptismal regeneration was not incompatible with Anglican orthodoxy. His Protestantism was nurtured alongside his Erastian belief that the Church of England should be subservient to the government. This seemingly simple and straightforward Erastianism was to get him into trouble when others within the Church of England were unable to accept that his policies were those of a man merely abiding by the law. Both elements of his convictions were anathema to the Tractarians, and Sumner's apparent blatancy was to be a source of difficulty as a bishop and as archbishop when he allowed his partisan Protestantism and his inflexible Erastianism to exacerbate situations which were already difficult; but his personal piety was genuine.

The partisan nature of Sumner's thinking can be most easily understood by referring to his fifth *Charge* to the clergy of his diocese in June and September 1841, which he went on to publish "at their request". On a casual reading, it is a largely uncontroversial document, but it does not conceal an attack on the Tractarians. John Henry Newman had published his unwise *Tract 90* in January of the same year and created a storm with which he was emotionally unable to deal. He had tried to calm the situation by publishing an explanation in a public letter to R. W. Jelf, an Oxford contemporary who was principal of King's College, London. *A Letter addressed to the Reverend Dr. R. W. Jelf* appeared in March 1841, and so was still a current issue when Sumner was writing his *Charge*. There is no explicit identification of the Tractarians as Sumner's target within the text of the *Charge*, but it was clear whom he meant, and a footnote removed any lingering uncertainty: "The divinity of the Oxford Tracts has been completely refuted in all its parts, as any erroneous opinions can ever be refuted." He sniped at the Oxford men as "those who have studied religion in the closet rather than in the world, or who know more of other history than of the history of the human heart"; similarly, he was critical that "whilst learned men are elaborately proving that outward rites and services are the only means of holiness on which we can depend, that 'bodily exercises' and 'voluntary humiliation' are the proper mode in which the sinner may approach his God, the plain preacher of the gospel is confuting them, not by words, but by faith."[89]

It is necessary to discover the basis of Sumner's reasoning. As one who had written extensively on the New Testament, he also had a considerable knowledge of the history of the early Church, including the period which produced the Creeds which were later incorporated into the Book of Common Prayer. It seems that he rejected accretions to the faith that occurred in the centuries that followed the composition of the Creeds, and which were in his opinion swept away at the Reformation. When the Tractarians "studied religion in the closet", Sumner thought that they were intent upon reversing the achievements of the Reformation, and of course some later enthusiasts were, but not all. There was an original purity of motive in men like E. B. Pusey and John Keble, that was desirous of linking the Church of England with the non-papal and scriptural catholicism of the earliest centuries; this was reinforced by disciples such as Richard Church and Isaac Williams, and a little later by H. P. Liddon. However, Fowler noted that the endeavours of the Tractarian movement, "and the Catholic teaching and practice which it sought to revive were... unknown in the English Church, (save to the few who had studied her history and learned what her teaching and practice had been in primitive and mediaeval times)."[90] Their efforts to get back to it were often misunderstood by friends and followers who identified that early catholicism with later Roman Catholicism. The later history of the Oxford Movement was associated with those who did not share the full subtlety of the insights of Pusey and his colleagues. It was that which Sumner, and those who thought like him, sought to repudiate, though they also had no sympathy for Pusey's sometimes esoteric approach. This confusion was fuelled within a few years by the emergence of ritualism, which frequently aped contemporary Roman Catholic practice. In addition, much of the press leapt to condemn such "Romanizing" and brought it to the fore, although Sumner's ministry ended before the great controversies over ritualism that troubled several of his successors as Archbishop of Canterbury. It is also clear that with *Tract 90, Remarks on certain passages in the Thirty-nine Articles*, Newman himself strengthened immeasurably the identification of the Oxford Movement with Romanism, despite his protests that such was not his motive. There were many eager to follow where they thought he led. That was the phenomenon with which the bishops had to deal. They found themselves having to respond to the fears of lay people and of clergy who did not have the theological acumen of Pusey, along with the growing journalistic clamour.

The hostility of many bishops to Tractarianism is well known. Bishop Sumner was temperamentally a Protestant, and a conservative in his biblical scholarship. His evangelical training, sitting at the feet of Simeon at Cambridge, also strengthened his resolve to oppose the "new" teaching emanating from Oxford from the 1830s. Sumner's opposition to the Tractarians did not develop simply in response to Newman's final *Tract*. It was already well developed by the time of his fourth *Charge* to his diocese, delivered in 1838, five years after the series of *Tracts for the Times* began. That first episcopal denouncement of the Oxford Movement was soon followed by others. In it Sumner was outspoken: "under the specious pretence of deference to antiquity, and respect for primitive models, the foundations of our Protestant Church are undermined by men who dwell within her walls, and those who sit in the Reformers' seat, traducing the Reformation."[91] Newman's *Tract* contradicted Sumner's clear belief that the Thirty-nine Articles of the Book of Common Prayer were the "essential cornerstones of Anglicanism",[92] and in the revealing second Appendix to the *Charge* of 1841, he declared his own position:

> I consider that the Articles do contain "a system of faith:" that system, according to which those who subscribe them, are bound to regulate the tenor of their ministerial instructions.
>
> That any could hold a different opinion, I should never have conceived...

The Appendix to the *Charge* came about as a result of an effort by Pusey to clarify the situation. Newman's public letter to Dr Jelf had done nothing to allay the hostility of those opposed to the *Tracts*. Jelf was a friend of many on both sides of the disputes; he was learned and respected, but not involved. He was an ideal person to aid the search for clarity, even if his correspondents made things more obscure. In his effort to help, Pusey followed Newman's example with a public letter of his own to Jelf; but Pusey was not good at clarifying matters. His letter to Dr Jelf, *The Articles treated in Tract 90 reconsidered and their Interpretation Vindicated*..., consisted of 186 pages, with an appendix of an additional forty-one pages; its voluminous nature probably meant that few readers persevered with the whole document, although it did run to two editions.

It is likely that Bishop Sumner was one who did persevere. In the Appendix in his *Charge*, he was severely critical of the Tractarian position. He was kinder to his readers than Pusey, because he confined his remarks to just three pages,[93] but he was emphatic, and his words exposed the unbridgeable gulf between him and the Tractarians:

> Contrary to my original intention, I find myself constrained to add a few words . . . as a result of Dr. Pusey's recent letter to Dr. Jelf . . .
>
> I understand the Articles subscribed officially before me, as articles, not of the Universal Church of Christ, but of the United Church of England and Ireland, of which the subscriber is a member. They do not, therefore, admit of interpretation borrowed from any remote or undefined authority, professing to be that of a church calling itself, or imagined to be the Church Catholic.

In the remainder of his short Appendix, Bishop Sumner picked his way briefly through a number of the Articles where he disagreed with Pusey's attempts to explain Newman's *Tract*. What comes across, however, is Sumner's conviction that the Articles of Religion are somehow above dispute. He did not acknowledge that they were composed in the sixteenth century, and reshaped in the seventeenth, with an ambiguity which was probably deliberate. He also ignored that they were never intended to be a definitive statement of Christian doctrine but were set to deal with theological controversies current at the time. He did not seem to recognize that they were subject from the beginning to a variety of interpretations. Despite the equivocal nature of the historical evolution of the Articles, Sumner was unwilling to admit of any interpretation other than his own:

> It does certainly require an elaborate system of argument, such as is attempted in the writings referred to, in order to prove that persons holding the opinions here excepted against, are consistent members of the Church of England.

Sumner's Erastianism had led him to a self-defining perception of the Protestant nature of the Church of England.

The ministry of his predecessor Bishop Blomfield in the Diocese of Chester had been short, four years, so his energetic personality had little time to make a lasting impact. Consequently, Sumner found that there was a great deal of work to do, and he set about it with zeal. He did not pull his punches: "Our own diocese, Reverend Brethren," he said in his 1841 *Charge*, when he had been in post for twelve years, "did present, some years ago, a specimen of religious destitution, which might well be deemed in every point appalling." The diocese then contained within its boundaries the great and growing Lancashire industrial towns of Manchester, which did not become a separate diocese until 1847, and Liverpool, which remained in the Diocese of Chester until 1880. Sumner recognized the significance of the two and acknowledged the growing population across his whole diocese which he said, according to the 1841 census, stood at just over two million. He "worked nobly within his sphere, building churches, founding schools and doing all in his power to make the Church of England the Church of the people."[94] The reference to "founding schools" is important. Sumner did a very great deal to encourage such work and deserved to be remembered for it. High among his priorities as Bishop of Chester was to encourage elementary education, and he was to carry his enthusiasm to Canterbury. He reported in his *Charge* of 1838, ten years into his time at Chester, that fifty-nine new schools had been started, in conjunction with the National

Society. This impressive number grew from the bishop's conviction that the poor could be brought into contact with Christianity through the schoolroom. It is "sometimes hardly inferior to a church. The stranger to the church is more likely to enter it than a church. The poor who are unwilling to exhibit their poverty and rags in a church might well enter a schoolroom."[95] With the same motive, Sumner also supported the training of teachers for the schools that the Church founded and was active in setting up a training college for teachers in 1839. By the close of his Chester episcopate, the number of new schools had risen to the remarkable total of over 670. Notwithstanding his remark about the reluctance of the poor to enter churches, in another Appendix to his *Charge* of 1841 Sumner listed many examples of new church buildings for the growing population of his diocese. By 1847, near to the close of his Chester episcopate, he had consecrated more than 200 churches, having set up a church building society in the diocese to assist and coordinate the work. He held the straightforward view, which he shared with many contemporaries, that the Church, as a priority, should ensure that there was adequate provision of pew accommodation in parish churches in order to provide for the growing population in the diocese. He regretted the legal difficulties encountered by plans to build new churches. These were often due to the rights of existing incumbents. No such problems existed for nonconformists or Roman Catholics who wished to erect churches. In a Canterbury *Charge* in 1857, he expressed his frustration:

> In future times men will be slow to believe, that the members of our Church were the only parties who were forbidden by law to provide the means of worship for themselves, and so to maintain proper ecclesiastical discipline and order.

In the course of these initiatives, Sumner travelled throughout his diocese and got to know his clergy. He preached and confirmed in many of the parish churches. He recorded his visits to individual parsons in his own hand and made notes about their circumstances.

As early as 1829, at the beginning of his Chester episcopate, he had urged the clergy to greater efforts, and had recommended his longstanding practice, used effectively at Mapledurham: the use of lay visitors in parishes, following the example he had learned from Simeon. As Bishop Longley was to find in the nearby Diocese of Ripon, it was sometimes difficult to attract new clergy into the diocese, but Sumner persevered and did manage to staff the churches that were built in his time, and a large proportion of those whom he appointed shared his evangelical convictions. After leaving the diocese, he looked back fondly on his time at Chester. It had been full of interest and stimulating work. In his 1853 *Charge* to the Canterbury clergy, Sumner allowed himself to reminisce about Chester:

> In that extensive and populous territory there was always an abundant supply of interest, in the various circumstances belonging to its overgrown parishes; great local wants, and great local exertions; much spiritual destitution to report, and much success in relieving that destitution; many difficulties in promoting education, and proportionate zeal in converting factories into schools.[96]

Sumner's tenure of twenty years as Bishop of Chester was unusually long for the see. In his early days, it was relatively poorly endowed, and bishops often sought to move to more lucrative appointments: so a local adage had it that "the Bishop of Chester never dies". Sumner was helped financially by his other preferments, and was better off from 1836, when the Chester stipend was raised from £1,700 to £4,500 per annum. The improvement in the stipends of relatively poor bishoprics, like Chester, was a direct result of the establishment of the Ecclesiastical Commissioners under Archbishop Howley and Bishop Blomfield, so Sumner benefitted from the work of his predecessors in both his dioceses, although as Archbishop of Canterbury he did not enjoy the wealth that Howley had commanded.

—

Clearly, he found the years at Chester fulfilling, despite his bereavement just after he began work there. After so many years, and in his late sixties, Sumner probably expected to end his days in the diocese. But in the wider Church, as has been noticed, the Hampden controversy was working its slow way towards resolution as Archbishop Howley became increasingly frail. As noted above, the number of candidates to succeed Howley was not large, because so many bishops had put themselves beyond Russell's patronage by their vociferous opposition to Hampden. Russell could not choose the new archbishop from among the dissentients, if he hoped to close the Hampden issue. The episcopal protest against Hampden's appointment had been signed by more than half of the existing bench of twenty-five diocesan bishops. In addition, some bishops who did not sign had written privately to Russell remonstrating against Hampden's appointment; also, two sees were vacant at the time. Consequently, the choice of available candidates was restricted by more than the usual considerations such as age, infirmity, competence, and (of great importance to Russell) political acceptability. Samuel Wilberforce, aged only forty-three and Bishop of Oxford since 1845, would have been a good candidate for the primacy, as he was well aware, but he had led the opposition to Hampden's appointment; later he was to believe that his prospects for the primacy were permanently damaged by his actions at that time. Russell's decision to recommend John Bird Sumner to the Crown meant that Sumner had the rather unusual distinction of having been appointed a bishop by a Tory prime minister and archbishop by a Whig. Sumner came to Canterbury with the Hampden consecration as his most immediate task. Although it was (and is) possible for an ordination to the episcopate to occur when there is a vacancy in the archbishopric, the custom is for the Archbishop of Canterbury to be the chief consecrating bishop in the Southern Province (as is the Archbishop of York in the Northern). The protest against Hampden's appointment was, according to a modern author, the first serious objection to the developed system of Crown appointments.[97] With such a contentious candidate as Hampden, there clearly needed to be no possible hint that his consecration was hurried through in an interregnum, so the selection of a successor to Howley needed to be speedy, and there could be no hint of any unsuitability in the nominee. The announcement that the next Archbishop of Canterbury was to be Sumner came speedily, after only eleven days.

The Queen had suggested Sumner to Russell before Howley died, and the Prince Consort also strongly supported Sumner as the best candidate.[98] Several years later, in 1856, the Queen was content with the way Sumner confirmed the sixteen-year-old Prince of Wales in St George's Chapel, Windsor, but she was irked that he made no mention of confirmation in his sermon when he confirmed the Princess Royal. Russell already knew that the royal couple liked Sumner's evangelical convictions and personal simplicity. His Protestantism also appealed to Russell, but Sumner's appointment was not universally welcomed. Any candidate who enjoyed the approbation of the Crown was unlikely to be agreeable to high church people in general, and the Tractarians had good grounds to dislike Sumner. Nevertheless, his obituary in *The Times* fourteen years later claimed it had satisfied nearly everybody. Whatever the misgivings of high church people, his piety and his reputation for being an efficient diocesan bishop went before him. All acknowledged that the new archbishop had exercised a devoted ministry at Chester, where he had

> set himself to work in good earnest ... arousing, in a variety of ways, a considerable amount of zeal for the work of the Church among the two hundred and fifty-five parishes under his episcopal charge. This was due not only to his activity, but to the deep personal piety which he was universally acknowledged to possess.[99]

Unfortunately, Chester had not prepared him for the rigours of the archbishopric, and his years at Lambeth were to be undistinguished. As Archbishop of Canterbury, Sumner's Protestantism was less marked than at Chester, but he became noticeably indecisive. He was described in 1854 by Bishop Samuel Wilberforce, not perhaps the most objective of commentators, as "good, gentle, loving and weak".

Sumner came to the archbishopric under the financial arrangements which his predecessor had negotiated with the Ecclesiastical Commissioners. Having benefitted from the increased stipend allocated to the Bishop of Chester by the commissioners, at Canterbury he received the lower level which had been fixed under those arrangements, £15,000 per annum. Sumner was not an avaricious man. He lived simply and accepted without complaint the reduced stipend and was also content with the reduction in expenditure which Howley had sought to put in place for his successors.

The new archbishop's decision not to join the protest against Hampden's appointment to Hereford can be attributed to his Erastianism. Although Sumner had repudiated Hampden's Bampton Lectures, Hampden had undoubtedly been selected lawfully to be the Bishop of Hereford. In a letter to Samuel Wilberforce on 6 December 1847, Sumner wrote of Hampden's preferment: "after the offer [was] made I do not see how it can be withdrawn." In the same letter, he had conceded a point made by Wilberforce about Hampden's unorthodox teaching. He had been reluctant to join the objection without reading more of Hampden's work, but having read a pamphlet of his on the Thirty-nine Articles Sumner had concluded that the objectors were right. In his letter to Wilberforce he asked whether the "remonstrance can have the result of withdrawing the mitre from the head already bent to receive it?", and shrewdly noted that "the offer might have been prevented if the [Prime] Minister had done like other Ministers and taken wise advice."[100] Sumner had hoped that the lapse of years since the publication of Hampden's Bampton Lectures meant that they were no longer a defining statement of the man's views, but Hampden had done little in those intervening years to dampen the accusations of heresy. Archbishop Sumner proceeded with the consecration of Hampden to the Bishopric of Hereford, but he did so cautiously. In order to eliminate the prospect of protests at the service, it took place in the chapel of Lambeth Palace at the end of March 1848. Sumner was assisted at the consecration by the Bishops of Norwich, Llandaff, and Worcester; his own brother, the Bishop of Winchester, and Blomfield of London declined to take part. The timing was tight; the consecration took place on 26 March 1848, after Sumner's election as Archbishop of Canterbury had been confirmed at Bow Church, but before his enthronement in Canterbury Cathedral. Hampden, duly consecrated, went off to his diocese, which he administered faithfully for two decades until his death, and so disappeared from the chronicle of Queen Victoria's Archbishops of Canterbury.

—

In contrast to Howley's lack of stature and diffident manner, Sumner was tall and appeared to have a commanding presence, although Lord Aberdeen described him as "vain". The contrast between the old archbishop and the new was by no means confined to their physical differences. Howley, whom no one thought of as vain, had accepted the pomp that surrounded the life of the Archbishop of Canterbury even in his domestic circumstances, although it sat ill with his personal humility. Sumner was also an essentially unpretentious man, and he was content with the change of circumstances ushered in as a result of the establishment of the Ecclesiastical Commissioners in the previous decade and did not lament the loss of archiepiscopal splendour. His wife had died many years before he became archbishop, and he was accustomed to living simply; he was known to get up early and light his own fire before starting his desk work. He walked around happily with his umbrella under his arm, and on long journeys he often travelled with only one servant, eschewing the splendour of the archiepiscopal carriage. Theologically, the two were also very different. Howley's old high churchmanship was utterly foreign to Sumner as a committed evangelical. Again, unlike his predecessor, he showed a lack of sympathy towards those who did not share his views. Sumner's churchmanship was described by his supporters as moderate, but it was underpinned by his Protestant evangelicalism, although that trait was less evident in his years as primate. Owen Chadwick noted that, until Sumner, there had not been an archbishop as committed to Reformation principles since the middle of the seventeenth century.[101] Consequently, Howley's death meant that the influence of the Hackney Phalanx and its understanding of the Church of England ended. Sumner was prone to letting his personal convictions prevail to the extent that, not infrequently, they clouded his judgement. However, he was consistent, if not always successful, in seeking to reduce disagreements within the Church. He had a tendency to seek assistance from individuals from whom he expected to receive congenial replies, and was disadvantaged by a certain poverty of judgement when assessing advice.[102] Although he was the first evangelical for generations to be appointed to the archbishopric, other evangelicals served alongside him as diocesan bishops. Among them was Henry Ryder, Bishop of Gloucester from 1815 and afterwards of Coventry and Lichfield until his death; he was the first evangelical to be appointed to a bishopric. Another was Sumner's younger brother, Charles Richard Sumner (1790–1874), who had been appointed Bishop of Llandaff in 1826, which he held in plurality with the Deanery of St Paul's; he was translated to Winchester in the next year, at the early age of thirty-seven, less than a year before J. B. Sumner was appointed to Chester. Although he was also considered for the primacy by Russell in 1848, some resentfully believed that evangelicals had been deliberately excluded from episcopal preferment by those responsible for appointments.[103]

The fact that Sumner had not joined the bishops' protest against Hampden had been enough, in Lord John Russell's opinion, to make him eligible for appointment to Canterbury, but there was more to him than his Erastianism. His conscientious work in the Diocese of Chester over many years had put him among the growing number of bishops who raised the standard of episcopal work during that time. His other qualifications for the Archbishopric of Canterbury were not so clear. Gladstone did not want Sumner to be appointed to Canterbury; he was "deeply pained", although as a young man he had rejoiced at Sumner's appointment to Chester. Gladstone was later to confide in Wilberforce his regret about Lord John Russell's policy "of elevating fierce Low Churchmen or latitudinarian nonentities to the chief offices in the Church".[104]

Unlike his predecessors for 133 years, Sumner decided to be enthroned as archbishop in person in Canterbury Cathedral, a wise decision which was appreciated by the clergy and parishioners of his new diocese. The ceremony took place on 28 April 1848 and was called the "Enthronisation", and the service followed roughly the pattern of Howley's enthronement by proxy twenty years before. The archbishop was installed in the so-called "marble chair" and later brought to the quire throne which had been provided by Howley. The service ended when the new archbishop was placed in the dean's stall from where he gave the final blessing. Sumner seemed bemused by the ceremonial, according to Henry Wilberforce, a brother of Samuel and an eventual convert to Roman Catholicism. He was an incumbent in the Diocese of Canterbury and attended the service. He returned in a good mood, remarking that it was "important as a precedent to have J. B. C[antuar] walk in *procession, chanting* the *Psalms* from the Chapter nave through the cloisters, in at the North door, then down the N aisle to the West end, then up the Nave into the Choir."[105] There was a very large congregation which witnessed the first enthronement in person of an Archbishop of Canterbury since 1716. Woodruffe and Danks in 1912 described the occasion as the "beginning of a new order of things", simply because of Sumner's presence, "and though the day was cold and wet the crowd of worshippers and spectators was too great even for the great spaces of the cathedral."[106] One unanticipated element was a protest which Henry Wilberforce also described with amusement: "outside stood a man with a huge playbill—and on the other side opposite one with a huge placard 'Ridiculous Farce—Carrying the Pope in Procession'. Only think of poor Chester after 68 or 69 years turning into the Pope!" A small irony was that when Henry Wilberforce converted to Roman Catholicism, he wrote to inform the archbishop of his resignation of his living and expressed the hope that Sumner, who was his second cousin as well as his diocesan bishop, would one day receive the blessing that Wilberforce believed his conversion to be. Wilberforce's wife had converted before her husband, who initially wished to keep things quiet; Sumner had "quite approved" of the desire for discretion and responded with "extreme kindness, which nothing could exceed".[107]

Archbishop Sumner did not find his diocesan work in Canterbury as stimulating as the work in Chester, and after five years in his new diocese he told his clergy so:

> Our Diocese, Brethren, is one in which the Church, comparatively speaking "has rest". The population of parishes, generally, instead of affording a boundless field of labour, is barely sufficient to awaken the interest of its pastor, or to excite its energies; and I have no affecting accounts to set before you, of thousands who wander among the mountains, as sheep who have no shepherd to tend or fold to contain them.

Aware that his listeners may not have been impressed by the implicit criticism of their conscientiousness, he continued:

> Still, I must not be understood to say, that there is nowhere in Kent a want of additional Church accommodation: much less should I be unmindful of the zeal and liberality which had been manifested where that want has been seen to exist ... It is due to the same zeal in the same good cause, that many outlying hamlets hitherto so far removed from the eye of their nominal pastor as to be beyond the reach of his practical superintendence, have now their own Church and resident clergyman.

In footnotes to the published version of his *Charge*, the archbishop listed new church buildings put up in eight rural locations in the diocese, and referred in the text to "six new Churches in five of our most important towns", rejoicing to say that with "the churches the hearers also are multiplied". Another footnote provided a list of the particular towns.[108]

Sumner's policy for establishing schools was similarly energetic in his new diocese, although in Canterbury the scale was smaller. Once again, his Canterbury diocesan *Charge* of 1853 is a valuable source of information.

> Next in importance to the Church itself comes Education, as the handmaid of the Church. And here I have the satisfaction of congratulating you on the establishment ... of a system of Diocesan inspection, which promises, I trust, to fulfil the expectations of its promoters.

There were no fewer than 406 schools in the diocese under the inspection scheme, and the archbishop rejoiced in "a particular and general account of the education afforded by the Church to most of the parishes in the Diocese ... few places remain where there is not access to a National School ... The schools of the more important parishes are in a state of much efficiency, while some have attained great excellence." He acknowledged that most of the educational provision was due to what he called "the laudable exertions of the clergy", which had often been at the cost of "great personal sacrifices, though not without the liberal assistance of the laity". Similarly, he praised the efforts of the parish clergy in obtaining properly "trained schoolmasters" and only lamented that many children left school early in life; this phenomenon was also tackled by the clergy with their commitment to Sunday schools.[109]

It is clear that Sumner was well informed about the life of the Diocese of Canterbury by that mid-point of his archiepiscopate. Whatever his underlying disappointment, he continued the active diocesan ministry that he had exercised in Chester and went about his new diocese, "every part of which was personally known to him", again frequently travelling almost unaccompanied. As a diocesan bishop, Sumner was conscientious, and his reputation benefitted, as he had abandoned some of the partisan churchmanship that he had exhibited in earlier years. However, the work of the Archbishop of Canterbury was less domestic and diocesan than that of an ordinary bishop, and Sumner was less able to deal with the larger issues which challenged him in the wider role.

In relation to his wider responsibilities, he continued to be strongly opposed to the Oxford Movement and emergent ritualism and was particularly alarmed by the spread of the practice of sacramental confession. Sumner turned his attention to the subject in his *Charge* of 1853. His argument was based on the conventional low-church view that the authority of the Lord's apostles to forgive sins was not passed to their successors as leaders of the nascent Church. He said: "We have therefore no authority from the Apostles for the system, the want of which has been complained of as a defect of the Church of England."[110] He reinforced his argument regarding the lack of subsequent apostolic authority: "If, therefore, we can be satisfied to take our views from Scripture, we cannot justly complain of our Reformed Church because the Sacrament of Penance, or the practice of Confession and consequent Absolution, is no doctrine of our Church." More than twenty pages of the *Charge* were taken up with refuting what he believed to be the "Roman" doctrine of the Church, whilst "far from intending to use severe language concerning all who have been nourished in it or have adopted it as their own."

As a bishop who ordained new priests he was, of course, aware that the Church of England Ordinal in the Book of Common Prayer is clear that priests are charged with the duty of absolution, and he turned to that issue in Appendix V of his *Charge*. This he answered with a curious argument from silence. The Reformers, he claimed, consciously wanted to alter the Ordinal as little as possible, "and finding the exact words of our Saviour employed in the Popish ritual, they, instead of removing them, made such a change as they thought would modify any wrong use that might be made of them." In attempting to deal with the other specific reference to absolution in the Book of Common Prayer, the Visitation of the Sick, Archbishop Sumner resorted to a similar theological contortion, claiming that the priest has no power to absolve but just to say that God absolves; the priest is there not in a "judicial" sense but in a "ministerial" one.[111]

However, in a Canterbury *Charge* delivered in 1857, when he was roughly two-thirds of the way through his archiepiscopate, Sumner was less negative and revealed some optimism. He reflected in general terms on the state of the nation and the Church. He asserted "the age is an age of progress" and continued:

> Everything is advancing. Wealth, knowledge, art, science, have advanced, within the last 50 years, in a manner which we cannot contemplate without astonishment. Things which would have once been deemed impossible, are become familiar to our thoughts; things which would have been pronounced incredible, are daily brought before our eyes. It might therefore have been a trial to our Faith if, whilst everything else was making progress, the religion of the Gospel alone remained behind. But let thanks be given to our Divine Head, the Gospel is liable to no such disparagement. Much there is to be lamented, much there is to be amended amongst us, no one can compare the present state of religious feeling in this country with its state at the beginning of the century, without a sense of gratitude.

"Christianity", he added, "affords just grounds for encouragement."

Unfortunately for the archbishop, however, his troubles were by no means all over. His Erastianism, clearly revealed by the Hampden affair, was to be similarly exposed in other doctrinal controversies concerning the orthodoxy of belief, or otherwise, of clergymen. The first of them was the case of George Cornelius Gorham. This problem, like Hampden, was business left over from Howley's primacy. It took several years to resolve. G. C. Gorham (1787–1857) was a clergyman who held a living in Cornwall, which at that time was part of the Diocese of Exeter. Henry

Phillpotts (1778-1869) had become Bishop of Exeter in November 1830 and remained there until his death. He was strongly opposed to the Calvinistic Protestantism which was dear to the heart and soul of Gorham. Phillpotts tried to control appointments within his diocese, even when he did not hold the patronage himself. He had a powerful and bellicose personality and was famed for his belligerence; Sydney Smith, with unkind exaggeration, coined a witticism that Phillpotts was "so like Judas that I now firmly believe in the apostolical succession". In reality, Phillpotts was profoundly orthodox in his views and strove to impose doctrinal conformity and liturgical uniformity throughout his large diocese across Devon and Cornwall. For his part, Gorham also relished a battle; he was no weakling and no stranger to theological controversy. He had been ordained in 1811 by Bishop Dampier of Ely, who had initially threatened to refuse him ordination because of his unorthodox views on baptism. That obstacle had somehow been overcome, but Gorham consistently taught that regeneration was entirely dependent on a conscious decision of the baptism candidate to accept Christ as his or her saviour. Gorham rejected the doctrine that at baptism a person becomes regenerate, or born again, as declared in the Book of Common Prayer.

Bishop Phillpotts was a politically and theologically deeply conservative, old-fashioned high-and-dry clergyman, a last representative of the "Church and King" school of the eighteenth century,[112] but he was not Erastian like the archbishop. He held that the tenets of the Christian faith were unalterable, and he had little sympathy for evangelicals. Sumner and Phillpotts had both been canons of Durham, and so knew each other from those days. Coincidentally, Phillpotts had been appointed Dean of Chester in the same year that Sumner became bishop. However, he had only held the deanery for two years before becoming Bishop of Exeter. Despite their shared background, it is unlikely that the two would have worked harmoniously for long, had they remained colleagues in Chester; their temperaments as well as their convictions were widely different. By the time Sumner became archbishop, the forthright Phillpotts's reputation was already established well beyond his diocese as a litigious man of fixed opinions, considerable moral courage, and theological expertise.

In 1846, Phillpotts, perhaps unaware of Gorham's views, had instituted him into the isolated living of St Just with Penwith in Cornwall. Within a few months, they had quarrelled over a fundraising leaflet published by Gorham. Matters were made worse when the bishop saw that Gorham had advertised for a curate, stipulating that candidates must "be free from Tractarian error". Phillpotts condemned Gorham's terminology, asserting that it would "encourage party spirit". However, in due course he did license the curate whom Gorham had chosen, but the correspondence between the two men showed that a rift existed. It became unbridgeable.

Gorham, who had married late, soon found that St Just was too remote for the satisfactory education of his young family of six children and sought a move. In August of the following year, 1847, he was presented to another living in Phillpotts's diocese by the Lord Chancellor, who was the patron; it was the parish of Brampford Speke. He accepted the new parish even though the income was substantially less. In Phillpotts's mind, Gorham had become a marked man, so he created an opportunity to investigate Gorham's doctrinal position before deciding whether or not to institute him to his new parish. The bishop's chaplain quizzed Gorham for many hours over a period of several days spread across the winter of 1847–1848. The bishop required satisfactory answers to 149 questions, so the process was meant to be thorough! The outcome was that Phillpotts decided the man's opinions were unsound, and that it would not be appropriate to admit him to a new parish, so he refused to institute him. Phillpotts had acted similarly on other occasions with clergy whom he judged to be heterodox, but Gorham was not the man to accept such a ruling without a fight and appealed to the Court of Arches, the Consistory Court for the Province of Canterbury and therefore a court of the archbishop. This was effectively the ecclesiastical court of appeal. The Court of Arches decided that Gorham was wrong and, therefore, that Phillpotts was acting properly in refusing to admit him to the new parish.

The Court of Arches had acted on behalf of the Archbishop of Canterbury but without his personal involvement. Gorham appealed against the decision of the Arches to the Judicial Committee of the Privy Council, which led to Archbishop Sumner becoming directly involved. Sumner went on to create a litigious muddle by his subsequent actions. As Archbishop of Canterbury, he had the right to sit as a member of the Judicial Committee to hear Gorham's appeal, and decided to do so. The other members of the committee were Archbishop Musgrave of York, Bishop Blomfield of London, and seven lay judges. Inevitably, Phillpotts's counsel protested at Sumner's presence. Their objection was simple. As the Court of Arches was the court of the Archbishop of Canterbury, it was Sumner's court, they maintained. Therefore, if Sumner sat as a member of the Judicial Committee, he would be acting inappropriately; he would be adjudicating an appeal on a matter which had already been decided on his behalf. Astonishingly, Sumner did not step aside. His presence as a member of the Judicial Committee, although legally permissible, was in practical terms unwise. Theologically, his personal sympathies were known to be closer to those of the vicar than to those of the diocesan bishop; indeed, shortly before he became archbishop he had written sympathetically to Gorham.

The committee set aside the judgement of the Court of Arches and found for Gorham. It instructed Phillpotts to install Gorham in the parish of Brampford Speke. Phillpotts refused to obey the Judicial Committee's instruction. Gorham's next move was to appeal to the Archbishop of Canterbury as metropolitan against Phillpotts's refusal. Sumner found himself expected to adjudicate an appeal against the Bishop of Exeter's refusal to obey a decision that Sumner had been party to making as a member of the Judicial Committee. When it is recalled that the Court of Arches acted on behalf of the archbishop, the absurdity of the situation which Sumner had created around himself is hard to credit, and there can hardly have been a better illustration of the wisdom of the objection lodged by Phillpotts's counsel at the Judicial Committee hearing. The case attracted much publicity in the press; a war of pamphlets and books ensued, more than sixty in all, and the case became famous.

Phillpotts was understandably furious. He wrote and published an intemperate pamphlet, *A Letter to the Archbishop of Canterbury from the Bishop of Exeter*, which eventually achieved twenty-one editions. Coming from Phillpotts's powerful pen, it was dogmatic, and its author was unable to avoid sarcasm. Any pretence that it was genuinely a letter was nonsensical. It was an essay of about 25,000 words and ran to more than ninety pages. Phillpotts focused his attention on Sumner's book *Apostolical Preaching Considered in an Examination of St. Paul's Epistles*. As has already been noticed, this volume had been published originally in 1815 and had had several editions. It was an entirely conventional statement of the doctrine of the Church of England from a Protestant evangelical perspective. Sumner thought fit to reissue it in 1849–1850 in a revised form. Phillpotts noticed that the revision was such as to support the views held by Gorham. He hit the archbishop hard over the changes. Following the thrust of his argument demonstrates the depth of feeling around the Gorham case; it also reveals the belligerence of theological disputes in the mid-nineteenth century. Even if a reader tries to bear in mind that the author was hostile to the archbishop, the essay sadly reveals limitations in Sumner's perception of unfolding events. Phillpotts wrote, with a hint of malice:

> I cannot adequately express my regret, that now, in your advanced years, and exalted station, you should materially impair and almost contradict the sounder teaching of your earlier years—teaching, through which your Grace's name would have gone down as a benefactor to the Church.[113]

The whole tone of the *Letter* was an accusation that Sumner had changed his views, as set out in 1815, without acknowledging that he had done so; that he had reissued the book without pointing out the amendments, seemingly to avoid charges of inconsistency. Phillpotts, like Sumner a scholarly man, mentioned the Fourth Council of Carthage, held in the early sixth century, which set out the standards of orthodoxy required for appointment as bishops with regard to baptismal regeneration in particular. "Thus it appears that no one in the Primitive Church could properly be ordained a bishop, without it being first ascertained that be believed original sin to be remitted in baptism."[114] He continued: "I hope that your Grace, when you were made bishop in 1828, did hold this doctrine, as you certainly did in 1815 when you first set forth your work on Apostolic Preaching." Phillpotts saw Sumner's inconsistency revealed in the judgement of the Judicial Committee:

> But if self-contradiction were all that I had to object to your Grace's book, I should not think it necessary to trouble you or myself, much less the Church at large, on the matter. My

complaint is of a much graver character. My Lord, you were summoned to attend the hearing of the late cause before the Judicial Committee of Her Majesty's Council, in order that you might assist them in dealing with the questions of doctrine which were involved in that cause—and I grieve to think, that, instead of leading, you must have misled those whom you were to instruct, not only by mis-stating the matters on which you advised, but also by misquoting all, or almost all, the authors cited by you in confirmation of your statement.

When Phillpotts got to Gorham in particular, he was completely emphatic:

The heresies, then my Lord, which came out in my examination of Mr Gorham, and for which I refused him institution. Are these: 1st. That by declaring original sin to be a hindrance to the benefits of Baptism, he denied the Article of the Creed, "One Baptism for the remission of sins"; 2nd. That he separated entirely "the inward and spiritual grace" from the Sacrament, inasmuch that he stated "regeneration" to *precede* Baptism, when Baptism was rightly received ... I can hardly describe with what amazement I found these heresies glossed over, or almost unnoticed in the judgement.[115]

Phillpotts could not resist a final thrust when he conceded that "lay judges might err in this way", but the theologically informed should not; that he could not understand "how even your wish to see everything as favourably as you can, can have betrayed you into countenancing such entire misstatement of unsound doctrine". Phillpotts reached the summit of his rhetoric when, although without naming the archbishop, he wrote:

I protest, in conclusion, that I cannot without sin—and by God's grace, I will not—hold communion with him, be he who he may, who shall so abuse the high commission which he bears.

The threat was clearly absurd, but it did indicate the level of anger over the controversy which did nothing for Sumner's or Phillpotts's reputation. It cannot be known whether Phillpotts thought he could intimidate Sumner into giving up Gorham by exploiting the archbishop's inconsistency and weakness. If so, he miscalculated Sumner's Erastian reverence for the law. He remained unmoved by Phillpotts's foolish threat of excommunication and did not react publicly to Phillpotts's broadside. The archbishop was, naturally, obedient to the court's direction, and Gorham was instituted into his new parish on 6 August 1850 by a commission issued by Archbishop Sumner. Inevitably, the relationship between the two bishops was strained, even though Phillpotts signed his long *Letter* as "Your Grace's affectionate friend for nearly thirty years", adding, in case Sumner had not got the point, "and now your afflicted servant, Henry Exeter". Unsurprisingly, the Bishop of Exeter at his next visitation and on other occasions spoke of Sumner in somewhat intemperate terms.

It is difficult to see Sumner's actions in the Gorham case as anything other than unwise, even without such fireworks from Bishop Phillpotts. His personal involvement had made a difficult situation worse. There is more than a hint that his own convictions had moved closer to Gorham's, and the suspicion remains that his personal opinions overcame a necessary objectivity, and that his absolute conviction of the Church's subordination to the State prevailed. He believed that he was acting in accordance with the law, and he was correct in that belief, but this Erastianism was revealed to the detriment of his reputation. The case became one of the most celebrated ecclesiastical lawsuits of the nineteenth century. However, a decade later, the personal rift was patched up when Phillpotts sent an affectionate message as the archbishop lay dying in 1862, which Sumner warmly accepted.

Even with Gorham safely in his new living, the controversy did not die down immediately. Sumner's actions caused a good deal of distress and resentment among high church people in particular. The final outcome caused a small number of such clergy to secede to Roman Catholicism. The archbishop had failed to perceive the depth of disillusionment into which those who converted felt themselves to be plunged. In his 1853 *Charge* he did acknowledge that such conversions came "at a cost which gives sufficient proof of their sincerity", but they did not cause him any disquiet and did "not diminish our surprise at a course which seems to be nothing less than an infatuation". Many of those who felt compelled to leave the Church of England for that of Rome felt that the former had abandoned any claim to be part of a universal Church, and that the sixteenth-century gibes that the Church of England was a "State Church" or a "Parliament Church" proved unanswerable in the face of the Gorham litigation.

Ironically, one priest who seceded to Rome was Phillpotts's chaplain who had conducted the examinations into Gorham's orthodoxy. The Gorham case also led to the conversion of Henry Wilberforce, who had commented wittily on Sumner's enthronement, and that of another Wilberforce brother, Robert, an archdeacon in Yorkshire, who was to follow in 1854. Robert Isaac Wilberforce was a significant theologian, and his secession, just a few years before his untimely death, robbed the Church of England of one of its most useful intellects. Historically the most significant among the converts was H. E. Manning, brother-in-law to the Wilberforces, who converted in 1851 and, a mere fourteen years later, became the Cardinal Archbishop of Westminster.

—

Only a month after the conclusion of the Gorham case, Sumner faced another significant issue, but this time he handled it with wisdom, even though there was much public perturbation. It was the announcement of the Vatican's plan to set up a Roman Catholic hierarchy in the British Isles. The plan became public towards the end of 1850. It will be recalled that two decades earlier, newly appointed to Chester, Sumner's vote in the Lords for Roman Catholic emancipation was consistent with a surprisingly moderate attitude towards Roman Catholicism. Back in 1829, he thought that Roman Catholicism in England was in terminal decline and declared that Roman Catholicism was no sort of threat to the status of the established Church of England. He had even been sanguine, back in those days, about the management of appointments to high office in the Church of England should a Roman Catholic ever become prime minister (a prospect that some raised as a spectre at the time). He faced, and passed, the more stringent test in 1850 and kept himself from foolhardiness when faced with what many of its opponents at the time called the "Papal aggression". His tolerant attitude surprised many who expected him to be opposed to it because of his personal churchmanship, and his vehement opposition to what he believed to be the "Romanizing" tendencies within the Oxford Movement. He saw that the establishment of a Roman Catholic hierarchy would prove to be of little significance in the long run for the Church of England; he somehow retained his conviction that the Roman Catholic Church was a declining force in England.

It was in September 1850 that the Roman Catholic plans for the setting up of territorial dioceses became known. The Roman Catholic bishops in England were known until then as Vicars Apostolic, and they tended to live quietly and to govern and serve their flocks discreetly. As a result, the ancient animosity towards Roman Catholics had largely died away, except in the minds of extreme Protestants. The Vicars Apostolic had wanted proper diocesan status to be accorded to them since around 1837, and reorganization was overdue. The driving force behind the plan was the redoubtable and flamboyant Nicholas Wiseman (1802–1865), who became the Archbishop of Westminster under the new system. He was a man entirely unsuited for the delicacies of diplomacy. He lacked tact and antagonized those who disagreed with his floridly emphatic opinions; he also lacked the necessary administrative ability and subtlety to achieve his ambitions without causing disruption and dismay among many. He had a mistaken idea that great numbers of conversions from Anglicanism to Roman Catholicism, particularly from adherents of the Oxford Movement, would follow the process.

Wiseman went to Rome in 1847 at the behest of his colleagues to petition Pope Pius IX to restore the hierarchy in England. He succeeded in his mission, but it became controversial to an extent that surprised everyone, although Sumner held his nerve. The plan was put into operation with the issue of a Papal Bull in September 1850. Wiseman was appointed the first Cardinal Archbishop of Westminster. He aggravated the tense situation whilst still in Rome with a very rash "pastoral letter", run through with inappropriate triumphalism and exuberance and lacking in tact.[116] However, he sought to mitigate the situation with a later pamphlet entitled *An Appeal to the Reason and Good Feeling of the English People*. But a good deal of damage had been done.

When the announcement came in 1850, it was a bad time for Archbishop Sumner. The Gorham controversy was a very recent memory, and the Oxford Movement was just beginning to find expression in ritualism, although neither phenomenon was linked to Roman Catholic ambitions.

> Had the hierarchy been restored in say 1847, without undue publicity and with a discreet leader, and the change represented as a matter of internal organisation of interest only to the Roman body, it would probably have passed without widespread notice.[117]

Coming when it did, nearly three years later and with Cardinal Wiseman having stoked any potential fires, the proposal excited great populist opposition and was much resented by the English public. The newly restored Convocation as one of its first actions "put forward an energetic protest against the new papal hierarchy".[118] The anti-Roman feeling, which ran high in the popular mind, was fuelled by elements of the press. November 5 and Guy Fawkes provided opportunities for mob reaction.

It is to his credit that Archbishop Sumner took little or no part in the excitement, even when the potential titles of the new Roman Catholic sees became a burning issue to some. Eventually the matter reached Parliament, and a Bill was passed in 1851 regulating and restricting the use of territorial titles by Roman Catholic dioceses. Known as the Ecclesiastical Titles Act, it prohibited Roman Catholic use of the names of existing Anglican dioceses. Sumner does not appear to have taken part in the debate, sharing Gladstone's view that the matter was, in reality, unimportant. Sumner's modern biographer appropriately devotes only a passing reference to the matter. The Ecclesiastical Titles Act was repealed in 1871, having been recognized as an over-reaction by Parliament, and the Pawleys recorded that the fine of one hundred pounds for adopting the title of an Anglican diocese was never imposed. The Act was, they correctly claimed, "a damp squib".[119] The new Roman Catholic arrangements were enacted and life went on as it had before.

—

Archbishop Sumner, however, found himself facing a significant new issue within the Church of England with the restoration of Convocation. The Church had no means of debating its own business or making its own decisions. The ancient ecclesiastical assemblies of Convocation, whose origin is buried in the eighth century, had long ceased to function in any meaningful way. Bishop Longley, who was to be Sumner's successor at Canterbury, in a *Charge* delivered in 1853 to the clergy of his diocese of Ripon, described the origin of Convocation. He referred to King Edward I as the monarch under whose authority Convocation came into being as "the body properly designated by this term in the sense in which we apply it at the present day".[120] Consisting of a House of Bishops and House of Clergy in each of the Provinces of Canterbury and York, they had lapsed in 1717, except for formal meetings with no agenda at the beginning of each Parliament. Their long slumber followed a command of King George I, who prohibited meetings in order to protect Bishop Hoadly of Bangor from censure by Convocation over unorthodox theological views expressed in a sermon. It had not met since that date, except as a formality, and many of its members habitually absented themselves. Fowler described the Convocation as having been "practically the Parliament of the Church", but in the nineteenth century its suspension meant that the Church of England had no voice. Although there had been a modest attempt to secure its revival as early as 1826, the lack of such a facility caused little or no difficulty until the upheavals of the middle of the century began to stir the Church and the nation.

Although the Reform Act of 1832 had not been a direct threat to the Church of England, the fear that it would soon face attention from the government was felt acutely, as has been noticed. That possibility sharpened, in the minds of some, a sense of the need for Convocation to be active in the hope that it would give the Church a voice regarding its own future. The fear had been partially realized the next year with the introduction of the Irish Church Temporalities Bill. This added to the anxiety of some churchmen that other reforms would soon come, and that the Church would not be able to respond through any formal mechanism. That fear had been behind John Keble's famous Assize Sermon. Attempts at revival became almost frequent; one was made in 1847 and another in 1850. There was a debate about revival in the House of Lords in 1851. Those who wanted to revive Convocation as a forum within which debate could occur hoped that the Church would be seen to have a voice. In 1850, "a society for the revival of Convocation was set on foot."[121] Wilberforce and Blomfield were episcopal champions of the revival, although the desire for revival should not be exaggerated. Chadwick estimated that most of the laity and nearly half the clergy, Archbishop Sumner emphatically among them at this stage, were not in favour of the revival, and Sumner's brother was described as "lukewarm" about it. Archbishop Thomas Musgrave of York was so opposed that the eventual revival in the Northern Province did not take place until Longley succeeded him before following Sumner at Canterbury in 1862. Prince Albert did not approve of a revival, a fact of which Sumner must have been aware and to which he instinctively attached importance. Archbishop Sumner went so far as to declare elsewhere that the authority of the Crown would be reduced if Convocation were to meet with the intention of transacting business. In fact, Convocation could only meet at the invitation of the monarch, but Bishop Phillpotts thought that was not the case.

The threat that Church reform might be imposed by a hostile government had receded by Sumner's primacy, but the controversy over Hampden, which his appointment had brought to an end, also fuelled the move within the Church towards a revival of Convocation. The Gorham case, which the archbishop so palpably mishandled, also added impetus to the agitation for revival. Sumner used his *Charge* of 1853 to declare his hostility to the idea and told the clergy of the Canterbury Diocese, "I can think of no better opportunity of explaining the reason why I am opposed to such a revival." His explanation ran to twenty pages in the published version of the *Charge* and reveals a good deal about his thought processes and why his critics believed him to be fundamentally weak. He seemed to be aware that he had said too much when he ruefully admitted "this subject, Reverend Brethren, has occupied me longer than I should have felt myself justified in pursuing", although he sought to excuse his loquacity by adding that it had "led me to consider a course of remark that is practical rather than theoretical".[122]

Nevertheless, the desire for revival grew and could not be ignored. By chance, a general election happened while the Hampden affair was working out, and automatically triggered one of the formal meetings of Convocation. This juxtaposition of events naturally increased the pressure for revival. Similarly, when the Gorham controversy raged, the desire for the matter to be considered in Convocation gathered momentum. Bishop Phillpotts discovered that, under a long-forgotten Act from Tudor times, he had the right to ask Convocation to consider the issue. It is more than unlikely that Phillpotts was seized by a sudden desire for a more democratic Church, and his ruse certainly did not succeed; but his voice added to the gradually developing but still muted clamour.

Sumner was not impressed either by the campaign, or with its ultimate success, and in his *Charge* of 1853 he said:

> The revival of Convocation would not tend to promote the great interests of our ministry, the establishment of personal religion amongst our people or the advancement of religion generally throughout the land. Nay, I would go further, and express my belief that, it would be more likely to impede than to assist the progress of religion.[123]

A further objection which Sumner voiced was that the proceedings might be too controversial at that time, although this did not prove to be true in the event. Samuel Wilberforce's biographer was right to opine that Sumner thought that "it was most improper that Convocation should in any way place itself in hostility to the Government".[124] At that stage no one was suggesting, however, that there should be any additional meeting or meetings, but only that after the legal requirements were concluded, meetings should be extended to allow some business to be discussed. But Sumner wanted to avoid even that; he did not want Convocation to become a forum where doctrinal matters might be debated. He also feared that the content of the Book of Common Prayer might be altered by an ambitious Convocation at some future date and argued that the Church's liturgy was authorized by Parliament and that no other body, such as Convocation, had the authority to make changes. It is interesting to note this fact because Sumner himself had suggested to the Queen, in 1854, the alteration of the marriage service, expunging its "coarseness",[125] knowing that the Queen disliked the carnal references contained in the

Prayer Book version of the service (although in the event no changes were made). Also, of course, the Judicial Committee of the Privy Council, in respect of the Gorham case, had already set aside the doctrine of baptismal regeneration as defined in the Prayer Book.

An additional reason for Sumner's opposition to the revival of Convocation was his awareness that the Tractarians and their followers, who regarded themselves (with some justification) as a persecuted minority, were eager to see Convocation restored. Part of their enthusiasm for its revival was a hope to avoid future doctrinal debacles such as had arisen with the Gorham case. Dr Pusey believed that it could be the authentic voice of the clergy of the Church. But the Tractarians were not alone, and their view, at least in part, was shared by many moderate church people, although most evangelicals were opposed. Gradually, Bishop Samuel Wilberforce emerged as the episcopal champion of the supporters. At the height of the campaign, Wilberforce tried some unofficial persuasion of the prime minister, Lord Aberdeen. The prime minister was initially opposed to the movement for revival, declaring that it must be stopped, asking "do you think I am going to tolerate them by a side-wind because the archbishop is a poor, vain, weak, silly creature whom they can bully with impunity?"[126]

At the formal meeting of Convocation in 1852, Wilberforce proposed that a petition be addressed to the Crown for permission for the meeting to be given some substance. Sumner tried to prorogue the meeting on the grounds that he had not been given notice of Wilberforce's intention. Wilberforce accepted the ruling, and out-manoeuvred Sumner when he gave notice that he would bring his petition to the next meeting. As a result, an address was made to the Queen in 1853. When Sumner delivered his *Charge* to the clergy of the Diocese of Canterbury in 1853, he deflected the issue away from the concerns of the wider Church. He concentrated on the drawbacks of revival, as he perceived them, from the point of view of the parochial clergy. Rhetorically, he asked whether they found the absence of Convocation a hindrance in their work. He was convinced that parish clergy had a unique role but his words, later in the same *Charge*, were rather disingenuously designed to lead his hearers away from the real question of the usefulness of a revived Convocation:

> I am altogether unable to perceive how any clergyman's efficiency or success in the various departments of his parochial duty can be promoted by the deliberations of an assembly constituted as Convocation is constituted.[127]

A few minutes later he added:

> I know not what suggestions they could propose, or what advice they could offer which would be generally applicable or beneficial; so as to give any pastor of a parish the assistance which he needs towards reclaiming the dissolute members of his flock, towards awakening the thoughtless, or promoting the edification of the better disposed.

He also pointed out that a revived Convocation would not have the "power to provide more Church buildings [and] so could have no relevance in expanding the mission of the Church". That, of course, was true in a literal sense, as was his assertion that Convocation would not be able to assist the Church as a whole in the increase of the number of schools in parishes. Sumner did not have much time for abstract ideas as to what ought to be done,[128] but faced with the reality of its revival, by 1854 he had begun to change his mind, as had the prime minister. But Sumner was a difficult man to read. His inner feelings were never on display in his public life, but his opposition to the revival seemed to have reduced.[129] This was apparent when, having arrived more than five hours late for a meeting, he was rebuked by the prolocutor, and apologized and declared that he had thought the meeting to be just the usual formality. Sumner had somewhat undermined his case in 1853 when, arguing against reviving Convocation, he asserted that a revived Convocation would need to be different from the form in which it existed at the time of his *Charge*.[130] That was exactly the point being made by those who sought revival. He had also declared that, if Convocation were to be effectively revived, it would need to "represent every part of the country, including, as has been justly stated, not only the province of York, but Ireland and the Colonies".

The pressure for a revival of Convocation for the Province of Canterbury was maintained, and Wilberforce's tactic in 1852 meant that it was likely to succeed. Despite Sumner's *Charge* of 1853, the first business meeting for more than 130 years was held between the sixth and ninth of February 1855 and did much valuable work. Sumner, however, rarely involved himself in discussions when he chaired the meetings of the Upper House during the remainder of his primacy. Slightly cynically, Bishop Wilberforce felt that Sumner's opposition to Convocation had, in the end, worked in favour of its revival. He wrote privately to his brother Robert:

> In my opinion, his Grace has almost as effectively done his great work of proceeding gradually to revive our synodical action, by thus making the struggle real, as if he had let the Committee [sic] sit. May God bless all for the Church's good and His Glory.[131]

As the two Wilberforce brothers anticipated, the revival of Convocation proved to be a significant event in the life of the Church of England and Sumner's misgivings were misplaced. His Erastianism was clearly exposed, and so was his lack of sympathy and his obstinacy despite the pragmatism of his gradually softening. He did not emerge well from the revival campaign. It is not difficult to assert, as did his opponents, that Sumner was fundamentally timorous and afraid of the very idea that the Church of England should have a synodical voice in its own governance, and no longer be obliged to leave everything to the bishops in the House of Lords. In reality, his apprehension had a rather firmer base; he was fearful that a revived Convocation would make claims or put forward petitions that would undermine the established relationship of Church and State. His opposition was fuelled by his Erastianism.

When Sumner commented on the appropriateness of representation for colonial dioceses, if Convocation was to be revived successfully, it was not merely part of his filibustering. Colonial bishops sometimes sought advice from the Archbishop of Canterbury, especially as the numbers grew after the establishment, during the primacy of William Howley, of the Colonial Bishoprics Fund in 1841. Also in Howley's time, Sumner had been enthusiastic about the setting up of the Jerusalem bishopric,[132] and like many of his contemporaries, Sumner had supported societies within the Church, a good proportion of which promoted mission at home and in the colonies.

He recognized the importance of the Church Missionary Society (CMS), with which lay his personal sympathies, and preached one of the Jubilee sermons in 1848, shortly after his translation. He was both a friend and counsellor to Henry Venn, the long-serving head of the CMS, who consequently had ready access to the primate.[133] Sumner also took the chair at one of the society's anniversary meetings when Lord Chichester, the designated chairman, was unable to be present. He was cautiously supportive of CMS plans to establish a "native pastorate" in Sierra Leone in 1852 and was willing to share with Venn a suggestion he received of the idea of a "Native Church" with its episcopate under the authority of the Crown in the same way as that of the Church of England.[134]

Sumner was always appreciative of the need for missionary outreach to the colonies, but was cautious towards high church moves in that direction. At first, he was reluctant to endorse the high church initiative which was the foundation of St Augustine's College, Canterbury. This was the first of a number of missionary colleges established in the nineteenth century for the training of men for overseas missionary work. However, he was won over and gave the plan his support to the extent that, soon after his translation to Canterbury, he consecrated the college chapel and preached at the service; he also accepted the role of "Visitor".

Sumner's involvement with the Society for the Propagation of the Gospel in Foreign Parts (SPG) was part of his response to missionary outreach, which always had his keen support although the SPG was not his preferred organization. In 1851, the SPG had been in existence for 150 years, and there was a natural desire to celebrate the anniversary. Sumner supported the plans and agreed to write to all the bishops in Britain and in the colonies. He also wrote to the bishops of the Protestant Episcopal Church in America, to "manifest the essential unity of the sister Churches of England and America". It was in North America that the society had done some of its earliest work until the time of American independence.

In his letter he invited them to share in the celebrations of the 150th anniversary of the founding of the society at Westminster Abbey, and to celebrate the society in their own country.[135]

He received a reply from the Bishop of Vermont, John H. Hopkins, a moderate high churchman, who had read Sumner's communication "with great interest and satisfaction". Hopkins later became the Presiding Bishop in the USA. He and his American colleagues rejoiced in the closeness of the relationship of their Church to the Church of England, and Hopkins expressed what he believed to be a common wish:

> For my own part, I would that it were much closer than it is, and fervently hope that the time may come when we shall prove the reality of that communion in the primitive style, by meeting in the good old fashion of Synodical action. How natural and reasonable it would seem to be, if "in time of controversy and division" there should be a Council of all the bishops in Communion with your Grace![136]

Celebrations held to commemorate the Third Jubilee of the SPG stretched between the summers of 1851 and 1852, just a few years after the CMS celebrations. These commemorations were of great importance in developing the self-awareness of Anglicanism as a communion, as, similarly, was the case with the CMS celebration.[137] The SPG celebration at Westminster Abbey took place in June 1852 and was attended by the English bishops, with others from America and from the Scottish Episcopal Church, as well as some from the colonies. It was described in almost euphoric terms by one present, Henry Caswell. It began with what he said was "such a procession as the Anglican Church has never before witnessed".[138] Sumner's willingness to be involved with the SPG is a demonstration that he was not as rigidly partisan in his churchmanship as primate as some of his contemporaries asserted, or as he appeared to be in his Chester days. Indeed, in 1841, he had helped to achieve an understanding between the CMS and the SPG, which had led to the two archbishops and a number of bishops becoming members of the CMS.[139] Among the English bishops particularly interested and supportive of the celebration of the SPG's significant anniversary was C. T. Longley of Ripon, and it was certainly a factor that contributed to Longley's successful calling of the First Lambeth Conference.

It should be remembered to his credit that J. B. Sumner had played a positive part in the early relationship between the Church of England, the colonial Church and the Episcopal Church of the United States. The work of the missionary societies was another happy element in Sumner's primacy, but he was to be involved in another doctrinal dispute and his involvement was, again, less than successful. It arose as the pressure was growing to restore Convocation in the Province of Canterbury and, like the Gorham case, demonstrated the archbishop's lack of wisdom and competence in leadership over doctrinal matters. This time the furore was brought about by the theological teaching of the Archdeacon of Taunton in the Diocese of Bath and Wells, who was also a parish clergyman, the Vicar of East Brent, George Anthony Denison (1805–1896). His brother was the Bishop of Salisbury and had been a schoolboy at Eton when Sumner was an assistant master. The archdeacon was convinced of the catholic character of the Church of England, and later became sympathetic to a modest degree of ritual in Church services. He had opposed Hampden's appointment to a bishopric and had protested at the outcome of the Gorham case, although his profile then was not high enough to have a practical bearing in either case. Denison, as a high churchman of rigid views, enjoyed a good argument and was endowed with a taste for litigation. He believed absolutely in baptismal regeneration and the doctrine of the real presence of Christ in the sacrament of Holy Communion. As an archdeacon, Denison was one of his diocesan bishop's examining chaplains and interviewed candidates for ordination, several of whom he had rejected, because they "did not accept the full teaching of the Church on the subject of Holy Baptism".[140] The similarities with the Gorham case are obvious, although the doctrinal issues were diametrical opposites, and Denison, like Gorham, was not the sort of man to avoid a dispute. The evangelical individuals and societies which had supported Gorham looked for an opportunity to challenge the dogmatic archdeacon.

The Bishop of Bath and Wells was Richard Bagot, who had formerly been Bishop of Oxford at the time of the Tractarians' most energetic period and had some sympathy for them. By the 1850s, the bishop was aged and infirm, and rarely resident in his diocese, so he entrusted his episcopal duties to a retired colonial bishop named Spenser, who had served in Madras. When Denison's theological convictions were brought to the attention of Spenser, with the claim that they were erroneous, Denison declared that he was answerable only to Bagot. In order deliberately to fuel the developing controversy, Denison decided to nail his colours to the high church mast by preaching a series of three sermons in Wells Cathedral on eucharistic doctrine. He did so in August and November 1853 and May 1854. He published them and did not have to wait very long to get his battle. Early in 1854, before the final sermon was preached, a neighbouring incumbent, the Vicar of South Brent, Joseph Ditcher, who had the backing of the Evangelical Alliance and some non-Anglican Protestants, formally complained to Bagot about Denison's teaching and asked the bishop to prosecute him. Bagot, close to death and perhaps remembering the sadness that surrounded his disciplinary endeavours at Oxford twenty years before, declined to proceed and only gave Denison the mildest of rebukes after he submitted a statement to him. Ditcher was opposed to all things high church and pressed his case; he had powerful evangelical backers, the Church Association and Lord Shaftesbury among them, as well as the Evangelical Alliance.

Bishop Bagot died in May 1854 and was succeeded by Lord Auckland. He too decided not to prosecute. Ditcher and his friends discovered that they could appeal to the Archbishop of Canterbury to override the decision of the diocesan bishop. They exploited this loophole which existed because the diocesan bishop was the patron of Denison's parish. It was an arrangement originally intended to protect the interests of any incumbent who fell foul of his diocesan patron. Accordingly, Sumner was petitioned, and he behaved as Ditcher and his backers hoped. Two successive diocesan bishops had refused to prosecute Denison, but under a clause intended for the protection of an incumbent, the Archbishop of Canterbury decided that he could proceed against him and set up an enquiry into Denison's teaching.[141] Sumner selected as commissioners five evangelical clergy, leading even sober-minded Tractarians such as John Keble to declare that there was "a war of extermination against us".[142] Denison tried unsuccessfully to get the commission set aside by an appeal to the Court of the Queen's Bench. Sumner's commission of enquiry overruled objections that its members' churchmanship meant they were biased against Denison from the start. They also refused to hear any doctrinal evidence from either party. This was an astonishing decision, for the whole matter was a doctrinal dispute. Sumner sent a document to Denison which seems to be a copy of the complaint and which set out in detail the case against him:

> That the Body and Blood of Christ being really present after an immaterial and spiritual manner in the consecrated bread and wine are therein given to all, and are received by all who come to the Lord's Table, to those who eat and drink worthily, and to those who eat and drink unworthily the Body and Blood of Christ are given, and that all who come to the Lord's Table, by those who eat and drink worthily, and by those who eat and drink unworthily, the Body and Blood of Christ are received . . . that the universal reception of the inward part or thing signified of the Sacrament in and by the outward sign, is a part of the doctrine of the Real Presence itself . . . that all who receive the Sacrament of the Lord's Supper receive the Body and the Blood of Christ.[143]

John Keble, who had sought to defend the integrity of the Church of England back in 1833, was keenly alert to the underlying danger to the Church, coming this time from within; it would simply be revealed as a Protestant sect, if the case went against Denison, as Manning and his associates had concluded in 1850 over Gorham. Keble was "sorrowfully convinced that if the propositions attributed to the Archdeacon were 'declared untenable in the Church of England, a far more serious question would arise concerning the reality of our communion with the Universal Church than had yet arisen'".[144] Sumner possibly began to sense the danger of a theological rift to which he had brought the Church of England when, unsurprisingly, his commission decided that Denison should be arraigned before the archbishop's court. Having convened the enquiry despite the refusal of the current Bishop of Bath and Wells and his predecessor to proceed and having become aware of the potential gravity of the situation, Sumner seemed to be at a loss. This conjecture may account for the fact that having received the findings of the commission, and its recommendation, and despite a direct request from Ditcher, the archbishop delayed for a long time before being forced to proceed with the next stage of the prosecution of Denison. Ditcher and his friends were anxious to press on and sought a remedy through the courts for Sumner's inaction. The Lord Chief Justice expressed his regret that Sumner had not declined to proceed right at the beginning but granted Ditcher's request. The archbishop was obliged to hear the case. Denison refused to attend a hearing in London, whereas Sumner wanted it to be in the capital. Denison insisted it should take place within the diocese in which he served, so further wrangling followed over the appropriate location. Eventually, Sumner heard the case at a hotel in Bath in August 1856; he was assisted by two assessors, both of them clergy opposed to Tractarianism. Somewhat predictably, he decided against Denison, who was given until 1 October to recant. Denison was a man of steady nerve, and on the day before the deadline he formally declined to do so. On 22 October 1856 came the declaration that Denison was deprived of his living and his preferment.

The battle was still far from over. Denison appealed to the Court of Arches. The Dean of Arches, Sir John Dodson, tried to avoid the issue with a ruling that if he heard the case it would mean that the Archbishop of Canterbury's court would be hearing an appeal against a decision of the Archbishop of Canterbury. Sumner found himself in a situation similar to that of the Gorham case. The litigious Denison went to the Queen's Bench for a mandamus which compelled the Dean of Arches to hear his appeal. In April 1857, Dodson's judgement ruled that the whole prosecution was invalid, and that Denison should not have been deprived of his preferments. The Court of Arches' ruling was that the action was out of time, because more than two years had elapsed since the alleged offences, which were the cathedral sermons of 1853 and 1854. Even at that stage Ditcher and his backers did not give up. They turned to the Judicial Committee of the Privy Council. In February 1858, that body agreed with Dodson's judgement that the proceedings were invalid and that Denison's deprivation was an error.

Although this was satisfactory for Archdeacon Denison in terms of his temporal security, the process had, however, not vindicated his theological position, because the decision was based on the technicality of timing. This was a matter of concern for Denison and those who shared his convictions and had hoped for the vindication of the theological position expressed in the sermons. Denison's outspoken actions had been regarded with alarm by men such as Keble and Pusey and many who shared their doctrinal beliefs. But once the sermons were preached, and the matter out in the open, they had hoped for a declaration of Denison's orthodoxy. Their fear was that had Denison been declared unorthodox, and the views of his opponents had prevailed as the official doctrinal position of the Church of England, then the cherished convictions of high church people would have been deemed to be heretical. In such an event, all who held to those doctrines within the Church would have been liable to similar prosecution, and (in their view) the catholic nature of the Church of England would have been compromised. Many old-style high church people also feared the possible consequences of Denison's provocative actions, so the Tractarians and their followers were by no means alone in their dismay. In addition to the threat to his personal security, Denison had acted rashly in putting at risk the theological convictions of his friends, along with his own.

Once again, Archbishop Sumner had handled woefully a situation which he could easily have prevented from happening. His decision to set up his commission of enquiry despite the decision of two successive diocesans was hardly the act of a man interested in maintaining balance of the theological parties within the Church, and not that of a man who valued good relations with his fellow bishops. By filling the commission of enquiry with men known to be hostile to the accused, and by accepting their findings whilst aware that they had not heard the theological arguments, and by eventually holding his own hearing, he had assured the headstrong Denison of more sympathy and publicity than he deserved. Sumner's early failure to recognize the likely consequences of the line he followed, which had so agitated high church people, had shown a lack of insight into the comprehensive nature of the Church which he was charged to lead, and an indifference to the prospect of schism. As had been the case with Gorham, Sumner had once again revealed the limited nature of his grasp of the complexities of his office. Once again, he had damaged his personal reputation and weakened the public reputation of the Church of England.

The evangelicals suffered partly because the prosecution seemed so persistent, partly because dissenting money helped to finance the attack upon an Anglican archdeacon, and partly because Sumner appeared before the world as an archbishop in a muddle.[145]

Sumner was destined to have the end of his archiepiscopate overshadowed by yet another controversy, as he had at its beginning. This time it was to do with a theological book. *Essays and Reviews* was published in 1860. It was a collection by seven liberal theologians who thought that religious enquiry should be unfettered. The book attracted little attention at first. Controversy erupted, however, when Bishop Wilberforce wrote a hostile, although temperate, review in the *Quarterly Review* of January 1861. In February, he persuaded the bishops, meeting at Fulham, to condemn the book, and Sumner issued the condemnation shortly afterwards. The Lower House of Convocation also condemned the volume, and the bishops in the Upper House decided to take legal action against the essayists in the ecclesiastical courts, but Sumner's involvement was drawing to a close, and the case properly belongs to the next chapter.

—

Sumner was taken ill in May 1861, only three months after the Convocation debate about *Essays and Reviews*. Although he recovered, he did not regain his full strength. The end came on 6 September of the following year. On his deathbed, he replied in friendly terms to the conciliatory message from Bishop Phillpotts. His funeral took place at Addington on 12 September 1862, and *The Times* noted that the funeral service was one of great simplicity, and that not many invitations to the service had been issued. Samuel Wilberforce attended the funeral of his second cousin and noted in the privacy of his diary, "off to the funeral of the archbishop. The day beautiful. Gathering of many old friends. Bishop of Winchester greatly affected."[146] Sumner was the third Archbishop of Canterbury to be buried at Addington, the others being his immediate predecessors, Howley and Manners-Sutton. A memorial was placed in the nave of Canterbury Cathedral, a tomb chest with a recumbent effigy;

like the figure of Howley the effigy wears a cope, although it is unlikely that the living Sumner ever attired himself in that way.

So ended the life of an archbishop who was regarded by his friends as a moderate man, but who had antagonized many whose views he did not share. Nevertheless, he seems to have been a good and holy man; "a good old man", as *The Times* described him, but one who lacked the breadth of insight and sympathy necessary for the position in which he found himself. Little more than thirty years later, a chaplain of Archbishop Benson wrote of Sumner:

> He was better fitted for, and perhaps experienced a greater pleasure in, the fulfilment of his pastoral duties than of the wider questions of statesmanship in ecclesiastical matters.[147]

The Archbishop of Canterbury operates across a wide canvas, and Sumner lacked the capacity for the leadership that he was called to give, although he had managed well the Diocese of Chester as a conscientious diocesan bishop. He suffered from an inability to understand people who did not share the same views, and he showed definite hostility towards the emerging high church revival, a sad judgement on a hard-working and devout man.

CHAPTER 3

Charles Thomas Longley (1862–1868)

Viscount Palmerston was the prime minister responsible for nominating a new Archbishop of Canterbury when J. B. Sumner died. He was not especially knowledgeable about the merits of senior clergy and was not interested in theology, yet he knew that he wanted the Archbishop of York, the sixty-eight-year-old C. T. Longley, of whom he clearly had a high opinion. He knew and trusted him and regarded him as the only suitable candidate. Longley was also acceptable to Queen Victoria, but he was never close to her; his high churchmanship, although moderate, precluded that. Even though his appointment to Canterbury came less than a year after the Prince Consort's death in December 1861, the Queen did not resort to Longley in her grief. But at least the archbishop did not suffer a rebuff, whereas Bishop Wilberforce's well-meaning but clumsy encouragement that the widowed sovereign should consider Christ to be her "spouse" was dismissed by her as "twaddle". Longley did, however, develop a pastoral relationship with the Queen and her family. She wrote to him a personal letter about her trust in God after an attempted assassination of the Prince of Wales in 1868. In 1865, he had entertained the Prince and Princess of Wales to dinner at Lambeth and to luncheon on at least one occasion a year later. Also in 1865, he baptized Prince George, the Queen's grandson, who became King George V, and Longley stayed at Osborne for the confirmation of Princess Louise.

In selecting bishops, Lord Palmerston was, inevitably, interested in the political support that bishops could offer in the House of Lords. He tended to rely ecclesiastically on the advice of Lord Shaftesbury, whom he also respected and who was married to his stepdaughter. Shaftesbury, dubbed by some of his contemporaries as "the bishop-maker", had an encyclopaedic knowledge of the clergy. He had very strong evangelical opinions, was often prejudiced and preferred to recommend clergy from his own school of thought. The Bishop of Winchester, C. R. Sumner (1790–1874), the younger brother of the late archbishop and a man of similar evangelical opinions, was a possible candidate, but Palmerston was concerned about his age as he was already over seventy.[148] Shaftesbury would have preferred a man with such convictions, but he did not exclude broad churchmen from consideration. He did exclude Tractarians, but Longley was not one, despite some high church sympathies. Shaftesbury's approval of Longley was already apparent in the fact that Palmerston, during his first term as prime minister between 1855 and 1858, had translated Longley from Ripon to Durham in 1856 on the resignation of Bishop Edward Maltby. Four years later, Palmerston, back in office from 1859–1865, moved him to York where he served until Sumner's death. Longley's comparatively rapid rise through the senior levels of the episcopate came after he had laboured for twenty years as Bishop of Ripon. Long before his efforts were rewarded with further promotion, he had been commended by Sir Robert Peel for his "unremitting activity, zeal and piety".

A short biographical essay by an anonymous author, who seems to have been a personal friend of the archbishop, was "published under the direction of the Tract Committee" of the SPCK, with the title *Church of England biographies, second series*. It is in a collected volume of nine biographical sketches, of whom Longley is but one. No publication date is given, but it is a useful source of information because of the personal element of some of its contents. Another biographical sketch appeared in 1895 in the volume by Montague Fowler, *Some Notable Archbishops of Canterbury*. No full-length biography of Longley was published in the nineteenth century or since, and he remains the least well-known of Queen Victoria's Archbishops of Canterbury. Perhaps as a result, he has been neglected as of less importance to the history of the Church of England than some of his fellows. However, such neglect is unmerited, for it was under his leadership that the first Lambeth Conference took place. Lambeth Conferences have grown to become the primary expression of Anglicanism's self-understanding as a worldwide Communion, and they owe their modus operandi as well as their inception to the leadership which Archbishop Longley provided.

Samuel Wilberforce's diary for 25 September said that Longley had "received the offer of Canterbury and accepted. God be praised!"[149] Although his enthusiasm was genuine enough, it was strengthened by Wilberforce's ambition to follow Longley as Archbishop of York. To some extent he was the archbishop's protégé. Longley wanted Wilberforce to follow him at York and possibly also at Canterbury. Wilberforce wrote to Gladstone, putting his own case for York, but Gladstone, even though he was Chancellor of the Exchequer, proved unable to advance his friend's interest. A modern writer, Bernard Palmer in *High and Mitred*, thought that Palmerston's rejection of overtures made by Gladstone was, in part, designed to remind Gladstone who was in charge. Not only was Wilberforce destined for disappointment over York, he was not a little put out when William Thomson was translated there from Gloucester and Bristol only ten months after being elevated to the episcopate, Bishop A. C. Tait of London having declined it. Thomson had been Wilberforce's curate at Cuddesdon and was to serve as Archbishop of York until 1890.

Charles Thomas Longley, ninety-third Archbishop of Canterbury, was born on 28 July 1794 near Rochester in Kent. He was one of the seventeen children, not all of whom survived, of John Longley and his wife Elizabeth. The future archbishop's father was a lawyer who served as Recorder of Rochester and as a magistrate in London. He was the author of a book on jurisprudence and an occasional political writer. He was, however, not successful financially and found it difficult to maintain his large family, so they moved house periodically to smaller and cheaper dwellings.[150]

The future archbishop was educated at Cheam School until 1808, when he was old enough to be elected a King's Scholar at Westminster School, which is located in the precincts of the abbey. He enjoyed his Westminster days and many years later claimed, "to Westminster School I owe all my prosperity."[151] He was at the school until 1812, when he was elected to a studentship at Christ Church, Oxford. Longley graduated in 1815 with a first in classics; he was examined for his degree by John Keble. In 1818, he was ordained deacon, and priested the following year. Also in 1818, he took his MA; then his BD and Doctor of Divinity degrees in 1829. During his time at Oxford he was popular as a don, described as having a "handsome face and winning manner". He was examiner in the classical schools for two years, and a university proctor in 1827; between 1825 and 1828, he was tutor and censor at Christ Church. He was "a teacher of some ability", yet he found life at Christ Church tedious and longed to be involved in pastoral work. Decades later, in the Lords, he opposed the proposed reforms of Oxford University in 1854.

In the more immediate future, however, Longley's desire for a pastoral ministry led him to combine his college life with a curacy at Cowley under the incumbent, Thomas Vowler Short (1790–1872). Short had been a senior contemporary of Longley's at both Westminster School and Christ Church. Eventually he became Bishop of St Asaph and is not to be confused with another contemporary, Thomas Short, who was a tutor of Trinity College. Dr Pusey had been a favourite pupil of T. V. Short and revered him afterwards. Gladstone was another of Short's pupils. John Keble was a friend, and Short had examined Newman for his degree. From 1816, T. V. Short had the living of Cowley, but he left Oxford in 1823, before the Tractarians began their work. Longley succeeded him in the living and began to earn a reputation as a conscientious pastor. He combined his parish duties with those of his college until 1827. Longley was not planning to marry, so when he gave up his fellowship in order to be incumbent of the parish of West Tytherley in Hampshire, it was regarded as an unusual step to take. Before the university reforms, dons customarily resigned and took parishes in order to be free to marry. Longley did so in order to serve as a parish clergyman. The strong pastoral element in his nature was to be apparent in the years of his episcopal ministry.

Yet he was not destined to remain a parish priest for long. He was elected as Headmaster of Harrow School on 21 March 1829; his friend Short was instrumental in Longley's selection. The author of the anonymous *Church of England biographies* records that he had not sought the post and, when the offer was made, Longley "had only the interval between services one Sunday to decide whether to accept it or not".[152] Unfortunately, the reason for such urgency was not given. He did accept and was to become the first of Queen Victoria's Archbishops of Canterbury to have served as headmaster of a public school, coincidentally setting a pattern for the rest of the reign. Under his leadership, the school roll grew from around 115 at the time of his arrival to 165 at the end of his time. He also developed the syllabus. Among his staff at Harrow was a Cornishman, J. W. Colenso (1814-1883), whose later career was to prove problematic, when Longley was Archbishop of Canterbury and Colenso had become a highly controversial diocesan bishop in South Africa. Longley introduced frequent examinations to raise academic standards; also his religious influence on the life of the school was noticeable. On leaving Harrow, his farewell sermon was published at the request of the boys, but he did not have the reputation of a great headmaster. Despite his ability to attract additional pupils and make relevant changes to the curriculum, Longley's rule was described as lax in terms of discipline; drunkenness among the boys was a problem. Longley did, however, command the respect of no less a man than the great Thomas Arnold, the Headmaster of Rugby, whose career indelibly shaped public-school education. Arnold wrote, "with regard to my children's prospects on so small an income... if I live and Longley lives, I am inclined to send the boys to him" at Harrow.[153] It was alleged that at Harrow Longley became wealthy through capitation fees as the number of pupils increased. The *Church of England biographies* tract declared that Longley was able to save "a considerable sum of money, as was needful to one who had to depend on his own exertions for all that he had".[154] He still expected that when his time at Harrow came to an end he would resume his career as a parish clergyman. During his tenure as headmaster, Longley married. His bride was Caroline Sophia Parnell, and the ceremony took place in December 1831. The couple were to have six children, of whom four survived. Longley's wife was the eldest daughter of Henry Brooke Parnell, who became the first Baron Congleton.

Congleton changed his son-in-law's prospects by recommending him for a bishopric, just as T. V. Short had supported his earlier career. Congleton was a member of Melbourne's administration and served as Paymaster General from 1836 until 1841. Probably at the urging of Congleton, Longley left Harrow without another post in anticipation of receiving preferment. He was followed at the school by Christopher Wordsworth, who became Bishop of Lincoln and was later to be mentor to E. W. Benson. Longley's resignation was not as hazardous as it seems; he knew that he was likely to become a bishop, because he had already been offered the bishopric of Chichester by Lord Melbourne. Unfortunately for Longley, the offer had to be revoked by Lord Melbourne for unknown reasons, and William Otter became the Bishop of Chichester. The setback did not have any effect upon Longley's subsequent progress, as he was appointed to the new Diocese of Ripon in the same year.

The Diocese of Ripon was set up under the Established Church Act of 1836, and Charles Thomas Longley was its first bishop. In addition to districts taken mainly from the Diocese of York, the new diocese included part of the Archdeaconry of Richmond from Chester Diocese. The new diocese had within its boundaries the growing towns of Bradford, Leeds, Wakefield, Huddersfield, Halifax, Dewsbury, and Barnsley. In order to give the new bishop a seat in the House of Lords without increasing the number of episcopal seats, the two dioceses of Gloucester and Bristol were combined. However, the plan to create the Diocese of Ripon had excited some opposition, and legal niceties needed to be sorted out by Judge Stephen Lushington in his capacity as Dean of the Court of Arches. Because the Diocese of York had provided most of the territory of the new Diocese of Ripon, Archbishop Harcourt of York had managed to stipulate that the nomination of the new bishop should meet with his approval. The writer of the SPCK *Tract* believed that Harcourt had wanted Longley all along. Although Lord Melbourne expected his episcopal nominees to support him in the House of Lords, he declared himself willing to accept that Longley could not guarantee his support with regard to Irish church policy. Longley showed some steel in his approach; he had written to Melbourne,

> there are some questions connected with the Irish Church on which I should be unable to support your lordship's Government in the House of Lords, and should this circumstance prove an obstacle to my appointment to the See, however much I may regret the issue, it will not in the least diminish my feelings of gratitude and respect.[155]

Later, when Longley felt unable to support Melbourne on other issues, the prime minister was not pleased, despite having accepted Longley's initial hesitation, and his own declared magnanimity over Ireland.

Longley was consecrated in York Minster on 6 November 1836. The preacher at the service was Thomas Vowler Short, who was at the time Rector of Bloomsbury. The sermon was published as a pamphlet "at the request of the Archbishop of York". In his sermon, Short refrained from any mention of the episcopal candidate, but developed a picture of the qualities necessary among those called to the office of bishop; qualities which, by obvious implication, were to be found in Charles Thomas Longley. They were, he said, "very rarely found united in the same individual; and the more it shall please God to open the eyes of his exalted servants, the more will they discover how inadequate their own powers are for the important task to which they are called." He also enumerated the qualities required by all priests: they should "be a race of learned, holy, self-denying men . . . Beyond all this, the Bishop is called on to advise those who are under him, and that on every description of subject; to be an example to us, to lead us onward in everything that is good—to govern us, to be able to restrain and punish everything that is evil."[156]

The new bishop was enthroned in Ripon Cathedral early in 1837. Longley's cathedral was the former monastic church where St Wilfrid had been abbot. Wilfrid died in 709 having become Bishop of York, before the archbishopric was established. Ripon had been the centre of a diocese for a few years in the seventh century, but the bishopric had lapsed long before the Reformation. The great abbey church in Ripon was rebuilt in the eleventh century and was served by Augustinian canons until the Reformation. It was re-founded as a collegiate church in 1604 and was a parish church until it became Longley's cathedral in 1836; a major restoration under the supervision of Gilbert Scott took place in 1861, five years after Longley's departure. By the 1830s, however, the development of industrialization in Yorkshire, with its consequential growth in population and the expansion of towns, meant that the Church of England needed to expand its ministry in the area. The author of Longley's biographical sketch summarized the situation as follows:

> The sudden growth of manufactures in the north had presented to statesmen a most difficult and anxious problem. New centres of population had suddenly arisen, round which the circles had

widened with such rapidity as to alarm all who looked on. There were no clergy or wealthy class resident on the spot to guide safely the vast forces thus set in motion.[157]

The establishment of the new diocese was an early example of the Church's attempt to meet the urgent demands of increased urbanization. After the Dean of Arches had sorted out the legal quibbles, Longley was eventually able to deliver his first *Charge* to the Diocese of Ripon in 1838, "the Primary Visitation of the New Diocese". He commented on the large population of nearly "900,000 souls within its limits". Fifteen years later, in his *Charge* of 1853,[158] he returned to the matter of the population of the diocese. It was still growing rapidly, and he lamented that the great effort to build schools was unable to keep up with the growth, although Longley had set up an Education Board in the diocese.

The need for an increase in the number of bishops, which had brought Longley to Ripon, had been fuelled not only by the shift and growth of the population, but also by the needs of parish clergy. As the pace of life in the middle decades of the nineteenth century increased, parish clergy found that their duties increased, and so did the perception of many of them that a more professional approach to their work was necessary. This led to the desire of parish clergy for the bishops to be available for advice and guidance, to give leadership, and to be less remote from their work and their parochial concerns. The Evangelical Revival at the end of the eighteenth century also led church-minded evangelicals to see the need for increased support. The rather later spread of the insights of the Oxford Movement, which was gathering pace when Longley became Bishop of Ripon, elevated the episcopal office in the minds of its adherents with consequential demands for the bishops to be accessible, despite frequent disobedience to the actuality of episcopal direction. These elements were reflected in what A. J. Russell described as "the adoption by the clergy of a distinctive lifestyle which tended to mark out the clergyman and separate him from the gentry status group".[159]

At first, the new Bishop of Ripon lived in a house on the outskirts of the see city, but an episcopal palace was built between 1838 and 1841. The Ecclesiastical Commission voted £15,000 for the work as part of its plan to provide suitable residences for the episcopate. Longley found the location of his home and cathedral in his see city of Ripon to be convenient. He could reach the more heavily populated parts of his diocese with comparative ease, particularly when travelling became easier after the railway was opened in June 1848. Ripon was the principal station between Harrogate and Northallerton; from the latter there was access to the wider railway network which gave him ready access to London and thus to the House of Lords, and also to York.

Urban and industrial developments had not only brought very great numbers of people to live in the newly populous towns, they had also cut across ancient parish boundaries which had often defined administrative arrangements for the care of the poor. In 1836, the Church of England was still the principal provider of elementary education. Ancient parishes that had become the new urban areas were overwhelmed by the potential demand. Longley's Education Board did assist in building schools and gave grants towards salaries for teachers, but the Church's provision in the Diocese of Ripon was never quite as successful as he originally hoped. Nevertheless, he told the clergy that he was pleased with the initial efforts that had been made in this respect, for those efforts were by no means a failure even though the plans had not borne as much fruit as was hoped. Whilst conscious of the need for an increased provision of schools, he was also aware of the need for good quality teaching. In his *Charge* of 1838, he encouraged the maintenance of standards, particularly in schools which were not subject to inspection by the National Society. He wanted the Diocese of Ripon to be "among the first to try an improved scheme to widen out education throughout the Society's schools".[160] In addition to the efforts of the Church, Longley had firm views on the need for the State to provide a system of education. This was at a time when relatively few bishops or other leaders saw the need. He made the sharp observation that the defence of the realm was not financed by voluntary giving, and elementary education should not be funded in that way. Ripon, in partnership with the Diocese of York, founded teacher training colleges for men and for women; the women's college was originally located in Ripon from 1846 but later moved to York.

Another consequence of the growth and shift in population, of which Longley was naturally aware, was the provision of church accommodation; in Ripon, as Sumner had known in Chester, there was not sufficient.

Along with the establishment of schools, a notable part of Longley's Ripon episcopate included church building. Longley's own notes, accessed by Stephenson, record that on his arrival in 1836 there were 279 incumbents, and when he left the number had risen to 419. These numbers indicate the increase in the number of parishes, and it is a safe assumption that each new parish either had a church building or was expecting to build at least one. Along with the increase of incumbent-status clergy, there was a remarkable growth in the number of curates, which had almost doubled from seventy-six to 146. Longley always did his own ordinations, never sending candidates to other bishops for convenience sake, which was a not uncommon practice in the early decades of the nineteenth century. He conducted his ordinations in his cathedral and not in parish churches or even in his own chapel in Ripon, or in London.[161] In his *Charge* of 1838, he remarked that there had been an unacceptably high number of requests for curates to be ordained by letters dimissory, which was the process by which clergy could be ordained by bishops of other dioceses to suit their personal convenience. He told the clergy that he intended to conduct ordinations every January and July, and that he expected incumbents to present their potential curates at those times. Having them "under the roof of the Bishop" would, he declared, enable him to get to know the men being ordained into his diocese, so that he could develop an "intimate acquaintance with their habits of thought, their religious views, and the light in which they regard those sacred obligations which they propose to undertake".[162] In his first ordination address in 1837, Longley spoke movingly to the candidates,

> Let your people only perceive that it is from the fulness of the heart that your mouth speaketh—that you are addressing them, not in the formal language of a system, but are exhibiting to them the counterpart of those living realities which exist within your own bosoms—and you will have found an avenue of persuasion which will be inaccessible even to the highest natural attainments. For that alone will come home to the heart of the hearer which comes forth from the heart of the speaker; and he is truly eloquent who so expresses himself (no matter how few or how simple be his words), that while he feels *himself* the power of his

own language, he communicates that feeling to those whom he is addressing.[163]

Chadwick recorded, however, that during ten years, half of Longley's time at Ripon, he did not manage to bring into the Diocese of Ripon any curates who were graduates, although his recruitment efforts were noticed.[164] Charlotte Brontë in *Shirley*, published in 1849, recorded that "of late years an abundant shower of curates has fallen upon the North of England, they lie very thick upon the hills".

Longley revived the ancient office of rural dean to give support to parish clergy and to help with administration. He never felt able to call diocesan conferences during his Ripon years, regretfully judging that the time was not ripe. He was in favour of the revival of Convocation during his years at Ripon, and also wanted to achieve some sort of representation of the laity in the governance of the Church of England; he would also have liked to develop lay involvement in the governance of the diocese, but circumstances made that impossible until long after his death.[165] In the shorter term, his desire for the revival of Convocation in the Northern Province included a wish for it to have the authority to conduct business meetings. He devoted much of his *Charge* of 1853 to the matter. The revival of the Northern Convocation was to be the major achievement in his short time as Archbishop of York and will be examined below.

Although Longley was a good representative of the growing numbers of nineteenth-century bishops who worked conscientiously in their dioceses and beyond, he also took his part in the work of the Church at the national level, and in all his episcopal appointments was conscientious in attending bishops' meetings, which had been established on an annual basis by Archbishop Howley. In addition, he attended the House of Lords and made a contribution. He spoke in opposition to the Divorce Act in 1857. Also in the Lords he resisted a motion put by Lord Ebury for a modification of the Act of Uniformity which would have enabled a revision of the burial service in the Book of Common Prayer and a relaxation of the obligation of the clergy to subscribe to the Thirty-nine Articles of Religion. However, he supported Lord Shaftesbury's Bill to restrict the working hours of children in factories, drawing on knowledge gained in his Ripon episcopate.[166] He was present at nationally important events, such as the funeral of the Duke of Wellington on 18 November 1852 at St Paul's Cathedral.

He was also prepared to work behind the scenes, if he believed he could be more effective than entering upon public disagreements with regard to church polity. The best example of such activity is to be seen in his remonstrating privately to the prime minister, Lord John Russell, at the time of the controversy over the appointment of R. D. Hampden to the Bishopric of Hereford. He had declined to add his signature to the letter of thirteen bishops. His disagreement with the appointment, along with his reasoning, was set out in his letter to the prime minister dated 2 December 1847, which is given in the *Life* of Wilberforce.

> Although I do not feel myself at liberty to adopt all the expressions contained in the Memorial about to be presented by several of my Episcopal brethren to the head of Her Majesty's Government, on the subject of the rumoured nomination of the Rev. Dr. Hampden to the See of Hereford, I would, nevertheless, desire to join in most respectfully but earnestly expressing my conviction that, unless your lordship can be induced to pause before you press on the election of Dr. Hampden, and to wait until some means be found of proving the groundlessness of those apprehensions which it has excited, there is the greatest danger of the further interruption of the peace of the Church, and of the disturbance of that confidence which it is most desirable that the clergy and the laity of the Church should feel in every exercise of the Royal Supremacy.[167]

Within his diocese, as the anonymous writer of the biographical *Tract* claimed, he willingly visited parishes and individual parishioners, "villagers . . . the sick and afflicted, not officiously, but kindly, conversing with them in the meekness of love." He was able to deal effectively with hard-luck stories, and the same writer recorded an instance of Longley responding with financial help to an appeal. He investigated the circumstances and discovered that the indigent was a drunkard, but that his needs were real. He helped the family in such a way that the individual could not get access to the money. The man bundled up the correspondence and sent it to the well-known Baptist preacher Charles Haddon Spurgeon, anticipating sympathy. Spurgeon replied that Longley had responded like a good Christian gentleman to the man's importunity and sent the bishop a copy of his letter. The same pastoral spirit "carried him into the condemned cell at York Castle to hold up the Cross before the eyes of dying men, and awaken in cold hearts thoughts of contrition, faith and hope".[168] This unsung element of Longley's ministry to the condemned was paralleled much later by Bishop King of Lincoln and was rightly counted as evidence of his personal sanctity. Longley also went on confirmation tours and parish visits which took weeks at a time. Mrs Longley wrote ruefully to her mother about her husband's absence, that she did not expect to see very much of him during the ensuing three months because he was visiting his clergy. His plan was to provide confirmation services within reasonable proximity to where candidates lived, even if the services could not always take place in their own parish churches. This practice, he believed, would be a source of encouragement to them and their families. He set it out in his 1838 *Charge* and also commended the clergy on the arrangements that he had encountered for confirmations. He frequently stayed in parsonages across the diocese, and Elizabeth Gaskell recorded (in her biography of Charlotte Brontë) a visit to Patrick Brontë at Haworth. Some of the local clergy were invited to the house for the evening and began to "upbraid" Charlotte Brontë for "putting them into a book". The embarrassed Charlotte successfully appealed to Longley for support in her predicament. Later, she described him as "the most benignant gentleman that ever put on lawn sleeves". The occasion was regarded by the Brontës as a success: "his visit passed capitally well; and at its close, as he was going away, he expressed himself thoroughly satisfied with all that he had seen." Nevertheless, it had caused turmoil in the household: "it is all very well to talk of receiving a Bishop without trouble, but you *must* prepare for him."

Not all Longley's dealings in the diocese were untroubled, however, despite his efficiency and personal charm. In 1838, one of the new churches, St James', Bradford, was paid for by a generous individual. Longley licensed it for public services, but it is clear that the status of the new church in relation to the parent parish was not defined clearly enough. In 1839, a new vicar was appointed to the parish of Bradford who was not prepared to continue with an informal situation whereby fees taken in St James' were retained to pay the stipend of its priest. Despite Longley's efforts to resolve the situation, the original donor, who had spent nearly £14,000 on the church, a school, and a parsonage, forced it to remain closed for two years until the situation was resolved to his satisfaction.[169]

Church life in the great and growing town of Leeds was to provide Longley with much work and considerable anxiety. In May 1837, Walter Farquhar Hook was appointed vicar of the parish church of St Mary, Leeds, after a strenuous ministry in Coventry. His nine years there enabled him to assess quickly the needs of his new parish. Hook had a powerful personality and an understanding of parochial ministry that was second to none. He was a talented man, well-equipped for the work that lay before him, but his churchmanship meant that his arrival in Leeds was not universally welcomed. He had been inclined to support the Oxford Movement at first and had even tried initially to support Newman when *Tract 90* appeared. As the Tractarians became increasingly controversial, Hook's enthusiasm for their teaching waned considerably, but in Leeds the opposition to his appointment was because of his supposed high church views. The new Vicar of Leeds and the new Bishop of Ripon had known each other at Christ Church, Oxford. Both had held a studentship, and they were near contemporaries, although Hook had had an undistinguished and rather reclusive Oxford career and had been glad to leave in 1821. He had gone up in 1817, two years after Longley had graduated. In the late 1830s, the near coincidence of Longley's and Hook's arrival in Yorkshire meant that they "almost simultaneously began the labours by which they were destined under God to win back for the Church her long-lost supremacy in that part of the country".[170] The first census recorded that in 1801 the population of Leeds was 53,162. It rose inexorably, and by 1841, forty years later and five years after Longley was appointed Bishop of Ripon, Leeds had a population of 152,054. As he settled to his new work, Hook soon realized that the parish church was inadequate for its work. He set in train its rebuilding, which was completed in 1841 with seating capacity for 1,600. Longley consecrated it with a great service. Among the bishops attending was one from the

United States and one from Scotland. The American presence was an early indication of Longley's interest in the wider ministry of the Anglican Church beyond the shores of England and the British Empire.

Longley knew that Hook was one of the most effective clergy of his diocese, but their partnership endured considerable strain and never developed into a close friendship. The issue of churchmanship led to an unfortunate set of circumstances developing. It began with a meeting of the Pastoral Aid Society in Leeds in 1841. It was well-attended, not least by local clergy, some of whom "were most bitterly opposed to the vicar, and some of them in their speeches reflected rather severely upon his opinions and proceedings". Hook saw the meeting as a demonstration against him and his work. A few days later, there was a meeting of the Society for Promoting Christian Knowledge, also in Leeds. Longley was again in the chair. Many of Hook's friends and supporters attended this second event determined to support their man, who (his biographer was forced to admit) "spoke under the influence of strong excitement" and "with an overflowing heart". Uproar followed; the unfortunate Longley tried to restore order, making the error of saying publicly to Hook, "I, in Christian kindness beg my friend to consider whether he may not confine himself to the subject we are met to promote."[171] Naturally, in the heated atmosphere, this was taken as a public rebuke. Hook was wounded as much by the reaction to the bishop's words as by what was actually said, and the relationship between the two men was damaged.

Hook was very aware of the need for additional churches in the town if the Church of England was to be effective in its ministry, and Longley shared that view and supported Hook's endeavours despite the coolness that had developed in their personal relationship. In his *Charge* of 1838, the bishop expressed his concern, which he knew was shared by his clergy, at "the very inadequate provision which our Church as yet affords for the spiritual wants of this densely populated Diocese".[172] He proposed "to form a Diocesan Society, for building, enlarging and endowing churches, and for increasing, if possible, the provision for churches at present inadequately endowed".[173] This was to be a successful initiative. By the time he left Ripon, the number of churches in the diocese had risen from 307 to 432, according to Longley's own notes. But one new church in Hook's Leeds was destined to cause much trouble for Longley and for the vicar. It was one of eighteen erected in Hook's twenty-two years as incumbent, but certainly the most troublesome. The idea for it came from Dr Pusey, who also appreciated the needs of the town. In 1839, he offered anonymously to finance the building of a church in a destitute area of the parish. Pusey insisted on his anonymity to the extent that neither Longley nor Hook knew that Pusey was the sole financier of the project. His anonymity was maintained at some spiritual and emotional cost to Pusey, for he acted as the supposed intermediary of the donor, and so was not as detached as the bishop and the vicar assumed when problems arose.

Understandably, Hook was immediately enthusiastic at the prospect of building a new church. It was an ambitious project, with a seating capacity of 500. The location chosen was one of the most difficult parts of his parish, an area "untouched by the ministrations of the Church". It had a rising population of around 6,000.

> [It had] narrow streets, with low houses . . . inhabited by mill labourers and mechanics; and among or around these ran a branch of the river Aire whose waters were brown and thick with mud, and dye-grease, and drains. The physical discomfort was outdone by the moral degradation; every form of the foulest vice flourished, as was natural, in rank luxuriance.[174]

By 1840 Hook had already acquired land which he had hoped, at first, to use for a school, but there was space for a church to be built. The prospect of the new church, in addition to a school, in that neglected part of Leeds appealed to both men; they were of one mind at the start of Pusey's project.

Pusey's biographer asserted that Longley had approved the plans for the new church when they were submitted to him, and also that, later, he approved a planned series of sermons around the consecration date. It took Pusey a little while to set aside the funds for the building, and in the interim the Tractarian crises of the mid-1840s gathered pace. As they did so, Longley became increasingly cautious and began to raise objections and to question the work. From the start, Pusey had wanted an inscription set up in the church asking that "Ye who enter this holy place pray for the sinner who built it". Longley became very unhappy with that proposal. Not knowing the identity of the donor, the bishop had no way of knowing whether the person was alive or not; he feared that the inscription might unwittingly lead to prayers for the dead. Many in the Church of England disliked the practice and thought of it as "Romish". It was anathema to evangelicals, and even as a moderate high churchman, Longley would not countenance it. On being assured that the anonymous donor was still alive, he relented on condition that he would be informed of the death when it occurred. In the event, Pusey survived Longley by many years. Another objection of the bishop's concerned the dedication proposed. Pusey, for reasons of personal devotion, wanted the church dedicated to the Holy Cross. Longley vetoed it and said he had not been consulted about the dedication, but that is not likely to be the main reason for his objection for he was not small-minded. He said that he feared he might be committed to "some legend", if he allowed it. Eventually, it was agreed that the dedication should be St Saviour's. The tribulations Longley endured over building St Saviour's, Leeds, damaged his reputation among the Tractarians, but it is difficult to see how he could have acted differently in the circumstances of the Church of England as a whole in the period of the building of the church. Yet the problems were far from over.

The donor had hoped that the consecration of the new church would take place on Holy Cross Day, 14 September, but it was deferred until the feast of St Simon and St Jude, 28 October 1845. The agitated nature of Church life in 1845 was made much worse by the conversion of John Henry Newman to the Roman Catholic Church, which by coincidence happened little more than a fortnight before the date eventually set for the consecration of the new church in Leeds. This increased the nervousness of Hook and Longley, although the former had the moral courage to insist that Dr Pusey should be present, even though he had offered to stay away. During the lengthy building process, Pusey's teenaged daughter Lucy had died, and he had given communion vessels, engraved in her memory; sadly, Longley would not allow them even to be in the church during its consecration. On the day, Bishop Longley led a great celebration in which 250 clergy took part, and there were 500 communicants.

Despite the more-or-less satisfactory outcome of the scheme to build St Saviour's, the church was to be a cause of further anxiety for Longley,

Hook, and (by association) Pusey. Initially, St Saviour's was a district church under the control of the Vicar of Leeds, but it became a parish in its own right in 1846 following the Leeds Vicarage Act. At the start, the original plan was that a group of single clergy should live together in the clergy house and work as a team of curates under the incumbent, Richard Ward. He had been a curate of Hook's, who was pleased at the appointment. But tensions increased and erupted into a scandal. Ward's leadership almost immediately took church life strongly in an Anglo-Catholic direction and laid it open to the charge of Romanism. Complaints soon reached Longley, and he interviewed Ward on at least one occasion. Hook declared that he would have been able to deal with the emerging situation if he were still responsible for the new church, that is to say, if it had not been made into a separate parish. He claimed to have advised the patrons' committee as to the danger before it emerged.

Worse was to follow on New Year's Day 1847, when Ward informed Hook that four members of the church, including one of the curates, a man named Macmullen, who had been sent from Oxford on Pusey's recommendation, were about to secede to Rome.[175] Ward later resigned the living, to Longley's relief, but eventually he also converted. By February 1847, in a private letter, Pusey described St Saviour's as "a complete wreck", and Longley was coming to the same conclusion. He refused to licence a curate, whose name is not recorded, and referred to "the danger of the course which [Pusey] had been long pursuing", even though he remained ignorant of Pusey's real involvement in the scheme.[176]

The Evangelical Alliance issued a protest to Bishop Longley about St Saviour's, but it "did not meet with such a favourable response as some of them, perhaps, had anticipated. The steady support and sympathy, indeed, of his bishop was an immense consolation" to Hook,[177] but misunderstandings were inevitable in such circumstances, and Longley handled the situation with care and tact, but it took a lot of skill. Further secessions to Rome by clergy of St Saviour's occurred in the next few years. By the end of 1847, a new vicar had been selected, but Longley's caution had become such that he refused to licence two potential curates for the newly designated incumbent, Thomas Minster, who consequently withdrew his acceptance. Later, Minster accepted the parish, and one of the curates was licensed. At the end of 1848, Longley held a confirmation at Leeds Parish Church, and discovered that the fifty St Saviour's candidates had been taught "a regular system of confession". The bishop was unwilling to sanction the teaching of sacramental confession as a requirement of the discipline of the Church of England, although he did recognize that the practice was sanctioned in the Prayer Book for acute pastoral need. Minster wrote at length to justify his position to Longley, but was dissatisfied with the response, which he described as "cold". Longley visited the parish and took away some devotional literature, including a book written by Pusey. If the clergy were left in any doubt of the bishop's disapproval, that was dispelled when he sent a long letter to Minster in which he emphasized that sacramental confession should only be used for people who were dying, or whose consciences would not let them proceed to receive Holy Communion. The uneasy situation continued through 1849 and 1850, and Longley continued to receive complaints.

Eventually, at the behest of other clergy, Bishop Longley "opened a court of inquiry" in the vestry of Leeds Parish Church in December 1850. Thomas Minster, who had feared for his health from the start, became ill and had to be given a year's leave of absence; he subsequently resigned and eventually joined the Church of Rome. By 1851, no fewer than fifteen of the clergy connected with St Saviour's had converted to Roman Catholicism. The only significant priest from the staff of St Saviour's who remained loyal to the Anglican Church was A. P. Forbes, who went on to exercise a distinguished ministry in Scotland as Bishop of Brechin from 1847 and has been described as the "Scottish Pusey". When Pusey had secretly planned to pay for the building of St Saviour's in Leeds, he had expected it to be staffed by a small community of celibate clergy. Sadly, his vision of witness and ministry in a crowded slum was marred by the repeated secessions of so many of its clergy to the Church of Rome. St Saviour's has the unhappy distinction of being the parish which saw the greatest number of secessions of any in the country.

The Leeds situation has been described at length, as it was the most severe test of Longley's Ripon episcopate. Almost at the end of his life, Longley used it to reinforce a point in his *Charge* to the Diocese of Canterbury in 1868:

> It is now more than a quarter of a century since, in the course of my administration of the Diocese of Ripon, I came into collision with a movement in Leeds somewhat similar to that on which I am now animadverting. The clergy of a church there had adopted practices which appeared to me inconsistent with the principles of the English Church; that of Auricular Confession being the most offensive. I felt myself bound to revoke the licence of the Curate who had thus, as I considered, transgressed the limits of this office; he appealed to the Archbishop of the Province, who confirmed my decision. The course which I adopted was resented by the rest of the clergy of that church, and a secession to the Church of Rome was the consequence. Those who thus abandoned the Church of their baptism at any rate showed themselves in their true colours, and behaved honestly in openly avowing their true principles at the sacrifice of worldly advantage.[178]

Hook always regretted the problems of the early days of Longley's years in Ripon. Later, however, when the St Saviour's debacle was consigned to the past, their relationship improved. When Longley died, Hook wrote movingly:

> For the first ten years, our opinions, when he was my diocesan, on many points differed; for the last ten we were entirely one. I have known him therefore as an opponent almost, and as a friend, and I can truly say that I never met with anyone so just, so patient, so placable, so considerate and kind.[179]

The anonymous author of the *Church of England biographies* claimed to have had personal knowledge of the situation and described Longley's Ripon years in favourable terms, with an oblique reference to Hook. Longley's "Ripon episcopate is one of the brightest chapters in the later history of the Church of England. To him and to a fellow worker, still living (God long preserve him!), it is, under the Divine blessing, mainly owing that the Church of England has probably no stronger influence among intelligent men anywhere than in the West Riding of Yorkshire."[180]

It is convenient to consider Longley's position with regard to ritualism at this point. Much later in his career, whilst Archbishop of Canterbury, Longley served on a Royal Commission on ritual which was set up in 1867. Coming close to the end of the archbishop's life, the author of the Longley essay in *Church of England biographies* recorded the opinion of an unknown relative of Longley who believed the extra work of the commission was a factor in the fatal decline of his health.[181] Subsequently known as the Ritual Commission, it issued no fewer than four reports, but Longley's final words on the subject came in his second *Charge* to the Diocese of Canterbury of 1868. He was clear that parish clergy should not be free to do as they wished with regard to ritual in Church services.

> It is obvious that if any order or discipline is to be maintained in our Church, it will be impossible to allow each single clergyman to change the customs and ritual according to his own private opinion, and to set himself up as judge of what is lawful and what is not. Anarchy will be the fruit of any such system.[182]

He acknowledged that the precise meaning of the Ornaments Rubric is "complicated" but observed that it had only recently become problematic. With a hint of irony, he drew attention to the fact that over the preceding three centuries no less than 700 bishops had managed to make it work. The first report of the Royal Commission had condemned the use of eucharistic vestments, and Longley expressed his conviction that no clergyman in the Diocese of Canterbury had adopted vestments, and none used incense, although the latter was not considered until the publication of the second report in 1869. Longley said that clergy who do use vestments "are a noisy but not very numerous section of our Church". He said that the wearing of a preaching scarf and an academic hood was the legal vesture.

Turning to the doctrine of the Eucharist, he continued in his *Charge*, "in general I would say, without attempting to define accurately the limits of opinion on the Holy Eucharist, I cannot think that a clergyman is justified in propounding anything to his people save that which fairly represents the tone and language of the Church of England." After such an anodyne observation, he went on to cite Richard Hooker, Lancelot Andrewes, Nicholas Ridley, and Thomas Ken as theologians to support his view that "it cannot be denied . . . that the doctrine of the Real Presence is, in one sense, the doctrine of the Church of England".[183]

At the time of the 1868 *Charge*, Longley knew that he had not long left to live. He was consequently eager to set on record his beliefs and teaching about the Eucharist in the devotional life of the Church of England. To do so was his "last opportunity of bearing [his] testimony", and it gave him "abiding satisfaction" to speak,

> touching the Blessed Sacrament of the Lord's Supper, as plainly set forth in our formularies . . . of thus declaring my steadfast adherence to those principles upon which our Reformation was conducted, my rooted conviction that the doctrines respecting the Holy Eucharist enunciated by our Reformers are in full accordance with the language of Holy Scripture, as well as the ancient Doctors of the Church.[184]

Even though St Saviour's, Leeds, had given Longley the most intractable problems of his long Ripon episcopate, those problems were but part of the business of his ministry and among its occasional crises. One such crisis occurred in 1852, when the embankment of the Bilberry Reservoir above Holmfirth collapsed in the early hours of the morning of 5 February. There was widespread destruction of property, and eighty-one individuals lost their lives in the most serious flood to strike in that flood-vulnerable district. Longley earned much praise from newspapers and the general public for his visit to the scene and for the encouragement he gave to the rescuers and to the local clergy. The bishop's pastoral activity was not restricted simply to such disasters, and by the time that he reached the end of his time as Bishop of Ripon, Longley was loved and respected.[185]

There can be little doubt that Longley expected to spend the whole of his episcopal ministry as Bishop of Ripon; however, his twenty years there were to be just a long apprenticeship for higher office. It came to an end when Palmerston offered him the Diocese of Durham in 1856, in succession to Edward Maltby, also a former headmaster of Harrow.

Maltby had gone to Durham in 1836, the same year that Longley had gone to Ripon. Longley accepted Durham, although Samuel Wilberforce noted that he had declined Lincoln in 1853. His translation went smoothly, and Archbishop Tait later recorded in his diary a tale which he must have got from Longley himself. On 4 December 1856, he had paid homage as Bishop of London to Queen Victoria and recorded that Longley was also present to take his oath as Bishop of Durham. The ceremony was very seemly, but Tait remarked that Longley "had not escaped so quietly when he was consecrated Bishop of Ripon". That occasion had been before the accession of Queen Victoria, for Longley was one of the last bishops to be appointed in the reign of King William IV. Following Longley's homage, the king, who was incensed by the political problems of the day, said to him in a loud voice, "Bishop of Ripon, I charge you, as you shall answer before Almighty God, that you never by word or deed give encouragement to those damned Whigs who would upset the Church of England."[186]

Longley soon settled into Durham, even though a personal tragedy struck within two years of his arrival. Caroline Longley died on 9 March 1858 at Auckland Castle. Samuel Wilberforce visited Longley in October 1858: "by rail to Bishop Auckland Castle, where received most kindly [sic]. Dear Bishop Longley surrounded by his family and happy in them." However, by the time of his wife's death, Longley had already established a pattern of activity, and he worked in his characteristic fashion. In his short time in his new diocese he re-established the office of rural dean as he had in Ripon, and similarly began to increase the Church's educational provision and to get churches built. Wilberforce thought that the work in Durham was lighter than Longley had endured in Ripon and also recorded that he "enjoys the change to comparative rest and peace"; but Longley was not indolent; he travelled around the parishes and was conscientious in his administration of the diocese and his attendance in the House of Lords.

He was pastorally active and, as had been the case with the Holmfirth flood disaster, Longley had to respond to a tragedy. He visited Burradon Colliery after a great explosion in March 1860 caused the deaths of seventy-six men and boys. The colliery was not far from Newcastle, and at that time was in the Diocese of Durham. He visited the homes of the injured and bereaved and stayed for two hours. On 10 March, the Mayor of Newcastle had called a public meeting to raise funds for the families of the victims, and Longley sent a message of sympathy and support with a donation. The tragedy received much publicity across the nation, particularly as it happened at a time when the welfare of miners and their families was causing concern. Longley's care attracted attention and enhanced his reputation in his diocese and beyond.

———

C. T. Longley served as Bishop of Durham for only four years. Palmerston intervened once again by inviting him to succeed Thomas Musgrave as Archbishop of York. It will be recalled that the old archbishop had preceded Hampden as Bishop of Hereford. He died in London on 4 May 1860, and Longley was appointed on 1 June. Once again, he set about getting additional churches built, and soon established another church building society. However, his efforts in that field were not given time to mature as he was translated to Canterbury two years later, but he did initiate one very significant development for the Northern Province during his short archiepiscopate.

Longley's achievement as Archbishop of York was the revival of the Convocation of the Province of York, but it was an achievement whose arrival was overdue. The northern process of agitation for the revival was described by D. A. Jennings in an essay which was published in 1975, *The Revival of the Convocation of York, 1837–1861*. He recorded that it had been sought from as early as 1837, and that it had intensified after the appointment of Robert Isaac Wilberforce as Archdeacon of the East Riding in 1841, but he converted to Roman Catholicism in 1854 and had died before Longley was made archbishop. It was only with the demise of Musgrave and the arrival of Longley in 1860 that the revival of Convocation in the Northern Province became possible; Longley deserved much credit for achieving it.

Although of a liberal cast of mind, Archbishop Musgrave had feared that Convocation would become entrenched in dogmatic disputes fuelled by the growing strength of the Tractarian movement. He had been obliged to call the formal periodic meetings of Convocation required by law, but took to extending the dates between them, exercising an authority which he did not have. No one was able to protest effectively, sometimes because they did not know when the meetings took place, and on at least one well-attested occasion he kept the door locked, so that no one could attend.[187] Even when Lord Redesdale raised the matter in the Lords, which he did on three separate occasions, Musgrave had remained obdurate. He refused to attend the House on at least one occasion when the subject was to be raised, and even when threatened by the prospect of legal action from the court of the Queen's Bench, he remained unmoved.

Bishop Longley had devoted most of his *Charge* at Ripon, in 1856, to the subject of Convocation. That *Charge* encapsulated Longley's emphatic expression of support for Convocation's revival. He had refrained from mentioning it in two earlier *Charges* in 1841 and 1844, and he did not speak when it was discussed in the House of Lords in 1858. D. A. Jennings, in his otherwise very helpful monograph, noticed that Longley sought other ways for convening clerical meetings, but was incorrect in his observation that "Convocation as an instrument for such a purpose was not even considered".[188] He also opined that Longley decided to allow the York Convocation to meet in 1860 because he had his eye on his possible translation to Canterbury, and knew that the Southern Province had been meeting in Convocation since 1852.[189] However, expediency was not Longley's motive, and nor was cynical opportunism. His desire for the revival was a longstanding one. In fact, in his 1853 *Charge* to the Diocese of Ripon, Longley was quite clear that Convocation was the entirely right and proper place for clerical issues to be discussed and had then expressed strongly his desire that Convocation should be revived. Since 1717, Longley said, "Convocation has presented the appearance of an empty shadow" and was "virtually defunct". Later, he declared, "I cannot but believe that it would be acceptable to the clergy as a body to have representatives of their own who should have the opportunity of deliberating on their behalf."

Longley said that King Edward I was the monarch to whose reign the origins of Convocation, as the nineteenth century recognized it, could be traced, and he explained it in detail in his *Charge* of 1853. With the historical legitimacy of Convocation asserted, Longley made the bold claim that "nor can we escape the conviction that it is the inalienable property of every Church that it should be able to avail itself of the services of such a council, not only convened, but also acting in its behalf from time to time, should circumstances demand such action".[190] Next he dealt with the odd assertion, evidently put forward by someone opposed to revival, that the concerns of the clergy could be adequately articulated through the presence of the bishops in the House of Lords. His rejoinder was simple; bishops are not in the Lords as representatives of the clergy but as a result of royal command. He also dismissed the idea that Parliament could still be regarded as the appropriate source for church legislation. He made the familiar point that the House of Commons was no longer exclusively composed of Anglicans, but had among its members "Roman Catholics and Dissenters"; consequently he was anxious to ensure the Commons should not have a "voice in sanctioning the articles of faith and canons of our Church".[191] Convocation ought to provide that voice.

A tactic employed by some of the clergy who managed to attend the formal meetings of Convocation which Musgrave had sought to curtail had been to convene their own meeting immediately after the formal prorogation. This, of course, had been in defiance of the old archbishop, but in the course of his *Charge*, Longley mentioned this approvingly. He had, he said, "got legal opinion", which said that "after the prorogation of Convocation a committee, delegated by the whole body, may legally sit and confer upon matters that concern the interests of the Church and clergy; may draw up reports upon matters and present them to the body which commissioned them."[192] He recognized this expedient as a method of ascertaining "the sentiments of my reverend brethren in this diocese" but saw that it was outside the influence of the diocesan bishop to an even greater extent than would be properly convened meetings of the Lower House of Convocation. The reality of such meetings encouraged him to "entertain the idea of a diocesan synod". However, he did not do so immediately because he felt the need for unanimity among his clergy before proceeding; he did not want it to be a divisive step.

His final point in this first part of his *Charge*, before he turned to acknowledging the 150th anniversary of the Society for Propagation of the Gospel in Foreign Parts, was to assert that the judicial powers of a revived Convocation should be limited. He did not want it to become the "tribunal for the trial of offences against our Laws Ecclesiastical", although in a parting shot, he observed that no one wanted the Judicial Committee of the Privy Council to be involved in doctrinal matters either.

At that time, 1853, Longley's thoughtful desire for the revival of Convocation, as expressed in this *Charge,* had to wait seven years for its fulfilment even though the Convocation of the Province of Canterbury had already emerged from its long slumbers. After Longley succeeded to the archbishopric, the York Convocation had its first meaningful meeting on 16 August 1860. Although that meeting could be little more than a formality, it was apparent that the times had changed. Of course, as archbishop he was not present at the meeting of the Lower House, but Longley insisted that the prolocutor conducting the early meetings of that House should do so with extreme caution. This is likely to have been the exercise of common sense rather than timidity on Longley's part. He knew that there was likely to be a temptation to explode into action, after such a long period of suppression. More liberty of expression developed, but Longley soon moved to become Queen Victoria's third Archbishop of Canterbury.

—

C. T. Longley's stay in York was short, but the revival of Convocation in the Northern Province was a very significant achievement and earned him an honourable place in the modern history of the Church of England. He succeeded Sumner at Canterbury in September 1862, just over two years after becoming Archbishop of York. Samuel Wilberforce wrote to a friend: "I suppose that tomorrow's papers will tell you that York goes to Canterbury; quite surely an answer to prayer . . . We shall have peace and holiness and, a steady adherence to Church principles in him. God be thanked."

Longley was enthroned in person, like his predecessor, in Canterbury Cathedral on 12 December 1862. His appointment was generally welcomed, largely for the reasons Wilberforce recorded. He was known as a thoughtful and just man. Some regarded him a little dull, but this was to underestimate his character. He came to Canterbury with a well-deserved reputation as a competent bishop with long years of experience in administration and qualities of leadership demonstrated in the revival of Convocation. His work as a diocesan bishop had mirrored that of his predecessor with regard to increasing the provision of schools and churches, together with his extensive confirmation tours. His skill in handling the situation at St Saviour's, Leeds, had shown considerable ability in dealing with conflict. His ready response to the tragedies of the floods in Holmfirth and the colliery accident at Burradon showed a man of sensitivity in pastoral matters.

High on the list of things which claimed the attention of C. T. Longley after he became the new Archbishop of Canterbury was the growing theological controversy concerning *Essays and Reviews*. It will be recalled that the collection had been published in the autumn of 1860 to a mostly indifferent reception. It was the production of writers with whom Longley's predecessor had few shared convictions. Sumner, wisely after his experience with the courts, had counselled caution to a deputation seeking action which called on him at Lambeth. The underlying thrust of *Essays and Reviews* was to assert intellectual freedom in theology, especially in the light of the emerging insights of biblical criticism. The book owed its origin to the longstanding friendship between Benjamin Jowett and Frederick Temple, both of whom were well aware of the developments in biblical criticism, although those insights had not become an issue for most clergy, and consequently were largely unheard of in the parishes. According to Temple, he and Jowett had "frequently talked of the melancholy unwillingness of people to state honestly their opinions on points of doctrine ... We thought it might encourage free and honest discussion of Biblical topics", if such a volume was published.[193] Temple had the inevitable headmaster's anxiety about the reaction of parents and that explanation had been offered to a meeting of masters at Rugby School in February 1861. F. E. Kitchener, the author of the Rugby section of Temple's *Memoir*, was present at that meeting, which he said was called as the "ecclesiastical storms were raging", when Bishop Wilberforce persuaded his fellow bishops, meeting at Fulham, to condemn the book.

The seven different authors had each taken responsibility for his own offering. That was stated in the volume, but public and ecclesiastical opinion at the time was unwilling to accept the essayists' claim that each had worked separately; after all, it was reasoned, they were a group of friends and acquaintances and, therefore, were cognizant of each other's views. To the post-Victorian mind, the essays are innocuous, but theological developments were more anxiously analysed in the year after Darwin had brought the concept of evolution to general notice. Within the Church, the essayists managed to unite both high and low church people against them and generated one of the most significant ecclesiastical controversies of the century.[194] It fell to Archbishop Longley to offer leadership in managing the controversy. This he did with a light ecclesiastical touch and diplomatic skill.

Frederick Temple's essay was the first in the volume and will be examined in detail in the final chapter. Benjamin Jowett was Regius Professor of Greek at Oxford and a future Master of Balliol College (from 1870). He wrote "On the Interpretation of Scripture", and his essay was theologically weightier than Temple's. Both were uncontroversial, but both men were caught up in the ensuing controversy because, as Tait shrewdly observed to Temple, the book was judged as a whole. H. B. Wilson, Vicar of Great Staughton, who had been one of the co-signatories to the protest against *Tract 90* in 1841, was another contributor; his essay on the "National Church" was more radical than its title suggested. Mark Pattison, the Rector of Lincoln College, Oxford, wrote on "Tendencies of Religious Thought, 1688–1750". Rowland Williams produced an essay on Bunsen's *Biblical Researches*. He was Vice Principal of St David's College, Lampeter, but was also Vicar of Broad Chalke, which proved to be more significant in the saga of *Essays and Reviews*. Baden Powell, who died in June 1860 before the controversy broke out, wrote on the "study of the evidences of Christianity". C. W. Goodwin, a Cambridge Egyptologist and the only layperson among the essayists, wrote "on the Mosaic cosmogony".

The book had a "slow fuse" in that it received little attention when it first appeared, although Canon H. P. Liddon had soon begun to rally opposition to it. Another opponent, but with very different reasons, was Frederic Harrison. He had abandoned Christianity for disillusioned agnosticism and later embraced positivism; he wrote a review anonymously in the *Westminster Review* of October 1860. The controversy grew fierce after the volume was denounced in January 1861 in the *Quarterly Review* by Bishop Samuel Wilberforce, who asserted that the seven could not "with moral honesty maintain their posts as clergymen of the established church".

Gradually, considerable attention began to be paid to what the biographers of Archbishop Tait (at that time Bishop of London) called "the obnoxious volume", and "protests and memorials" soon reached the bishops and the archbishops. The growing agitation gave strength to Wilberforce's demand that the bishops should discuss it and, incidentally, helped improve Wilberforce's reputation among evangelicals. No official record of the bishops' meeting at Fulham exists, but Wilberforce's biographer reproduced an account which Wilberforce left.[195] The bishops decided that the appropriate way to announce their conclusion was to reply in detail to a formal complaint. They chose one which had come from the clergy of a rural deanery in Dorsetshire. The episcopal reply, dated 12 February 1861, included the following paragraph:

> We cannot understand how these opinions can be held consistently with an honest subscription to the formularies of our Church, with many of the fundamental doctrines of which they appear to us essentially at variance.[196]

A. P. Stanley, Regius Professor of Ecclesiastical History at Oxford, was the leading theological liberal of the time. He had declined to contribute to *Essays and Reviews*, believing the volume to be inopportune; a contemporary remarked that his absence made the volume "like Hamlet without the Prince". He did, however, publish a defence of the book in the *Edinburgh Review* of April 1861. Despite his support, a strong feeling prevailed that the book was indeed unacceptable as the expression of the views of clergymen of the Church of England. However, for more than a year, there was no obvious way of tackling the problem. Most of the authors were in employment which placed them outside the direct authority of the Church of England. Only two of them were susceptible to church disciplinary procedures, but those processes were complex and might produce a result which would satisfy no one. The two men vulnerable to such processes, and who became the symbolic targets of the book's opponents, were H. B. Wilson and Rowland Williams. The latter's parish was in the Diocese of Ely, and Bishop Turton of Ely was reluctant to initiate a prosecution. Eventually, he did permit another clergyman to act as plaintiff. H. B. Wilson's parish was Broad Chalke in the Diocese of Salisbury, whose bishop, Walter Hamilton, was the only follower of the Tractarians on the bench of bishops. He was also reluctant to proceed. Hamilton's biography was published in 1869 by Canon H. P. Liddon, who said that Bishop Hamilton believed *Essays and Reviews* to "contain propositions clearly at variance with the teachings of the Church. It was for that reason that the Bishop felt it to be his duty to take legal proceedings",[197] but even so, Hamilton took several months to reach his decision. Liddon felt it necessary to identify several reasons for the delay. Hamilton, he said, did not want to appear to be acting from "any feelings of indignation". More importantly, he "was afraid of appearing to assign to an ephemeral publication a degree of importance which did not belong to it. He was afraid of adding to its actual importance." Hamilton's most profound reason for hesitating, however, was a fear that the court might fail in its duty: "he was dissatisfied with the fitness of the courts of judicature 'for weighing in the fine balances of truth' the delicate questions which would have to be brought before them." Eventually, however, Hamilton overcame his reluctance and the case was argued before the Dean of the Arches, Dr Stephen Lushington. Wilson and Williams were each sentenced to one year's deprivation of office. Lushington based his judgement upon the Thirty-nine Articles of Religion and the Book of Common Prayer, although neither was claimed to be infallible.[198]

Williams and Wilson decided to appeal against the decision of the Dean of Arches to the Judicial Committee of the Privy Council. Longley, in the anomalous position adopted earlier by Sumner, sat with Archbishop Thomson, Bishop Tait of London, and several eminent lawyers. Lushington's judgement was overturned by the committee in June 1863: Wilson and Williams were not guilty of heresy. The majority included Tait, but both archbishops were in the minority in their belief that the two arraigned were guilty of heresy. Longley, in his dissent from the Judicial Committee decision, adhered to that of his own Court of Arches and so avoided the inconsistency which had been apparent in his predecessor's dealings with the Gorham case.

Afterwards, each of the archbishops issued a pastoral letter explaining his dissent from the majority judgement. Longley's lengthy pastoral was widely published as a pamphlet and in the press and gives valuable insights into his personal opinions and his theological convictions. He began on a rather diffident note, but explained that he received daily "many letters of inquiry expressing much perplexity and seeking counsel at my hands". Some of the correspondence came from eminent individuals who urged him to make some sort of public declaration. He had been reluctant to do so because he was sensitive to the confidential nature of the deliberations of the Judicial Committee, but was eventually convinced of the need to explain his position. He set out to explain that in dissenting from the judgement of the Judicial Committee he was abiding by theological convictions which he had always held and which informed his mind as he reached his decision about the case. What he said was masterly.

> It would be entirely unbecoming in me as a member of the Court to presume to criticize the terms of a judgment concurred in by the able and distinguished persons who assented to it; but on a question so momentous, involving as it does such grave issues to the Church of England, I must claim to myself the privilege of giving expression to opinions formed prior to the delivery of the judgment, and wholly irrespective of the terms in which it is couched.

When considering the parts of *Essays and Reviews* that concerned the authority of scripture, he felt no need to attempt any definition of inspiration, because "the Church had not thought fit to prescribe one". He had, however, felt bound to adhere to the "exact level" of authority and inspiration accorded to scripture by the Thirty-nine Articles of Religion and the liturgy of the Church of England. This was the basis from which he formed his decision about the theological opinions of the two clergy.

He first considered the essay by Rowland Williams and began by looking at the case in the light of Article 6 of the Thirty-nine Articles of Religion, "Of the sufficiency of the holy Scriptures for salvation", and Article 20, "Of the authority of the Church". In the latter, as Longley pointed out, the Scriptures are defined as the "Word of God", and the article requires that any passage from the Bible must not be expounded in such a way "that it be repugnant to another". Having developed this general (but hazardous) argument, the archbishop then turned to his dilemma: "It remained for me to consider how far the statements of Dr. Williams, respecting Holy Writ, were reconcilable with those express declarations of the Church in her formularies and Articles." He then summarized Williams's statements regarding the inspiration and authority of scripture in *Essays and Reviews*. He reached the conclusion that "to myself these [Williams's] views of Holy Scripture appeared entirely inconsistent with the terms of our formularies as cited above". He concluded that there was "an irreconcilable difference between the language of the 6th and 20th Articles representing Holy Scripture on the one hand and the statements of Dr. Williams concerning it on the other". In the light of that conclusion, Longley could only react by voting to uphold Lushington's original judgement of condemning the teaching of Williams.

The second part of Longley's pastoral letter was given over to an examination of H. B. Wilson's essay, which considered the concept of a national church. Wilson had referred to the "pivot Article of the Church"; again, this is Article 6 of the Thirty-nine Articles. It lists the Canonical Books of the Old Testament and refers to those of the New Testament "as they are commonly received". Wilson had noted correctly that there is no use made in the article of the phrase "Word of God". Longley said, "he would seem to infer hence that the Church never calls Holy Scripture by that name." He went on to refute Wilson's argument by finding references to "God's word written" in Article 20, as already noticed, and, he added, there is a reference to the Scriptures as the Word of God in the Church of England ordinal. His cumulative point is that "according to the mind of the Church, the terms 'Holy Scripture', 'the canonical Books of the Old and New Testament', 'the Word of God' and 'God's Word Written' appear to be equivalent." In a rhetorical question he then asked the extent to which Wilson's "language" was reconcilable with the expressed mind of the Church "on these points". He found to his satisfaction that Wilson's essay was not reconcilable,

> In truth, the inconsistency seems to me to be so great as to approach to a logical contradiction, the Church treating Holy Scripture as God's Word written without stint or qualification;

> Mr Wilson, on the contrary, maintaining that some parts of Holy Scripture are not the Word of God.

A little later, Longley declared that a momentous question was under consideration,

> whether a clergyman should be permitted to proclaim to his people that the term 'Word of God' is not to be identified with 'Holy Scripture'; whether in fact the Bible is still to be our guide in matters of faith, still to have any power for establishing doctrine, still to be canonical in the sense in which I hold the term to be undoubtedly used by our Church.

Having set out his convictions very clearly, Longley then turned to the question of the clergy and whether they have any liberty of interpretation. Here he was consistent, but his strictures were unlikely to have encouraged those who were engaged in biblical criticism. He was tolerant "as to questions of various readings, or the genuineness of a disputed text", but claimed that such matters were widely different from asserting that any part of an acknowledged "canonical book" is not the Word of God. He believed that,

> there is ample room for fair criticism; but criticism in the case of a minister of our Church must have its limits, in as much as he has bound himself to adhere to the plain meaning of the Articles and formularies. You will, I am persuaded, feel convinced that it cannot be agreeable to the mind of the Church that you should transgress these limits.

In the final paragraphs of his pastoral letter, Archbishop Longley turned his attention to the word "everlasting" in the "passage of our formularies which relate to the punishment of the lost". Once again, he adhered to the traditional doctrine that "everlasting" denotes a permanent state. He did recognize the harsh nature of this condemnation, and tried to put it in perspective by referring to its opposite, the blessedness of the saved, for whatever the meaning of the word ... in the case of the lost, the same must be its meaning in the case of the saved; and our certainty of never-ending bliss for penitent believers is gone if the word bears not the same significance in the case of the impenitent and unbelieving.

Longley reached the end of his long letter with words of encouragement for his readers, particularly the clergy to whom the letter was specifically addressed.

> You will, I doubt not, resolve to adhere steadfastly to those interpretations of the language of our Church which have been commonly accepted as agreeable to Holy Scripture and to the doctrine of the Catholic Church. You will reverence, and teach your flock to reverence, the canonical Scriptures as the Word of God.

His closing words were also pastorally sensitive, referring to the gospel,

> May we find and feel it to be our solace in sickness, and our strength in the season of temptation; our guide and comfort in life, our stay and support in the hour of death! May it be our privilege to preserve it, in all its integrity and purity, to this generation, and hand it down as the Word of God to all them that are yet to come.
> I am your faithful and affectionate friend and brother,
> C. T. Cantuar.

Essays and Reviews caused a significant controversy, and it presented the Archbishop of Canterbury with the usual problem of inconsistency when the civil courts reversed the decision of the Court of Arches, when Wilson and Williams appealed beyond it. Longley had been left with little room to manoeuvre when he and Thomson of York expressed their dissent from the majority verdict of the Judicial Committee, but they stuck to their guns. Their pastoral letters were attempts to deal with the situation, and Longley's letter breathed good sense and toleration. It added to his stature as Archbishop of Canterbury and demonstrated theological skill and diplomatic sensitivity of a significant order.

The controversy did not die down immediately. Eventually, a petition was signed by 11,000 clergy, declaring their belief in the inspiration of scripture and in the eternal punishment of the damned. Even so, as the signatures were gathered the importance of the volume was fading, and later scholarship was able to build upon the insights of the essayists without fear of prosecution.

—

Longley was not naturally combative, but he soon found himself embroiled in another controversy. Once again, it was not of his making, but he was called upon to give a lead in difficult circumstances and deal with the consequences of the English secular courts again making a theological ruling. John William Colenso had been an assistant master at Harrow under Longley's headmastership, and there is evidence that they liked each other. Colenso had also been a don and a mathematics tutor, but Longley's former subordinate at Harrow was the cause of much difficulty for Longley when he was Archbishop of Canterbury because of his theologically enquiring mind. He was the cause of a controversy that ran for a long time and was later to cause further difficulty for E. W. Benson, who was archbishop after Longley's immediate successor, A. C. Tait. For Archbishop Longley, the Colenso case was so significant that it was a factor, although by no means the dominant one as has often been claimed, in his decision to call the first Lambeth Conference in 1867, which will be explored below. Longley's initiative set in train the ongoing series of meetings which developed into the most important element of the self-understanding of the worldwide Anglican Communion.

J. W. Colenso, after Harrow and following his marriage in 1846, had become a parish priest in Norfolk. His wife had introduced him to F. D. Maurice, and the two became friends, although Colenso's developing theological opinions estranged them many years later. He had also been impressed by *Essays and Reviews*, but his dominant interest came to be in foreign missions. This drew him to the attention of Bishop Robert Gray of Cape Town, who was a combative man of high church opinions, strongly opposed to Erastianism. Gray was the son of the Bishop of Bristol whose house had been burned by a rioting mob in 1831 at the time of the Great Reform Bill and had been persuaded to accept the Bishopric of Cape Town by Archbishop Howley in 1847. He had a huge diocese, and when it was divided, he asked Colenso to become bishop of the new Diocese of Natal, although there was some opposition to his appointment because of his liberal scholarship. Nevertheless, Colenso was consecrated on 30 November 1853 in Lambeth Parish Church under letters patent. Colenso was a man of great energy and set out for Natal almost immediately, returning after nearly three months in order to raise funds. Back in Natal, he established his headquarters six miles east of Pietermaritzburg on 8,500 acres of Crown land and set out to rationalize the somewhat disorganized Anglican missions of the area, of which only one, he thought, was functioning properly. As a bishop, he regarded the indigenous people as his first responsibility, which earned him criticism from the white population. Some of them also objected to his unwillingness to condemn polygamy among his indigenous new converts. He disliked the practice, but saw that enforced monogamy tended to pitch rejected wives and children into penury, when their husbands embraced the Christian faith and abandoned them. Further trouble was also brewing. Colenso soon learnt the Zulu language and began to translate, with the help of assistants, the Bible and the Book of Common Prayer. In the course of doing so he found himself questioning the more savage events recorded in the Old Testament and was perplexed by the moral questions concerning them which were raised by some of his assistants. This experience radicalized his understanding of the Bible. He produced a commentary on Romans in 1861, a copy of which Gray sent to Archbishop Sumner. That book was followed in 1862 by the publication of the first of four volumes on the Pentateuch and Joshua, "critically examined". In South Africa, his books, when in turn critically examined by Gray among others, led to an accusation of heresy. In 1863, he was tried in Cape Town by Gray sitting with two other bishops and was deposed from his bishopric on 16 December. Colenso, who was not lacking in courage, ignored the sentence (except to protest against the jurisdiction of the court). He was excommunicated by Gray in 1866.

In England, Longley's opinion was clear, and was shared by his episcopal colleagues. He had hoped in vain that Colenso would resign. In October 1865, the Archbishop of Canterbury wrote to the Dean of Maritzburg,

> I do not see how you can accept Dr. Colenso as your bishop without identifying yourself with his errors. The bishops of the Church of England have, with scarcely an exception, either publicly prohibited Dr. Colenso from preaching in their dioceses, or intimated their unwillingness to allow him to do so.[199]

As was to be expected Colenso appealed against Gray's sentence; the appeal was to the Judicial Committee of the Privy Council in England. He appealed to the committee, but he did so as an ordinary citizen of the Empire who believed himself to be wronged, which meant that his appeal was not to the council in its ecclesiastical role. Nevertheless, the fact of the appeal immediately drew attention to the Erastian tension inherent within the legal system; it is difficult to believe that Colenso did not expect that to happen. Gray's court was a spiritual one, whereas the appeal was, once again, to a secular body; an old problem was receiving a fresh airing. Colenso's appeal was successful. That outcome was unsatisfactory because the judgement was based on the doubts about the validity of Gray's letters patent in the light of the change of status of South Africa. Gray's letters patent had been re-issued when his diocese was divided, but by the time that happened, South Africa had been granted constitutional government, which had arguably obviated the need for such authorization from the Crown.[200] Colenso was able to continue working in defiance of Gray, effectively as a schismatic, but one who retained the emoluments and properties of the Diocese of Natal. He continued in that anomalous position until his death in 1883. Despite Colenso's tenacious continuation to work, a new bishop, W. K. Macrorie (1831–1905), was appointed in 1869 in Colenso's place, designated the Bishop of Maritzburg. Macrorie was the first colonial bishop not to be appointed by the Crown, but was elected within Gray's province.

On a lighter note, not everyone took the situation with the seriousness that it required and which Longley believed to be acute. After the Lambeth Conference, the following anonymous verses appeared:

> The Archbishop:
> My dear Colenso, with regret,
> We hierarchs in conclave met,
> Beg you, you most disturbing writer,
> To take off your colonial mitre;
> This course we urge upon you strongly:
> Believe me, yours most truly, LONGLEY.
> The Bishop:
> My dear Archbishop, to resign
> This Zulu diocese of mine,
> And own myself a heathen dark,
> Because I've doubts about Noah's Ark,
> And think it right to tell men so –
> Is *not* the course for, COLENSO.

When Archbishop Longley wrote to the Dean of Maritzburg in 1865, his letter had given comfort to those anxious about the appointment of a bishop without the involvement of the Crown. That comfort did sound a little cool.

> As to the appointment of a new bishop, the Privy Council has pronounced the Church of South Africa to be just as independent as any of the Nonconformist communities, as under this view, it is, I conclude, competent to elect its own bishop without reference to the authorities in England either civil or ecclesiastical; nor, as I conceive, will such an act separate you from communion with the Church of England. The Scotch Episcopal Church is in communion with us, but elects its own bishops, and is not obliged to submit to appeal to the Judicial Committee of the Privy Council.[201]

It was consistent with that opinion that Longley refused to allow Macrorie to be consecrated in the province of Canterbury; in this Dean Henry Alford of Canterbury, in whose cathedral it had been suggested that the consecration took place, was of the same opinion as Archbishop Longley. Eventually, Macrorie was consecrated by Gray in Cape Town on 25 January 1869, almost exactly three months after Longley had died.

—

For most of the century and a half since his death, Archbishop Longley's reputation has been that of a mild-mannered man who achieved little in his time at the helm of the Church of England; more accurately, he had the disadvantage to be overshadowed by the more dominant characters of his successors as Queen Victoria's archbishops. However, he was, nevertheless, an effective man who knew his own mind, and his work with the first Lambeth Conference is of great importance in Anglican history. He was an efficient administrator, "proverbially" courteous and devout. When he became Archbishop of Canterbury, he had a wide understanding of the Church which he was called to lead and made a seminal contribution to the life and self-awareness of the whole Anglican Communion. It was the crowning achievement of his ministry and came near the end of his life when, in 1867, he called and governed the first Lambeth Conference of the bishops of the Anglican Communion. Randall Davidson, in 1896, when Bishop of Winchester, produced an important book on the early conferences: *The Lambeth Conferences of 1867, 1878, and 1888*. More recently, A. M. G. Stephenson chronicled the origins and development of the Lambeth Conferences in two important volumes: *The First Lambeth Conference* (1967) and *Anglicanism and the Lambeth Conferences* (1978). Stephenson rightly believed that the first Conference was "the greatest moment in Longley's life".[202] Any survey of Longley's life and work must seek to analyse his achievement with regard to the Conference, which was held on 24 September 1867 and the three following days. The archbishop's experience, and the general feeling of those meetings, concluded that any future gathering should be of greater duration, although Longley had no plans that there should be any second or subsequent Conferences. He could not know that the

Lambeth Conferences were to become a defining factor of the worldwide Anglican Communion and are very significant occasions: the second Conference, which will be assessed in the next chapter, was held over four weeks, and subsequent Conferences have been of a similar length of time. The brief duration of the Conference does not detract from Longley's wisdom in initiating what was, even at the time, such an important aspect of Anglicanism. As chair of the proceedings, Longley himself became a focus of the unity of the Communion, and that role has been sustained unquestionably until very recently by his successors as Archbishop of Canterbury.

Longley's decision to call the Conference was, primarily, the outcome of a growing awareness of the gradual expansion of the Anglican Church. This development started to become significant around the beginning of the reign of Queen Victoria, and a summary of the background is necessary for the comprehension of Longley's initiative. In 1840, there had been ten overseas Anglican bishoprics. By the time of the Conference in 1867, there were 151. When C. T. Longley became Archbishop of Canterbury, the Anglican Church was becoming inescapably aware of itself as a worldwide phenomenon. This was a process which had gained momentum throughout J. B. Sumner's archiepiscopate. It was noted above that the SPG had been founded in 1701 to provide the ministry of the Church for British subjects overseas, and to bring the gospel to non-Christian races. Similarly, the CMS had been founded in 1799 as the Society for Missions in Africa and the East. Under Archbishop Sumner, the CMS had enjoyed a favoured position through his friendship with its long-serving secretary, Henry Venn. But with the change of primate there was a shift of emphasis, because Longley was a moderate churchman, not an evangelical as was his predecessor. Regarding the appointment to colonial bishoprics,

> Venn was plainly aware of the new and less favourable conditions under which he was working since Archbishop Sumner's death. In Sumner he had had an archbishop who was a personal friend and counsellor, to whom he had easy access, and who was quick to appreciate the point of view he represented through theological and personal affinity.[203]

Venn wrote on 11 January 1864 to Bishop George Smith, a former CMS missionary in China and Bishop of Victoria (as the Bishopric of Hong Kong was known), complaining that the change of Archbishop of Canterbury from Sumner to Longley had altered, among other things, the way that colonial bishops were appointed. The process of selection was now in the hands of Longley and his closest advisors, whom Venn asserted were Bishops Tait of London and Wilberforce, who was still at Oxford. Venn's powerful influence regarding such appointments had come to an end.

At the commencement of Queen Victoria's reign, the two important Anglican societies were already well established and respected, and their work was readily acknowledged. Longley was not partisan in his approach to either of them, but as the British Empire grew, so did an awareness of the need for an ecclesiastical structure to develop the whole ministry of the Church, something more than even well-respected voluntary societies. In addition to the importance of foreign missions as a legitimate ministry among the indigenous peoples of the Empire, the growth of the Empire was significant for Anglicanism as members of the Church of England went to live across the world. Some of them wished to worship according to its familiar rites and to receive the ministrations of clergy as they had at home. At the same time, the Anglican Church was also growing in the United States and, as early as the reign of Charles I, Archbishop Laud had hoped to establish episcopal ministry in North America. He was unsuccessful, but in 1783 a number of clergy in Connecticut had elected one of their number to be their bishop. He was Samuel Seabury (1729–1796). They sent him to the Archbishop of Canterbury, John Moore, for consecration, but

> the perplexity of the archbishop of Canterbury was considerable. Seabury could not take the oath of allegiance to the House of Hanover, and the archbishop could not legally consecrate anyone who could not take that oath ... A way out of the difficulty was found by recourse to the persecuted Episcopal Church in Scotland.[204]

Seabury had received his consecration in Aberdeen on 14 November 1784, at the hands of Scottish bishops. The requirement to take the obligatory Oath of Allegiance to the British sovereign, which was (and is) required of bishops of the established Church, was eventually set aside by Parliament with regard to bishops for foreign states. The circumstances of Seabury's consecration, however, forged an early link between two unestablished Anglican Churches. Archbishop Longley recognized a subtle distinction between the Church in the United States and the colonial branches of Anglicanism in their relationships with the Church of England; "once a daughter, now a sister", he said graciously in his 1853 *Charge*.

Longley spoke with enthusiasm about the SPG in the same *Charge*, but he also commended in the *Charge* the work of the CMS. He was described by a modern author as a "good friend" of the society.[205] Further to the personal inclinations of Longley's predecessor, Archbishop Sumner, towards the evangelical CMS, he had sometimes seemed to have greater sympathy with nonconformists than Anglican high churchmen. Nevertheless, Sumner must be given credit for an important initiative: he wrote to the bishops of the Church in America and asked that the American Church would also commemorate the SPG anniversary. This approach was entirely new. It was appreciated by Hopkins, the American Presiding Bishop, who commented with approval on Sumner's reference to the "close communion" between the two churches in the reply to which reference has already been made.

It is also noteworthy that Longley, as Bishop of Ripon, had been hospitable when an American bishop visited his diocese. Bishop Doane of New Jersey attended the re-consecration by Longley of Hook's rebuilt parish church, St Mary's, Leeds, on 2 September 1843. Also present was the Archbishop of York, a Scottish bishop, and about 300 other clergy. Magnanimously, Longley waived his right as diocesan bishop to preach at the service, and the sermon was delivered by Doane, who thus became the first American bishop to have preached in England.[206] Shortly afterwards, Doane preached in Ripon Cathedral for Longley, another "first occasion". Doane went away with a warm regard for Bishop Longley. Longley's hospitable manner towards Doane was unusual in the middle of the nineteenth century and reveals that he had the courage of an innovator.

The anniversary celebration service for the SPG in Westminster Abbey, at which Archbishop Sumner had presided and which Longley attended, was a moving experience, he said. Afterwards, he devoted about a quarter of his 1853 *Charge* to the society and the celebration. He rejoiced that there were bishops from across the world; he mentioned America, Asia, Africa, as well as Scotland, and a number of English bishops. There were nineteen bishops at the service, according to Stephenson, although Longley thought the number was fifteen. The gathering was for Longley "a happy demonstration of the unity between the different members of the Reformed Catholic Church throughout the world . . . a living and lasting testimony of pure doctrine and primitive truth". He went on to remark that there were 125 bishops, 23,000 clergy, and many millions of worshippers "in the four quarters of the globe", all part of the Anglican Communion. It was around the time of the SPG celebrations that the phrase "Anglican Communion" began to be used with regard to the worldwide Church which had its roots in the Church of England.[207]

By the end of Archbishop Sumner's life, it was becoming apparent that a need was growing for a proper ecclesiastical structure to which the growing number of colonial bishoprics, their clergy and people could relate. Longley rose to the task to respond to the needs and concerns of the Church in the Empire, and the increasing pressure from the bishops in the colonies, in America and Scotland. Sumner had never taken up a suggestion by Hopkins for "Synodical action". It was left to Longley to carry this work forward, which he did after receiving more specific and pressing expressions of the wish which the American bishop Hopkins originally articulated. Specific expressions, however, came first from the Church in Canada. A provincial synod, held in Montreal in 1865, asked the Archbishop of Canterbury to convene a synod of the "home and colonial Church". The Canadians wanted such a meeting to counter the influence of Colenso and to be a demonstration of unity. The letter sought a meeting that would "comfort the souls of the faithful". The phraseology of the request would have excluded the Church in the USA and Scotland, but there does not seem to have been a deliberate intention to exclude. In the event the first Lambeth Conference did include the whole Anglican Communion and was a clear expression of Anglican self-identity as a suggestion that Swedish bishops should be invited was rejected by Longley after consulting with his English episcopal colleagues.[208]

The driving force behind the Canadian letter was J. T. Lewis, the first Bishop of Ontario, who had been appointed in 1861. A. M. G. Stephenson wondered whether Lewis was in touch with Gray of Cape Town, as their forms of expression were somewhat similar, but he offered no conclusive evidence; certainly, they shared an anxiety about heresy. The Colenso case and *Essays and Reviews* had both raised problems with regard to authority within the Church, which Colenso had brought intensely to the attention of the Church in the colonies which were self-governing. The Church in the USA was, of course, not compromised by the colonial difficulties of the Church of England. Longley remembered happily the SPG celebrations and was increasingly aware that the Church of which he became primate in 1862 was very widely spread across the Empire and beyond. He was conscious of the importance of the Church as a worldwide communion and more than willing to be collaborative. Characteristically, his encouraging response to the Canadians was tempered with caution. He recognized that any meeting should not seek to establish doctrinal boundaries. He stuck to that conviction, although his determination was unwelcome to those who thought as Bishop Lewis and, indeed, Bishop Gray in South Africa did.

In his reply to the Canadian Church, he readily said that he understood their desire for meeting, and personally shared their wish: such a meeting was "not by any means foreign to my own feelings". Yet he was entirely consistent when he pointed out that he could not take "any step in so grave a matter without consulting my episcopal brethren in both branches of the United Church of England and Ireland, as well as those of the different colonies and dependencies of the British Empire".[209] When Gray learned of Longley's cautious welcome to the concept of a conference, he was delighted. Privately, he was determined that when it took place, he would secure the condemnation of Colenso and his opinions. In the event, Longley proved able to handle Gray's attempt to usurp the conference to that end. Gray managed to get Colenso on the agenda, but he did not secure his goal of declaring Colenso a heretic. Longley was to exercise firm leadership, when he "declined to allow any distinct resolution of condemnation".[210]

Longley's skilful response to the Canadian suggestion to hold a conference at Lambeth was, at first, as far as he felt able to go despite his personal enthusiasm for the idea. He took the same line when, later in 1866, Bishop Lewis called on him at Lambeth. On that occasion Longley said that such a meeting was without precedent and Lewis replied, "That may be so, but let Your Grace make a precedent." The archbishop was not a vain man eager for his place in history, and Lewis's plea would have come to nothing had it not accorded with Longley's own conviction that such a precedent would be desirable. As was to be expected, Longley did not get anything approaching unanimity when he consulted his "episcopal brethren", but he got enough support to feel able to proceed and that was strengthened when the Lower Houses of Convocation endorsed the plan, after being assured by Longley that he would not be willing to allow the conference to define doctrine. The idea received publicity when Bishop Francis Fulford, the Metropolitan of Canada, preached at an ordination conducted by Wilberforce in Oxford and spoke of his hopes for a meeting, which he described as Pan Anglican, thus bringing a new term into the debate. This was on 23 December 1866, by which time Longley's plans were well advanced. Longley had drafted the invitation himself but had submitted it to the scrutiny of a committee convened to assist him in the work. He began to sign each individual invitation to the bishops in the early weeks of 1867; in all he sent 144.[211] It was inevitable, but nevertheless noteworthy, that Colenso was not invited to the Conference. The advisory group also worked on the programme for the Conference but responded only in small part to a request for suggestions for its content which accompanied the archbishop's invitation. Suggestions included the question of reunion; the problem of ritualism; the revision of the Authorized Version of the Bible; a few, some of the most vociferous, sided with Gray in wanting to discuss the Colenso case.

Throughout the planning, and with considerable success during the Conference, Longley insisted on his assertion that the meeting should not attempt to define doctrine. He was also determined that it should not become a single-issue gathering. He was also emphatic that the gathering would be a conference, not a synod. Here too he was battling against powerful opposition. Bishop Charles Wordsworth, of St Andrews in the Scottish Church, wanted it to be a synod which would control the

Communion, and campaigned for that. Longley argued, with unusually Erastian sleight of hand, that a synod could be called only at the behest of the sovereign, and the Queen had not asked to call one! The planned meeting would not have authority to "enact canons nor do anything contrary to the wishes of the Crown". Nor could the conference be a general council, because the ancient necessity of the involvement by all Christian communities could not be met.

The realities that Longley faced meant that from the very beginning the Conference would not pass smoothly. The secular press in England opposed the idea, in part out of pique that they were to be excluded from the sessions of the Conference. *The Times* eventually supported the archbishop's action, and afterwards regarded the Conference as a "seed sown". The partisan ecclesiastical press was divided. Evangelical publications, such as the *Record*, were opposed, and the evangelical CMS was not represented, even though the moderate high church Longley continued his support for the society. Opposition also came from clergy best described as broad church, such as Dean Stanley. The high church press and the Tractarians were supportive, as was the high church SPG.

Longley persevered with his plan, convinced that there was a need to be met. He was proved correct, and his determination, and the leadership which he offered, were vindicated by the subsequent history of the Anglican Communion. The programme was compiled in the spring and summer of 1867, and although it varied in the event, the original plans shaped the Conference. There was a celebration of the Eucharist at 11.00 a.m. on the opening day in the chapel at Lambeth Palace, which the archbishop celebrated and prefaced with some opening remarks. Longley hoped for the support of Archbishop Thomson of York and had wanted him to preach at the opening service. He was disappointed when Thomson declined to attend, offering no explanation, on receiving the programme. The preacher was Bishop Whitehouse of Illinois, who had accepted the privilege reluctantly. It was a dull and incoherent sermon, criticized afterwards by some of the bishops present as not equal to the occasion; perhaps Whitehouse knew his limitations. A nice touch was the use for the Communion of bread made from wheat sent from Bethlehem and wine from Jerusalem. The Conference proceeded at a leisurely pace; by the end of the first day, it was already clear that it would be too short in duration. Longley acted throughout as chair, and all agreed that the archbishop conducted it with grace and skill. He began with an opening "Declaration". This had been the subject of dispute even before the Conference as it touched on matters of authority and discipline within the Church as a whole, but Longley knew his remarks needed to avoid banality. He presented the "Declaration" adroitly, and he was soon seen to be a focus of unity; a role which, ideally, the Archbishop of Canterbury continues to hold within the Communion.

The most contentious issue was that dear to the heart of Bishop Gray and his supporters, whose determination to raise the issue of Colenso cast a shadow before the Conference even began. Longley enlisted the assistance of Samuel Wilberforce, who (in turn) enlisted the help of Bishop Hamilton of Salisbury in his efforts to persuade Gray not to press for the Colenso case to be raised. A hint of irritation is apparent in Longley's letter to Wilberforce regarding Gray's attitude, for the decision not to invite Colenso to attend had been deliberate.

> I really cannot think it reasonable to write as though nothing had yet been done, as regards the Conference, in repudiation of Dr. Colenso, and in support of the judgment against him. No words can more significantly express the mind of the Conference than his absolute exclusion from it.[212]

It was later alleged that Longley had promised the eminent Bishop of St David's, Connop Thirlwall, that the Colenso matter would not become an issue. Indeed, that aged and learned man had delayed his acceptance of the invitation "until the official agenda-paper or programme" was published.[213] It was said that he had only agreed to attend on that condition; however, Longley had never made such a concession, as Thirlwall confirmed at a later date. When Longley was forced to concede a debate on the final day, Thirlwall was unhappy. Stephenson noted an unpublished comment in Bishop Tait's diary regarding Thirlwall's anger, when he discovered that the issue was to be discussed, "I wish I could have had a photograph of the old man" as he spoke "with the utmost vehemence and solemnity". Longley apologized to Thirlwall that the subject had been raised.

As chair of the Conference, Longley opened his home at Addington, as well as at Lambeth Palace, to the visiting bishops. Several bishops stayed at Addington, and one wrote to his wife and described how the archbishop's carriage had met his train at Croydon railway station with "four splendid horses". He went on to describe how,

> at nine in the morning the bell rings and all the family go to the chapel in the house, some twenty or thirty servants included, where the chaplain, in full costume reads prayers, the Archbishop sitting on a kind of simple throne.

After spending the day "in London", they returned for dinner. "Everything is easy and unconstrained as possible."[214]

Also at Addington, "though Longley had been widowed since Durham days, his guests were well entertained by his daughters, Frances and Rosamund, whose sweet singing charmed even a stern musical critic", later identified as the son of Bishop Hopkins.[215] On at least one occasion Archbishop Longley entertained the American bishops to dinner, and it is likely that there were similar events for others; certainly Tait and his wife, over at Fulham Palace, also entertained bishops attending the Conference.

Reference has already been made to Longley's efforts to exclude the Colenso issue from arising at the Conference despite Gray's determination otherwise. Longley's stance was strengthened, if that was necessary, by the opinion of the American bishops that the case was a concern of the Church of England and the colonies and not of the whole Communion. The problem arose when Bishop Gray persevered in his efforts and persuaded G. A. Selwyn, Bishop of New Zealand, to introduce a resolution into the Conference programme, which had already been amended. Thirlwall tried to make his protest, but was forestalled by the American, Hopkins, who condemned Colenso at length and in forthright terms.

Longley did not give the Conference a direction, which led later to the mistaken accusation that his leadership was weak, but his non-intervention cleverly gave the Conference a "safety-valve", as Gray later described it. Longley repeated that the Conference was not in a position to condemn Colenso; he had not called it in order that it should do so. He was willing to concede that a committee could look into the matter. Selwyn eventually proposed forming a committee which should report to Archbishop Longley, and so the sting was drawn from the issue. Longley's apparent procrastination effectively moved the Conference in the direction which he desired. He had to endure the irritation expressed by Thirlwall, but their relationship recovered.

Later in the day, when a motion to form a committee to consider the election of colonial bishops was discussed, Gray endeavoured to raise the issue yet again. He tried to get the Conference to approve a date for the consecration of a new Bishop of Natal but did not succeed. An angry Bishop Tait thought Gray succeeded in giving the erroneous impression that the Conference had supported him, which was not so. In fact, Longley was able to refute the allegation. The Conference had done no such thing, and Longley had by then told Gray's preferred candidate, W. J. Butler, the Vicar of Wantage, that he should not accept the post and had obtained his agreement to stand down.

The Conference ended with a service in Lambeth Parish Church. Originally it had been hoped to hold it in Westminster Abbey, but Longley was rebuffed by the dean (A. P. Stanley). Stanley was to incur considerable criticism for his attitude, especially as his grounds for declining appear to be somewhat insubstantial. His first biographer, R. E. Prothero, quoted Stanley's reply to a letter Longley sent asking the abbey to host the service. In it, Stanley gave two reasons. First, that the absence of the Archbishop of York and most of the northern bishops meant that the Conference was unrepresentative of the Church of England as a whole; further, the absence of bishops from India and Australia and "other important colonial or missionary sees" meant that it was not representative of the whole of Anglicanism. Stanley's second objection was "the absence of any fixed information as to the objects to be discussed and promoted by the conference". Prothero gave a third reason, which did not appear in the correspondence which was published. It revealed a more substantial fear on the part of Stanley, one which necessarily had to remain undeclared by the dean.

> In the uncertainty that Stanley felt as to the purposes for which the Conference was summoned, he feared that it might be used for party objects, such as giving support to the Bishop of Capetown [Gray], repudiating the Judgement of the Privy Council, and confirming the alleged deposition of the Bishop of Natal.[216]

He did not want either Westminster Abbey's or his own reputation to be caught up in what he feared might become a heresy hunt against Colenso, and which might produce a narrowly defined orthodoxy. Even though Stanley had a high reputation as a liberal theologian himself, he did not share all Colenso's opinions. He tried to draw the sting of his decision by inviting the bishops to other services being held in the abbey; he also wrote later at length to Bishop Hopkins of Vermont, which elicited an excoriating reply.

Eight reports of the committee work of the Conference were produced and discussed at a meeting at Lambeth on 10 December by bishops who were still in England. Of the eight, only seven were published. The one which "referred to Bishop Colenso's deposition" was "received and printed", and the thanks of the session was "given to the committee for their labours", but Longley's wish that it be not circulated was accepted.[217] That meeting was unavoidably an anti-climax as it was confined to a single day and so few of the bishops, "less than a score", were present.

—

The anonymous writer of the *Church of England biographies* claimed, perhaps a little optimistically, that Longley's "hope for the Conference coming happily to an end was fulfilled, and it left naught but pleasant memories behind it". Fowler, in *Some Notable Archbishops of Canterbury*[218], correctly declared that the Conference "is the great event with which the thought of his primacy is associated". When the Conference ended, Longley was exhausted. His health had begun a gradual decline from around the middle of 1867, but he showed no signs of weakness in the face of the demands of the Conference. Afterwards, he went to Whitby, but it was not to be a cheerful holiday. He had been called there because his daughter, Caroline Georgina, was unwell. She died on 30 October

1867. He had already returned to Addington, arriving at three o'clock in the morning, when he heard of her death. At the funeral, the archbishop "had a calmness not of earth" about him. Despite his bereavement and his declining health, he continued with his duties as archbishop and took the ordination service in Canterbury in Advent 1867. He struggled on until Easter 1868, when he preached as was his custom. Eventually, he accepted the advice of his doctors and went on holiday to Salzburg, hoping that the "air" would benefit his bronchitis, and the change of climate help his rheumatism. At the front of his mind during his convalescence was the preparation of his planned second *Charge* to be delivered to the Diocese of Canterbury. But Longley was still a sick man when he returned from Austria; he suffered some sort of seizure at Brussels on his way home. He did manage to conduct the Michaelmas ordination, and arranged for his sermon to be published. That service was his last appearance at public worship. He was, however, still anxious about the *Charge*. He was too unwell to deliver it personally and arranged for it to be read as "intended for delivery", as Henry Lyall, the Dean of Canterbury, noted. The published document, Longley had written, "was to be considered rather as a draft of a Charge; but I felt very anxious to let my opinions be on record at this critical period."[219]

The *Charge* contained an expression of regret that he had been unable to devote his "whole attention" to the Diocese of Canterbury. However, he said that he had confirmed 17,585 persons since his last "Visitation Charge" and rejoiced that the annual number of communicants in the diocese had risen by a thousand. He was also pleased to report that there had been a significant increase in the provision of school places for children and urged the clergy not to refuse a place in a church school to any child whose parents were opposed to it being taught the Church catechism. Of particular regard to the Diocese of Canterbury, which was in large part a rural area and not industrialized, he told them that he hoped that the educational obligations imposed by the Factory Acts would be extended to "agricultural districts". A minor reference in the *Charge* was made to the abolition of compulsory Church rates, which had passed into law that year, "and have now ceased for ever".[220] He also discussed the matter of ritualism, the Ornaments Rubric and eucharistic doctrine, as was noticed above.

Longley concluded his *Charge* with a poignant reference to his own situation: "it will be an abiding satisfaction to me to have taken this last opportunity of bearing my testimony to that which I believe to be the mind of the Church of England."[221] This was a fragment of a sentence in which he dealt with the "Blessed Sacrament of the Lord's Supper", but it was clearly his acknowledgement that the end of his life was near and that the *Charge* was his farewell to the Church and diocese which he had led with unassuming determination.

It was Longley's mildness and persuasiveness that acted against the enduring of his reputation as an effective Archbishop of Canterbury, but he was able to show determination. After the Lambeth Conference, he was regarded by many as an insightful leader. More recent assessments have characterized him as weak, but that is unjust. E. Carpenter's opinion that he was an honest but undistinguished man also does him less than justice.[222] His successor as archbishop paid him a generous tribute at the second Lambeth Conference. Tait recalled the Archbishop of York saying in a sermon, "that many who were here at our last gathering had gone to their rest." Tait took up the thought in his opening speech of the Conference:

> I will not speak of any excepting him who held my place at that time. All of you of the small remnant, for it is after all but small, who were, eleven years ago, present here, will remember the kindly, gentle, Christian influence which proceeded from this Chair, and which, among many difficulties, regulated all we did.[223]

Followed as Longley was by the tough A. C. Tait, then the self-absorbed Benson, and after him by the rock-like Temple, it is not surprising that Longley's reputation suffered. The writer on Longley in the *Church of England biographies* shared the opinion that the archbishop was brought down, in part at least, by overwork in addition to his personal sorrows. However, the same author recorded an accurate judgement of Charles Thomas Longley:

> [In] all matters, he steered the vessel of the Church, on the whole, with the skill of a watchful pilot, contenting himself with

counselling peace and patience. Many a difficulty was soothed, and many a breach healed, by the interposition of his mild and persuasive authority.[224]

Severely afflicted by the bronchitis, Longley died at Addington Palace on 27 October 1868, just a few weeks before Disraeli's government fell. It was characteristic of Longley that his last intelligible words were those of the *Gloria in Excelsis*.

CHAPTER 4

Archibald Campbell Tait (1868–1882)

Disraeli, as the incumbent prime minister, called a general election which took place on 10 December 1868, but Gladstone won. However, in the meantime, Disraeli had moved swiftly to fill the vacant archbishopric. If Gladstone had been the one to decide, it is likely that Samuel Wilberforce would have been nominated as archbishop, for the two had a longstanding friendship. Wilberforce had to be content when Gladstone moved him from Oxford to Winchester in 1869. Longley's deathbed lingering deprived Samuel Wilberforce of his last chance to become Archbishop of Canterbury, as he was killed in a riding accident before the next vacancy.

Disraeli's initial choice was C. J. Ellicott of Gloucester and Bristol, who he believed would rally Conservative voters. This was Disraeli's last attempt to manipulate the appointment to the archbishopric for political gain. It revealed his fundamental lack of concern for the welfare of the Church of England, because everyone, apart from the prime minister, thought that Ellicott would not do for the post of primate. Queen Victoria had her own ideas. She wanted Archibald Campbell Tait, the Bishop of London, for whom she had a high regard. Letters to and from the Queen and Disraeli, bearing the names of their nominees, crossed in the post. The Queen's determination won the day. On 12 November 1868, Disraeli offered Tait the archbishopric in a suave letter which gave no indication of any disappointment he felt in having to make the offer. Tait accepted at once, to the delight of many. Tait wrote conventionally in reply to Disraeli, but with no hesitation:

> I have this morning received your letter of yesterday. I accept with
> a deep sense of responsibility the offer which you make in terms

181

so kind and considerate, and I pray that, by Divine blessing, I may be guided aright in these difficult days.[225]

Tait's wide experience, after twelve years as Bishop of London, had prepared him for the primacy, and he was fortunate that his health had significantly improved after bouts of serious illness endured during his London episcopate. He was at the height of his considerable abilities, and he became the most distinguished of Queen Victoria's Archbishops of Canterbury. Of them all, Tait was to be the first of whom a biography was published. It was the work of an old friend, William Benham, with Tait's son-in-law, R. T. Davidson, who was himself later to serve as Archbishop of Canterbury. The two-volume biography was published in 1891. Unfortunately, the biography of A. C. Tait offered relatively little insight into the man and his personality, although it chronicled his work excellently in close detail.

Tait was an unusual individual: there was a certain earnestness about him which made Edward Carpenter speculate that he would have made a judge, for he was able to face problems in a cool and dispassionate manner.[226] This objectivity sometimes made him seem insensitive to the feelings of others, but he rarely succumbed to irritation and was not without humour. Combined with his intellectual ability were considerable powers of self-discipline. His temperament, as well as his Scottish background, meant that he is to be understood as a low church Protestant, not an evangelical. Tait's personality was not narrow, and he was a man with breadth of character, which inclined him to a tentative theological and political liberalism.

As a student in Glasgow, in a student debating society, Tait supported parliamentary reform, but asserted it was inexpedient to abolish rotten boroughs. He also supported the maintenance of Church establishments. Along with these rather contradictory views when young, he also supported Roman Catholic emancipation, although the mature Tait distrusted and also disliked the Roman Catholic Church, which he regarded as superstitious and corrupt, although he could be individually friendly to its clergy.[227] This, however, was not much of a problem for an Archbishop of Canterbury in the second half of the nineteenth century, even after the Roman Catholic hierarchy was set up in England in 1850 and following the decrees of the Vatican Council of 1870. Less objectively, he feared that the Tractarian movement within the Church of England inclined its followers to "Romanism", and this earned him the dislike and distrust of a significant and growing minority within his own Church. The growth of Anglican ritualism was foreign to both his understanding and his sympathy. Curiously, he was tolerant of the sisterhoods which developed as a facet of Anglo-Catholicism, but he may have gained insights from Harriet Monsell, the first Superior of the community at Clewer, who was his wife's cousin.

Tait was described by A. P. Stanley, Dean of Westminster, as "our first Scottish archbishop". The family home was in Edinburgh on the outskirts of the Old Town. He was born in 1811, the youngest in a family of nine children. Shortly before his birth a brother suddenly developed paralysis, and another died while A. C. Tait was still young. Archibald Campbell Tait himself was born with his feet, in the words of his much older sister, "completely doubled inwards". The unfortunate child was forced to wear "tin boots" day and night, but the treatment was eventually effective in correcting the disability.

Another misfortune befell Tait while he was still in his infancy with the sudden death of his mother in 1814. The family was dispersed, and Tait was cared for, along with a disabled brother, by their old nurse, Betty Morton, who seems to have also been some sort of governess. She imposed a strict regime of lessons and her own Sabbatarianism. He remembered that she instilled in her charges an "unusually thorough acquaintance with the details of scripture history". Young Tait was fortunate to have older sisters who endeavoured to provide some of the love which the motherless boy otherwise lacked. His sister Charlotte (who became Lady Wake on her marriage) was twelve years older and survived him by six years. She provided background information for his biographers.

The Taits were members of the Church of Scotland, but he had early contact with Anglicanism through a neighbouring family to whom they were related, that of Sir Archibald Campbell after whom, presumably, A. C. Tait was named. The Campbells were members of the Scottish Episcopal Church, and the children of both families mixed freely; as boys A. C. Tait and Ramsay Campbell often went together to services at St John's Episcopal Church. But it was not until Tait was at Oxford in 1830 that he was confirmed in the Church of England by Bishop Bagot. The young Tait had a sense of the reality of God from an early age, although there seems to have been no indication that he would seek ordination, despite some of his family teasing him with the nickname of the "little bishop" from about the age of six. More significant evidence of his early spiritual awareness was found in a private note found in his desk after his death. In it he recorded a night when he was "some ten or twelve years old . . . awaking with a deep impression on my mind of the reality and nearness of the world unseen, such as, through God's mercy has never since left me".

In October 1827, A. C. Tait matriculated as a student of the University of Glasgow. He lived in lodgings and was cared for by Betty Morton, who kept a close eye on him and guarded him rather jealously. Tait's career at Glasgow was "uninterruptedly successful", and his biographers declared that, with only one possible exception, "he stood foremost among the students of the University."[228] That exception was James Halley, who was sometimes introduced in later years as "the man who beat Tait".

Despite the Calvinism of his family, when Tait went to Oxford in October 1829 he had no difficulty in subscribing to the Thirty-nine Articles of Religion of the Church of England, which was an obligatory part of the process of becoming a member of the university. Oxford was to remain Tait's base until his appointment as Headmaster of Rugby in 1842. Even so, he felt out of his depth in his early days there. However, his natural shrewdness enabled him to carry off successfully his interview with the Master of Balliol College, Doctor Jenkyns, and his intellect came to his rescue in his examination by the College Tutor. Indeed, his ability was recognized almost immediately when he won a college scholarship within a month of his arrival. By the time he graduated, Tait had suffered another personal tragedy with the death of his father in May 1832. His sister recognized that he had lost the one who was "both a motive for exertion and a reward for success". Soon afterwards, Betty Morton died on New Year's Day 1833, holding his hand. The young Tait was only twenty-two and already no stranger to bereavement.

—

In November 1833, he took his Oxford degree, a first class in Final Classical Schools, but he was never a theologian.[229] Tait was awarded his Oxford degree just a few months after John Keble's famous Assize Sermon and when Newman began the *Tracts for the Times*, against which Tait's Protestantism and regard for legality and order reacted. Gradually, his disquiet at the general thrust of the *Tracts* and their authors grew.

As the *Tracts for the Times* continued to be published, Tait was becoming a senior figure in his college; he was elected to a Balliol Fellowship on the same day as his friend W. G. Ward in November 1834 and appointed a tutor at Balliol College in 1836. He was ordained deacon by Bishop Bagot of Oxford on Trinity Sunday 1836, and priest, also by Bagot, on the equivalent Sunday in 1838. His biographers emphasized that he had desired ordination before it became a necessity for his career. Tait was a conscientious don and had confided to his diary his desire to work "for the good of my fellow men". From the time of his election to his fellowship Tait became interested in introducing reforms in the college.[230] Indeed, in 1839 he spent the summer visiting Prussia examining university administration and teaching in order to widen his understanding of the possibilities.

Before he could do much with regard to his plans for Oxford, he was troubled by the issues raised by the *Tracts for the Times*. No stranger to the Thirty-nine Articles, Tait was convinced of their meaning, which, he believed, was not at all what Newman was arguing in *Tract 90*, which was published in January 1841. It bore the title *Remarks on Certain Passages in the Thirty-nine Articles*. W. G. Ward, an excitable man, was one of several among his friends who was very enthusiastic about the *Tracts*. It was the somewhat unstable Ward who first showed him *Tract 90*. He burst into Tait's room shortly after it appeared and threw down the pamphlet, exclaiming, "Here is something worth reading." Tait did not agree. *Tract 90* became the ultimate trigger for his public opposition to the Oxford Movement. Like the earlier *Tracts,* number *90* was published anonymously. Few doubted that Newman was the author, as he had been of so many in the series, and it was not long before he acknowledged the fact. The argument of *Tract 90* maintained that there was nothing in the Articles, despite their protestant origin and sense, which contradicted catholic doctrine. But *Tract 90* was the product of Newman's unsettled mind which, despite his evidently sincere protestations of loyalty, was already thinking its way out of the Church of England.

It was Tait's sense of duty, combined with his deep-seated protestant loyalty and a concern about the legitimate limits of interpretation, that caused him to react so strongly against Newman's special pleading. According to Benham and Davidson, Tait was among the first to decide that a response was needed. He had feared from the beginning that the Oxford Movement would lead susceptible undergraduates towards Roman Catholicism and was sure that *Tract 90* would certainly work to that effect, distorting the Articles beyond consistency with the doctrine of the Church of England. In March 1841, with three colleagues, T. T. Churton of Brasenose College, H. B. Wilson of St John's, and John Griffiths of Wadham, he wrote an open letter "to the Editor of the *Tracts for the Times*". Tait's biographers asserted that the letter "did but lay a match to tinder which had been long preparing",[231] and it certainly caused a conflagration. Tait's biographers claimed that what the four tutors wrote was a "calm and reasonable document". They also claimed that Tait was the principal author of the letter because of its similarities to a document which he had earlier drafted but not sent. The tutors' letter began with the assertion that the *Tract's* "contents is of so painful a character that we feel it our duty" to write, which they did in the hope that "the situations we hold in our respective Colleges will secure us from the charge of presumption in thus coming forward to address you".[232] The letter went to the core of the tutors' distaste in its second paragraph:

> The Tract has, in our apprehension, a highly dangerous tendency, from its suggesting that certain very important errors of the Church of Rome are not condemned by the Articles of the Church of England—for instance, that those Articles do not contain any condemnation of the doctrines
>   1. Of Purgatory,
>   2. Of Pardons,
>   3. Of the Worshipping and Adoration of Images and Relics,
>   4. Of the Invocation of Saints,
>   5. Of the Mass,
> as they are taught authoritatively by the Church of Rome.

A little later they continued,

> The Tract would thus appear to us to have a tendency to mitigate beyond what charity requires, and to the prejudice of the pure truth of the Gospel, the very serious differences which separate the Church of Rome from our own, and to shake the confidence of the less learned members of the Church of England in the Scriptural character of her formularies and teaching.[233]

The letter ended with a swipe at the author's anonymity and marked the opening of a long process of controversy and condemnation which propelled Newman into despair and led to his secession to Rome in 1845. Although not a creative thinker, Tait had "a powerful intellect and high moral tone" and was the most theologically well-informed of those who ranked themselves against the Tractarians, according to his lifelong friend W. C. Lake, Dean of Durham (1869–1894). Lake also said Tait was "throughout life rather a man of action than of the deepest thought".[234] Having been prominent among those who acted to resist the influence of Newman, he had to endure in later years the reputation of being one of those who "hounded Newman out of Oxford".

Tait had combined his Oxford work with a small curacy in Baldon near Oxford, which gave him an element of ordinary parochial experience and insight, but the even temper of his Oxford life was not destined to continue. As early as 1838, the year of his ordination as a priest, he had declined a Glasgow professorship, preferring the relative intellectual freedom of Anglicanism and Oxford rather than having to subscribe to the Calvinistic Westminster Confession within a much smaller institution which the Glasgow appointment would have represented.

———

Thomas Arnold had been Headmaster of Rugby School since 1828, and he is rightly seen as a seminal figure among nineteenth-century public-school headmasters. His headship had revitalized the school and established a pattern which was to be widely followed. In June 1842, Arnold died, and two of Tait's friends, Stanley and Lake, encouraged him to let his name go forward as a candidate for the vacancy. Both of them had known Arnold well; indeed, Stanley was to be Arnold's biographer, and Lake believed that he had been "a man of real genius and extraordinary force of character". Both were convinced that Tait would be a worthy successor to Arnold, although there was to be little convergence of style. However, there were some similarities in the views of the two. Both men were convinced of the validity of the link between Church and State, and Arnold had also opposed the Tractarians. Tait's opposition to the Tractarians was thought to have strengthened his candidacy among the governors. The intellectually and theologically liberal Tait, with his Oxford experience and reputation, was a strong candidate, despite being only thirty years old and having had no personal experience of English public schools. He did not, however, share Arnold's charisma, but any successor to Arnold would have been the subject of unfavourable comparison. Tait did not avoid that, but he did enjoy the support of Arnold's family and friends. Despite his contentment in Oxford he was appointed to Rugby only a month after Arnold's death.

The following year, on 22 June 1843, he married Catharine Spooner in Elmdon Church, where the bride's father, the Archdeacon of Coventry and a cousin of Samuel Wilberforce, was the rector. Miss Spooner was born in 1819, had grown up within the evangelical ethos of the Church of England, and yet had become sympathetic to the Oxford Movement through the influence of a future brother-in-law, Edward Fortescue, who later converted to Roman Catholicism. When she learned that a candidate for the headship of Rugby was one of the "Four Tutors", she hoped that he would not be appointed. In future years she "often told" Tait of her early prejudice, but within less than a year the two were married.[235] Mrs Tait also told her husband that, when a young girl, she had been advised by an elderly man "not to marry a drunkard or a Sabbath-breaker".[236] An unexpected benefit of his marriage, which the mature Tait recognized in relation to his ministry, was that his wife brought him some appreciation of the impact of the Oxford Movement on its more ordinary followers. It never reconciled him to the growth of ritualism, but served to temper "whatever might otherwise have been harsh in his judgments of the good men from whom on principle he differed".[237] It is clear that the couple became a source of strength and comfort to each other, both in the extraordinary stresses of their family life and in the demanding work of the future Archbishop of Canterbury. William Lake described the Taits' marriage as "most happy". Tait's biographers offered a conventionally idyllic picture of their relationship, and Mrs Tait's own words in her description of the tragic events at Carlisle reinforce the degree of affection, trust, and respect in which the Taits held each other. His wife enjoyed their Rugby life, and their first three children were born during that time. She said that the Rugby days were the "happiest of her life", but Tait doubted that many years later.

It is doubtful that Tait regarded his period as a headmaster as a time of complete success, and others also had reservations. One who was uneasy was George Bradley, a former Rugby pupil, who was an undergraduate at Oxford at the time of Tait's appointment. Bradley was to become an assistant master at Rugby under Tait; much later, he was to be Stanley's successor as Dean of Westminster (1881-1902). Bradley's reservations were the result of mature consideration; he acknowledged Tait's "quite indefatigable earnestness and industry, and of his throwing himself heart and soul into the Rugby tradition" but continued with the observation that he was not "a born schoolmaster". In an attempt to ameliorate his criticism, Bradley did admit that Tait's "tenure of the Head-mastership was a very remarkable instance of goodness and good sense (and, I need hardly add, very good abilities), enabling a man to fill a post for which he was not specially designed".[238] Indeed, it is noteworthy that even before Tait was appointed, Stanley had come to doubt his suitability, despite his earlier enthusiasm for his friend's candidacy. Stanley's biographer recorded his "fit of despondency as to Tait's qualifications in the matter of scholarship [and how] in a fever of excitement he wrote hither and thither, endeavouring to procure Tait's withdrawal".[239]

Tait brought his capacity for disciplined work to his new role as headmaster. Arnold's legacy gave him relatively little room to manoeuvre, and his reserved nature contrasted with the exuberance of his predecessor. Some of the staff were among those who resented his appointment, but it is likely that they would not have welcomed any successor to Arnold. Tait was a conscientious headmaster and instituted a number of minor reforms. Significantly, the school roll had expanded under his leadership, although some of that may have been due to the enduring reputation of Arnold. His wife helped with history lessons and supervised the school accounts, and supported him in what he called "my anxious life at Rugby".[240] The couple made a genuine contribution to the ethos of the school, but A. C. Tait only won the affection of the boys after a severe bout of rheumatic fever in February 1848. So severe was this illness that his doctor told him he was about to die; he made his will, and his siblings were summoned to Rugby to make their farewells. It was, he said, "one of those quickly-gathering dark clouds which at intervals God has sent to overshadow my bright life".[241] Eventually, he recovered and was able to continue with his duties, but his biographers said he was left with "a weakened heart", and he believed that his health had been permanently damaged, although to judge by his subsequent career he recovered fully. However, by the following year, it had become clear that he needed a change of work and he was fortunate to be appointed Dean of Carlisle in 1849. When he left Rugby, he had won the affection and respect of his pupils. Bradley recorded that his carriage was "drawn down by the boys, and there was the greatest possible excitement".

In the middle of the nineteenth century, the appointment to a deanery was considered to be a place where life could be lived with ease:

> The position of a Dean was regarded as one of dignified retirement rather than of active usefulness . . . It is not too much to say that this view of decanal responsibilities was at the time almost universal.[242]

When Tait first visited Carlisle, he thought that the cathedral had a "somewhat forlorn air", and he was not the sort of man to subside into genteel inactivity. He was installed as dean on 5 January 1850, yet agreed to return to Rugby until the spring, but immediately began to tackle his new responsibilities. He noted in his diary that on the Feast of the Epiphany, the day following his installation, there were only nine or ten communicants at the cathedral. He set to work immediately:

Some days [in fact, about a month] were spent in a vigorous inspection, not only of the Cathedral precincts and all belonging to them, but of the condition generally of the various parishes in the town. He noted the want of order in one of the National Schools, the fact that there was no chaplain at the Infirmary and many other details of cathedral and parochial shortcomings; he issued new orders regulating the Minor Canons' interchange of duty and the attendance of the bedesmen at divine service.[243]

Having demonstrated that he was not the sort of man who would be content with a quiet life, A. C. Tait then returned to Rugby. He moved into Carlisle Deanery in May 1850, with his wife and family of two daughters and a son.[244] Mrs Tait was thankful that her husband had "escaped alive" from his Rugby work.

Tait began his work at Carlisle at a time when cathedral finances were in the process of reform and takeover by the Ecclesiastical Commission, which generated a good deal of anxiety and opposition among deans and chapters. It was a nettle which Tait readily grasped with respect to Carlisle, and in 1852 the cathedral estates were transferred *en bloc* to the Ecclesiastical Commission in exchange for a fixed annuity. Carlisle and York were the first to make the arrangement, but it was a process which was soon entered upon by the other cathedrals. Some members of the Carlisle Chapter were not happy with the plan, and the fixed annuities were ultimately to prove inadequate; but it did simplify the process of lease renewal on properties in the chapter portfolio, and ironed out some of the financial anomalies that had previously been sources of discord. Tait was irked by the complexity of the negotiations, but later claimed that they had given him useful experience for when, as Bishop of London, he became a member of the Estates Committee of the Ecclesiastical Commissioners. However, he was pleased that the commissioners agreed to the expense of £15,000 on the cathedral fabric as part of the negotiations. This enabled the roof to be "entirely rebuilt". The east wall and windows, which had been in very poor condition, were also rebuilt, and a new door was opened in the south transept.

The vigour which Tait had displayed during his short stay after his installation as dean continued to be a hallmark of his ministry in Carlisle.

His health improved in the Carlisle years, and his family grew, but he sometimes found the work difficult. An undated quotation from his diary, given by his biographers, records, "this day in Chapter I was betrayed into unseemly anger." And a few days later he recorded: "at times I feel greatly depressed here by the uncongenial spirits among whom I am thrown."[245] As was often his practice, however, he concluded the entry with a prayer which was a sort of self-exhortation. Tait was a busy man as dean, constitutionally unsuited to "dignified retirement". He recorded that he had his "hands full with the attempt to reorganize the Cathedral Grammar School, and with the restoration of the cathedral building".[246] He also gave lectures in what he called his "night school", and he preached in the cathedral and elsewhere. His diary records some of his activity; Sunday, 22 December 1850 seems to have been typical: "I have preached twice and visited the workhouse. I have been very busy for others. Lord, grant that the growth of holiness in my own soul may keep pace with my activity for others." Shortly afterwards he visited "a man apparently dying; one of our cathedral almsmen, very ignorant and self-satisfied".

In 1853, Tait feared that cholera would spread from Newcastle, where it was rife, and he tried to help with preventative measures in Carlisle. In fact, Tait can be seen as an early example of a newly emerging cadre of energetic deans who, with their chapters, were to reinvigorate and renew the life of many of the nation's cathedrals. Examples of the type included George Peacock (1839–1858) and Harvey Goodwin (1858–1869), successively at Ely, Howson in Chester, E. W. Benson as the first bishop and dean, combined, at Truro, and, twenty years later, Dean Richard Church at St Paul's. Tait, and all these others, enabled the growth of cathedral ministry in the decades that followed.

In the year Tait was appointed to Carlisle (1850) the prime minister, Lord John Russell, invited him to be one of seven members of a Royal Commission into the administration and teaching of Oxford University. Russell was aware that Tait had long been interested in reforming Oxford, and that he had written on the subject both before and after his move to Rugby. Despite being very newly settled in Carlisle, Tait accepted immediately. There was his natural delight at the prospect of working on something he had long regarded as important, and perhaps he saw it as an antidote to early stresses within cathedral relationships and as something which widened his horizon beyond the remoteness of Carlisle. In the chair was Samuel Hinds, the Bishop of Norwich, and the secretary was A. P. Stanley. The situation which the Royal Commission faced with regard to Oxford was a society dominated by Anglican clergy. Only one college did not have an ordained man at its head; most permanent fellowships were held by clergy, and most of the tutors were also ordained. Even the majority of undergraduates were planning to be clergy, as had been the case back in the days of Archbishop Howley. Unsurprisingly, there was little cooperation from the university, and not a lot of enthusiasm for reform. The commission met for the first time at 10 Downing Street in October 1850 and was still working when Russell's government fell in 1852. The members of the commission were surprised that their work was allowed to continue. This was, in part, due to some shrewd manoeuvring by the chair, who went to see the new prime minister, Lord Derby. In a letter to his wife Tait described the bishop's strategy as that of "a canny old boy".

Tait sustained his early enthusiasm about the Royal Commission and saw his role as a member giving him "a new means of great usefulness [which] was opened up to me, and a very solemn responsibility", but he was not sanguine as to the reception that the commission would receive from the entrenched interests within the university. Indeed, the heads of houses at Oxford were almost unanimously opposed, although Jeune, the Master of Pembroke College, was a member of the commission; another member, H. G. Liddell, was later to become Dean of Christ Church. Hostilities broke out with protests and a pamphlet and newspaper war. There was even an attempt to deny the legality of the Royal Commission, which was questioned in Parliament by W. E. Gladstone, who represented the University of Oxford in the Commons. He intervened forcefully but to little effect; he spoke for an hour and a half in stubborn opposition, although the eventual Report of the Commission caused him to change his mind.

The report was issued in April 1852, and his biographers recorded that "Dean Tait was recognized in the letters of his brother Commissioners as largely responsible for its final shape, and especially for the form of its practical recommendations". A convenient summary of the outcome of the commission is that given by P. T. Marsh:

Half of Oxford's fellowships were opened to free competition, colleges were empowered to fill one-quarter of their fellowships with laymen, and the path was cleared for introducing and developing the study of natural science and modern humanistic disciplines such as English literature and contemporary languages. A way round the religious tests was also provided. Private halls which need not demand any oath or declaration upon entrance could be founded; but the M.A., the prerequisite for office in the university, was still restricted to Churchmen.[247]

Early in 1856, the Bishop of Carlisle, Hugh Percy, died suddenly, and Dean Tait's name was soon mentioned among those speculating about his successor. The deanery at Carlisle was described as a very bright and happy home, and by the time of Bishop Percy's death, the Tait family had grown to seven children. Their seventh child, Lucy, was born on 11 February 1856. Despite his domestic happiness, Tait found some of his work frustrating, but he told himself firmly in his diary that even

> if there be in my lot here some discouragements, let me think of the far greater comforts and blessings. Truly, [he continued in a prayerful musing] Thou hast caused my cup to overflow,—a loving wife and dear children, competent health, means sufficient far beyond most of my contemporaries, a good house, ample leisure, and great means of usefulness, blessed with the hearty good-will of the poor around me.[248]

Tait himself knew of the speculation; some of his friends "had made exertions to promote me to a greater sphere in this neighbourhood". He also knew that Lord John Russell had wanted to promote him to a bishopric. In the event, Henry Montagu Villiers was appointed to be Bishop of Carlisle. He was translated to Durham in 1860, by which time Tait was well established as Bishop of London: Villiers was eventually to be one of Tait's consecrating bishops. Tait learned to live with his "discouragements", and although he was cushioned by his material well-being, his biographers doubted whether he and his wife ever really enjoyed their time in Carlisle. They also speculated that he might not have accepted the deanery if he had known how complete would be his recovery from the illness that marked his last months at Rugby.

The end of their time in Carlisle was to be overshadowed by bereavement, and the Taits cannot have looked back on those days with anything but grief. Shortly after the birth of Lucy, their happiness was destroyed in a few weeks. The "storm", as the biographers called it, "broke upon Carlisle Deanery in that sad spring."[249] Five of their six daughters died of scarlet fever between 6 March and 8 April 1856. Mrs Tait chronicled the events in close and moving detail. Her account was published after her death in 1878, as she had requested. It records the children's fortitude and the strength of her and her husband's faith and the devout characters of the parents and each of the children. *Catharine and Craufurd Tait* appeared in 1884, with a preliminary section by the archbishop; it was edited by the indefatigable and loyal William Benham.

At the beginning of May, Tait felt able to resume his journal. He had "not had the heart" to do so before. "When last I wrote I had six daughters on earth; now I have one, an infant. O God, thou hast dealt very mysteriously with us ... They are gone from us, all but my beloved Craufurd [his only son] and the babe." The biography by Davidson and Benham was written very much from an ecclesiastical point of view, and it is in a footnote that Tait's acute personal suffering is poignantly acknowledged: "page after page of [Tait's] diary is filled with tender references to the children 'safe with the Lord, now their life's brief day is past',"[250] and there were many diary references to a reunion in the life to come. When he left the deanery for the last time, he recorded how he visited what had been his daughters' school room and wept.

—

The sense of devastation of Tait and his wife was such that they abandoned the deanery and spent the summer in a borrowed house on Ullswater with seven-year-old Craufurd and their newly born daughter. Tait continued with his work as dean whilst based at Ullswater, but the couple knew that the time for a return to their own house was drawing near. It was before their return, however, that Tait received an unexpected offer of the Bishopric of London from the prime minister, Lord Palmerston.

Four sees were vacant in 1856. London was the most significant, vacated at last by Blomfield; the others were Carlisle (which Tait may not have wanted after his family tragedy), Norwich, and Ripon. London certainly came as a surprise; it was "a post which I should never have dreamed of for myself". Indeed, only once in two hundred years had a man not already in episcopal orders been appointed Bishop of London, and even his biographers (describing Tait's preaching) had to admit that he was "thoughtful and earnest rather than brilliant".[251] He immediately determined to accept, and told himself that he was not "rash" to do so, as he had "not sought it". The offer was conditional upon his willingness to accept the future division of the Diocese of London into a smaller unit, an eventuality which did not occur in his time, and that the estates attached to the see would be placed under the management of the Ecclesiastical Commissioners, although his predecessor continued to enjoy the Fulham estate until his death the following year.

R. T. Davidson and W. Benham deduced three factors which had influenced Palmerston's choice of Tait in addition to his likely usefulness in the Lords to a liberal administration. First, he had a reputation for competence in handling difficult issues. This had been earned through his service on the Royal Commission on university reform, his Rugby headmastership, and his previous work as a don. Next, his theological position meant that Lord Shaftesbury, ever Palmerston's advisor on ecclesiastical matters, regarded Tait as the best of what he thought of as the Arnoldian school of thought, although he also thought Tait to be more suited to Norwich than London. Finally, it was alleged that the recent family tragedy had brought the Taits to the sympathetic attention and support of Queen Victoria.[252] Indeed, Tait was to establish a close relationship with the monarch which lasted for the remainder of his life; in 1882, the Queen asked for a lock of his hair, when she learned of his death.

When Tait was appointed as the 102nd Bishop of London, he was relatively unknown in the capital. His predecessor was Charles James Blomfield, who, it will be recalled, had been moved from Chester in 1828, when Howley moved to Canterbury. Blomfield was seventy years old and failing. His retirement could only be facilitated through a special Act of Parliament, which was brought in by Palmerston for Blomfield and for

Bishop Maltby of Durham, who was also frail.[253] Only when Blomfield died were the Taits able to move into Fulham Palace. Blomfield had been an energetic Bishop of London, who had worked well with Archbishop Howley. Sydney Smith said that Blomfield had "an ungovernable passion for business". He had set out to have fifty new churches built in London to accommodate the increasing population; this plan had been so successful that he eventually consecrated nearly 200, one of which, St Stephen's, Hammersmith, he funded personally. He had been much involved in the wider life of the Church of England, and a leader of the reforms which established the Ecclesiastical Commission. He had supported the revival of Convocation in 1851 and had also been involved in the Hampden controversy in 1847, and the Gorham case in 1850. Unfortunately, his last years had been overshadowed by ill health, following a fall at Osborne House, which left him with facial paralysis and slurred speech for several months. Disability had brought depression, although some thought that it was latently present after he failed to succeed Howley at Canterbury. Blomfield remained ill, and a fresh attack of paralysis in October 1855 had made retirement a necessity. He recognized that someone younger and fitter was needed, but was saddened at having to go, despite the retention of Fulham Palace estate.[254] It was very clear to everyone that new vigour was needed for the leadership of the Diocese of London. The untested Tait was the man to provide that leadership, and he was consecrated bishop on 23 November 1856 in the Chapel Royal, Whitehall, having stayed at Fulham with his wife for five days in October as Blomfield's guest. He was enthroned in St Paul's Cathedral on 4 December. Immediately he began to adapt and carry forward Blomfield's policy, although he was not at first convinced of the pressing need for more church buildings, which had dominated Blomfield's approach, having learned that some of the new churches were underused. He soon saw that there was, in fact, a need for more new churches, and less than a month after his enthronement he promoted a plan to raise funds for twelve, declaring "we must be very careful to use every means to bring in the poor". A few years later, in a *Charge* of 1862, he proposed to raise money for expansionist work with his Bishop of London's Fund, an initiative which became important.

More immediately, on the Sunday after his consecration in a sermon at St James's, Piccadilly, Tait emphasized the need for more evangelistic work. At an ordination service shortly afterwards, he urged the clergy "to go forth into the highways and hedges, and to proclaim in the simplest words at their command the Gospel of a living Saviour". Tait obeyed his own injunctions. From almost the beginning of his time in London, he preached in the open air, "in the streets" across much of London, often scandalizing more traditionally-minded churchgoers who were shocked at his "undignified and almost Methodist proceedings". Tait's biographers give a rare insight into the humanity of his approach, and the following gives an early description of Tait's busy life as Bishop of London.

> His diary shows him going off from the House of Lords to speak to a shipload of emigrants in the Docks, from Convocation discussions on Church Discipline to address the Ragged School children in Golden Lane, or the omnibus drivers in their great yard at Islington. He preached to the costermongers in Covent Garden; to railway porters from the platform of a locomotive; to a colony of gypsies upon the Common at Shepherd's Bush, and this without in any way relaxing the round of confirmations and sermons and committees which must always occupy a bishop's time in addition to his huge business correspondence.[255]

Although not narrowly an evangelical, Tait was more sympathetic to many of their endeavours than he was to the approach of the high church faction and, to the dismay of many of the latter, attended at least one of the Sunday evening services held in Exeter Hall in the Strand, under an initiative of Lord Shaftesbury, which brought "some of the foremost evangelical clergymen in England"[256] to give addresses. Tait's attendance brought a formal protest, which became public, from the incumbent of the parish in which the hall stood. This led Tait to advise the discontinuance of the services for a time, but he turned it to the advantage of his policy and secured the establishment of Sunday evening services "for the people" at Westminster Abbey, and at a rather more reluctant St Paul's Cathedral, where the dean (H. H. Milman) and chapter unfortunately did not make the arrangement permanent. The first such service was held in the abbey on 3 January 1858 and attracted an overflowing congregation. When Tait himself preached at St Paul's on Advent Sunday 1858, the numbers were such that thousands were turned away from the packed cathedral, a phenomenon repeated a few years later when Canon H. P. Liddon's sermons drew great congregations to St Paul's.

The bishop was cautious in 1859, when "A Conference of Christians of all Evangelical Denominations" claimed that he supported their plans for services to be held in London theatres, and the organizers further asserted that he "cared not whether Churchmen or Nonconformists conducted the services". In the House of Lords, Tait declared that he had not promised the support claimed by their organizers. His regard for legality meant that he could not endorse them, as they were irregular actions of private individuals. Nevertheless, he said he would not use his authority to try and stop them, but intended to watch their development closely, and hoped that they might raise the moral tone of theatres generally. To the continued dismay of many staunch church members, Tait was sympathetic to the position of nonconformity. He was willing to engage to a limited extent with its leaders, although his "concern was to cultivate common areas of Christian action rather than to air nice points of theological difference".[257] This was true not only of his time in London, but also when he was archbishop.

From the commencement of his episcopal ministry, he was a committed member of the House of Lords, where he was eventually to establish a well-earned reputation as a man who had a considerable contribution to make as a statesman. He devoted a great deal of his time to his attendance in the Lords, thereby demonstrating to members and staff that he took his role seriously and was convinced of the importance of the House. This meant that, when he became Archbishop of Canterbury, he was listened to with respect; indeed, it was claimed that, when they knew he was likely to speak, some peers made an effort to be present. One of the first debates in which he took part was on the 1857 Divorce Bill. He voted with the government, thereby demonstrating his cautiously liberal approach, and spoke in favour of a clause which gave clergy the liberty to refuse to "celebrate the remarriage of the guilty party".[258] His contribution on that occasion was brief, but as his ministry developed he spoke more often and at greater length; what he said was always relevant to the issue under debate and members came to appreciate his practical Christian wisdom. It is clear from the biography by Davidson and Benham that he willingly devoted a good proportion of his time to his work in the Lords, and he seemed happier in his dealings with the House of Lords than with Convocation. This may have been because of his preference for the company of lay people, a contrast to a sometimes apparent unease in his dealings with the clergy, particularly high churchmen. The new bishop rapidly grew into his responsibilities, and his health continued to improve under the stimulus of all his activities. He did not hesitate to put it at risk when cholera broke out in 1866, although in that year he did have an unrelated bout of illness. Tait and his wife visited the affected areas of London together; Mrs Tait took part in nursing some of the afflicted, along with Mrs Gladstone and a Miss Marsh, dubbed "the three Catharines" in one newspaper, as Tait himself noted with a hint of pride. It was at this time that he first met A. H. Mackonochie, a ritualistic priest in east London, whom he grew to respect for his pastoral dedication, even though he rejected his liturgical practices.

Tait was fully engaged in the work of his diocese, although there were many issues concerning the wider life of the Church of England that also claimed his attention, as is inevitable for any Bishop of London. An example of his diocesan involvement at the end of his first year in London was to be seen in a special series of Sunday evening services, which he planned to hold in Bethnal Green during part of Advent 1857 to enable him and the parishioners to "meet each other", as a placard proclaimed, so that the latter could "hear the message which I and the other clergy . . . are commissioned to deliver to you on Christ's behalf".[259] Another and more far-reaching insight can be gained from a decision which he made in 1862, with the inauguration of the Bishop of London's Fund. He was then about halfway through his time as Bishop of London and convinced of the need, as his biographers put it, "to strengthen and enlarge his diocesan work in all its forms". He hoped the fund would run for ten years and raise half a million pounds. In the end, it was so successful that it raised twice the original target sum. The objects of the fund ranged from church building, funding "missionary clergy", the endowment of curacies, paying for parish work, and funding "Scripture readers" to financing women's work, clergy housing, schools, mission rooms, and also the endowment of work in specific districts. Tait's biographers claimed that setting up the fund was "the greatest and most memorable act" of his

London episcopate. The fund was a very significant achievement and its aims and objects reveal a bishop who was in touch with the needs of his diocese and had a clear idea as to how to sustain a considered approach to its problems and opportunities.

—

When *Essays and Reviews* was published in 1860, the archiepiscopate of John Bird Sumner was drawing to its close, and although Longley as his successor had dealt with the debacle that followed, Tait was not free from involvement. This was in large part because he was personally known to several of the essayists. Frederick Temple (destined to be Queen Victoria's last Archbishop of Canterbury) was a personal friend and had been Tait's pupil at Balliol and a successor of Tait as Headmaster of Rugby. Benjamin Jowett was another former pupil of Tait's. In 1860, he was Regius Professor of Greek at Oxford and finished up as a renowned Master of Balliol College. Like Temple's, his essay was uncontroversial, although theologically weightier. Mark Pattison, the Rector of Lincoln College, Oxford, wrote on "Tendencies of Religious Thought, 1688–1750", and H. B. Wilson had been one of Tait's co-signatories to the protest against *Tract 90* and was one of the two prosecuted. In a letter to A. P. Stanley, Tait exonerated the essays by Pattison, Jowett, and Temple from culpability. He agonized for some time as to whether he should sign the condemnatory document, which the bishops produced at their meeting at his house in Fulham. Eventually he did so, and then found himself personally in a difficult situation largely of his own making. Unsurprisingly, he incurred the wrath of Frederick Temple. The two had met shortly before the bishops' meeting, and Tait had not told Temple of his reservations about the volume. In Tait's defence, however, it is likely that he did not make up his mind until the last minute. Also in his own mind he made a distinction between the essays which had caused offence and those which had not. Temple regarded Tait's action as a betrayal. Even Davidson and Benham could not disguise how distressed Temple felt, especially after Tait referred to his "somewhat arrogant over-estimate of the infallibility of your own opinion". Their correspondence was sad rather than angry, but Temple concluded a lengthy exchange of letters by writing:

> The greatest kindness you can do me now is to forget till all this is over that any friendship ever existed between us. That at any rate will save me from such mischief as your speech in Convocation yesterday is certain to do me.[260]

Their relationship was never quite restored, and it was unfortunate that Tait was ill and unable to officiate when Temple was consecrated as Bishop of Exeter in 1869.

The Lower House of Convocation was particularly condemnatory of the volume. Archdeacon Denison had been characteristically outspoken with a reference to the dangers of hell resulting from the reading of *Essays and Reviews* by the young. Tait's speech in Convocation as an attempt at damage limitation. He made a specific reference to his friendship with two of the essayists, and he mentioned Temple by name. Tait objected to extracts from the book being used to condemn the whole, but he did feel that the volume was "likely to do great and grievous harm". He hoped that the offending essayists would make some sort of declaration about their orthodoxy of faith. His speech achieved little. In 1864, however, he was one of only two bishops who voted against the condemnation of the book in the Upper House of Convocation. But overall, Tait did not come out of the controversy well; aggrieved friends, such as Temple and Stanley, were not mollified and opponents, particularly evangelicals, thought that he had failed to defend scripture from destructive critics. Eventually, the prosecution of Wilson and Williams was reversed by the Judicial Committee of the Privy Council, of which Tait was an assessor.

One problem which endured throughout the whole period of Tait's episcopal ministry, and beyond, was ritualism. His concern with it falls conveniently into the two parts of his episcopacy. The London episcopate was more generally involved with the cases of individual parishes and clergy, whereas his involvement when Archbishop of Canterbury was more to do with policy and his overall approach, although this distinction is not absolute.

The impulse of the Tractarians had initially been doctrinal. Pusey's opinion was "that the reassertion of Catholic truth must not be hindered by unnecessary provocation in ceremony". But Pusey did not prevail; it was ironic that enhanced ritual came often to be known as "Puseyism". Tait's opposition, perhaps as a result of his Scottish Presbyterian background, was based on a rejection of Tractarian doctrine and an abhorrence of elaborate ceremony. In addition, he was guided by his high regard for the law, but occasionally that inhibited his effectiveness. He seems to have believed that if he delineated the legally permissible limits of ceremonial, the clergy under his rule would see where their duty and obedience lay, and the problem would be solved. Although this was a little more subtle than the Erastianism of Sumner, he was unsympathetic to those who rejected his advice or orders, after he had spelled out to them what he believed to be the definitive position under the law of the land. He acknowledged this later, when he said that his wife's liking for some elements of Tractarianism occasionally served to check his rigour.

Tait was temperamentally and intellectually out of sympathy with ritualism and believed that toleration of it would propel more converts towards Rome. He believed that the doctrinal and ceremonial elements of the Anglican catholic revival were dangerous. He never forgot the row over *Tract 90*, the conversion of Newman in 1845 and later some of his disciples—such as Tait's former friend and colleague W. G. Ward. When conversions happened, he felt that his worst fears were justified. His strong dislike of Roman Catholicism was by no means uncommon, and his antipathy to it gained greater prominence in his mind after the so-called Papal Aggression of 1850.

Bishop Tait was acutely aware of his duty as a bishop to maintain law and order in his diocese and to deal justly with the intransigent, including those among the clergy who followed the Tractarians, and who, whilst remaining in the Church of England, came to believe that Roman Catholic liturgical practices and dress expressed the ancient doctrines which they believed. This led to a tendency to imitate contemporary Roman Catholic practices through liturgical innovation within the Church of England, and to the adoption of post-Reformation Roman

Catholic practices and dogma. It is clear that such Anglo-Catholicism strained Tait's composure. Personally, he was content with the liturgical practices that were customary before the emergence of ritualism. He knew that the ancient creeds recited in Church of England services expressed catholic doctrine and believed that doctrine to be expressed in worship offered in accordance with the Book of Common Prayer. He saw no need to add to what the Prayer Book provided by additional ritualistic acts, nor to adopt vesture beyond the stipulations of canon law. A secular element in this phenomenon which is sometimes overlooked was the development of romanticism in the arts.

The growth of ritualism provoked protests and stimulated legal action by those who thought it could be overcome by Erastian measures. Opposition led to intransigence among some of the Anglo-Catholics. Tait was properly concerned that the Church was called to reach outwards in mission to the unchurched masses in London and elsewhere and recognized that absorption with quarrels over liturgical detail wasted both energy and resources. Unfortunately, he had little room for manoeuvre in his London episcopate, partly as a result of the attempts of his predecessor to deal with the issue. Blomfield had tried to tackle Tractarianism at an early stage, and back in 1842 he had condemned *Tract 90* and those who enthused about it. Shrewdly, he recognized that he could not prevent ritualists from tampering with the Prayer Book to suit their opinions unless he forbade low church people from doing the same. Blomfield had gone into some detail as to what he regarded as permissible with the intention of achieving uniformity, but created a situation, which Tait inherited, where his episcopal authority was undermined in his own diocese. Back in 1850, the situation in the Church as a whole had been exacerbated by the Gorham judgement, the outcome of which many regarded as a triumph of protestant doctrine. This, in turn, had the effect of creating some sympathy for high church people and encouraged some of them to assert their doctrinal convictions through "an advance in outward ritual".[261] It had added an unsought element to the problems which Blomfield had tried unsuccessfully to solve, and thus to the confused situation when Tait took over in London in 1856.

Between the announcement of Tait's appointment and his consecration as a bishop, he received complaints about the situation in the parish of St

George's in the East, Stepney, so the problem was immediately brought to his attention. The parish was described by Tait's biographers as "in one of the roughest neighbourhoods in London". It had a population of more than 30,000, but a church attendance of only about sixty. The Rector of St George's was a difficult individual named Bryan King. He had been appointed in 1842, the year of Blomfield's unfortunate *Charge*, and in the years before Tait's arrival King had alienated many of his parishioners. He was described by Tait's biographers as "earnest but ineffectual". A flashpoint came in 1856, when King announced that he intended to adopt the use of eucharistic vestments. Although there are a number of recorded instances of the use of vestments around that time, they were few and far between. King's decision, therefore, was innovative and produced a strong reaction which was not helped by his abrasive manner. Tait interviewed him on 2 December 1858. He recorded what passed between them in a letter to King the next day. He referred to King's "green vestments, stoles or whatever they may have been", and plunged straight on to emphasize:

> I very deeply regret that you should think it right to assume the unusual garments you described to me. I am convinced there is no sufficient warrant for it, and if you continue this, it is against my express order. Surely, if in any matters a bishop is entitled to require the canonical obedience of his clergy it is in such a case as this.[262]

King, he said, could have no "legal obligation" to depart from the "usage of our Church, as explained and enforced by her living authorities". The letter to King was a lengthy document and included other issues apart from "the garments", which he described as "foolish vestments". Additional factors that pressed upon Tait's mind and strengthened his personal conviction of the folly of King's behaviour was that two of his curates had "lately joined the Church of Rome", and also the emptiness of King's "great church" set in the midst of 30,000 parishioners. The short passages quoted give an insight into Tait's mind as that of someone to whom the legal position was self-evidently paramount. King's argument that the rubrics governing the taking of services permitted, or even required, a more elaborate ceremonial and that, without it, the Church of

England was acting unlawfully, was incomprehensible to Tait. He wanted his clergy to adhere to what he regarded as the customary interpretation of the Ornaments Rubric. He concluded his letter with a promise that, if King would alter his "course", Tait would be eager to support him in his ministry, but it is likely that he doubted whether King would either obey him or ever achieve much in the parish.

There the matter rested, although the bishop continued to receive complaints. Another crisis came soon afterwards. The parish vestry, by an old Act of Parliament, had the right to elect a "lecturer" with the right to give addresses. Despite King, they chose a man named Hugh Allen, renowned for his opposition to "popery". Under the law, Bishop Tait was obliged to licence him and admit him to office, which he did on 17 May 1859. Allen acted in a high-handed and provocative manner; he denounced the vicar, his doctrinal beliefs, and liturgical activities. Allen's supporters were vociferous, and King responded; unseemly behaviour erupted in St George's, and rioting ensued. Police were called, but the disturbances continued: "Sunday after Sunday... disgraceful scenes. The riot, disorder and buffoonery grew worse instead of better, and the civil authorities believed themselves unable to interfere."

The churchwardens wrote to Tait in August 1859; he replied at length and tried to calm things down. Sadly, he found himself describing the limits of episcopal authority:

> Within a certain range defined by law, [the bishop] has the power to give orders and enforce obedience to them by penalty of law. Over a much wider range, he has authority from the good feeling of all well-disposed members of the Church, who voluntarily accept his paternal advice and guidance.

In other words, he was helpless in the face of the intransigence of both Allen and King. The situation at St George's was even raised in Parliament, and Tait spoke about it in the House of Lords several times. Even with policemen in the church, disorder continued.[263] The situation dragged on until Thomas Hughes and Tait's friend A. P. Stanley persuaded King to have a year's leave of absence. He went to Bruges, and the parish was put in the care of Septimus Hansard, who soon resigned. Eventually,

King was appointed to a rural parish in the Diocese of Salisbury, and new arrangements came into force at St George's in the East. Two of King's former colleagues, A. H. Mackonochie and C. F. Lowder, ritualists both, but loyal to the Church of England, persevered with greater emollience in their London parishes, and eventually they were held in high esteem among their people.

Another ritualistic matter which Tait inherited concerned the parish church of St Barnabas, Pimlico, which had been consecrated by Bishop Blomfield in June 1850. It had been erected as a result of the successful work of the incumbent of St Paul's, Knightsbridge, W. J. E. Bennett, himself an early ritualist. His successor was the Honourable and Reverend Robert Liddell, who had continued and enhanced Bennett's ritualism in both churches. By the time of Tait's arrival, the case, which was not specifically about the ceremonial in the church but rather furniture and furnishings, had attracted legal action, and was the subject of an appeal by Liddell to the Privy Council after losing in the Court of Arches. By virtue of his new appointment as Bishop of London, Tait was one of the assessors for the Privy Council, together with Archbishop Sumner, and judgement was delivered on 21 March 1857. The contentious objects included a stone altar with a cross on it and both objects were deemed to be illegal, along with "embroidered altar linen ... various coloured frontals and hangings for the Holy Table [and] a credence table". Also subject to the judgement were "architectural ornaments" and items that might have attracted "superstitious reverence". Liddell was required to replace the stone altar with a wooden table and to remove the cross, which he later tried unsuccessfully to persuade Tait to agree could be erected in the reredos. The linen and hangings also had to go, but Liddell was not as rigid as Bryan King, and a reasonable relationship was established between him and Tait, whose biographers record that "so far as Mr Liddell was concerned the judgement was not disobeyed". Liddell and Tait seem personally to have had a regard for each other's position. In addition to the Privy Council judgement, Liddell had also accepted that he could not have lighted candles on the altar at celebrations of the Eucharist unless they were needed for illumination. But another priest in the Diocese of London took issue over the point. The Reverend Edward Stuart was Vicar of St Mary Magdalene, Munster Square, and was one of the founders of the Church of England Protection Society in 1859, which was renamed the English Church Union in 1860. The object of the society was to promote and defend catholic principles in the Church. Stuart was delated to Tait for using lighted candles as a matter of course. He declined to accept Tait's directions and argued that the bishop was incorrect in his interpretation of the rubric. Tait was not willing to be lectured on the legal position and made his view very clear in a letter which, as in the King case, summarized a meeting which had taken place at Tait's house the previous day. He tried to be tactful and readily acknowledged Stuart's personal devotion and his conscientious ministry, but the law was clear in his view, and Stuart was breaking it by following what Tait described as his "private judgement". Stuart complained that the bishop "(unintentionally, of course) had transgressed the limits of that authority which the Church of England has committed to her bishops".[264] Stuart based his opinion on what the ritualists claimed was an accurate interpretation of the Ornaments Rubric, which was the substantive issue behind all the quarrels over ritualism. Tait, of course, rejected Stuart's view and was entirely convinced that the protestant understanding of the rubric was the only one permissible in law. Tait was far too great a man to be crushed by such differences, and Stuart was another "advanced" ritualist whom Tait grew to respect, despite their differences. He always gave credit for hard work by his clergy.

For Tait and those who thought as he did, a related anxiety which was more subtle than the adoption of the externals of catholic worship was the growth within the Church of England of the practice of sacramental confession. Tait was familiar with the rubric in the Form of Prayer for the Visitation of the Sick in the Book of Common Prayer that permitted the "special confession of his sins". Then, "after which confession, the Priest shall absolve him." He knew also, of course, that the Church of England ordinal authorizes the exercise of the ministry of reconciliation, but such practices were outside his experience and outside what he believed to be permitted except in the most extraordinary circumstances. So, when Tractarian-inspired clergy began promoting confession as part of normal Christian discipline, Tait and many others felt that a boundary had been crossed. The situation was made worse, in the eyes of many, when Roman Catholic publications were adopted, or adapted, by Anglican clergy in order to instruct parishioners and others in the discipline. Further, when it became apparent that some clergy were asking probing questions of their penitents, particularly regarding sexual sins, the agitation against confession grew and could not be ignored by the bishops, especially when the protesters' allegations were proved to be correct, and that such questioning effectively made sinful suggestions to the innocent.

An example of a case of this sort occurred in 1858. The parish, once again, was St Paul's, Knightsbridge, and the clergyman was a curate named Alfred Poole. He was accused of asking "outrageous questions" of people who came to him for confession. Tait investigated and concluded that the accusation was not true. He wrote to Poole to tell him of his conclusions, but continued, "I regret to say that, quite independently of that evidence, I am led by your own admission to regard the course you are in the habit of pursuing in reference to Confession as likely to cause scandal and injury to the Church."[265] As a consequence, Tait "with great pain" decided that he had no choice but to withdraw Poole's licence as curate of St Barnabas. Poole replied temperately but at length seeking a specific statement from the bishop. Although Tait said that he had "a sincere personal regard" for Poole as a "conscientious and upright man", he declined to give one. Poole was not mollified and took his case to the Judicial Committee of the Privy Council. The whole process took three years; the committee heard the case in detail but eventually concluded that no right of appeal existed, and the case was dismissed. The length of the process generated pamphlets and letters from many quarters which gave the dispute a wider interest than might have been the case if it had been dealt with more expeditiously. Tait, however, never wavered from his conviction "that the inculcation of the practice of habitual auricular confession was contrary to the doctrine and practice of the Church of England".[266] The Poole case was not unique, but it revealed an effort of fair-mindedness in Tait's dealing with clergy with whose position he had very little sympathy. Tait devoted no less than twenty-five pages of his first London *Charge* to the practice of sacramental confession, after which the controversy died down. However, in May 1873, a proposal for the "education, selection and licensing of duly qualified confessors" was put forward in a petition to Convocation. Tait was, as would be expected, opposed to the idea and spoke on it not only in Convocation but in debates in the House of

Lords. Eventually, the Lambeth Conference of 1878 acknowledged that the practice, while by no means essential within Anglicanism, could in "exceptional cases" be available "for troubled consciences" and "for the sick". The Conference stipulated that the special circumstances did not authorize a priest to require individuals to make their confession, and that absolution should only be given "when the sick man shall humbly and heartily desire it".

Tait learned of Archbishop Longley's death whilst staying at his recently acquired family home, "Stonehouse" in Kent. He had bought the "small estate" on the Isle of Thanet in the spring of 1868, as a refuge from the capital. He felt the need for somewhere that could provide "a considerable vacation every year ... without this alleviation, no human constitution could stand the pressure of constant work". He returned there after the funeral of Archbishop Longley at Addington. The decision to do so suggests that he was not anticipating being offered preferment. He thought that Archbishop Thomson of York would be appointed, and that Samuel Wilberforce would go to York (which Tait had declined in 1862). Of course, he knew that he was a possible candidate, and naturally friends and relatives were among those who speculated that he would be offered the vacant archbishopric. He admitted to catching some of the excitement generated by his guests' speculations, so it was not a total surprise when the call came to serve as Archbishop of Canterbury, although even in the privacy of his diary he claimed it was unexpected. He had served as Bishop of London for twelve years and so was immensely experienced in episcopal ministry. Physically he was in good health and seemed well-suited to his new role:

> An imposing figure: tall ... clean shaven ... with dark wavy hair parted in the middle and reaching almost to his shoulders, but in total effect unquestionably manly. He bore himself with great but natural dignity: he looked every inch the primate.[267]

He received the prime minister's letter on 13 November 1868 and went to London with his reply. Later, he had an interview with Disraeli, which he described as "curious", and continued:

> The servant announced me as Archbishop of Canterbury, on which I said that was not *my* mode of announcing myself. This led [Disraeli] to say that he had hoped to keep the matter secret till all his appointments were ready. Then he harangued me on the state of the Church; spoke of rationalists . . . He spoke at large of his desire to rally a Church party, which, omitting the extremes of rationalism and ritualism, should unite all other sections of the Church; alluded to his Church appointments as aiming at this . . . Remarked that, whether in office or out, he had a large Church party . . . I stated my views shortly and we separated. I have seen him only once since. Within a very short time he had resigned office.[268]

A few days later, and still before his appointment was announced, the consecration of a new Bishop of Peterborough, W. C. Magee, took place in Whitehall Chapel, where Tait's own episcopal ministry had begun exactly twelve years before. Tait was one of the consecrating bishops, along with York, Oxford, and Ripon, and he sent them confidential notes. The announcement came the following day.

As was to be expected, Tait received an avalanche of letters of congratulation. Many of them were predictable in their sentiments, but it is clear that his was regarded by many as a good appointment. Some of the disciples of the Tractarians were equivocal, but one of the most penetrating comments came from Walter Hook, who had become the Dean of Chichester. He had long expected that Tait would earn more preferment and wrote of "the peculiar talent you possess for 'ruling without showing that you rule' the most unruly of men, the clergy".[269]

—

The new Archbishop of Canterbury was to become the most influential primate in 200 years.[270] He was immediately faced with a political issue with significant ecclesiastical consequences; one which tested his undeniable abilities as a statesman. By the time he went to Osborne to pay homage to the Queen on 5 January 1869, Gladstone had been in office for some weeks with a substantial majority, and the new Parliament was the most radical since 1832. A principal issue of the election campaign had been the disestablishment of the Irish branch of the Church of England, still a minority body and disproportionately wealthy. Gladstone, anxious about Ireland, had advocated disestablishment there for some years, believing that reform was overdue and that disestablishment would go some way to ameliorating the political situation, just as Wellington had used Roman Catholic emancipation for the same end. The outcome of the general election meant that Irish disestablishment was inevitable. For Gladstone, the concept of Irish disestablishment had the happy result of uniting his Liberals, of forcing the Tories from office, and winning many Nonconformist votes. The irony of his position was that he was personally devout, had always been a committed disciple of the Tractarians, and had formerly been a powerful advocate of established religion. This was not lost upon the high church faction, but even prominent Tractarians, such as Doctor Pusey and Canon Liddon, were not so devoted to the establishment as to think that it was essential to Anglicanism's survival in Ireland. Tait was a realist and saw that outright opposition to Gladstone's plan would achieve nothing. Indeed, his Erastian awareness meant that he felt obliged to accept that the electorate had spoken definitively. Nevertheless, he hoped that he could reduce the impact of the proposals. An additional but unspoken consideration in the mind of Archbishop Tait throughout the Irish Church crisis was the old fear that a successful attack on the Irish Church might trigger something similar in England.

On 6 May 1868, a few months before his death, Archbishop Longley had chaired a public meeting in London, in St James's Hall. Tait had described it as a "great Church and State meeting". It was called in response to the government's plans and had twenty-five bishops, forty-nine peers, and numerous members of the House of Commons on the platform. Tait had moved a "strong resolution", which called upon the proponents of disestablishment to make clear precisely what was intended. A few days afterwards, he wrote to his son, who was an undergraduate at Oxford, "I never saw a meeting so wild with enthusiasm. The speakers had been carefully arranged so as to represent all parties." Bishop Wilberforce, "eloquent and indiscreet as usual", was "hissed" until the "chief hisser" was hurled "down the stairs"; Dean Stanley, declaring himself "as a Liberal of the Liberals" was "roared at . . . till he stopped". Tait said that he, Archbishop Thomson of York, and Lord Harrowby "had full opportunity of setting forth our view that there was no need of destroying the Irish Church in order thoroughly to reform it". Tait wrote that Gladstone was "certainly a good Christian man" but expressed his wish that he was not "so strangely impetuous". A few days later, Tait and his wife walked home with Mr and Mrs Gladstone after a church service, during which time they had a useful conversation.

Once legislation was certain, Tait set about trying to salvage what he could; most of the bishops were also keen to reduce the impact of the pending Act, and the Irish members of the episcopate were understandably opposed to disestablishment. At first, Tait hoped to influence the drafting of the Bill, which was inevitably complex, although he refrained from approaching Gladstone with any suggestion of this. The prime minister drafted the Bill himself, but he was careful to keep Tait apprised of his progress. Tait found the situation difficult but appreciated Gladstone's courtesy and had been encouraged by the knowledge that Queen Victoria was also uneasy at the prospect of Irish disestablishment. When the Bill came to the Lords, Gladstone's prior involvement of Tait, although limited, meant that the archbishop did not oppose the second reading, although he did not vote in favour of it.

Tait was pleased to discover that Gladstone intended to avoid unnecessary changes to the laws of the Church, except in so far as they must be modified by the separation of the Irish Church from the State. The second reading of the Bill in the House of Commons took place on 23 March 1869, and it was carried by 368 votes to 250. The following day, Disraeli, in opposition, wrote carefully to Tait in a private capacity, emphasizing the importance of the "course" to be pursued in the House of Lords. The letter went on to encourage Tait to call a meeting of about a dozen relevant peers at Lambeth Palace, and he suggested several of differing political persuasions. Tait acted on this advice and the meeting took place on 8 May 1869, although no agreements were reached. For Tait, it was part of an exercise where "the friends of the Irish Church should set themselves to obtain such fair and equitable conditions as might mitigate the severity of the now inevitable blow". Tait's next problem lay in his awareness that the bishops in the House of Lords needed careful management. He diligently consulted them and believed himself to know "the present views of the Irish Prelates". Walter Hook's dictum about Tait "ruling without showing that you rule" was proved apposite within weeks of him becoming archbishop. In the event, there were sixty-two amendments carried in the Lords, although thirteen English and three Irish bishops opposed the second reading. The Archbishop of York and Bishop Wilberforce joined Tait in abstaining; the only bishop to support the government was Thirlwall of St David's. Tait might have hoped for more abstentions, but he remained optimistic that he could secure amendments in Committee.

Tait had not been completely successful with his strategy for amendments. He failed to retain seats in the Lords for the incumbent Irish bishops. He was more successful in his endeavours to protect at least some of the endowments of the Church in Ireland, but he did not achieve as much as he hoped. He believed that the preservation of a good proportion of the Irish Church's financial resources, particularly those funds received by the Church since the Reformation, would help to ensure its independence. His success was somewhat limited, but he secured more than was originally proposed when Gladstone agreed to the sum of £500,000 as representative of private endowments made since 1660. Other funds of which the Church in Ireland was to be deprived should, he thought, be used for educational purposes; he did not manage to secure this. He did prevent superfluous church buildings, and property such as houses and glebe, and the like, being given to the Roman Catholics, and did his best to ensure that disestablishment did not increase the power of Roman Catholicism in Ireland. Ultimately, some funds were used to provide houses for Roman Catholic priests and Presbyterian ministers. This was effectively the outcome of proposals which had become known as "concurrent endowment". A more technical concern was that the disestablished Church would not be a new legal entity but would be "as far as possible" the same body which it was before. The amendments which Tait had sought were practical: to make the best of the situation as far as the future life of the Church of Ireland was concerned, and largely his efforts were successful. The Church in Ireland was disestablished in May 1871, after a postponement of four months. Tait was not reassured by the improvement regarding the endowment. His efforts were of value to the Church and for Ireland, but he recorded in his diary that the Act left Ireland and the Church there in depressing religious circumstances. Even so, when the controversy ended, Tait "received warm expressions of thanks from the Queen, from Mr Gladstone, and from the Irish bishops".[271] Nevertheless, he still incurred a great deal of criticism from people who thought that he had sold out, particularly because of his abstentions from voting in the Lords. The strongest expression of disapproval, which he failed to moderate, was "the extreme tone of the address to the Queen against disestablishment which Denison persuaded the Lower House of Convocation to put forward".[272]

However unhappy he was with the outcome, the letters of appreciation received from those on both sides of the issue were a tribute to what his biographers correctly described as his "practical statesmanship [and] persistent energy". He had had to be pragmatic and knew that he had no other option. Not unnaturally, Tait hoped that the passage of the Bill into law would be followed by a period of calm, in which he could get on with other things: "O Lord, grant that quiet time may now be given me to look after my own soul and the souls of my diocese ... Keep me near Thee in prayer and quiet Christian living, through Jesus Christ", he wrote in his journal. But the stress of the early months of his primacy took its toll on his health. In November 1869, he suffered a series of strokes, and it was again thought that his life was at its end. His son was called from Oxford, and Mrs Tait wrote to her sister that they were "simply waiting for the end". *The Lancet* published a pessimistic assessment of his situation. To the surprise of everyone, however, he gradually rallied and was to live another thirteen years, although he never regained the full use of his left arm. He was largely out of action for most of 1870 and spent the winter at San Remo. As he recovered, the plan to appoint a suffragan Bishop of Dover was implemented by Act of Parliament. His former pupil at Rugby, the Archdeacon of Canterbury and his current domestic chaplain, Edward Parry, was appointed to ease the burden of the archbishop's diocesan work. Although in Tait's case, Parry was appointed as a result of the archbishop's ill health, the principle for the consecration of bishops to assist diocesans was re-established. At the same time, a suffragan Bishop of Nottingham, then in the Diocese of Lincoln, was appointed. Such appointments had long lapsed in England, but there was a general acknowledgement that since the early years of the Queen's reign the workload of bishops had increased intolerably. This was to be reflected further in the establishment of no fewer than six new dioceses during Tait's primacy. Perhaps the most noteworthy was the Diocese of Truro, whose first bishop, E. W. Benson, was to be Tait's successor at Canterbury.

—

By the spring of 1871, Tait was almost restored to his former vigour. An entirely theological issue arose between 1871 and 1873 over the use of the so-called Athanasian Creed. This statement of belief is to be found in the Book of Common Prayer, where it is known by the Latin words with which it begins: *Quicumque vult*. The Prayer Book stipulates that it must be recited at certain services. It had, however, long been neglected, and some thought it should be removed from the liturgy, or at least its recitation made voluntary, because its "damnatory clauses" were regarded as distasteful by many. The suggestion was made by the Ritual Commission of 1869, and Tait was content that its use should be curtailed in some way, but it stirred up a hornets' nest of opposition from conservative churchmen. A leader among them was the famous Canon Liddon of St Paul's, who also held an Oxford professorship and was by far the greatest theologian among the second generation of the followers of the Tractarians. He went so far as to threaten to retire from public life and to write at length about his reasons for so doing if the Creed was altered in any way or the occasions for its use were reduced. Tait was disliked by Liddon, who had a wide following as an inspiring preacher and spoke on behalf of many Tractarians, not least the venerable Doctor Pusey. Eventually, Liddon accepted that there was no abandonment of principle in a suggestion of Bishop Wilberforce's that incumbents could ask their bishops in writing for permission to dispense with the recitation of the Athanasian Creed on specific occasions at services which were not eucharistic.[273] Such was Liddon's influence that the tension was reduced, but the controversy did not end there because a committee of

Convocation affirmed at the end of 1872 that although the Creed should stand, there should be the addition of an explanatory rubric. In the New Year, a protest meeting was held in London at St James's Hall; Liddon guessed that 3,000 attended, and he was a principal speaker. As a result of this obvious demonstration of strength, all plans to alter the usage of the Creed were abandoned. Tait accepted the inevitable but could not resist referring in a *Charge* to the Diocese of Canterbury "to certain eminent men, whom we greatly respect", who had threatened to retire into "lay communion". He was undoubtedly referring to Pusey and Liddon, and Bishop Hamilton of Salisbury, who had uttered the same threat.

—

The dispute over the Athanasian Creed was more or less an internal Church concern, but, by the autumn of 1873, the matter of ritual was receiving much wider interest. Tait's two predecessors had not stemmed the rising tide of ritualism within the Church of England, and Tait's concern with it in his London years has also been noticed, although back in February 1851 he had heard Pusey preach in Oxford and observed that "the exhortation to calmness and love with which he ended was very good". Ritualism now became a significant issue for Tait's archiepiscopal ministry, although in a somewhat different guise than that which had troubled his London work. Admittedly, Tait had sat as a member of a Royal Commission on ritual created in 1867 and chaired by Longley. This, combined with his practical experience of the phenomenon whilst Bishop of London, meant that he had wide experience of the complexity of the problem. Nevertheless, it is strange that he failed to perceive the profound depth of the ritualists' convictions, continuing to regard their practices "as an illegal eccentricity [rather than] a matter of deeply-felt conviction which they could not abandon", as Edward Carpenter accurately observed.[274] The archbishop came to believe that if legislation could strengthen the authority of bishops in their dioceses, subsequent episcopal rulings would be obediently followed by the clergy. In the summer of 1873, he hoped that Parliament would act and enable the bishops to deal with ritualism within their dioceses. He knew that Queen

Victoria strongly disapproved of ritualism, and the suggestion has been made that she urged him to take action.

The issue was discussed at a meeting of bishops held at Lambeth Palace in January 1874. At that meeting the two archbishops were entrusted with the preparation of a Bill which could be presented to Parliament and, at the same time, work its way through Convocation. It was envisaged that Tait and Thomson would come up with proposals consistent with "advice" from Convocation given four years previously, asking for legislation "for facilitating, expediting, and cheapening proceedings in enforcing clergy discipline". That is what they tried to do, although Tait knew that Convocation did need careful handling if any sort of workable plan was to be devised. Tait's biographers gave a succinct summary of the outcome of the archiepiscopal deliberations:

> In every Diocese a Council or Board of Assessors was to be formed under the presidency of the Bishop, consisting of three incumbents and five lay Churchmen, elected respectively by the clergy and churchwardens of the Diocese ... in addition to the Chancellor, the Dean, and the Archdeacon ... Any complaint made to the Bishop as to ritual irregularity might be referred by him to his Council, which should, if necessary, hear evidence, and advise the bishop whether, in the light of local circumstances, it seemed desirable that further proceedings should be taken.[275]

If the council advised the bishop to proceed, he would issue "such admonition or order [as] he deemed necessary". The bishop's action would have the force of law. A clergyman would be able to appeal to the archbishop, who would be obliged to hear the case in person, but there would be no further means of appeal. In this way the two archbishops hoped to contain any future disputes about ritual as internal Church business and eliminate the secular courts, although they were aware from the start that there would be opposition both within and outside Parliament to what they planned.

An unexpected difficulty arose later in January when Gladstone abruptly decided to call a general election. Tait was astonished at Gladstone's decision. He knew at once that it would not be possible for his proposed legislation to be considered by Convocation at the same time as it went through Parliament, even if the new government was willing to proceed with it. The electorate dismissed Gladstone. The Tories came in with a large majority although Disraeli had not expected to win. They came to power without a proposed programme of legislation. Tait shrewdly saw the new government's lack of a programme as an opportunity and decided to press on with the bishops' intention to ask for legislation. He knew the need to be urgent for several reasons. There was a widespread sense that something needed to be done, a view also held by the Queen, who urged him forward; politically more important was his awareness that the Church could lose the initiative if lay pressure from Lord Shaftesbury and his friends, who had tried for a number of years to introduce legislation to outlaw ritualism, resulted in proposals (as was quite likely). Archbishop Tait wrote to Disraeli within days of the election result and was encouraged by the premier's response. Someone said that Tait had more influence during that period than any Archbishop of Canterbury since the days of the ill-fated Laud, who was eventually executed by the Puritans in 1645. On hearing the comparison Tait wryly said that he hoped not to suffer the same fate. He wanted a simple piece of legislation and hoped that the bishops' proposals would recommend themselves by their reasonableness. They did not want to change the law but to clarify it, remove obstacles to its enforcement, and achieve a system that was relatively inexpensive to operate. Tait believed that the plan for Diocesan Councils would achieve this and eliminate controversy, but this did not happen when the Act became law. He wisely wanted to retain episcopal control over matters of ritual and keep liturgical issues outside the courts. To this end, he insisted that prosecutions should only be pursued with the agreement of the particular bishop in whose diocese any alleged offences were committed. The existing ecclesiastical courts, he envisaged, would continue to hold sway over matters other than ritual. The stage was set for what was to prove to be the last time that Church of England business would dominate Parliament for a whole session. The Public Worship Regulation Act also proved to be the final occasion when Parliament legislated on Church matters without the prior agreement of Convocation.

Tait moved the first reading in the House of Lords on 11 May 1874, and it attracted controversy from the moment of its publication. The opposition of high churchmen was to be expected; one called it "the Persecution Bill". Liberal church people feared that a rigid enforcement of the rubrics would restrict their freedom of interpretation of the Prayer Book, and some evangelicals were concerned in case the Act might be used against them in the same way. Immediately after its first moving, amendments were proposed. Lord Shaftesbury's were the most significant and would have altered the whole Bill if they had all been carried. The substance of his amendments was drawn from his previous efforts to introduce legislation against ritualism, and some of them were drafted for him by an eminent ecclesiastical lawyer, Archibald Spens. Tait opposed Shaftesbury's amendments, but discovered at a late stage that they had been privately endorsed by the government. This led him to realize that the whole Bill could fall if the amendments were rejected, so he spoke against them, but did not oppose them in the divisions. Shaftesbury wished to have a lay judge, although he conceded that he should be appointed by the archbishops. He did not want any diocesan jurisdiction or preliminary enquiries, rather a central court. Tait strongly disliked the plan to change the authority to a judge, rather than the bishop of the diocese, but he hoped to mitigate the potential harm by giving bishops a power of veto before cases could be brought before the judge. At first, Shaftesbury rejected the idea of the episcopal veto, but came to see that his amendments would only survive if he conceded. Tait, therefore, conceded the appointment of a lay judge, whilst remaining firm on the veto; it was "the very essence of the Bill", he said. Tait was proved right. The liberty of the veto was employed by the bishops and prevented most ritual cases getting as far as the courts. It was to prove the redeeming factor in what turned out to be a bad piece of legislation.

Convocation met in July 1874, and there was some agitation about undue haste and the lack of consultation about the Bill, but it was then too late to influence its contents. Despite Tait's initial hope that the Bill would run in some sort of parallel between Parliament and Convocation, the absence of Convocational involvement actually gave him greater flexibility in dealing with the amendments proposed by Shaftesbury and others. The Bill went before the House of Commons, where Tait had no voice, for its third reading in early August. He had earlier written to Disraeli urging that its progress should not be prevented by pressure of other business; he did not want it to be carried over to the next session as he feared it would not survive. The Queen also let Disraeli know that she wanted the Bill to be passed, so he threw his weight behind it. There was a considerable debate. Gladstone opposed it at length, although eventually he withdrew his objections. It was in Disraeli's speech at the end of the debate that his two famous phrases about ritualism were coined. The Act was designed, he said, "to put down ritualism", which he defined as "the Mass in masquerade". Royal assent was granted in early August, and the Public Worship Regulation Act passed into law. However, its progress convinced many that Parliament was not a suitable forum for debate about the doctrine of the Church of England and the regulation of its worship.

Even Tait's biographers, customarily so careful of his reputation, could not disguise his failure with regard to the Act. They believed that he never fully realized the weight of the ritualists' convictions, "riding roughshod over the obstacles in his way, he unintentionally gave more pain than he was at all aware of, both to his opponents and to his friends."[276] Events were to demonstrate the inadequacy of the Public Worship Regulation Act. In 1881, Tait himself, in a letter to Disraeli ennobled as Lord Beaconsfield, wrote that he had to "confess that the Act of 1874 has not worked very smoothly". The Act has been described as "a fiasco" and as Tait's "greatest blunder". The Act resulted in a number of hard-working ritualistic clergy being sent to prison for contempt of court when they refused to obey the judge's demands. In the last months of his life, Tait was anxious that Sidney Fairhorn Green, Vicar of Miles Platting in the Diocese of Manchester, whose ministry he came to admire, should be released from prison if only on the technicality that his benefice could be deemed to be vacant because of his prolonged absence from it. "Why Green was singled out for prosecution remains a mystery", Tait wrote. "He is evidently much beloved by his congregation." He was in prison from March 1881 to November 1882. Imprisonment was an outcome that no one anticipated for any ritualists, and it led within a few years to the virtual abandonment of the Act. In defence of Tait's reputation, one anecdote shows that he had some sensitivity towards the ritualists' doctrines. A consecrated wafer (wafer bread being regarded as a mark of extreme ritualism at that time) had been obtained by an anti-ritualist who had posed as a communicant with the intention to use it later as evidence in court. As a piece of evidence, it was kept for some time by court officials. Tait was horrified at the possible sacrilege and asked to be given custody of it, whereupon he "reverently consumed it". This caused some concern about his health but showed that he knew there were limits that ought not to be overset. The best that his biographers could say of the Act was that, by the time they published in 1891 nearly a decade after their subject's death, there had "been only some seven or eight prosecutions under its provisions". However, there remains the distinct possibility that repressive legislation might have been passed if Tait had not seized and retained the initiative after the 1874 general election. Even so, the final years of Tait's archiepiscopate were lived under the shadow of a well-meant, but unsatisfactory, Act of Parliament.

When he was Bishop of London, Tait had not been very enthusiastic about the first Lambeth Conference in 1867, but he had attended loyally, and even assisted in the committee work. As was noted in the previous chapter, that Conference had been held without any expectation that others would follow, but as the years passed there developed a call to have a second. Tait was still cautious, and he was not alone, but, as had been the case in 1867, Canadian churchmen were prominent in promoting the idea of another gathering as early as 1872, and Bishop Selwyn of Lichfield raised it in the Canterbury Convocation in 1873. Moreover, the years after the first Conference had seen some significant changes which affected the developing Anglican Communion, not least the growth of autonomy among its branches. Initially, colonial bishops had been appointed by the Crown. Their later successors were not appointed under letters patent and so did not have the same authority within the English establishment. Consequently, it was necessary to define carefully their relationship to the Church of England in a manner which noted the change of legal standing and respected their autonomy. A significant factor, already noticed as emerging in Longley's time, was more pronounced by the 1870s: that

Anglicans in the United States of America were in a different situation to other parts of the Communion and were increasingly influential. As church people of an independent nation, and not a colony, the Americans saw their Church as a "sister" to the Church of England, rather than as a branch of it, and certainly not in a filial relationship with the English Church. Despite the misgivings of some of his brethren, one of the American bishops, J. B. Kerfoot of Pittsburgh, who had been present in 1867, was a strong advocate for the second Conference. In addition, the disestablishment of the Church in Ireland had created another new relationship with the Church of England, and this too served to focus the need for some sort of mechanism which would enable various branches of the Church to interact.

Some Anglicans had begun to entertain a suggestion that the authority of the Archbishop of Canterbury should be defined in terms of a patriarchy. This probably arose as a result of the Roman Catholic Vatican Council of 1870, which had strengthened the authority of the papacy with the doctrine of infallibility and caused the question of authority to assume a greater significance. No such concept was entertained among Anglicans. The very idea of a patriarchy was anathema to Tait, and he got rid of it as soon as he could from the preliminary work for the Conference, although further efforts were needed to prevent it becoming an issue during the Conference. Additionally, the issue of ritualism was an unavoidable subject of discussion in a second Lambeth Conference; this was probably a consideration in Tait's lack of enthusiasm for calling it.

Whatever personal reluctance Tait felt with regard to having another Conference, Bishop Selwyn was enthused by the idea. He was a near contemporary to Tait in terms of age, having been born in 1809. Previously, he had been Bishop of New Zealand from 1841 and was largely responsible for the constitution of that Church, which included synods for clergy. Selwyn had been enthusiastically present at the 1867 Conference, the year of his move to Lichfield, and at the end of that Conference, as noticed in the previous chapter, he had been appointed Corresponding Secretary of the Anglican Communion. With his colonial experience he was an obvious choice for such work. He had been well able to appreciate the value of Longley's Conference, and naturally had high hopes for its successor. A man of vigour and insight, he set out to convince Tait that it should go ahead, and by 1875 he had persuaded him. In addition to working on Tait, Selwyn turned his attention to the American Church and became the first English diocesan bishop to visit the United States. Selwyn was such a success that the American Church presented a commemorative alms dish to St Paul's Cathedral in appreciation of his visit. He then visited Canada, where his work was made easier by the already existing desire for another Conference. In December 1872, five of the Canadian bishops had already written formally to Tait in his role as President of the Convocation of Canterbury, using Selwyn as their intermediary, to

> humbly and earnestly petition that the Convocation of Canterbury will take such action as may seem most expedient to unite with us in requesting the Archbishop of Canterbury to summon a second meeting of the Conference. We are persuaded that such meeting will be most efficacious in uniting the scattered branches of the Anglican communion, and in promoting an extension of the Kingdom of God throughout the world; and we, therefore, pray that it may be again convened at the earliest day that may suit the convenience of the Archbishop of Canterbury.[277]

The Canadian communication was supported by similar suggestions and requests from other parts of the Communion, not least the West Indies, and also Australia. When the Canadian document of 1872 was presented to Convocation by Selwyn, he was supported by Samuel Wilberforce, who made the suggestion that Tait should consult Archbishop Thomson of York. It may be that Wilberforce knew that Thomson, despite his refusal to attend the first Conference, would support the proposal. Tait was informed of the support of the Convocation of York in February 1875 and Thomson also told him that all the bishops had been consulted. In *The Lambeth Conferences*, R. T. Davidson reported that Tait was "fortified by the concurrence of the Northern Convocation".[278] At that point in his career, Davidson was the archbishop's resident chaplain, and he helped throughout, "unofficially" he said, with the secretarial work.

A few weeks later, Tait raised in the Southern Convocation the prospect of a second Lambeth Conference "to gather the bishops together from all parts of the globe". He asked for agenda suggestions, being "disposed, by the advice of my brethren, to request that our brethren at home, and also at a distance, will state to me as explicitly as possible what the subjects are that it is desirable to discuss". He emphasized that there could be no attempts to define doctrine; "our doctrines are contained in our Formularies." With these assertions, made almost three years before the Conference took place, Tait sought to avoid the ambushing tactics by which Gray had tried to coerce Longley into action against Colenso. Accordingly, in 1876, Tait wrote to all the bishops of the Communion to see how they felt about the prospect of a second Lambeth Conference, "if it shall seem expedient, after the opinions of all our brethren have been ascertained"; but as early as July 1874 a committee had been appointed by Convocation to consider the matter. Selwyn made a second visit to America two months later and was encouraged afresh by his experience there.

Even when the principle of holding another Lambeth Conference was accepted, there were difficulties about the date. Some wanted it to take place in 1876, but Tait wanted to devote time in that year to a *Primary Charge* to the Diocese of Canterbury. He suggested 1877, but the American Church had a General Convention planned, and did not want both events in the same year. So it was that 1878 was chosen, beginning on 2 July and to last for four weeks. That meant it would be a very different sort of gathering than the few days of Longley's. After consultation with Selwyn and a committee of bishops, six subjects were chosen to form the agenda. The items were similar to those of a decade before with the addition of a new fifth one: "Modern forms of infidelity, and the best means of dealing with them."

Across the world there were 173 Anglican bishops in 1877, and Tait invited them all; 108 accepted, although not all arrived. About a hundred bishops attended; Tait said during the Conference that there were ninety-eight attendees. Among the English diocesan bishops, only two declined to attend, both of them evangelicals: Baring of Durham and Philpott of Worcester. Less than three months before the Conference began, Bishop Selwyn died on 11 April 1878, and Tait lost a central figure on whose support he knew he could rely. But, in personal terms, worse was to come. The archbishop's only son, Craufurd Tait, was incumbent of the parish of St John's, Notting Hill, and had been unwell at the time of his recent appointment. He had previously made a useful contribution to the relations between the Church of England and the American Anglicans. He visited the United States specifically to reinforce his father's invitation to the next Conference and was welcomed by the House of Bishops of the American Church on 5 October 1877. His visit had been a notable success, and he was held in high regard by the Americans, but the young man had died at the end of May at the family home in Kent. He was not quite twenty-nine years old, and there were only weeks to go before the Lambeth Conference began. Both his parents were devastated that tragedy had struck again. Mrs Tait in particular never recovered from the loss of their only son. Tait referred to the relationship in poignant terms, "nothing could exceed in tenderness the affectionate friendship which bound the mother and the son."[279] His final days were chronicled as lovingly as those of his sisters had been twenty years before. He was buried on 4 June 1878 in the churchyard at Addington. Once again, the reader of *Catharine and Craufurd Tait* is shown an example of Christian fortitude in the face of death. Despite her loss, his mother persevered graciously with her duties as hostess at Lambeth Palace. One of the American bishops remembered after the Conference her unflagging courtesy as she "ministered—pale and sorrow stricken—to the multitude of guests ... he could scarcely believe that such fortitude and self-constraint were possible." Later it was feared that the loss shortened Mrs Tait's life. Archbishop Tait's strength of character was similarly demonstrated by the way he carried out all his duties at the Conference. When he welcomed the American bishops to the Conference he made a particularly poignant reference to Craufurd's visit; "partly for our Church's sake, partly for my sake, partly also for something you discerned in himself, you welcomed someone very dear to me last autumn."[280] Awkward though his words were, everyone present knew that Tait spoke as he did from a full heart.

Before it opened formally, new bishops for North Queensland and Nassau were consecrated, and so was Selwyn's successor as Bishop of Lichfield. A major service was at Canterbury Cathedral on St Peter's Day, 29 June, at which Tait spoke powerfully from notes written "in narrow columns on folded quarto paper, sometimes crossed and re-written till they seemed illegible"; it was the occasion when he alluded to the death of his son in the manner already quoted. Tait spoke from St Augustine's "throne", set up in the quire of the cathedral, and put the Conference in its global and historical perspective:

> My brothers, representatives of the Church throughout the world, engaged in spreading the Gospel of Jesus Christ wherever the sun shines, I esteem it a very high privilege to welcome you here today, to the cradle of Anglo-Saxon Christianity ... I am addressing you from St Augustine's Chair. This thought carries us back to the time when the first missionary to our Anglo-Saxon forefathers, amid much discouragement, landed on these barbarous shores. More than twelve centuries and a half have rolled on since then. The seed he sowed has borne an abundant harvest.[281]

The formal work of the Conference began with a lengthy speech from Tait to the bishops assembled in the Great Library of Lambeth Palace. His biographers provided a summary made from a "shorthand report". It was a small masterpiece and shows how Tait was fully conscious of the complexities of the authority of the Conference. He began by pointing out that the individual bishops were more than representatives, but less than plenipotentiaries. He noted that they worked under different forms of constitution and governance. They could not expect to make decisions that would bind the constituent Churches of the Communion, and he said that they should not desire to do so. The role of their meeting was to confer; they might make suggestions, but it would be the responsibility of the individual constituent Churches of the Communion to implement or reject those suggestions. From this point he progressed to a description of the situation of the Church of England as an established Church, explaining the creative nature of the three-fold relationship between the Church, the legislature and the sovereign. He indicated that, in his opinion, there was unlikely to be a change in those relationships until "something better" was conceived, and his tone indicated that this was not an appropriate topic for the Conference to consider.

From the English situation, he went on to describe the situation of "our brethren from India"; he described it as "the most distinctly Established Church in the world", despite the country's status as "more or less" a conquered race. The Church in India was funded by the State, through Parliamentary grants, and the "Indian bishops cannot leave India without the consent of the Governor-General". He seemed to hint that he was sympathetic to any disquiet about the situation which might be felt by the bishops from India, "but at all events, that is what it is at present." He then dealt briefly with "our Churches in the Colonies", claiming that only three persons in England could give a correct description of the constitution of a colonial Church, and said, "I rather pride myself on being one of the three", and then said that he did not want to enter into "tedious" details. His final example of a different sort of constitution was that of the Church in the United States. Again, Tait was brief; he was sure that the American bishops would be willing to speak for themselves, and the reader detects that he was being deliberately cautious in his dealings with that Church. Whatever he had been told by his son or by Bishop Selwyn, or had learned from his earlier correspondence, he was acutely aware of the sensitivities of the sister Church.

Having established the parameters of what he expected to happen, Archbishop Tait then moved to what he called "one or two principles", which he believed to be desirable for their deliberations. First came the "Christian virtue" of tolerance. As he developed his theme, he reached the conclusion that "this toleration is the same as Catholicity". With a quick reference to the narrowness and intolerance of "sects", he applied the principle of tolerance to a wider world than the Lambeth Conference. It is possible here to read into what Tait was saying a very oblique reference to the Roman Catholic declaration of papal infallibility made at the Vatican Council of 1870, but he was much too shrewd to be specific. He used the plea for tolerance to expand on the need to overcome differences within the Anglican Communion with regard to "ceremonies", asking that the bishops should not allow their Conference to adhere to developments of the "last forty years" (clearly a reference to ritualism), nor to the insights of the Evangelical Revival, nor even of the Caroline Divines, both of which he mentioned explicitly, nor of the "undivided Church, not even the Church of the first three centuries".

> We desire to be guided by our Lord and Master, Jesus Christ, and His recorded Word, and the words of His Apostles. Here

we build our faith: and we believe that in the changing ages, this everlasting Gospel will become more and more adapted to the ever-changing circumstances of the human race which it was destined in all its varieties to save.[282]

As Tait drew to the conclusion of this early speech, he made reference to Thomson's sermon, and paid his generous tribute to Archbishop Longley as the man who had called the first Lambeth Conference eleven years before, and then to Selwyn. He ended, characteristically, by commending the proceedings of the Conference to Almighty God.

There was a sensible degree of flexibility with regard to the arrangements of the agenda. Tait chaired a committee which proved to be influential in the conduct of the Conference. Its brief was "to receive questions submitted in writing by bishops desiring the advice of the conference on difficulties or problems they have met in their several dioceses". As Archbishop of Canterbury, Tait presided over the general debates, and took an active part in the deliberations of the Conference. He was described as sympathetic to the issues of the different bishops and their dioceses. "Fair and equitable in his address and rulings, and at the same time astute in feeling the temper of his auditors and brethren." When it came to the committee work of the Conference, meetings took place at Fulham and Farnham, the latter being the home of the Bishop of Winchester, as well as at Lambeth and several other places. Tait largely worked from Lambeth, where he took the chairmanship of the committee which deliberated on the consequences of the Roman Catholic Vatican Council of 1870. One unanticipated consequence of that council had been the establishment of the Old Catholic Church in Europe. The relationship of that breakaway movement with Anglicanism was considered by another committee under the chairmanship of Archbishop Tait (eventually full communion was established between the Anglican Church and the Old Catholics, but not until 1932). Tait also interested himself in the constitution of the West Indian dioceses and, as was to be expected, the "home troubles about ritual and the confessional".

Tait's steadiness of character served him well, and it also served the Conference well. The bishops "recognized in him, if not a patriarchal dignity, a pre-eminence willingly and reverently accorded" to him as the

Archbishop of Canterbury. He was not to be distracted by subsidiary issues and chaired his committees with wisdom and tact. Certainly, he earned much approbation during and after the Conference, despite the inevitable criticism that appeared in some periodicals, and notwithstanding yet another skirmish with Pusey following the cautious observations about sacramental confession made at the Conference.

Tait was the sole signatory, although not the sole author, of the encyclical which was published after the Conference; Thomson refused to sign any such document, and there had been some disagreement as to the contents of the report. However, Tait managed the situation well, and the Conference ended with widespread acknowledgements of his skill and breadth of character; "the archbishop's presidency was above praise", wrote one bishop.

> While avoiding all appearance of dictation, his presence and position were always felt; and the harmony and unanimity of the Conference were largely due to his uniform affability and good temper and his masterly leadership ... He impressed us profoundly with his eminent fitness for the trying though dignified position he has been chosen of God to fill.[283]

—

With the Lambeth Conference safely behind him, there was a brief interlude of happiness when the Taits' daughter Edith, who was born during his time as Bishop of London, married his chaplain Randall Davidson. The wedding took place on 12 November 1878 in the chapel at Lambeth Palace, which had been recently restored. After the wedding, the rest of the family went to Edinburgh to stay with a brother of the archbishop. They had an invitation to break their journey at the home of the Bishop of Carlisle. Tait thought his wife would like to visit the graves of their five daughters, as she had done every year. Mrs Tait declined, giving as her reason her continuing distress over the recent loss of their son. Her health had started to decline and soon Tait had to face yet another bereavement when she died, aged fifty-nine, in Edinburgh on Advent Sunday 1878. Tait's record of his wife's death in *Catharine and Craufurd*

Tait, which was edited for publication by Benham, was another example of his profound piety, although he was a changed man afterwards. His busy life continued, but, as Davidson noted, "after the sorrows of 1878 ... he became almost suddenly an old man."

Tait returned to the duties of a Victorian Archbishop of Canterbury. His diocesan work continued, and he continued to lead Convocation. The latter overlapped with his constitutional duties when the government decided to deal with what had become an anomaly regarding the burial of the dead. Tait benefitted from his well-deserved reputation as an effective member of the House of Lords when he began his next foray into legislation. He was substantially more successful with the Burials Act of 1880 than he had been with the Public Worship Regulation Act six years before. At the beginning of Queen Victoria's reign, almost the only places for burial of the dead were the churchyards of parish churches and cathedrals, which soon could not cope with the increase in the number of deaths consequent upon the growth in population. The establishment of municipal graveyards had already eased the problem, but a right of burial in churchyards continued to exist where the only permitted funeral rite was that of the Church of England, and Anglican clergy were the only persons permitted to conduct funeral services in them. Clergy were required by law to use the Prayer Book burial service even for funerals of parishioners who rejected the Church when the bereaved sought to exercise the right for the deceased to be buried in a churchyard. Disraeli's administration tried to mitigate the situation after his 1874 general election victory. Lord Beauchamp proposed "a Bill of a few short clauses, providing for the interment in consecrated ground, without any service whatever, of those for whom such a funeral could be claimed". This satisfied no one, and "was resented rather than welcomed by those whom it was intended to pacify". Pressure grew for the legal toleration of nonconformist graveside burial ceremonies in Anglican churchyards. Although there were occasions when incumbents turned a blind eye to irregularities, much distress and anger was generated. For a number of years, the matter had, as Tait's biographers put it, "slumbered". Archbishop Longley had tried to defer the matter, but Tait, whilst Bishop of London, "thought that some measure of relief might be accorded". In 1880, Gladstone won the general election, and a Burials Bill was proposed. The central proposal of the Act permitted the interment of the remains of a deceased who had the civil right of burial in a churchyard, according to the wishes of the relatives and friends or even the person's lawyers, either in silence, or with appropriate Christian prayers of their choice. Tait, in a speech in the Lords, expressed his desire for the Church of England to maintain its position as "a National Church, wide as the nation, ready to embrace all in the nation who are anxious to join it, and not making narrow sectarian distinctions between those who adhere very rigidly to one or another set of opinions".[284] He believed that the new Bill would demonstrate to nonconformists that Anglicans genuinely regarded them as brethren; that both parties' faith was indeed held in common, and that all Christians were working for a common cause in "resisting those who are opposed to our social system and family life". Other Church people feared that if churchyards were made accessible to non-Anglicans as a result of parliamentary action, it was conceivable that church buildings might be made the subject of similar legislation at some point in the future. Tait answered that objection judiciously, but not with much comfort to those who had identified it, "I think it is a dangerous principle not to give men what is right because there are unreasonable persons who demand more."[285] He steered a skilful course which preserved the position of the Church, although many Church people did not appreciate the subtlety of his efforts. The strength of feeling was expressed in a powerfully colourful speech by Bishop Christopher Wordsworth of Lincoln in which he described the legislation as "an Act for the martyrdom of the National Church . . . a burials Bill, and I venture to predict that if it becomes law, it will be an Act for the burial of the Church of England herself, not indeed as a church, but as a national establishment of religion."[286] While Wordsworth had been speaking, a petition was passed by the Lower House of Convocation which deplored the proposed Act. Tait was informed of that, as was Wordsworth, and responded to it in his reply. He paid tribute to Wordsworth's character and his ministry, but wondered aloud about the nature of the "martyrdom" of which the bishop had spoken and defined the principle which the Bill sought to establish, "to allow the burial, with religious rites, of persons who at present suffer under the grievance of being prevented from being buried with those religious rites."[287]

The petition of Convocation was, of course, moderate in its language, but its message was clear. It indicated a widespread, but ultimately groundless, fear held by many of the rank and file clergy and forcibly expressed again by "a stream of alarmed and indignant protests... from country parsonages". The doughty archdeacon Denison was among a number of indignant incumbents who wrote to tell Tait that he and the bishops who voted with him in the Lords were deficient in their duty. Several were quoted by his biographers; one cried, "Shame, shame on all those bishops who support this most iniquitous measure! Most fearful will be their responsibility, and retribution, who are thus doing their utmost to assist the enemies of the Church to destroy her." Similar clarity was expressed, with even less charity, in opprobrium directed personally at the archbishop; at a meeting of the Church Defence Institution he was told that he should be shot. In the House of Lords, most of the bishops joined Tait in supporting the new Burial Act in 1880, which, despite the hysteria, resolved many pastoral difficulties. As always, Tait's approach had been to accommodate cautiously the pressure for change. A rather heated exchange with the Bishop of Peterborough later elicited an eirenic exchange of letters.

Tait was proved correct in his assumption that the concessions to nonconformists in the Burials Act would not harm the Church of England. His biographers recorded that "he had judged more truly than his critics". Such was his success in protecting the position of the Church in the nation that they continued,

> Ten years have passed, and it is already difficult to realise the spirit of fear, and even horror, with which at its birth the Bill was looked upon by sober men... Will anyone contend that the Church is weaker today than she was before the dreaded Bill passed into law?[288]

—

By the time the Burials Act was passing into law, Archbishop Tait was drawing towards the close of his distinguished ministry. His personal faith remained strong and serene. Friends had noted how he had aged, but he continued to work, although he took to dictating only important letters to his chaplain, and left him to use his initiative with others, giving only brief instructions. He continued to attend the House of Lords, and he continued to be heard with respect by his peers almost until the end, although he recognized with sadness that his final speech was a failure. Convocation continued to demand his time, and he did not abandon his preaching ministry, although the occasions became markedly fewer. In the Diocese of Canterbury much of the burden was shouldered by Bishop Parry. Tait's interest in the wider life of the Anglican Communion remained, and he was involved in the appointment of a bishop in Japan in the closing months of his life. Similarly, his ministry to the Royal Family continued: in early August 1882, he prepared what he called a *Charge* for the confirmation of Prince Albert Victor and Prince George, which took place at Osborne House in the middle of that month. He was glad to get back to Addington, aware of his increasing weakness. He continued to struggle with the consequences of the Public Worship Regulation Act, recognizing that Parliament would not come to the rescue of the Church by repealing or amending it. A nice point is that, as his life drew to its close, he rejoiced to learn that A. H. Mackonochie, one of the more colourful ritualists with whom he had worked pastorally in his London days in the cholera epidemic of 1866, had taken his advice to avoid the courts by resigning his benefice.

As he became aware that his own death was imminent, Archbishop Tait gave thought to his successor, and thought that Bishop Harold Browne of Winchester, or possibly Edward Benson of Truro, might succeed him; but he would not let Davidson talk to Dean Wellesley of Windsor about either of them. In the event, Dean Wellesley died before Tait. The autumn of 1882 was a time of increasing weakness for him, and friends and family surrounded him. Tait died at the archiepiscopal residence, Addington Palace, on Advent Sunday 1882, the same day in the Church calendar as that on which his wife had died four years earlier. Tait was aged seventy-one. The Dean and Chapter of Westminster immediately offered to his family that he should be buried in the abbey. He had wanted to be buried at Addington with his wife and son, with which his family agreed, but they felt that the Queen should be consulted as to his resting place. She said that the family's wishes should be respected, and that was what happened. Queen Victoria felt genuine affection for Tait. She treasured the lock of his hair which she requested after his death. Almost certainly he was her favourite among her six Archbishops of Canterbury, and he was the greatest of her long reign.

A grand recumbent memorial to Tait was placed in the north-east transept of Canterbury Cathedral. Its inscription pays him a fine tribute: "A great archbishop, just, discerning, dignified, statesmanlike . . . he had one aim: to make the Church of England more and more the Church of the people."

CHAPTER 5

Edward White Benson (1883-1896)

E. W. Benson (1829-1896) became archbishop in 1883. Of the six Archbishops of Canterbury who held office during the reign of Queen Victoria, Benson is the one about whom most has been written. This is due, first, to the willingness of his family to write about themselves and each other; second, aspects of the archbishop's personality have continued to attract attention; third, the Bensons were an unusual family, and continue to intrigue. As a result, posterity knows more than is usually the case about the ninety-fourth Archbishop of Canterbury. First in importance among all the material is an extensive biography in two volumes written by his second and oldest surviving son, Arthur Christopher Benson (1862-1925). It is a carefully discreet account of a remarkable man, reticent regarding its subject's personality and about family relationships; fortunately, it is supplemented by other material by Arthur Benson and also his brother E. F. (Fred) Benson. There is less contrast between Arthur Benson's book and the biography of Archbishop Tait than might be imagined. Tait's biographers wrote with an inherent caution to protect the Church of England; Benson's biography was a memorial to the public life of the archbishop. Both biographies give the reader a good picture of the Church while concealing the personality of each of the primates. A "portrait" of the Benson family, *Genesis and Exodus* by David Williams, was published in 1979, and a biography of the archbishop's wife by Rodney Bolt was published in 2011, *As Good as God, as Clever as the Devil*. Both usefully supplement A. C. Benson's substantial work.

Edward White Benson was nominated to the primacy by W. E. Gladstone, then serving for the second time in the premiership. The only other bishop who appeared to be a serious contender was Harold

Browne, the Bishop of Winchester, of whom the Queen did approve, and with whom Tait would have been content. Browne was eliminated from consideration because Gladstone, aged seventy-three, described the seventy-one-year-old bishop as "no longer equal to such duties as the primacy would entail", and he carried out successfully the difficult job of informing Browne. When the next Canterbury vacancy occurred, Browne was dead, and Frederick Temple, then aged seventy-five, was considered to be equal to the duties of the primacy by a younger prime minister. Despite Tait's desire that Browne should follow him, the dying archbishop also regarded Benson as suitable, even though decades earlier, when Bishop of London, he had rejected a suggestion by A. P. Stanley that Benson could be his domestic chaplain. Unusually, there was a priest who was not a bishop but was thought to be a candidate for the archbishopric. He was Richard William Church, the distinguished Dean of St Paul's, friend of some of the original Tractarians, a man whom Gladstone regarded highly. He had, however, previously informed Gladstone that it was "out of the question" that he would ever accept any episcopal appointment. In 1882, Dean Church knew that "the newspapers have been taking liberties with my name". But it was not only newspapers; some of his friends thought he would be a very good choice. Church himself, however, maintained that Benson would be the ideal candidate: "he is quiet, and he is enthusiastic, and he is conciliatory, and he is firm."[289] Although he did not say so in the biography of his father, Arthur Benson in *Trefoil* (published in 1923) saw the appointment rather differently, concluding that his father had not been a suitable person to be archbishop but had accepted the primacy because of "what had always been a temptation of his, the love of ruling". Arthur Benson also thought that his father's lifelong propensity towards depression was exacerbated in his later years by the stresses of the primacy.

In Archbishop Benson's Canterbury years can be seen the development of a good example of the type of episcopal and archiepiscopal ministry with which the post-Victorian Church of England has become familiar. Benson was conscientious in his progress around his diocese, particularly in his Truro ministry, but to his friend B. F. Westcott he complained that "diocesanism is a new force of dissent as virulent as Congregationalism ... if every shepherd is to tell his own tale alone, we shall be cut off in detail." Westcott did not give the circumstances that led to Benson's heartfelt cry, and the archbishop himself did not let such a feeling show in his travels around the parishes. He was probably complaining about the increase of conflicting calls upon his time in a period when the Archbishop of Canterbury was required to give national leadership to an increasingly vigorous Church. Further, there was the increasing international commitments of the Archbishop of Canterbury relating to the growth of Anglicanism as a worldwide Communion. The Lambeth Conferences of 1867 and 1878 were a clear demonstration of this, and Benson enthusiastically involved himself in the 1888 Conference and in preparing for 1896. The House of Lords continued to demand and receive the archbishop's time, but the legislative and secular aspects of the work of the archbishopric had begun to decline, a process unwittingly accelerated perhaps by Benson's evident unease in the Lords.

Edward White Benson shared the same names as his father; their middle name was a homage to an eighteenth-century benefactor of the family.[290] The future archbishop was born on 14 July 1829 in Birmingham and was the eldest of a family of eight children, although two had died young. The elder E. W. Benson was a scientifically minded businessman, who had inherited what his grandson was to call a "modest competence". In 1838, in partnership with some friends, he built a factory and began to manufacture white lead. Benson senior was always reluctant to discuss money, and the venture failed in 1842. This catastrophe was compounded for his family by his death the following year, aged forty-three. Consequently, the future archbishop knew bereavement and straightened circumstances as a very young man.

After the collapse of the business, the family lived in a small house within the abandoned "works", and the children were able to do as they wished among the buildings. Young Benson was already pious and made an oratory in a disused room, an indication of his later fascination in liturgical matters, although in later years his churchmanship was difficult to define; Arthur Benson said it was "not mystical, but of a disciplinary and liturgical type".[291] At around the age of fourteen, he decided that the ordained ministry would be his life's work. He was fortunate that a benefactor enabled his mother to continue with his education at King Edward's School, Birmingham. One of Benson's contemporaries at the school who became a lifelong friend was Joseph Barber Lightfoot (1828–1889), who was consecrated Bishop of Durham in 1879, when Benson had been at Truro for about two years. Another, slightly older, friend from Birmingham days was Brooke Foss Westcott (1825–1901), who was to become Lightfoot's successor at Durham in 1890. The work of the three friends was a significant partnership in the life of the Church of England in the late nineteenth century. Benson, however, made his contribution more as a result of his position in the Church of England for, although gifted, he did not share the same profundity of scholarship as his two friends. Their headmaster was James Prince Lee (1804–1869), later to become the first Bishop of Manchester in 1848; his influence on Benson was lasting. Lee's career as a headmaster was outstandingly successful, but his episcopate was not, being marred by acrimony, litigation, and increasing intolerance.

Benson was a conscientious pupil and went from Birmingham to Trinity College, Cambridge. However, whilst still an undergraduate Benson had to deal with a double family tragedy. His sister Harriet had died of typhus in her mother's arms in May 1850, and, before the funeral, Mrs Benson died unexpectedly in her sleep. As the eldest of the family, it fell to E. W. Benson to make arrangements, not only for the funerals but also the care of his younger siblings. It was discovered that Mrs Benson had virtually no money left. Benson had previously forbidden his mother from starting her own business using her dead husband's assets. One of his cousins, Christopher Sidgwick "of Skipton", and other members of his mother's family gave the bereaved family generous help, but Benson rejected an uncle's offer of help for his younger brother, including to make him his heir, on the grounds that the potential benefactor was a Unitarian (as Benson's mother had been originally). Benson would not tolerate his younger sibling living with people of such beliefs. At this time, Edward Benson was still an undergraduate but had enough grace to regret if his side of the correspondence was "bigoted"; it was, and he was convicted by extracts from it quoted by Arthur Benson in the biography.

Throughout his adult life, Benson suffered from bouts of depression, and the experience of his early years may have contributed to that affliction. However, back at Cambridge, there was another benefactor, the Bursar and later Vice-Master of Trinity, Francis Martin, who made it possible for Benson to continue his studies despite his reduced circumstances. A lasting friendship developed between the two, and Francis Martin was generous to other members of Benson's family, providing dowries of five hundred pounds each for Benson's sisters.[292] Later, he also remembered Benson in his will. Benson graduated in 1852 with the added distinction of winning the Senior Chancellor's Medal. The news was brought to him in Bristol, while he was staying with one of his Sidgwick aunts, by Francis Martin, who travelled there for the purpose; years later Benson named his first son Martin as a sign of affection and respect for his friend. In 1854, Benson travelled on the Continent with J. B. Lightfoot and in Rome saw Pope Pius IX, who seemed keen to give audiences to pious young Anglicans, for H. P. Liddon had a similar experience a couple of years before.

After graduating, Benson was offered employment as an assistant schoolmaster at Rugby School by Tait's successor as the headmaster, E. F. Goulburn. He accepted on the understanding that he would have time available to read for his Cambridge Fellowship. He found his Rugby way of life congenial, and although elected a Fellow of Trinity in his first term at Rugby, he never went into residence. In 1854, he was ordained deacon by James Prince Lee at Bury, and in 1856 he was ordained priest in Ely Cathedral. Goulburn left Rugby in 1857, after a relatively ineffective tenure at the school. Goulburn eventually became Dean of Norwich but was followed as headmaster by Frederick Temple. Benson was fortunate to establish with him a good relationship which grew into a lifelong friendship. When Temple was nominated as Bishop of Exeter, Benson had no difficulty in defending him in a letter to *The Times* concerning *Essays and Reviews*, even though he disliked the rest of the book.[293] Temple was still at Exeter when Benson became the Bishop of Truro and, although the older of the two, was to be Benson's successor at Canterbury in 1897, the last Archbishop of Canterbury of Queen Victoria's long reign.

Edward White Benson was an energetic man who loved riding and was already described as "masterful". As a schoolmaster, his powerful and domineering personality began to be revealed. He earned a reputation for sternness as well as competence but was feared by staff and pupils because of his temper and his readiness to beat the boys. At first, he lived in lodgings but was soon invited to make his home with a widowed Sidgwick aunt and her sister, along with several cousins. They had just moved to Rugby to facilitate the education of her sons. Benson's own sister Ada also resided there. Ada Benson was described as "a clever attractive girl . . . fully determined as himself" by Benson's first biographer, her nephew, who perhaps unwittingly also provided an insight into E. W. Benson's character when he continued, "my father, though not even nominally the head of the house, naturally dominated a society in which he lived."

As early as October 1849, when Benson had first met his young cousin, Mary Sidgwick (1842–1918), he had described her in a letter to his mother as "a sweet little girl", who, he said, was knowledgeable about biblical history, English history, geography, drawing, and Latin grammar; Benson concerned himself with Mary's education, and his interests became her dominating concern. By 1852, when he began work at Rugby, Mary Sidgwick was ten years old, and Edward Benson was in his early twenties. They were inevitably brought into closer proximity when Benson moved in with her family. He decided that he loved her and resolved that eventually he would marry her. He recorded his affections in his diary, as their son put it, in "many entries too sacred for quotation".[294] It is clear that Benson submitted Mary, whom everyone called Minnie, to a great deal of pressure. David Williams, in *Genesis and Exodus*, made the plausible suggestion that Benson's attentions at such an early age affected her psychological development. When she was eleven, he told her startled mother of his feelings, declaring that he knew he must wait. Benson's precipitant declaration is not, perhaps, as strange as it seems to later generations, because the age of consent for girls in England was twelve until 1851, when it was raised to thirteen. Mrs Sidgwick expressed reluctance to permit the relationship; she repeatedly refused his frequent requests that he might speak to the girl about his feelings. Bolt, in *As Good as God, as Clever as the Devil*, gives a detailed account of Mrs Sidgwick's attempts to divert Benson's attention away from her young daughter, but he was not to be dissuaded, and extracted Mrs Sidgwick's eventual consent to talk to Minnie about their future together when she was twelve. He told her that he acknowledged she was too young to "make any promise" but said that he would wait for her. The young Minnie knew that she must become more serious, or else Edward ... would be disappointed with her. She admired him, she revered him, she was not ever the least afraid of him, as many others were, but was she at all in love with him? She was happiest, she confessed, when she knew he was happy, but not necessarily when she was with him.[295]

Their engagement was eventually announced on her seventeenth birthday. Fred Benson, always devoted to his mother, said that his father placed an "intolerable burden" on the girl and wondered about his parents' relationship. Arthur Benson also tried to be discreet, but, writing of his parents' marriage, he recorded, "my father had an intense need of loving and being loved; his moods of depression, of dark discouragement, required a buoyant vitality in his immediate circle." Arthur Benson also thought there was a fundamental incompatibility between his parents; he was pained on reading his mother's diary after her death, "because it shows how little in common they had and how cruel he was."[296]

Frederick Temple officiated at the marriage of Minnie Sidgwick and the thirty-two-year-old Benson on 23 June 1859 at Rugby, the year after Benson had moved from the school. Benson's biographer son recorded that at Rugby, "about 1857 my father's health began to break down: he was attacked by bad neuralgia and general nervous prostration", and a doctor suggested that he should leave Rugby, although, apart from his depressive interludes, there were few references to poor health in later times.[297] It is clear that he was a domineering husband, although he came to see that he needed Minnie's support more than she needed his, and he turned a blind eye to his wife's strong attraction to members of her own sex. As the years passed, she had many profoundly intense relationships with her special women friends. The most intimate and long lasting was with Lucy Tait, the infant survivor of the Tait family tragedy in 1856. So close was she to Minnie Benson that she was invited by the archbishop to live with the Bensons as a member of their family shortly after the death of their daughter Nellie in 1890, and she remained for the rest of Mrs Benson's life. On the couple's return from a honeymoon in Switzerland, Benson threw himself into his duties as the first headmaster of Wellington College with his customary energy and attention to detail.

Minnie was desperately miserable but supported him to the best of her own considerable ability; many years later Gladstone said she was "the cleverest woman in England", then he corrected himself: Mrs Benson was "the cleverest woman in Europe".[298]

When Frederick Temple succeeded Goulburn at Rugby, he had recognized Benson's vigour and abilities. In 1858, Temple recommended Benson, who was not yet thirty, to Prince Albert as a candidate for the headmastership of Wellington College.[299] The college was a new foundation and opened in 1859. It was initiated by the Prince as a lasting memorial to the Iron Duke, who had died in 1852. It was planned as a place where impecunious orphaned sons of military officers could be educated, and the funds raised for a permanent memorial to the duke were appropriated to the venture. Despite enjoying the support and friendship of the Prince, and later Queen Victoria, Benson always felt that he did not have the complete confidence of the governors (Disraeli attended one meeting and never went again). The governors' caution may, in part, have been due to the relative youth of the Prince's nominee at the time of his appointment. They may also have feared that his success in developing Wellington as a public school with a high reputation would overwhelm the original intention of the founders, but Benson's recognition of the need to expand the pupil base of the college helped to ensure its survival and rapid prospering. His feeling of unease at governors' meetings persisted, and over the years he frequently told his wife that he expected to be dismissed.

In his fourteen years as headmaster, Edward Benson worked hard to establish the reputation of Wellington College as a public school, despite the low levels of achievement of some of the early pupils. He tackled his responsibilities vigorously but was sometimes afflicted by his underlying depression. A problem for Benson was the Prince Consort's ambition that the school should not simply follow the public-school pattern, which Benson believed to be essential. The Prince had required Benson to visit Germany and study the education methods there, but he was unimpressed and complained to Lightfoot that the visit had been "dullish". Indeed, E. F. Benson later wrote that "he came back with a profound conviction that English methods were vastly superior to those he had gone abroad to study".[300] Prince Albert had no doubt expected

Wellington to follow German and Prussian methods under Benson; if so, he was to be disappointed. Benson was his own man and had sufficient self-confidence to take the college in the direction he thought best, yet he did not lose the trust of the royal couple as he did so. The school opened with just under eighty pupils on 20 January 1859, and the Queen soon visited with Prince Albert. Bishop Samuel Wilberforce preached at the ceremony of the consecration of the chapel, finishing preparing his sermon in the vestry as the congregation, including the royal couple, gathered in the chapel and waited.[301]

Benson soon recognized that the school was essentially underendowed, substantial though the Wellington memorial fund had been, and that fuelled his determination to establish the college as a public school, and thereby increase the fee income; coincidently it established his reputation as a leader and man of business. At Wellington, the curriculum was very similar to that of Arnold's Rugby, although chemistry, French, and German were included through the influence of Prince Albert, a concession to his hope that the college would break away from the traditional classical education of British public schools.

The headmaster was typically in the tradition of strict disciplinarian headmasters and was often impatient with the boys. Arthur Benson wrote:

> his severity had in it something painful, because it was with him, though he did not fully realize it, so unnecessary; he could have ruled by the tongue, and yet he did believe in and use corporal punishment to a conspicuous degree.

Benson never won the affection of the boys because of that severity. Another aspect of the headmaster's character was his aesthetic side, and it was much engaged in the development of the school. He was appointed before the building work was finished and involved himself in its design. Characteristically he was particularly interested in the college chapel, and personally designed some of the stained-glass windows in such a way as to encourage the pupils to work out for themselves the biblical themes depicted. Amusingly, years later on a visit, he admitted to his diary that he could no longer remember what some of the windows illustrated and confessed that he was unable to "read" them! He worked out the details for the liturgical arrangements of the chapel, described in his own words and quoted at length in A. C. Benson's biography.[302] He even compiled a hymn book himself, supervising the musical content even though he had no skill as a musician. College life on Sundays revolved round the chapel, beginning with a service at 9.00 a.m. and ending with another in the evening.[303]

—

It was during his middle years at Wellington that Benson became acquainted with Christopher Wordsworth, formerly Headmaster of Harrow, when one of the latter's sons, John (later to be Bishop of Salisbury), became an assistant master for a short period in 1866. The acquaintance had already blossomed into friendship when Christopher Wordsworth became Bishop of Lincoln in 1869; initially he declined the bishopric, and Benson was among those who persuaded him to change his mind. Eventually, Benson even got Wordsworth to contribute a mosaic of St Cyprian to the chapel at Wellington. Benson was made one of Wordsworth's chaplains for examining candidates for ordination, and Temple, who had become Bishop of Exeter in the same year, also made him an examining chaplain. By that time Benson had been at Wellington for more than a decade, and he grew restless. He had long believed that he would find "cathedral work" congenial and saw that there did exist a valid and particular ministry for cathedrals within the Church of England, despite a general belief at the time that they had nothing to offer. His conviction of the relevance of cathedrals was expressed in an article about cathedral ministry published in the *Quarterly Review*; later he contributed to a collection of essays on the subject in 1878, edited by Dean Howson of Chester.[304] Even later, he articulated his opinion when preaching in Norwich Cathedral on 1 May 1894. He said: "the cathedral exists to pour ... virtues upon our souls, to breathe ... sanctities over our faces. It is no museum; it is no historical monument; it is the House of God. Outside we have to practice what we have learned within." Wordsworth discovered that they shared similar views about cathedral ministry, and so invited him to become Canon Chancellor at Lincoln in 1873. There was not much doubt about his decision to accept the residentiary canonry, but Benson did claim to hesitate before doing so, saying he needed to consult "two friends and my dear wife". The unidentified friends were almost certainly Lightfoot and Westcott, and both advised acceptance. "My mother was away in Germany for her health", her son recorded.[305] Mrs Benson was indeed unwell, although Arthur Benson said no more in the biography. She had had some sort of breakdown and had gone to Wiesbaden to visit Christopher Benson and his family. Minnie Benson's diary recorded her distress, and Bolt explored the circumstances in *As Good as God, As Clever as the Devil*. Her husband was fearful that she might not return to him, but she did eventually after many anxious letters. Before her return, Benson accepted the canonry and told Wordsworth that his wife had "always and eagerly loved the every thought of a cathedral home", but "if that opinion is adverse . . . I will communicate by telegraph, and I will act upon it entirely", although it is unlikely that he would have accepted his wife's veto if she had tried to exercise it. He moved to Lincoln before Mrs Benson returned.

When the appointment was made, however, he complained privately that his income was reduced by at least half as a result of the move; this was of some importance, as he and Minnie had six children. When Benson went to Lincoln, the widely held opinion that cathedrals were notoriously irrelevant places of clerical repose was already beginning to change, as cathedrals all responded to the energetic Victorian world. As the externally calm life of the Bensons at Lincoln gathered way, the energetic Benson tackled his work with his customary gusto. He first had to adjust to his new situation; as a residentiary canon Benson was part of a group and not in charge, as he had been at Wellington for fourteen years. The Dean of Lincoln, J. W. Blakesley (1872-1885), was more cautious than his new canon chancellor and tried to restrain Benson's more energetic ideas and his tendency to dominate, but Benson ploughed ahead with his plans. He loved the "stately devotion", as his son described it, and notwithstanding the ancient nature of the cathedral foundation he managed to function as an innovator. Lincoln gave him the opportunity to put his ideas into effect and to make a contribution to the Church which was greater than the simply local aspects of his new ministry. Lectures, Bible studies, and night schools for men and boys (with up to 400 attendees) were initiated by Benson. His greatest Lincoln achievement was, however, the establishment of a theological college, which, with two students, began life in 1874 as Scholae Cancelarii, and served the Church of England for well over a century. Benson sought to establish working relationships with parochial clergy in the Diocese of Lincoln, and Mrs Benson later formed a passionate friendship with the wife of an older ordinand whom she nicknamed "Tan", and another with a woman named Ellen Hall.[306] Benson accepted invitations to preach in parish churches and elsewhere. On at least one occasion he preached at Windsor in the presence of the Queen; there he spent time with Gladstone. He was also a preacher at Westminster Abbey "on three not very auspicious occasions". An undated anecdote about his experience was recorded by E. F. Benson in *As We Were*:

> (i) The first time I preached in the Abbey, I lost my voice, so nobody could hear me.
> (ii) The second time there was six inches of slush, and violent rain after snow, so there was nobody to hear me.
> (iii) The third time, tomorrow, owing to the fog I believe there will be no light in the sky, and so there will be no one to see me.[307]

When he was archbishop, however, it was crowded with listeners eager to see if "I should stimulate church hatred" on 30 June 1889.

Such an able and energetic man as E. W. Benson was soon to be considered for appointments beyond Lincoln. In 1875, he rejected a suggestion that he should submit his name as a candidate for the Hulsean Professorship at Cambridge, on the probably valid grounds that he was not intellectually suitable for such an appointment. He declined the Bishopric of Calcutta, suggested to him informally in May 1876, because he felt that he should not leave behind Minnie Benson and their children, the oldest of whom, Martin, was only sixteen. Not only were those considerations relevant but, despite his depression and his anxiety about his health, he was happy in his busy life in the city, cathedral, and diocese of Lincoln. That sense of domestic, pastoral, and capitular contentment was not destined to last. It was apparent to many that an illustrious future was likely to be Benson's. One friend, Canon Crowfoot, wrote later to

Benson's son, "Lincoln came between Wellington and Truro. At Lincoln the headmaster was gradually transformed into the bishop."[308]

When the Bishopric of Truro was offered to Benson in December 1876, he was more prepared for the episcopate than even his public ministry had suggested. For some years, he had been making a special study of the work of Cyprian, bishop of the prosperous North African city of Carthage for about ten years until his martyrdom in the year 258 under the persecution ordered by the Emperor Valerian. Cyprian left a considerable archive: 111 letters and about a dozen treatises. Over the years Benson became completely familiar with this surviving work. He had begun at some point during the Wellington years. The suggestion to study Cyprian was made by Lightfoot, as A. C. Benson reported in his *Prefatory Note* to his father's "big book" (a phrase that the archbishop himself used in relation to the finished work).

> When he was Headmaster of Wellington College, he found that his professional work was so absorbing that he felt himself losing sight of study, of erudition, of antiquity, and resolved . . . to undertake some definite work, which might provide both a contrast to and illustration of modern tendencies and recent problems.[309]

Benson was a good scholar, although not as profound as his friends Westcott and Lightfoot. He devoted his spare time for much of his life to Cyprian. He planned that it should appear as a book, which "he had promised his patient publishers should be ready in six months for certain, but which was to occupy him for twenty-two more years instead, and still lacked at his death its final revision".[310]

In the third century, Carthage was an important North African city of ancient origin and a significant centre of population. Its bishop was a Christian leader of international significance in the Roman Empire. Cyprian was wealthy and had been a lawyer before his conversion in the year 246. Benson always had in his study what his son called a "Cyprian table", where he was able to leave his work undisturbed at times, when he was perforce unable to attend to what was, in effect, a hobby. Sometimes weeks passed between opportunities to work on Cyprian, but Benson always returned to him, and recognized that it helped keep his many activities in proportion. His book, *Cyprian: his life, his times, his work*, was completed only shortly before his death and was posthumously published in 1897, after being finally edited by A. C. Benson. The study of Cyprian ran through so much of his life that it was a permanent influence upon his approach to his episcopal work. It is appropriate to examine his study of Cyprian for the light it sheds on Benson's understanding of episcopacy and authority.

His approach is revealed by his useful chronological table of dates, names of important consuls and particularly emperors, and then "events", and finally Cyprian's treatises and letters. Benson's introductory chapter was given the title "Carthage and her society". Its tone of immediacy and almost delight confirms it was written late in the life of the project, soon after Benson's visit to North Africa in 1891. The trip, wrote Arthur Benson, was "to him a kind of pilgrimage, though but for my mother's urging he would never have gone to the places where in thought he had so often dwelt". Later he continued, "it was this journey which enabled him to finish in more detail his chapter on the cities of north Africa and to give so vivid a description of Carthage in his *Cyprian*."[311] The rest of the book, which comprised eleven chapters and is probably about 250,000 words in length, is partly chronological and partly thematic in its arrangement, so the following can only be the merest summary. Cyprian's ministry came at "The Last of the Long Peace", a time when a lengthy period of freedom from persecution had been enjoyed by Christians, and Benson used that phrase as the title of his first substantive chapter. Under the Emperor Decius, who reigned from 249 to 251, that peace ended in persecution. The Christian population was unprepared for such exigencies, and many believers lapsed from their faith and worshipped the imperial cultus. This, perhaps understandable, behaviour created great difficulty when such persons sought also to worship as Christians. Two approaches were in contention: one rigourist and exclusivist and the other more humane, a willingness to re-admit after appropriate penance. Cyprian, like other bishops, had to maintain some sort of equilibrium, and he sought to accommodate penitents, many of whom had only denied their faith after suffering cruelly. A more recent scholar observed of Cyprian that "his approach was practical and even legalistic, owing much to analogies borrowed from Roman law";[312] this was unsurprising when Cyprian's background is recalled. It commended itself to Benson, because his cast of mind was also practical and, although he was not a lawyer, he recognized the necessity for probity. The North African policy did not commend itself to the Church in Rome, particularly under Pope Stephen. From Rome, said Benson, there came "no request that he should reconsider his judgment, or recognize theirs. They simply reversed his verdict and regarded their reversal as final." Cyprian and his fellows sent a long reply to Rome, which "treats the decision of the Bishop of Rome as simply and gravely mistaken, and therefore to be set aside".[313]

Cyprian himself was exiled or had moved from Carthage at the behest of those who did not want to lose his leadership to martyrdom, but his absence did not still his pen. Because of the importance of Carthage as a city, the diocese was a leader among those of its locality, and Cyprian soon became sufficiently authoritative for him to be able to call five councils of bishops over the decade of his episcopate; one such council, in the year 256, was attended by eighty-seven of the approximately one hundred incumbent bishops in the area. Cyprian held that the Church was founded on the bishops, and Benson himself recognized the importance of a phrase of Cyprian's regarding the cooperation of the episcopate; theirs was a unity held together by "the cement of mutual concord". Cyprian also believed that each diocese is a microcosm of the whole Church, and, although each bishop enjoys autonomy, to him it was vital that they worked together for the common good. Benson, like his master, held to a similar view. This was seen in a specific instance, when Bishop Edward King faced ritualistic allegations, which will be examined below. Then Archbishop Benson sat as the only judge, assisted by episcopal "assessors".

At times, the Church in Rome continued to endeavour to overrule Cyprian and the North African dioceses and congregations, so the question of authority was inevitably behind some of his thinking and writing. Cyprian did not concede to Rome any juridical primacy or any right to determine how he dealt with believers who had lapsed under persecution. Rather he acknowledged Rome as a starting point for unity and "the leading Church". In Benson's book this led to chapter IV, entitled " . . . of the Unity of the Catholic Church". He quoted Cyprian: the "tangible bond of the Church's unity is her one united episcopate, an Apostleship universal yet only one." He developed this statement with references to the Old Testament and to St Paul, and Benson followed with another quotation from Cyprian, where the saint drew on the natural world for his metaphors. Benson described it as a "famous and beautiful passage on the natural analogies of this spiritual unity".

As is well-known, Cyprian was martyred in September 258, having refused to go once again into exile. His courage at his execution became a lasting inspiration to suffering Christians, and Benson asserted that "to the victorious firmness and sweet persuasiveness of Cyprian it was due that in his age Christianity did not melt into an ethnic religion or freeze into a sect".[314]

Benson's book reveals its slow and prolonged gestation; indeed, Benson wrote in his diary in 1896 about sending to the publisher some material that "certainly cannot have been later (if so late) than 1865, and I have today sent that originally written list and notes, with fresh notes made today . . . So that my copy is at least 30 years apart in its work." However, there is no doubt that Benson's study of Cyprian increased his theological insight, and it provided a welcome change from his customary work. In practical reality it informed his own episcopate and brought insights from history to bear upon the problems of the Victorian Church of England.

—

As prime minister it was Disraeli (in the same year that he was ennobled as Lord Beaconsfield) who invited Benson to become the first Bishop of Truro. The diocese had been created by an Order in Council dated 15 December 1876, but that was the end of a lengthy process, and Disraeli's letter had come a few days before. It was opened by Benson in Lincoln only minutes after telling his wife of his contentment; his "own impulse was to refuse. He did not think that he ought to leave his Lincoln work so soon."[315] The appointment was the most significant ecclesiastical appointment of Lord Beaconsfield's second term as prime minister, and it received the warm approval of the Queen, who liked Benson as a result of the confidence placed in him by Prince Albert over Wellington College. Many of his friends and contemporaries expected him to go to the See of Rochester, which was vacant as a result of the aged Bishop Claughton's decision to move from there to the newly created Diocese of St Albans. However, the Bishopric of Truro was a post with a great deal to be done. E. W. Benson was aged only forty-eight at the time of his consecration, and the work was attractive and gave much scope to his powerful personality, and he rejoiced to be in charge once again. The Diocese of Truro was almost coterminous with Cornwall and was created from the large and ancient Diocese of Exeter. The longstanding friendship between Benson and Temple meant that the latter was pleased to have him as his episcopal "neighbour". Stanley, by then the Dean of Westminster, told the prime minister in a private conversation, "It is an excellent appointment. The Bishop of Truro is a very old friend of the Bishop of Exeter, and therefore they are sure to work well together."[316] In earlier centuries there had been a diocese in Cornwall, but it had been merged with Exeter before the Norman Conquest. The revival of the ancient Cornish see, to be based on the county town of Truro, appealed to Benson's antiquarian instincts, and the new work was to exercise fully his considerable abilities. He had shown his skill at establishing a new institution at Wellington and had shown much initiative in his canonry. He was a good candidate to lead a nascent diocese, although he told Lightfoot of his concern that the stipend was barely adequate "for a person without a private fortune", echoing his earlier concern as a canon. Another insight into Benson's personality can be glimpsed in the arrangements made for his accommodation. With the cordial assent of the Vicar of Kenwyn, for whom a new house was provided, he chose to live in Kenwyn vicarage. About a mile outside Truro, it was considered to be too large for a vicarage even in those more spacious days and had been under consideration for use as an episcopal residence from before Benson's appointment. Nevertheless, despite its size, Benson wanted more room, and he was able to use a special fund which had been set up in Cornwall in anticipation of the formation of the new diocese. Two additional wings were built with a library, new kitchens, and stables. The old kitchen was converted into a chapel with, he wrote to a daughter, "colours very soft and very quiet, and yet rich, and the screen, our only bit of *form*, very taking." Even so, Benson and his family lamented that, "with these additions the house is hardly of adequate size." With an eye to historical associations, Benson named the house *Lis Escop*, old Cornish for "Bishop's Court". E. W. Benson's episcopal consecration took place at St Paul's Cathedral on 25 April 1877. His oldest friend, Lightfoot, preached at the service, and the bishop designate was presented to Archbishop Tait for consecration by two other episcopal friends, Bishop Wordsworth of Lincoln and Frederick Temple. When he was enthroned in St Mary's Church, Truro, on 1 May 1877, the service was conducted by Frederick Temple.

However, a personal tragedy early in his Cornish episcopate left him permanently damaged emotionally and psychologically. Martin Benson, his first son and the apple of his eye, had been born in 1860; Westcott and Lightfoot were the boy's godfathers. He was a schoolboy of great promise at Winchester when he died relatively suddenly in February 1878. He was seventeen, and the cause of his sudden death was probably meningitis. Benson struggled to reconcile the disaster to his faith, and the moving correspondence quoted in A. C. Benson's biography reveals the costliness of his endeavours to see the will of God in what had happened. "It has changed all my views of God's work as it is to be done both in this world and the next, to be compelled to believe that God's plan for him really has run on sweetly, and rightly for him and for all—and yet—he is dead."[317] The parents' grief was acute, but Mrs Benson seemed to bear it better; the bishop's tendency to depression meant that he never adjusted completely to the loss. Benson wrote to his old school friend Frederick Wickenden, with whom he had also been at Cambridge, "We are learning not to withhold him from God in our hearts, and my dear wife is the mothers' example." An immediate way in which Benson tried to cope with the loss was by writing, a week after the tragedy, a lengthy and poignant account of Martin's life and death. This was noticed by David Newsome in *Godliness and Good Learning* as providing insights into Victorian domestic life and of the high emotion and idealism which was typical of the period and very much a part of E. W. Benson's personality. Whenever possible, in later years they visited Martin's grave on the anniversary of his death, and their sadness remained real for the rest of their lives. David Newsome was correct in the assertion that Benson never really understood why Martin had died. This is confirmed when, a decade later, on Benson's sixtieth birthday, in 1889, he wrote in his diary of his "inexpressible" grief for his son and made the comment, "to see into that will be worth dying."

Eventually, despite his great capacity for work he began to find the "languid climate" of Cornwall a trial. His depression and the bereavement exacerbated and deepened his self-questioning and self-doubt, but these feelings were concealed from his public life. Anglicanism was weaker in Cornwall than in many other parts of the country, for "dissent" had thrived. Consequently, there was much to be done. The weakness of the Church was due in part to the difficulty of getting around the unmanageably large Diocese of Exeter before Cornwall was taken from it. Before the appointment of Frederick Temple as Bishop of Exeter, Devon and Cornwall had suffered as a result of the infirmity of the aged Henry Phillpotts, who had ruled the diocese for nearly forty years, from 1830–1869, very much in the earlier tradition of bishops who did not travel much around their dioceses. By 1860, his age had rendered him immobile and at the end he was bedridden. He had, however, anticipated that a Cornish diocese would eventually be created, and had arranged the residentiary canonries at Exeter in such a way that the income from one of them would be available for Cornwall.

Benson made himself read a good deal about nonconformity in preparation for his new work. Methodism, in particular, was strong but, he thought, "far narrower" in Cornwall than in Lincolnshire. The new bishop had to promote the development of parochial life and he set about travelling through his diocese, "driving on long tours", to get to know the people and places under his care. Some of the parishes had not been visited by their bishop for generations, and many of the clergy lived in poverty and were depressed by the lack of a response to their ministry. Sometimes he found parish churches to be ruinous. Occasionally, Benson took responsibility for a parish in order that the incumbent might get a holiday. As part of his strategy he held annual Diocesan Conferences. This was a new and growing practice in the Church and was intended to allow the laity to be heard in the management, but not the governance, of dioceses. The first at Truro was held in October 1877, and Benson felt that his initiative had been a good one. At that first conference, he gave an extensive address, part of which dealt with the issue of nonconformity in

Cornwall in relation to the Church of England. He was anxious to strike a positive note but was completely frank:

> We withhold not our sympathy from every company which loves the Lord Jesus Christ in sincerity and truth; and we are bounden to tenderness for our own people who have lived and laboured for higher and more delicate, as against ruder, less articulated forms of faith, remote, unknown, all but despondent. Yet our sympathy can only stimulate even while it softens our energy . . . I shall lay it down as an axiom that, irrespective of every other work of our own, and of every work done by every other body in Christ's name, it is the final and ultimate duty of this Church to provide Church worship and Church instruction wherever there is a group of our people out of reach of them.[318]

But his addresses were not simply domestic; he took his people beyond the confines of Cornwall when, for example, in the conference in October 1881, he included a reference to the Commission on Ecclesiastical Courts on which he served. On other occasions, Benson looked even further afield. His attitude to Rome, informed by his study of St Cyprian, and as will be seen in his later dealings with Lord Halifax, was distinctly cool and did not agitate the Protestantly-inclined minds of Cornish nonconformity. His personality and manner earned him the respect of many Cornish dissenters, as did his journeying around his diocese. A friend wrote after Benson's death:

> I doubt if he always satisfied the Dissenters of his being a "converted" man, for neither his mind nor lips could shape the kind of pious speech to which they attach such value. But they felt the knowledge of them and their surroundings and their history, and his interest in them, was quite boundless—and the best of them—at any rate, yielded readily to his spell.[319]

When he referred to what he called "Home Reunion" at the 1881 diocesan conference, what was in his mind was a reunion which would have seen the insights of dissenting bodies being merged into what he regarded as the greater spiritual richness and subtlety of the Church of England. Benson was completely content with the concept of the established status of the Church of England, but he felt that the nation benefitted most from the situation. His brother-in-law, Professor Henry Sidgwick, in a reminiscence provided for the biography, referred to Benson's "strong conviction of the importance of the union of Church and State", and continued, "I ought to add that this was not due to any belief in the special value of establishment to the English Church—regarded as one denomination competing with others." Rather, as the archbishop himself wrote, "what we believe as Christian citizens is that a Church freely established as it is in England, is the best mode of advancing the best interests of Religion."[320]

At the heart of his work was the task of effectively establishing an entirely new body ecclesiastic in the far west of England. It was a task which very much appealed to Benson's innovative instincts, as others noticed. Canon F. E. Carter of Canterbury, who contributed some reminiscences to the first volume of the biography, remarked: "I have often dared to think that his greatness was more apparent as Bishop of Truro than as archbishop."[321] But in both of his episcopal appointments Benson's study of Cyprian informed his mind in ways which he could adapt to the very different circumstances of his own episcopal work in the Victorian Church of England. At Truro his interests were necessarily focused upon his diocese. However, there was not the sort of commitment to developing elementary education such as Sumner had in Chester. This may have been because Parliament had in 1870 passed the so-called Forster Act, which had brought into existence a national system of elementary education to cover the gaps and inadequacies in the provision of voluntary or religious schools..[322] Some of the urgency had gone, but it is possible that there would have been more Church of England schools in the Diocese of Truro if his time there had been longer and he had been free to work at issues which were less immediately pressing. Certainly, as a young man he claimed that he wanted to teach the poor. Also, in Cornwall the relative strength of the nonconformist bodies made the concept, and the fundraising, difficult for the setting-up of Church of England schools. When he moved more into the centrality of national and Church life as archbishop, he championed the work of the

National Society and spoke in the Lords in defence of church schools. He was instrumental in the appointment, in 1886, of a Royal Commission to enquire into the working of the Education Acts of recent decades. Even so, an early practical result of his ambition with regard to education did lead Benson to set up a high school for girls in Truro, and his daughters were pupils there. He "believed firmly in the higher education of women, and from the first hoped that his daughters would have a University training—a wish that was carried out."[323] In this, he shared the view of his sister Ada, who was described by her nephew as "one of the pioneers of the High School movement". She was successively headmistress of the High Schools of Norwich, Oxford, and Bedford.

—

Part of the work which ignited Benson's enthusiasm, understandably with his interests and with his supervision of the construction of the chapel at Wellington, and his work at Lincoln, was Truro Cathedral. The Truro Bishopric Act, which had formally brought the new diocese into existence, stipulated that St Mary's Parish Church in Truro should be the cathedral church, but, characteristically, Benson felt the diocese should not "content ourselves with a magnified parish church". His biographer sums up succinctly the thinking behind Benson's ambition:

> To build a Cathedral, a holy and seemly House, as a visible sign and symbol of Church energy and influence, and a radiating centre of sacred activities, was one of the Bishop's most congenial hopes: in old days the aesthetic aspect of the question would have been paramount with him, but now he had been too long a patient disciple in the school of deeper truth to base his desire or his claim upon any but the sternest of practical reasons. A Cathedral was a necessity to efficient Church work; that it should inspire and stimulate and consecrate and bind together were potent but secondary reasons for making it, in beauty and costliness, worthy to be the first Post-reformation Cathedral.[324]

He drafted its statutes himself, a task he found very congenial, and soon inaugurated a committee for building his cathedral, with St Mary's to be incorporated into the entirely new edifice. The new bishop reasoned that the energy which had led to the creation of his new diocese could be harnessed for the good of the Church of England in Cornwall. He shrewdly asserted that the idea of building a great cathedral church which would be funded from across the whole country could be identified with that vision, but "England would not have helped to build a Parish Church". Benson omitted to mention that they already had "a Parish Church" in St Mary's. So he spoke about his scheme wherever he could. He went to see individuals and groups who might be generous, although he professed that he did not like asking for money. The cathedral in Truro was short of funds from the start, with only a low income but with heavy expenses. What it did have was somewhat erratically sourced and totalled a little less than one-tenth of the financial resources of Exeter Cathedral.

> The entire organisation was founded on (1) an Exeter canonry of £1,000 ... which they divided into two canonries; (2) a private gift from Benson to make a canon missioner at £100 per year; (3) a gift of £800 a year which Temple of Exeter gave from his stipend when the see was founded; and (4) the stipend of [the rector of] St. Mary's (under £100 a year) who continued as sub-dean.[325]

As is to be expected, he did his best to fire his diocesan conferences with enthusiasm for the plan. At the 1879 conference, Benson was pleased with the progress the diocese was making. Turning to the plans for the new cathedral, he enthused about the work of the committees on various parts of the project as presenting "a brightening and inviting view of church work. Over all this particular tint there broods a solemn light. The whole of it is grave, serious, determined. There is no dilettantism in it." He was, however, practical. The cathedral had to be appropriate; as he said, to "fit the future". And he emphasized that there should be no debt upon the Church as a whole.

The architect for the project was John Loughborough Pearson, RA. Until 1887, a temporary wooden structure stood on an adjacent site and served as a temporary cathedral. The last time it was used for cathedral worship was in 1896, by sad coincidence on the day that Benson died. It had seating for 400 people but was too cold for comfort in the winter and too hot in the summer. Benson had to set about building cathedral life from scratch, acting as dean himself, initiating the statutory daily services and even establishing a form of daily prayer, later changed to weekly, for the workmen engaged on the building work. It was in the wooden building that Benson inaugurated what was to become a permanent part of the Church of England's Christmas celebrations with a service of nine lessons and carols. He compiled the liturgy in collaboration with G. R. Sinclair, who was the cathedral organist.[326] Sinclair was seventeen years of age when Benson appointed him organist at Truro, and his later distinguished career from 1889 at Hereford Cathedral demonstrated good judgement by Benson in making an imaginative appointment. When he appointed residentiary canons, one, G. H. Whitaker, was designated Diocesan Missioner. His was the first such appointment of its type. Another canon was Arthur Mason, whom he later moved to Canterbury. Both of them were former members of Benson's staff at Wellington. He also exercised his right to appoint honorary canons, giving them stalls named after Cornish saints rather than simply numbering the stalls as in many cathedrals, and in a letter he described this as "a brilliant idea"!

Later generations were as proud as Benson that Truro was the first cathedral church to be built in England since Salisbury in 1220. The foundation stone was laid on 20 May 1880 by the Prince of Wales, in his capacity of Duke of Cornwall, with whom Benson was friendly. The bishop preached on the Sunday following at an open-air service attended by, he said, 4,000 people; many walked miles to come. He also spoke of the occasion with enthusiasm at the diocesan conference in October of that year. Pending the completion of the cathedral endowment, the bishop was designated as Dean of Truro in the measure which established the new diocese, although, some years before, he had opposed a suggestion that the role of bishop and dean should be combined in English cathedrals. He felt that bishops should be involved in cathedral life, but not in the day-to-day running of the place. But despite this conviction, this dual role appealed very much to Edward Benson as it enabled him to be involved in the progress of the building and gave an outlet to his liturgical interests and his love of detail. Indeed, his character was such

After his nomination Benson wrote a very tactful letter to Browne. The process of the appointment went smoothly. Benson's election to the office of Archbishop of Canterbury was confirmed in Bow Church on 3 March 1883, and he was enthroned in Canterbury Cathedral on 29 March 1883, having allowed his hair to grow long in what he believed to be "the tradition of the primacy"! Presumably he was pleased with the added authentication of having inherited Archbishop Howley's gold shoe-buckles, and to be placed in the quire throne which Howley had given to the cathedral, and in addition in the "marble chair" of St Augustine. In later years, particularly after the appointment of Canon Mason, Benson managed to influence the liturgical arrangements in Canterbury Cathedral; among his achievements was to have a chapel set aside for private prayer, getting the cathedral to host "quiet days", and the establishment of chapter retreats. In 1895, he secured the eastward-facing position for the celebrant to stand at the altar at the early Communion service.[330] At the time of his appointment to the primacy, Benson was aged fifty-three, but had not attained sufficient seniority at Truro as a diocesan bishop to sit in the House of Lords, so he took his seat as archbishop on 12 March 1883. He made his maiden speech in May on the Cathedral Statutes Bill, which was introduced by the Bishop of Carlisle but later failed in the Commons. It is recorded that Benson spoke rather nervously. According to Arthur Benson, it proved to be a sphere in which his father did not excel.[331] However, he supported the extension of the franchise in 1884 with a speech in the Lords which impressed Gladstone, and a few years later spoke in support of the establishment of parish councils in a debate on local government. Unlike Tait, however, he did not have the instincts to manage successfully the political aspects of the archbishopric, so his work was somewhat more ecclesiastically focused than Tait's.

The Times claimed, at the time of his death, that he had been appointed to calm the troubled waters of ritualistic controversy, which had plagued the primacy of Archbishop Tait. Apart from the immediate legacy of the archbishopric, Benson knew that he was also entering on an ancient heritage; his skills as an innovator had to be very differently directed. He was not as free to act at Canterbury as he had at Truro and at Wellington, sweeping all before him by the force of his personality and intellect. His immediate recognition of this reality caused him to hesitate for a week that it is difficult to imagine that he would not have interfered if there had been a separate person appointed as dean. It was in 1887 that, as Archbishop of Canterbury, Benson returned to Truro and consecrated the quire and the transepts of the new cathedral, although work was not finally completed until 1910 with the dedication of the west tower many years after his death.

Benson's powerfully capable personality and notable energy were ideal qualities for the pioneering work of a new diocese, but those assets were needed by the wider Church and after only six years he was invited to follow Tait at Canterbury. Despite the evidence that Tait had thought E. W. Benson could be his successor, Benson's biographer son conventionally declared "the idea never ... crossed my father's mind", although the ailing Tait is alleged to have raised the matter with him, notwithstanding the possibility that he probably had had a similar conversation with his old friend Bishop Browne, who visited him on his sickbed. The prime minister's handwritten letter offering the primacy to Benson was dated 16 December 1882, just a fortnight after Tait's death. The letter informed him that Gladstone had already obtained Queen Victoria's approval for the offer to be made, and Benson later received a personal letter from the Queen.[327] As was his practice as prime minister, Gladstone's exercise of patronage was not as influenced by political considerations as had been the case with other prime ministers, and Benson was politically of a conservative persuasion.[328] He shared the distinction of receiving preferment to Truro from the Conservative Disraeli and to the archbishopric from the Liberal Gladstone. Benson's son told the story of the Canterbury appointment:

> It was just about Christmas time that the primacy was offered to him; the first post came before breakfast, and he used to read his letters at breakfast. I remember the meal well: he read his letters as usual, made no remark, but shortly after breakfast called us into his study and told us that the offer had been made.[329]

before writing his letter of acceptance to Gladstone. Benson's new work was very different to that in Truro, but, having taken it on, he set about it with all his powers. Benson had been long aware of the more demanding nature of diocesan work than had been the case in earlier times and had been busy in Cornwall. The Archbishop of Canterbury is bishop of his diocese in Kent, but the reintroduction of suffragan bishops in 1870 meant that much of the work was undertaken by the Bishop of Dover. Edward Parry had been appointed specifically to assist Tait when he was unwell, and he continued in office under Benson until he died in 1890. Nevertheless, Benson was as conscientious in his diocesan work as his other commitments permitted and enjoyed his local work. His involvement in the cathedral was limited, as has been noted, and he had little outlet for his liturgical skills, certainly nothing similar to what he had enjoyed when he was able to combine his episcopal role with that of the dean. Two men served as Dean of Canterbury in his time, and both were opposed to liturgical innovation. In addition, there was no archiepiscopal residence in Canterbury, so with his family he lived as much as possible at Addington Palace and to a lesser extent at Lambeth Palace, and his work was heavily concentrated in the capital. Benson recognized what was being asked of him. His friend, J. A. Reeves, recalled him saying that in Cornwall he had surrounded himself with "moderate high churchmen". "'Now', he went on, 'I shall be archbishop of the *whole* Church, but' (with a bright look in his eye) 'I mean to rule.'" This was a point of similarity between the new archbishop and his hero Cyprian. The latter said, "the Church is one ... And in her we preside ... For her honour and unity we do battle." And Benson added, "such was his [Cyprian's] estimate of his duty and responsibility."[332]

An important initiative of Benson's was his success in establishing a House of Laymen to complement the revived Convocation in the governance of the Church of England: this too was at least partly inspired by his reading of the letters of Cyprian. Despite the ancient parallel, it was not appreciated by all and its legality was questioned at first, but it was an early step in recognizing that lay people should have a chance to contribute to the modern life of what he had called "the *whole* Church". It was a prophetic move which reached its fulfilment in the twentieth century with the creation of the Church Assembly and later the General

Synod. Benson's House of Laymen met for the first time on 16 February 1886. It was a significant achievement for the archbishop.

Benson's intensity and concentrated masterfulness was well known by the time he became primate, and he never worried about asserting his authority. Consequently, his archiepiscopal ministry was very different from that of his predecessor, who had ruled his clergy, in Walter Hook's phrase, "without showing" that he did so. Benson was aware of the "grandeur" of the archbishopric, but also knew that "it is chiefly by suffering and by enduring hardship, that men are able to win the greatest victories for Christ".[333] It may be that his depression and his sense of "mere emptiness" in facing his new challenge caused Benson's confidence to flag at this time, despite the determination to "rule".[334] Wisely, he invited Tait's chaplain, Randall Davidson, to continue at Lambeth as his own chaplain. Benson and Davidson formed an excellent relationship which endured throughout Benson's primacy, even though Davidson left Lambeth to become Dean of Windsor in 1883 whilst still in his mid-thirties. Benson was fully involved in Davidson's appointment to Windsor and declared his support in response to a letter from the Queen seeking his advice and written, as she said, "in the first person as I can better express myself".[335] The appointment of such a young successor to Dean Connor, who had died after only a few months in post, excited some comment, but as the archbishop replied to Queen Victoria, "with regard to his youth . . . it has the advantage of spring and freshness, while it does not carry him away into any intemperate expression . . . much less into rashness." Benson could only reply in the affirmative to the monarch's question as to whether he could manage without Davidson so early in his own primacy. In his letter to the Queen, he also observed that the new Dean of Windsor already had "a most wide and very thorough knowledge of the clergy and others", due to his years at Lambeth with Tait.[336] Davidson had been close to Archbishop Tait as his son-in-law as well as his chaplain, having married Edith Tait in 1878. He was, however, to be completely excluded from the confidence of Archbishop Temple on the death of Benson. In the meantime, however, Davidson continued to be Benson's friend and trusted advisor, and came to fill the same role ecclesiastically for the Queen; it made a very workable arrangement which lasted fourteen years. Davidson was often consulted by Queen Victoria, and she always trusted

Benson. In 1887, the Queen and the archbishop corresponded directly about plans for a service at Westminster Abbey to celebrate the fiftieth anniversary of her accession, and Davidson was also consulted by them both. Benson drew up the "Form of Prayer" himself, and the monarch later expressed her gratitude to him for it, having made, as Davidson wrote, "a few slight suggestions".

Benson was approached in 1885 by several well-to-do ladies, led by the Bensons' particular friend, Lady Tavistock, who became the Duchess of Bedford, with the suggestion that he might form a devotional study group at Lambeth for them and their friends.[337] The idea appealed greatly to Benson, because it gave him an opportunity to offer some religious teaching to a receptive audience, and in that way exercise a ministry somewhat different from the usual work of an archbishop. He enjoyed impressing female company and proposed a weekly service on Friday afternoons in Lambeth Palace Chapel, to be attended by invited individuals. He gave as much thought as he could in a busy life to choosing the subjects and preparing his addresses. It seems that eventually the practice evolved into lectures each Lent. The meetings continued for the whole of his time as archbishop, and he claimed to find them a source of mental and spiritual refreshment, describing them in 1888 as "the green pasture in this wilderness of dry work". In March 1891, the group presented an "eagle" lectern to the chapel at Lambeth, in memory of Benson's sister. The chapel was full for the event. As late as March 1896, he recorded in his diary, "3rd Lent Lecture in Chapel. It has been full each time with about 144 ladies—ladies in 'Society'", and in an address he tackled the Second Letter to the Corinthians, "trying to get them into deep waters".[338] When Queen Victoria got to hear about the meetings, she was told that the initiative had been Benson's and that his motive was to "reform Society". The much-trusted Davidson was asked to make enquiries and reported to Sir Henry Ponsonby, the Queen's Private Secretary, that the initiative had come from the ladies themselves and that there was "no sort of idea of any general scheme for the improvement of Society or anything of that kind".[339] The Queen was evidently mollified to learn that the Archbishop of Canterbury was not seeking to improve society! Nevertheless, she forbade the attendance of the Princess of Wales. This delicate situation was successfully navigated by Benson, as was another potentially more difficult one which involved the Prince of Wales. The details can be outlined briefly. At Tranby Croft, near Doncaster, a house party was disrupted by an accusation of cheating at a card game. The Prince was present, but he had known nothing of the circumstances. The dispute led to a court case with the Prince called as a witness, and the press made much of it. The Prince heard an allegation that Archbishop Benson was behind reports that the Church condemned him "as a gambler and worse". Benson was summoned to see the Prince and assured him that he had not made such claims. Somehow, he managed to talk to the Prince about the evils of gambling without alienating him. They parted amicably with the agreement that Benson would send a letter expressing his personal views and also clearing up the situation. It began:

> Sir, The utterances of various religious bodies have been so painful and ill-judged that I am anxious to assure Your Royal Highness more explicitly than seemed possible in our conversation, how entirely erroneous are any assertions that I had in any way countenanced or encouraged such tone of criticism ... My attachment to the person and honour of Your Royal Highness is so heartfelt and of such long standing that it would give me the acutest pain to think that I sympathised with [the critics'] proceedings. The Church has, I am sure, felt throughout that if there were a word to be said about the Tranby Croft affair it must be said in a perfectly different spirit and manner.[340]

Benson's letter ran on for another couple of pages and elicited a gracious reply from the Prince which brought the matter to an end. Whether the Queen knew of the exchange, Fred Benson did not reveal, but it is unlikely that the newspaper reports were not conveyed to her.

The controversy surrounding Bishop Colenso, which was described in the chapter on the archiepiscopate of Longley, reignited shortly after Benson's appointment to Canterbury, when, in June 1883, Colenso died at the age of seventy-nine. Colenso had enjoyed support within South Africa from Church people; he was held in considerable affection within his diocese. Some people, of course, agreed with his views, and there were those who felt that he had been harshly treated. Following Colenso's excommunication in 1866 by Archbishop Gray, a new diocese had been contrived which covered an area that included the entire territory of Colenso's original diocese; W. K. Macrorie had been appointed Bishop of Maritzburg and Natal, but Colenso had continued his ministry. He secured legally the Natal cathedral and diocesan endowments for his continued use. Inevitably, the supporters of Colenso, who were known as the "Church of England in Natal", were not willing to accept Macrorie's ministry. Colenso's followers included seven clergy, although Macrorie thought there were only five, and that Benson had largely over-estimated the total number of other supporters. The number of followers of Colenso were indeed small, but A. C. Benson said they were "socially influential". They applied to Benson and the Archbishop of York for the appointment of a successor, and had included the Bishops of Worcester, Manchester, London, and Liverpool in the application.

Benson believed that the best way forward would be the appointment of a bishop who would be acceptable to both sides of the dispute. By chance, the Bishopric of Bloemfontein was vacant, and Benson suggested that Macrorie should be moved. The ensuing vacancy in Maritzburg and Natal, along with the Colensoite vacancy, would have created the opportunity for the appointment of an acceptable compromise candidate. Within South Africa, however, there was some doubt as to the practicality of such a step, and the Archbishop of Cape Town feared that it might exacerbate the situation, rather than resolve it. However, Benson wrote to Macrorie, believing that he had expressed, "from your own lips", a willingness to stand aside "if England wished for a successor to Bishop Colenso who could begin freshly, unbiased by, and independent of, any section in Natal". Benson was soon disillusioned when Macrorie denied that he had said anything of the sort, and was resolved to stay in his current diocese, although he admitted to a moment of tolerating a "cowardly thought of the comparative freedom from strife which Bloemfontein offered".[341] His ultimate conviction was, "I may truly say that I have never wavered in the conviction that God's call to me is as clear as ever to remain in my post."

Foiled in his attempt to secure what he believed to be the most sensible answer to the problem, Benson called a meeting at Lambeth of the bishops whom the Colensoites had approached. Although the Archbishop of York was absent, a common mind was reached and a long letter was sent to the leader of the faction, Archdeacon Colley, who was described as the "President of the Church Council in Natal". In the letter, which all the relevant bishops signed, including the Archbishop of York, Archbishop Benson characteristically went into considerable detail and concluded:

> We have to consider, not only the immediate effect, but the possible and the even probable, consequences of such action on our part as that to which you invite us; and we cannot think that such a step would be conclusive to the welfare of the Church of Christ in South Africa, by whatsoever designation it may be known, nor to the cause of peace, unity and brotherhood, in the Christian world.[342]

The Colenso party were not pleased and sought to choose independently a successor to Colenso. They lighted upon Sir George Cox, but the archbishop refused to apply for the necessary Queen's mandate for the consecration, and they were unable to find a way legally to overturn that decision. And there the matter lay until Macrorie did resign in 1891, whereupon the Colensoites nominated someone, and again the archbishop refused to accede on the grounds that a genuine opportunity had occurred for the appointment of a candidate acceptable to both sides. Eventually, both groups agreed to accept a nominee of the Archbishop of Canterbury, who eventually chose A. H. Baynes, Vicar of Christ Church, Greenwich, a former domestic chaplain. Unsurprisingly, Baynes took some persuading and was the recipient of several detailed letters from Benson before he agreed. He was consecrated in Westminster Abbey on 29 September 1893. Baynes held office until 1901 but was not successful in uniting the two elements of the Church in South Africa, but by the time of the death of Queen Victoria in the year that Baynes resigned, there were only two Colensoite clergy left, although the schism lingered for another ten years.

—

The appointment of an Anglican bishop in Jerusalem had been a joint venture with German Lutherans under the initiative of the Chevalier Bunsen in 1841; this topic was discussed in chapter two. By the time that Benson embarked on the primacy, the Jerusalem bishopric was vacant following the death of the third holder of the office, Bishop Joseph Barclay, in 1881. There was a general consensus that the scheme had proved impracticable; in 1884, Benson himself expressed the view that it had "been of little use", and in 1886 described the bishopric as "ill-compacted". This last remark in his diary was recorded after a meeting with Canon Liddon, who was one of the most vociferous of the high church opponents of the arrangement. The grounds of their objection have already been noticed as fundamentally two-fold: first, that the joint nature of the appointment with the German Lutherans was heterodox; second, that Jerusalem was already very well-served by episcopal ministries, albeit not Anglican. The problem had been exacerbated by the personalities of Liddon and Benson, as the latter's biographer accurately observed. "The two men were by nature essentially dissimilar. To the eager practical temperament of the archbishop the subtle metaphysical element of Canon Liddon's mind was wholly antagonistic."[343] There was also the suggestion that high church people may have been disappointed that the new archbishop's appointment had not led to a greater sympathy for their views. Liddon, however, was rarely sanguine about the men appointed to the episcopate and believed that Benson had "meddled" in regard to the Jerusalem bishopric, and had also been too tolerant of those Liddon described as "the Puritans". Benson, though, believed that the local opposition to the scheme in Jerusalem, which Liddon asserted to be strong, was virtually non-existent and so he decided to proceed with a new appointment. At about the time of the announcement of the next bishop's name, Benson had to contend with an "address", signed by a number of high churchmen, but probably drawn up by Liddon, which appeared in *The Times* on 22 March 1887. Other signatories included

Dean Church of St Paul's and several heads of Oxford colleges, as well as a number of influential laymen. The nearest that it got to offering an olive branch to those who wished to appoint a successor to Bishop Barclay was a suggestion that an appointment should only be made with the concurrence of the existing Patriarch of Jerusalem. That was unlikely to commend itself to Benson, who never doubted his authority to appoint a new bishop *in*, not *of* Jerusalem. The archbishop's reservations about the original plan were, at least partially, alleviated by an important change which also offered a crumb of comfort to the signatories of the "address". The arrangement with German Protestantism was brought to an end with the new appointment, and the Jerusalem bishopric became a purely Anglican affair. In addition, another objection was at least partially acknowledged when Benson wrote letters of introduction to the Patriarchs of Jerusalem, Constantinople, and Antioch, although he stopped short of asking for their approval. Archbishop Benson's personal involvement in the bishopric in Jerusalem came to an end with the consecration of George Popham Blyth, formerly Archdeacon of Rangoon, to the post. He continued in office until 1914, long after Queen Victoria's reign had ended and all her Archbishops of Canterbury were dead and buried.

—

In the weeks before the Lambeth Conference of 1888, Archbishop Benson became embroiled in a legal nightmare which went on for more than two years. The situation was not of his own making, although Benson's handling of it elicited criticism which was probably deserved. The case concerned the Bishop of Lincoln's ritual practices, and tested Benson's political skills and moral courage. It also demonstrated his scholarly ability to sift through evidence and revealed that his fascination with detail was combined with an ability to assess its relevance and to reach a reasonable conclusion. In all, he emerged well from the case, which revealed a good deal of his character. It appealed to his fascination with liturgical minutiae but revealed his unattractive strand of self-importance. It was, in the opinion of Arthur Benson in his biography of his father, "indubitably the most important contribution to Ecclesiastical History in my father's life." At the time it attracted widespread publicity and raised passions across the whole Church and was important because it virtually removed the spectre of prosecution from the activities of high churchmen. More than a century later, it seems remarkable that such an issue should have been so important, but the case strengthened the liberty of the Church of England in its relation to the nation. By avoiding the pitfalls that lay around Tait's unsatisfactory Public Worship Regulation Act, it was an important part of the process of establishing liturgical freedom in the conduct of public worship.

Benson was regarded as a "moderate" high churchman and described his own churchmanship with that adjective; certainly, he had some sympathy for high church practice. By contrast, the Bishop of Lincoln from 1885 to 1910, Edward King, was known specifically as a high churchman in his own right. Indeed, his appointment to Lincoln had been contentious for some; the Archdeacon of Lincoln had refused to attend King's formal election, as did the Dean, although the latter was unwell and nearing the end of his life. He died on 18 April 1885 and was replaced by King's friend William Butler later in the year. Bishop King was a person of great holiness of life, tolerant of ritualistic practices among his clergy and acknowledged as a bishop who cared deeply for his people and clergy whatever their churchmanship. Benson and King were both born in 1829, and so were exact contemporaries, although of very different character and background. King's leadership was self-effacing, and he did not like the limelight, but Benson seemed to enjoy the unfolding drama in which the two were involved. Both were serious and convinced Christian leaders, but Benson's mind was more of the cast of a bureaucrat and administrator; it also had a dramatic element which was wholly lacking in King. Like Benson, King had already had a distinguished career before his appointment as a bishop. He had been Vice Principal and then Principal of Cuddesdon Theological College, and afterwards Regius Professor of Moral Theology at Oxford. By the time of his appointment to Lincoln, more than a decade after the passing of the Public Worship Regulation Act, ritualism was slowly becoming less of an issue, but still had intransigent opponents to whom it was an object of horror. They wanted ritualism to be declared illegal, along with the doctrines such actions implied. They believed that the prosecution of offenders was the only way to preserve the Protestantism of the reformed Church of England. This was the nub of the issue.

The organization which campaigned against ritualism, and which tried to tackle King, was the Church Association, which had been founded in 1865 by a number of prominent evangelicals at the height of the ritualistic controversies. It sought specifically to ensure the maintenance of Protestant ideals, worship, and doctrine in the Church of England. It battled to prevent what it regarded as the spread of Roman Catholic beliefs and practices in the Church of England. After its successful prosecutions of a number of clergy, it was anxious to bring a "test case" in the expectation that it would be vindicated once and for all. As has been noticed in the previous chapter, the Public Worship Regulation Act gave diocesan bishops the right of veto over prosecutions for ritualism. Several had exercised that right, and King was among them; he was known to have done so in 1886 when one of the clergy from his diocese was threatened. The membership of the Church Association believed that Edward King represented, at a senior level in the Church, the very things that they abhorred. Low on funds, the Church Association nevertheless had a number of wealthy members and felt able to finance the case against King. Benson rather cynically remarked, "there is something in 'Protestant Truth' which is very concordant with wealth."[344] The motive of the Church Association in its decision to take action against Edward King was to force the courts to impose a prohibition on the ritualistic practices to which they objected, using his known practices as the basis of the case. There is some evidence that the association recognized that attacking King was a risky stratagem, but it acted in the belief that the successful condemnation of a diocesan bishop would ensure the permanent eradication of the "problem" of ritualism. The trigger for the action was the simmering discontent of Ernest de Lacy Read, a churchwarden in a parish where King had prohibited a prosecution in 1886 by the use of his veto. Read had tried to get the original case referred to the archbishop, but had failed; consequently, he was quite willing to make a common case with the Church Association and attack Bishop King.

The Church Association was the instrument of the evangelical Anglicans, but high churchmen had founded the English Church Union to promote and protect their interests. The two societies were utterly opposed, and the English Church Union supported King and his practices. Between them, said Benson in his diary on 8 June 1888, they were "set on the destruction of the Church of England, and perhaps they will succeed. Well we must stop them."[345] Shortly after writing those words, he received the Church Association's denunciation of Bishop King on 22 June 1888, and a few months later he lamented the situation when writing to Davidson, "When a horse bolts downhill it's safer to guide than to stop him . . . would that it had never begun."[346]

The Church Association presented a petition to Archbishop Benson in which it alleged that King was guilty of illegal ritual acts at celebrations of Holy Communion. The petition cited in particular that King had committed the offences in a celebration in Lincoln Minster on 4 December 1887, and at another in the parish church of St Peter at Gowts in Lincoln on 18 December. It was alleged that King faced eastward during the prayer of consecration, rather than standing at the north end of the table facing south; this meant that the "manual acts" of consecration, as required in the Book of Common Prayer, were not visible to the congregation. In addition, that there were lighted candles on the altar for purposes other than illumination, that water was mixed with wine in the chalice, that King permitted the *Agnus Dei* to be sung after the consecration prayer, and that he made the sign of the cross at the blessing at the end of the service, as he had also done at the absolution after the confession of sins; also that there was a visible washing of the communion vessels after the administration of Communion. The case was not whether King had done or authorized the actions; there was no doubt that he had. The assertion of the Church Association was that in so acting he had broken the law. It was clear from the outset that some sort of plea for toleration would have been unacceptable to the association, and that the case would have to be dealt with in court. There was a sense in which a proper trial would be an advantage for the whole Church, because in most previous ritual cases the alleged offending priest had refused to plead his case. Those instances meant that the defendants were undoubtedly guilty of contempt of court but, more importantly, it meant that it was impossible to establish whether such practices with which defendants were charged were illegal or not. Pursuing a revered bishop, whose actions were common knowledge, meant that the association could claim not only that he was guilty, but it would also show that he was indifferent to the law. Benson realized that if he heard the case himself, he could hope to clear up the question of permitted ritual once and for all. Benson was encouraged in his view that the Archbishop of Canterbury had authority to deal with the case as a result of the findings of the Royal Commission on ecclesiastical courts, set up in 1881 at Tait's suggestion, and of which Benson had been a member. He found support for his view in the opinion of the immensely learned historian Bishop William Stubbs of Chester, then of Oxford from 1889, who had also been a member of the commission.

Concerning the Lincoln case, Benson received much advice, "asked and unasked", he observed. King's biographer captured the dilemma which the Church Association presented to Archbishop Benson. Everyone wondered whether he should hear the case:

> A vast commotion arose. What would the archbishop do? Some great authorities doubted whether he possessed the requisite jurisdiction; some thought that he would be unwise to exercise it; some held that he possessed it and should exercise it by dismissing the suit; some said that, if he attempted to try the bishop, he would be restrained by the secular courts; others that, if he declined to try, the secular courts would compel him to do so. Beset by these many and conflicting difficulties, the Archbishop conferred freely with legal flesh and blood.[347]

Among those whom he consulted privately were Davidson at Windsor and Joseph Lightfoot, who believed that Benson was acutely aware of the danger of the situation for the Church, and both counselled great caution. For Benson, the situation regarding his legal competency to hear the case was complicated. If he exercised his veto, there was then a chance that he might be compelled to hear the case by the Court of the Queen's Bench, to which the Church Association was likely to appeal. High churchmen would have seen this outcome as conclusively and unacceptably Erastian: it would have proved to them that the secular courts, if they could so compel the archbishop, were authoritative over ecclesiastical courts. Bishop King's supporters were relieved that the association had not gone straight to the Queen's Bench without having petitioned the archbishop, for the same would have been true.

Notwithstanding the authority which seemed to be conferred by the recent Royal Commission, a precedent of sorts did exist of an archbishop hearing a case against a diocesan bishop, but it had been back in 1699 and the cases were so different that it could not remove all doubt. It had concerned Bishop Watson of St David's, who had been charged with simony, and there were suspicions that the judgement had been politically biased. The wise and holy Dean Church called the authority of the archbishop to act "altogether nebulous" and the precedent, "fishy". Archbishop Benson also suspected that the precedent was arguably inapplicable to the King case, despite Stubbs's assertion that it did apply. He was pleased when it proved possible to authenticate his authority by a different means. Amongst the advice he received was the suggestion that the Judicial Committee of the Privy Council should rule on whether he did have the authority to proceed to hear the complaint. Benson thought it to be good advice, even though there was doubt as to whether it was necessary to approach the Judicial Committee at all. In due course, on 3 August 1888, the committee recommended that he could go ahead. In the minds of high churchmen this ruling was irrelevant and had no bearing upon his right to proceed, for they did not believe that the Privy Council's view mattered anyway; they would have thought the same if the archbishop had been ordered by the Queen's Bench to hear the case against King. On the other hand, Benson knew that the Church Association and its friends would not be able to argue afterwards, if they disliked his findings, that the archbishop lacked the authority to hear such cases.

The prospect of hearing the case, and the likelihood that he could clear up the ritualism issue once and for all, appealed to Benson with his love of liturgy and his high opinion of archiepiscopal authority. Newspapers such as *The Times* believed that Benson would have preferred not to be obliged to hear the case, and he had said as much himself. Nevertheless, the biographies of both Benson and King unwittingly reveal a hint of relish in the archbishop's approach. His considerable ability to handle detailed matters supplemented his liturgical skill and meant that he was personally qualified, and legally obliged (at least in his own opinion), to handle the case. However, some high churchmen, of whom Dean Church and Canon Liddon were among the most distinguished, wondered if Benson realized the gravity of what he was undertaking, but it is clear that he did have an acute sensitivity towards the situation. He remembered that Cyprian saw his episcopal role as, in part, that of a judge, but he also knew that his hero consulted "presbyters, deacons and laymen" in decision-making. In his situation, Benson could only seek advice from other bishops, when the lawyers were done, so his decision to sit with six episcopal assessors was a shrewd move, although he retained decisive authority. These were Frederick Temple, by this time Bishop of London, Bishop Stubbs, Thorold of Rochester, John Wordsworth of Salisbury, Atlay of Hereford, and Browne of Winchester. The latter in the event was unable to take part, but disagreed with Benson's conviction that he was acting as sole judge, as did Stubbs; they thought the assessors should be part of the decision-making process and not merely advisory. For his part, King was advised to contest the competency of Benson's plan to hear the case, but his dislike of secular courts making ecclesiastical law would have been at the front of his mind; so King decided to let events take their course. However, as proceedings began, he declared,

> I appear before your Grace in deference to the Citation which I have received, and in accordance with my Oath of "due reverence and obedience" to your Grace and the See of Canterbury; but I appear under protest, desiring, with all respect, to question the jurisdiction which your Grace proposes to exercise.[348]

King thought that, if he were to be tried at all, the proper court would be the whole bench of bishops, sitting with the Archbishop of Canterbury in the chair. Benson, though, was wise enough to realize that the wide variety of episcopal opinions regarding ceremonial would lead to the inability to reach a meaningful decision. To Benson's mind, there was an additional reason for not making the assessors fellow judges: he would establish a precedent which reserved the responsibility of judgement to the archbishop alone. As ever, Benson was keen to preserve archiepiscopal rights.

The hearing began on 12 February 1889 in the library of Lambeth Palace and was open to anyone who cared to attend. Stubbs, who had not wanted to serve as an assessor, grumbled that it was not a court, but "an archbishop sitting in his library". Liddon commented on "the great ecclesiastical ladies", who "flitted" in and out of the place; one of these was Benson's daughter Margaret, who was unimpressed by the issue and described it as "a storm in a teacup" and a "tremendous fuss". Another of Benson's daughters, his eldest, Mary Eleanor (Nelly), was taken ill around this time and died of diphtheria at the end of November 1890, casting the archbishop into an understandable depression and the whole family into mourning. She was twenty-seven years old.

Nevertheless, the proceedings moved forward, but only slowly; but at last, on 21 November 1890, Benson delivered a judgement which "was long and learned, the fruit of much study in liturgical history". It took an hour and a half for him to do so. Benson declared that the eastward-facing celebration of Holy Communion was legal, as were the lighted candles and the mixed chalice (provided that the mixing took place before the service in private); he also declared legal the *Agnus Dei* and the ablution of the vessels at the end of the service. However, he did rule that the manual acts at the consecration should be visible (which was not possible for a celebrant to achieve facing eastwards), and he decreed that the sign of the cross should not be used. J. A. Newton, in an article in the *Ecclesiastical Law Journal* published in July 1999, noted that Benson "took for granted the continuity of the English church across the Reformation divide", something that high Anglicans "warmly endorsed".[349] Benson's judgement gave a degree of liturgical freedom to the Church of England and was another nail in the coffin of the Public Worship Regulation Act. The Church Association was still low on funds, and the case against Bishop King was its last major effort. Benson was successful in his manoeuvres, and it stands to his credit that he was willing to trust his scholarship and risk his reputation with a course of action which he hoped would enhance the peace of the Church. Dean Church later described Benson's judgement as the "most courageous thing to come from Lambeth for the last two hundred years".[350] This, as G. W. O. Addleshaw noted in 1941, was "not so much for [Benson's] decisions on the particular points at issue", but for his recognition "that the rules employed by temporal lawyers in the interpretation of statutes make nonsense when applied to the liturgy" and that the liturgy "is something living, only to be understood in the light of the Church's life and history".[351]

The Church of England was fortunate that King was a good and holy man, for he accepted the judgement. The Church Association, however, appealed to the Judicial Committee of the Privy Council, but the appeal was rejected on 2 August 1892. Inevitably, King and his high church friends did not recognize the authority of the Judicial Committee regarding ritual matters. The rejection of the appeal was a relief to Benson, because it brought the matter to an end, although a clash between the Church (or at least its high church members) and the authority of the State was prevented by King's intimation that he would respect the judgement of the Judicial Committee even if it had gone against him. The case did help Benson meet one of the expectations at the time of his appointment: that he would somehow draw a line under the more virulent quarrels over ritualism.

—

The trial of Bishop King was important for the Church of England, but it was an interlude in the life of the developing Anglican Communion. In July 1886, Benson had announced that he planned to call a third Lambeth Conference. The news came as no surprise. "It was virtually settled at the Conference of 1878 that a third Conference should be held at Lambeth, ten years later, and the death of archbishop Tait . . . made no difference to these arrangements."[352] Benson was following the pattern established by Longley and Tait, but was conscious of the Cyprianic precedents. He was looking forward to the event, although his biographer son noted that, despite the offer of the Bishopric of Calcutta ten years earlier, he "did not find that the question of Foreign Missions occupied any great space" in his father's thinking in earlier days. However, as Archbishop of Canterbury, Benson knew he had to engage in all aspects of the life of the emergent Communion and the idea appealed to his imagination. With his commitment to synodical consultations in his own diocese, along with his churchmanship and a well-developed view of the primacy of the See of Canterbury, it was an entirely consistent act. The initiative was his, and he threw himself into the planning with enthusiasm. Having received suggestions for the Conference agenda, he worked with a number of other bishops in a preparatory committee, including Thomson, who was still the Archbishop of York. As he did with so many things, he also consulted Dean Davidson of Windsor, acknowledging his assistance as the "Honorary Assistant Secretary". He established the agenda in advance, unlike his predecessors, which may have been an endeavour to establish his control of the Conference from before the start.

This was the programme of subjects:

1. The Church's practical work in relation to (A) Intemperance, (B) Purity, (C) Care of emigrants, (D) Socialism.

2. Definite teaching of the faith to various classes, and the means thereto.

3. The Anglican Communion in relation to the eastern Churches, to the Scandinavian and other Reformed Churches, to the Old Catholics, and others.

4. Polygamy of heathen converts. Divorce.

5. Authoritative standards of doctrine and worship.

6. Mutual relations of dioceses and branches of the Anglican Communion.[353]

On his own admission, but echoing Longley and Tait before him, Benson did not regard the Conference as a synod; it was not competent nor powerful enough to make binding decisions on doctrines or discipline or on relations between the constituent Churches. Benson had some idea of what was involved, having already participated in the second Conference as Bishop of Truro in 1878. The invitations for 1888, totalling 211, were sent out in November 1887, with the intention that the Conference would begin on 3 July 1888 and conclude on Friday, 27 July. One hundred and forty-seven bishops accepted the invitation, of whom 145 attended.

Early on Benson showed a good grasp of tactics when dealing with a suggestion that the bishops should process in copes and mitres at Canterbury and at Westminster. The idea came from some high church bishops and would have been unacceptable to many others. As such, it was a more significant matter than it appeared to be at first sight. Benson issued an edict that black chimeres should be worn, and not red, as was another suggestion. This secured obedience from the bishops and the potentially divisive question of copes and mitres never became an issue. Proceedings began with a great service in Canterbury Cathedral on 30 June 1888, which all the bishops attended, most of whom arrived in Canterbury by special train from Victoria Station. The arrangements pleased Benson, who wrote in his diary:

> First, I was taken by [the] Dean and Chapter to [the] West Doors inside [the] Nave. Doors were opened, and 100 Bishops entered in double file, dividing to right and left as we greeted each other, and passing up the Nave and the great steps of the Screen, and so into the Choir, the Minor Canons and singing-men and choir-boys standing in three lines . . . and singing all the time the procession was going up . . . we followed and went up the lower flight of the sanctuary steps, and there was placed the great grey "Chair of Augustine"; when I reached it we knelt in silence and then stood and sang Te Deum gloriously, the whole Choir and Aisles full of people as well as the Aisles of the Nave.[354]

Benson, impressed, "sate [sic] and gave them a short address from St Augustine's Chair exhorting all to obey the Church and not themselves, if they wished any loyalty to be left in the Church." Randall Davidson thought Benson's words "wise and generous if somewhat obscure" and compared unfavourably his "eager, apologetic, and involved utterance *read* from the Chair" with "the big simplicity of the words *spoken*" by Tait from the same place a decade before.[355] Benson spoke at greater length at another crowded service held in Westminster Abbey on 3 July, where G. G. Bradley had succeeded A. P. Stanley as dean in 1881. The archbishop's sermon lasted three quarters of an hour and was on the text of Ephesians 4:16 ("The whole body, joined and knit together by every joint with which it is supplied"). He believed that he held everybody's attention for the whole time. Privately, he thought the latter service was "more impressive" than that held in Canterbury Cathedral. In his diary, reminiscent of Cyprian's precedent, he wrote:

I continued to press the Church to keep its diocesan centres very strong, not comminuting their resources, not reducing the size of the dioceses so that the strong influence of each ceases to radiate through all. Then I pressed extension of organisation,—new religious orders free from the snares of the past, in intimate connexion with dioceses—and thirdly to hold no work true which is not absolutely spiritual work.[356]

After several days of deliberation, the Conference adjourned until 23 July to allow the various committees to discuss their topics in depth. On reconvening, the Conference had before it the reports of the committees, but one report was never published. This was that of the second agenda topic, and the reason for the secrecy was because of the "geology and Genesis" controversy, which the bishops believed to be a too contentious issue. Possibly they were afraid that public and press reactions to the work of that committee would overshadow the other work of the Conference.

An important outcome of the 1888 Lambeth Conference with regard to an element of Anglican self-understanding in relation to other Christian bodies was the document which eventually became known as the "Lambeth Quadrilateral". It had originated from the General Convention of the Episcopal Church of the United States, held in Chicago in 1886, but was slightly modified by the Lambeth Conference. It was in Davidson's *Report of the Lambeth Conference* that it was published for the first time in England and was the work of a committee charged to discuss "Home Reunion". This document set out, from the Anglican standpoint, the essential elements for Christian reunion as follows:

A. The Holy Scriptures of the Old and New Testaments, as containing all things necessary for salvation, and as being the rule and ultimate standard of faith.

B. The Apostles' Creed, as the Baptismal Symbol; and the Nicene Creed, as the sufficient statement of Christian faith.

C. The two Sacraments ordained by Christ Himself—Baptism and the Supper of the Lord—ministered with unfailing use of Christ's Words of institution, and of the elements ordained by Him.

D. The Historic Episcopate, locally adapted in the methods of its administration to the varying needs of the nations and peoples called of God into the Unity of His Church.

Not all the bishops were happy with regard to the Quadrilateral. In particular, some of those whose ministry was worked out alongside "non-episcopal communions" were concerned about the last element of it. Nevertheless, the adoption of the Quadrilateral was to prove significant beyond the immediate environs of the Lambeth Conference, and it became an important part of Anglican self-understanding. The Lambeth Quadrilateral was to remain influential when, in the twentieth century, ecumenical relationships became important between churches episcopal and non-episcopal. Curiously, in the light of its importance, the Quadrilateral is not mentioned in the biography of Benson.

A considerable number of other important issues were discussed, but few had such far-reaching consequences. One, which arose from the group working on "Purity", urged that a "life of chastity for the unmarried is not only possible, but is commanded by God... We declare that no one living an immoral life ought to be received in Christian society." Similarly, the same group considered the problem of divorced persons receiving Holy Communion and took a line which was entirely predictable within Victorian society.

An amusing incident occurred when the question of "socialism" was reported upon. Bishop Potter of New York, who described the event, recorded that a speaker whom he left unidentified, inveighed against servants wearing clothing that identified them as "liveried menials". When the speech ended, Benson announced that luncheon was due to be served and, said Potter, he declared, to a "shout of laughter from the Conference", and "with a charming twinkle in his eye, 'the liveried menials will show the way to the dining room.'" One thing did annoy Benson. The Australian Anglicans had decided that the title of "archbishop" should be assigned to the primate of Australia and Tasmania. Benson was not consulted but thought he should have been; he did not think that the use of the title should be proliferated. He did, however, win a partial victory, for, although several other provinces did distinguish their senior bishop with the title, it was not used until the question had been discussed at the Lambeth Conference in 1897, but by then he was in his grave.

By a remarkable feat, Davidson, who was part of the secretariat, managed to produce the 1888 Conference Report within a few days and received much praise for his efforts. The third Lambeth Conference ended, as it had begun, with "a stately concluding service". It was held at St Paul's Cathedral, and the preacher was the Archbishop of York. For the first time, the closing service was attended by the clergy of the Lower Houses of Convocation, and by the House of Laymen. Benson received much praise for the successful conduct and management of the 1888 Lambeth Conference, and afterwards claimed to be exhausted. The American bishops presented him with an altar-cross for the chapel of Lambeth Palace. When it was all over, he wrote a summary which he sent to Queen Victoria, who replied that she was glad "I was pleased with the Lambeth gathering, and thinks that I must have enjoyed the opportunity of making many interesting acquaintances".[357]

In 1896, Benson had almost completed the programme for a fourth Lambeth Conference, but it took place in 1897 under the chairmanship of his successor Frederick Temple and will be considered in the next chapter.

—

Despite his audience with the Pope back in 1852, like many Victorian Church people, Benson had a deep dislike and distrust of the Roman Catholic Church. His theological convictions about the Church of England were rock solid, but he was not blind to

> the great strengths of the Church of Rome; yet he was firmly rooted in the ethos of the Anglican Church and was disposed to guide its destinies from the position of deep scholarship and tenacious loyalty.[358]

As a very young man, he had written to Lightfoot about the Roman Catholic Church: "in England it is not only in error, but in heresy, and schismatical." As Archbishop of Canterbury, he was more diplomatic addressing the National Society at its annual meeting in 1894: "Roman

Catholics held principles which were not the principles of the Church of England." Pastorally, he had objected on an earlier occasion to one such principle: "Confession insisted on, Confession enforced; the yoke, the terror, the deceivableness of Technical Confession."[359] In 1887, he wrote, once again privately to a friend (Canon Mason): "We are utterly guiltless of any schism. Till the eleventh year of Elizabeth, when we were as we are now, there was no thought of such a thing. Then we were impiously excommunicated." The archbishop had also written in his *Seven Gifts* of the regrettable historical relations between the papacy and the Church in the British Isles; that "foreign papal wedge . . . interposed and driven continually and ever more cruelly between the nation and Church". He was conscious of the irony of the existence of the Roman Catholic hierarchy in Victorian Britain, calling it elsewhere the "Italian Mission", and in the same letter to Mason, inveighed against its setting up in 1850, which he described as "the uncatholic and unchristian act of sending an Italian Mission to attack this ancient Church".[360] Benson's study of Cyprian also informed his thinking about the relationship between Rome and the Church in England, for there had been difficulties regarding the autonomy of the North African Church in relation to Rome at the time of the Decian and Valerian persecutions. The relative independence of the Church in England from Rome had been a longstanding phenomenon for several centuries before the formal split in the sixteenth century; it had been recognized in the assertion in Magna Carta, which declared "that the Church of England shall be free". Just as Benson objected to "the unfounded nature of the claims and doctrine of Rome", so he believed in the "true historic position of the Church of England", her "Apostolic Ministry" and the "masculine sense, the unsurpassed knowledge and the keen historic sense of her Reformers".[361] In short, Benson was sure of the ultimate strength of the Church of England; "I do not fear that the Italian Mission will make anything of our clergy or our people."[362] He admitted to being irritated that whenever he hesitated to support a society or function the organizers always told him that they hoped to get Cardinal Manning's support or presence; wryly he said, "when the dog won't eat his dinner, we call out, 'Puss, puss!'"

He was very sceptical when approached by Charles Lindley Wood, who became the second Viscount Halifax, a committed high churchman, who longed to see the Church of England (and the whole Anglican Communion) united, or reunited, with Roman Catholicism. In 1868, Halifax had been elected President of the English Church Union, and fully supported its endeavours to promote high church practices and to defend ritualist clergy. However, in 1890, whilst in Madeira, where he had decamped with a convalescent son, Halifax met a Roman Catholic priest named Etienne Fernand Portal, who had a deserved reputation in his native France as a churchman who sought the intellectual revival of Roman Catholicism. Halifax and Portal liked each other, and a firm friendship was established. This was encouraged by Portal's superiors, who hoped that Halifax would convert to Roman Catholicism, reasoning that a convert from the English aristocracy would strengthen the position of the Roman Church in England. Halifax was a loyal but very high church Anglican and was surprised at how little Portal knew of the Anglican Church. Portal had previously assumed the Church of England to be just another "Protestant sect". As Halifax's friendship with Portal developed, so his enthusiasm grew. They met on a number of occasions in 1891 and 1892, and Halifax did his best in their many conversations to deepen Portal's knowledge. He supplied him with a Latin translation of the Book of Common Prayer, and expounded the Thirty-nine Articles, emphasizing (according to Halifax's biographer) "the points of similarity". As Portal continued his studies their conversations eventually moved on to the possibility of reunion, and they concluded that the Roman Catholic perception of the Anglican ordinal was the central question. Portal, using the pen name F. Dalbus, wrote a pamphlet in French on Anglican orders, with Halifax's encouragement, but it received a dusty reception from other Roman scholars and a learned but lively controversy erupted in the high church Anglican journal *The Guardian* in England, and in the *Univers* in Paris. In England, Cardinal Vaughan, who had become Archbishop of Westminster in 1892, was deeply suspicious of these manoeuvres, and so he remained. Eventually, Halifax had lunch with Cardinal Vaughan. He imagined that Vaughan would be as enthusiastic for corporate reunion as himself. The matter of the validity of Anglican orders was raised. Halifax said that if Rome could reconsider its view of Anglican orders, a "great cause of irritation would be removed". Vaughan asserted that the authority of Rome should be first addressed. This exchange precisely demonstrates the dilemma. Halifax wanted Rome to concede the authenticity of Anglican orders; Vaughan believed that Anglicanism must submit to the authority of Rome. Halifax, however, continued to work towards his goal of reunion. In England, alarm stirred around Halifax's activities, and in 1894 Halifax carried his ideas to Benson, who reacted with proper caution. In July of that year, Halifax brought Portal to England and took him to see R. T. Davidson, who by that time had been appointed Bishop of Rochester (from 1891). It is unlikely that they would have got much from such a cautious man, and it is an indication of Halifax's optimism that he arranged such a meeting. It is easy to dismiss Halifax as naive, but he genuinely longed for reunion and undoubtedly believed that he might be God's instrument in starting the process.

When Halifax took Portal to meet Benson at Addington, the abbé thought Benson "a holy man and learned" but claimed to be "puzzled" by the Archbishop of Canterbury, and was surprised at his caution, unaware of the magnitude but relatively solitary nature of Halifax's ambitions. Benson wrote to Davidson that Halifax had "taken the greatest care of M. Portal. He has seen and heard nothing but with H's eyes and voice. He has been to St. Paul's, to the Ritualistic churches, to Cowley etc."[363] Halifax's biographer thought Benson "not quite fair . . . Neither then nor later did Halifax attempt to conceal from Portal the presence of the Protestant skeleton in the Catholic cupboard."[364] But the real situation was somewhat different, as recorded by Bernard and Margaret Pawley in *Rome and Canterbury through Four Centuries*:

> Any attempt at corporate union of the whole body of the Church of England with Rome at that time was entirely out of the question. Such a project would require a long period of mutual co-operation and education, with positive and deliberate attempts to remove bigotry and ignorance on both sides.[365]

Portal, only aware of Halifax's enthusiasm, could not have known the real situation. Benson had previously indicated that he would concede nothing beyond a courteous reception to Portal. It would have been surprising indeed if Benson had done more. Both his personal beliefs and the doctrine of the Church of England set the limits; in addition, the recent history of the papacy offered no help at all. In his *Cyprian* book, Benson allowed a moment of exasperation with the contemporary situation to colour what he wrote, referring "to the new malevolence, which since the dogma of Infallibility has made it necessary for papal advocates to bespatter each whitest robe that has not walked in the Roman train".[366] Indeed, Arthur Benson thought "the archbishop's view from the first seems to have been that an attempt was being made from Rome, working through the sincere and genuine enthusiasm of Lord Halifax and the Abbe Portal, to compromise the official chief of the Anglican Church". It cannot be known whether Portal and Halifax were being used in the way Benson suspected, as "unconscious agents", but a protracted correspondence continued for many months, together with a scheme devised by Portal for a series of meetings at a later date. Halifax spoke at a public meeting in Bristol and sent copies of his address to many English and Scottish bishops and, early in 1895, asked Benson how he, and the bishops, would react if a conference should be held in Rome on the subject of Anglican orders. Benson in reply asserted his continued desire for Christian unity. He described it politely and firmly as a "far-off desire and hope", even going so far as to say that "neither, I am afraid, can I give the most capable and trusted person leave to give any probable supposed question replies in my behalf in any specified direction." But Halifax did not give up. With Portal he had interrupted the archbishop's holiday in Devon and earned a rebuff; the two "were trying to make him commit himself, he protested, while the Pope remained uncompromised".[367] He also called on Benson when the archbishop was on holiday in Florence in April 1895 and submitted to him what Benson described as "four long memoranda", one of which he had also sent to the Pope; another was an account of his interviews in Rome. Archbishop Benson read them "very carefully", but he was clearly becoming exasperated. The situation was made worse from the Anglican point of view when, in the same month, Pope Leo XIII published an open letter to Roman Catholics. Its title was *Ad Anglos*, and it was addressed "to the English people who seek the Kingdom of Christ in the unity of the faith, health and peace of the Lord". Benson was incensed that no reference was made even to the existence of the Church of England, a fact which he drew to the attention of his diocesan conference in the summer of 1895. Some of what Benson said was subsequently included in a pastoral letter which he published in September of the same year. In it, he asserted the historical authenticity of the existence of the Church of England, and emphasized the validity of its orders, rites, and ceremonies. The Pope eventually appointed a commission to investigate the subject of Anglican orders and, in 1896, he declared Anglican orders to be null and void in an encyclical entitled *Satis cognitum*, which was issued on 29 June 1896. On 29 September 1896, Benson was sharply critical of what he called Cardinal Vaughan's "insolent speech on our Orders", and a report in *The Times* that the Pope was setting up a fund to assist Anglican clergy converts to Rome. He said: "If Rome had not for once overshot all prudence I am mistaken." Halifax's activities seem to have had precisely the opposite effect to what he hoped; Davidson, it was said, "like Benson was detecting the faint odour of a Popish plot about the whole business", and thought that a naive Halifax had been led to put policy before principle. Benson, equally shrewdly, said that Halifax "is like a solitary player of chess, and wants to make all the moves on the board himself, on both sides".[368] Halifax was mortified by the outcome of his sincere efforts, but Benson was vindicated when the papal bull declared Anglican orders to be invalid. This inevitably brought the whole issue of the Anglican relations with Roman Catholicism to a halt for the remainder of the Victorian period, and beyond. Benson made an initial response and began to work on a more thorough reply as he set out on a visit to Ireland in early October 1896.

The Church in Ireland had been disestablished in 1871, as has been noticed, but Benson was "received with warmth and welcome which came upon him as a delightful surprise", *The Times* reported on 12 October 1896. Among his other duties, he visited Dublin and also Kildare for the restoration of the cathedral. He described the visit as "very interesting", but admitted in a letter, "I have been over-travelled and overworked." His wife said when *The Times* reported his death, that "he had complained in Ireland of constriction across his chest and had been treated for it". On their return, they stayed with the Gladstones at Hawarden Castle. The two men talked for three hours on 10 October. The following morning, Benson made his communion in the parish church at Hawarden and returned later for Matins. It was during that service that Benson died of heart disease.

> A member of the choir observed a sudden peculiar twitching of the archbishop's arms. A gurgling noise from the throat was heard, and, attention thus having been attracted, a considerable portion of the congregation noticed his Grace drop forward from a kneeling position in a state of helpless collapse ... the archbishop never regained consciousness.[369]

So Benson's life ended abruptly, in what Gladstone called "a soldier's death". It had been a life which his biographer described, in a page heading, of "incessant work". *The Times* on 12 October 1896 said, in a tribute that was typical of many, "he has been taken from us in the midst of his work with his activity and influence at their highest." The funeral took place in Canterbury within a week of his death. Benson's body was brought by train and then taken through crowded streets to the cathedral. Queen Victoria and the Prince of Wales were represented at the service by the Duke of York and Prince Charles of Denmark. A large number of bishops attended, the Archbishop of York and Davidson (by then Bishop of Winchester) among them. Arthur Benson's description is of a service which was "one of the stateliest that it is possible to conceive; and the pomp of burial was sweetened by the evident and heartfelt grief of the great silent congregation, who seemed to feel that it was the laying to rest of a true father in Israel".[370] Archbishop Benson was buried in Canterbury Cathedral under the north-west tower, the first archiepiscopal interment inside the building since that of Cardinal Pole in 1558. Over the grave is a fine medieval-style monument slab, with alongside nearby a recumbent effigy commemorating the man and, incidentally, his taste for dramatic architecture. The dedication of the monument took place on 8 July 1899. It was another grand ceremony, with unexpected drama provided by the English weather. It took place on a very hot day, during a thunderstorm with "hailstones ... as big as eggs". As the Archbishop of York read a lesson, "there came a terrific peal of thunder and a great rumbling in the roof, followed by a cataract of water. The Cathedral had been struck by lightning."[371]

CHAPTER 6

Frederick Temple (1896–1902)

Queen Victoria did not want Frederick Temple for the primacy, when Benson died. She wanted her long-time favourite, Randall Davidson, and told him so in a letter. He had been close to the work of the Archbishop of Canterbury for almost twenty years as Tait's chaplain, and then as a friend and advisor to Benson. The Queen knew him well from his days as Dean of Windsor, and was additionally predisposed towards him because he was married to Edith Tait, a daughter of her old friend Archbishop Tait. However, still in his late forties, Davidson was regarded as rather on the young side. In addition, his career had seemed particularly gilded, so there was a sense in which he still needed to demonstrate his abilities; certainly, that was the view of the prime minister, Lord Salisbury, which he expressed to the Queen. She had wanted Davidson for Winchester as early as 1891, but she had had to wait four years; Lord Salisbury had argued then that Davidson "was able but not, as yet, distinguished". Later, he told the Queen that Davidson would be a serious contender to follow Temple, and so it proved: he was appointed to Canterbury in 1903, but neither the Queen nor Salisbury lived to see it happen.

The death of Benson consequently presented an unexpected and unwelcome problem. Salisbury considered that Frederick Temple, Bishop of London, was the obvious man, despite his seventy-five years.[372] Salisbury, by then in his last premiership, felt that there were no other suitable candidates, and was sure that the old man could do the work. He believed that the other bishops would readily accept Temple as their leader and chief, and so it proved to be. Some people thought that Davidson wanted the archbishopric when Benson died, but naturally he denied it. In fact, he claimed that Temple was his favoured candidate from the start. His biographer, G. K. A. Bell, referred to several letters in which Davidson's preference for Temple was expressed; one, penned after the appointment was announced, was to Lord Salisbury and thanked him for choosing Temple. If Davidson was disappointed, he did not say so but mastered his frustrations and worked diligently under Temple's leadership. Temple was certainly suspicious about Davidson's ambitions. Arthur Benson warned Davidson: "it is obvious that [Temple's] view of yourself is that you intended to obtain the Primacy, and were passed over, to your own chagrin . . . and that you are disappointed and vexed."[373] His source for Temple's opinion was impeccable; he had got the information from E. L. Ridge, who was his father's chaplain at the time of Benson's death, and then continued in the post for the first four years of Temple's primacy. The relationship between the two remained workable, perhaps through the private intervention of Mrs Benson, but Davidson was excluded from Temple's confidence.

The Queen's disapprobation of Temple was based on several factors, although she had not objected to his earlier episcopal appointments to Exeter and London. She certainly regarded him as too old for Canterbury in 1896. She was concerned about his failing eyesight, she thought him "ungentlemanly" with a rough accent and lacking in "social qualities" (which she knew Davidson had in abundance). She would have been aware of his reputation for brusqueness, which sometimes bordered on bad manners. He was the oldest man to be appointed to the Archbishopric of Canterbury, several years older than Harold Browne, who had been passed over because of his age when Benson was appointed. Temple was two years younger than the Queen, but she saw that there is a great difference between starting new work at a relatively advanced age, and simply continuing to fulfil a longstanding role.

The prime minister quickly prevailed over the Queen's wishes and prejudices and wrote to Temple eleven days after Benson's death:

> I am authorised by Her Majesty to propose to you that you should be nominated to the Archbishopric of Canterbury, vacant by the lamented death of archbishop Benson. I need hardly enlarge on the great office which is vacant, nor on your own pre-eminent position in the Church of England, which designates you as the fittest person to undertake it. I believe it will not involve any

labours in excess of those which are now incumbent on you and to which your strength is fully equal. If you should see your way to the acceptance of the office, I am convinced all who love the Church of England will regard the event as one of singularly auspicious promise for her welfare.[374]

Lord Salisbury had assured the Queen that Temple had the strength of character to decline the invitation if he doubted his own ability to fulfil the duties, and there is a hint in Bell's biography of Davidson that she hoped he would decline the offer of the primacy and was put out when she heard of his ready acceptance. He was as quick as Tait had been before him and replied the following day, characteristically feeling that he "had no right to refuse the call" and promising to do his "best to carry on the work of the late archbishop, my most intimate friend for forty years". There was no hint that he felt himself unable to rise to the challenges of the Archbishopric of Canterbury, and there was even a suggestion that the primacy would be an easier role than that of the Bishop of London, and he had been in his mid-sixties when he moved there from Exeter. Certainly, Temple thought so, for he declared, "I do not think I shall find the work very new." He was pleased to receive the opportunity; Benson's son told Davidson that Temple was delighted at the pending change; he is "in high spirits, and looks upon the change to Canterbury as a headmaster might accept a deanery".

Despite his enthusiasm for his new role, Archbishop Benson's death had been an immense shock to Bishop Temple. The foundations of their long friendship had been laid when Benson, as a very young man, had been an assistant master at Rugby when Temple became headmaster. Benson had sought Temple's advice when appointed to be the first headmaster of Wellington College and had publicly supported Temple when the latter was criticized over *Essays and Reviews*. They had been episcopal colleagues in the West of England, and Archbishop Benson had later sought "the judgment of the Bishop of London to an extent to which few persons were aware".[375]

Towards the end of his life, Frederick Temple declared that he did not want anyone to write his biography, but he was a figure too important to remain unrecorded in post-Victorian Britain. Accordingly, two volumes were published in 1906: *Memoirs of Archbishop Temple by Seven Friends*. The editor was E. G. Sandford, Archdeacon of Exeter and residentiary canon at Exeter Cathedral. He was well-placed to bring out what is effectively a biography, having been a lifelong friend of Temple. Sandford was a boy at Rugby School under Temple's headmastership and served as his domestic chaplain when Temple became Bishop of Exeter. Sandford's admiration of his former chief is clear, but he did not baulk at Temple's shortcomings, although he tried to minimize them. The book purported to describe his career, but inevitably contains much personal material. In that sense it is less guarded than the biographies of Tait and Benson. In 1998, a useful modern biography by Peter Hinchliff was published, *Frederick Temple, Archbishop of Canterbury: A Life*.

Temple served in the archbishopric for six years, but his best work was behind him, as the faithful Sandford admitted. In a "supplement" to the *Memoir*, printed at the end of volume two, Sandford noted, "the call to London, and still more to Canterbury, came to one whose convictions and character were already fully formed." And he added that Temple "was not quick in old age to take in new ideas from individual minds". G. W. E. Russell was later to describe Temple's primacy as "the least successful period of his career". Nevertheless, his Canterbury years demonstrated that Lord Salisbury's confidence was not misplaced. His solidly faithful ministry demonstrated his strength of character and capacity for work in his final appointment, and when Davidson assumed the burden of the primacy as Temple's successor he entered upon a goodly heritage.

Frederick Temple was born on 30 November 1821, one of the youngest of fifteen children, of whom eight survived infancy. His father was Octavius Temple, an army officer who was serving as sub-inspector of the militia in the Greek Ionian Islands. His mother, Dorcas, was the daughter of a Cornish gentleman named Richard Carveth. Frederick Temple was always close to his mother, and later she shared his home at Rugby, as did his youngest sister. Frederick was born on the island then known as Santa Maura, modern Lefkada. The family returned to England in 1830. Their new home was a farm near Culmstock, about twelve miles from Tiverton in Devon. Octavius Temple seems to have nursed some sort of idyllic dream and hoped to finance the education of his sons from the profits of the farm, but he was not successful as a farmer. It was probably financial need that led him to accept the post of Lieutenant Governor of Sierra Leone in 1833, where he died the following year. Mrs Temple had remained in England and was left with reduced means to raise her family. She struggled to continue with the farm, and her resident children often worked on the land. One recorded that she worked with the women servants and "the boys picked stones into heaps, took out weeds, docks and thistles, and laid the roots in heaps". Frederick Temple never denied his agricultural background and claimed to be able to plough a straight furrow. With at least one brother, he was initially educated by his mother at home. She was not a particularly competent teacher, nor well educated herself. What she lacked in skill, however, she made up in perseverance and conscientiousness, and the boy rapidly caught up when he began to attend school.

Temple was placed as a pupil at Blundell's School in Tiverton in January 1834, where he was joined by a younger brother the following year. He rose rapidly through the school and impressed those who taught him. He was confirmed around the age of twelve and enjoyed his new life, despite the need for careful frugality; in later life he often paid tribute to his school—"when I look back upon those days, my heart has leaped with pleasure"—and he rejoiced to become a governor in 1871, when he was Bishop of Exeter. When the time came for him to leave school and go to university, Temple was fortunate that Blundell's had links with Balliol College, Oxford. An ancient provision made it possible for boys from the school to win designated scholarships to the college. Temple, already showing great promise, gained one and he went up at Easter 1839. The Master of Balliol was Dr Jenkyns; Temple, through a piece of absent-mindedness, did not impress him at the beginning, but his capacity for hard work and his conscientious nature combined to earn him an enviable reputation. He lived frugally, endeavouring to keep within the limits of his scholarship in order to avoid asking his mother for money. His poverty was noticed to the extent that Jenkyns tactfully found an excuse to give him ten pounds, and in December 1839 Temple received a similar sum in an anonymous letter. He did not drink wine, which added to his reputation for seriousness. His lifelong support for the temperance movement and his personal commitment to total abstinence from alcohol was to become a significant aspect of his ministry in later life. His lack of funds also meant that he was unable to afford a coach to assist him in his studies, but some of his older contemporaries, recognizing his abilities, helped him without charge. W. G. Ward, whose censure by the university he later opposed, was one of them; A. C. Tait was another. In 1842, Temple, a somewhat awkward man with a lack of polish, was awarded his degree. He obtained a double first, in classics and mathematics. A younger contemporary, W. J. Farrer, wrote in 1903, "I do not think I ever remember anyone whose success in the schools gave greater general satisfaction."

In 1842, Temple became a lecturer at Balliol and later a Fellow of the College. He remained in Oxford until the end of April 1848, lecturing in classics and logic and, to more able undergraduates, mathematics. His teaching style was described by E. G. Sandford:

> Temple kept us alert, walking briskly about the Hall, talking very loud, turning suddenly upon us with questions, and greeting blunders with boisterous laughter. He always seemed to be in high spirits, as though the whole thing were very enjoyable. At the same time he exacted work, showing marked displeasure at any neglect or idleness, and using great plainness of speech.[376]

During his Oxford period, Temple gradually developed the liberal opinions which remained with him for the rest of his life. In 1847, Temple was among those who signed the petition supporting the nomination of R. D. Hampden to the Bishopric of Hereford. In the same year, he worked on Gladstone's election committee to Parliament as one of the members for Oxford University. Temple did not engage with the Tractarians, who were well-established as a powerful force in Oxford during his time, although he enjoyed hearing Newman preach.

Temple's departure from Oxford came in the early summer of 1848 as a result of a suggestion by James Kay Shuttleworth, who had been a Fellow at Balliol College with him. Kay Shuttleworth was the Assistant Secretary of the Committee of the Council on Education. This was a committee of the Privy Council; the brainchild of Lord Melbourne, its initial role was to administer the annual grant which Parliament had made since 1833 for financing of elementary education. Previously, elementary education had been almost exclusively in the hands of the Church of England, but by the time of Melbourne's premiership it was clear that the Church did not have sufficient resources. Kay Shuttleworth, effectively the administrator of the developing system, was convinced that the education of the poor, especially boys and youths, would regenerate society and reduce the number of criminals among the dispossessed. He wanted to reduce the influence of the Church, but he persuaded Temple, who became a civil servant attached to the department of the Committee of the Council on Education in May 1848. By this time, he had been ordained deacon in 1846 and priest in 1847 by Samuel Wilberforce, but was persuaded that his future lay in the developing scheme.

Benjamin Jowett, later the Master of Balliol College, who had become a personal friend, encouraged him in this change of work. But Temple was motivated by a sense of vocation and for the remainder of his life he was enthusiastic about expanding the education of the poor, and he spoke and wrote frequently on the subject. He shared Kay Shuttleworth's conviction that education was the best way to improve their quality of life, and Temple added to that belief his conviction that temperance was similarly important. To start with, Temple's work was that of an examiner in the office of the committee, which was located in Whitehall. He was employed in "revising the marks given by Inspectors for candidates, in order to ensure uniformity of standard". He had, however, other functions which related to the funding of institutions and "had to consider the reports of Inspectors and the information given by the Managers of Schools, and ascertain whether the rules of the department allowed a grant of public money to aid the elementary or training schools, whether for building or maintenance".[377]

The Committee of the Council had discovered that school masters for pauper children in workhouses were often "wretchedly supplied with books and apparatus . . . having often been themselves dependent on parochial relief and generally ignorant and unskilled".[378] They were always poorly paid and frequently held in low esteem by those responsible for the administration of workhouses, so part of the committee's thinking was to improve both the training and standing of such men. It embarked on the development of a special training college, Kneller Hall near Twickenham, around 1847. The intention, which was never achieved, was that it would have one hundred students training as teachers for workhouse children. Temple was appointed its principal with a salary of £800 per year, during the building work. The committee carefully regulated the daily life of the hall and was prescriptive about the curriculum, which was shared among four teachers, including the principal. He was responsible for working the curriculum, and for the wider pattern of life at the hall as he appointed himself chaplain. "The subjects of instruction were divinity (taught by the Principal), geography, English history and literature, grammar, mathematics, physics, agricultural chemistry, and music."[379]

Temple took a particular interest in what the *Memoirs* described as "industrial training". This was in the hands of the Kneller Hall gardener, but the principal often joined in the work and rolled up his shirt sleeves, for he enjoyed physical activity. A footnote tells of Temple setting to work cleaning a pig sty when a student demurred. This action was entirely characteristic on Temple's part. He was not above exploiting such an occasion to assert the strength of his personality and demonstrate the agricultural experience of his early years, but it revealed an element of moral superiority. He gave proper weight to all the subjects that the authorities required, but at the heart of his plan was that "religious instruction . . . is to be the centre of all the teaching". Temple unhesitatingly adhered to the teaching of the Church of England in his approach, although he willingly accepted non-Anglicans as students and thought that the liberality of his approach would be acceptable: "I do not expect to offend the Dissenters grievously. That on the whole the Church of England, more nearly than any other I know, represents the ideal drawn in the New Testament, I heartily believe and shall very heartily teach."[380] He expected, though, that his approach would offend stiff church people, and it did so.

Sandford's "Editor's Supplement" at the end of the second volume of the *Memoirs* reveals some of the frustrations which Temple experienced as principal of Kneller Hall. The scheme never attracted the number of students that was envisaged, in part because the salaries of workhouse schoolmasters, which were never high, were reduced. Kneller Hall was weakened by the outbreak of the Crimean War, which diverted the minds of "both country and Ministry" from education. Changes of government meant that the original impetus behind the establishment was lost and such a small experiment in education ceased to be regarded as important. By the end of 1853, Temple was frustrated. He was not successful in efforts to enlist support from politicians, and told friends that he was considering resignation; disillusioned with working in the public service, he said, "I have assigned them six months more in my own mind to do what I want: after which time—the Deluge."[381] The end came in 1855, when he resigned, aware that the authorities "have not, however, the audacity to propose to carry on Kneller Hall without me. They are going to make it a barrack or a lunatic asylum or something of that sort."

Temple planned, at least for the short term, to take up the Inspectorship of Training Colleges, but he was unhappy at the prospect, although he persevered until 1857. In his new work, he was plagued by a sense of failure and a "somewhat unreasonable bitterness against public men",[382] for he felt that he had been let down when Kneller Hall was allowed to fail. He was aware that his name had been mentioned in newspapers for the vacant Bishopric of Ripon, when Longley moved to Durham, and some other pieces of ecclesiastical preferment. He discounted the possibility in his correspondence with friends, and was right to do so, but the rumours added to his unsettled state of mind.

—

He was rescued when the headmastership of Rugby School fell vacant in 1857. Tait, at that time Bishop of London, urged Temple's candidacy upon the trustees and told them, "I have no hesitation in saying that I am acquainted with no man in England so fit for it as he."[383] He pressed Temple to submit to the selection process, and he did so; the prospect was attractive, and not entirely outside his imagination. Temple's appointment was supported by testimonials from colleagues and friends, but according to Sandford, "with characteristic self control, he never even read them." It was the second time that Tait had tried to persuade Temple. At the time of Tait's own departure from Rugby in 1849 to become Dean of Carlisle, he had hoped that Temple would succeed him as headmaster,[384] but Temple did not submit his name. Goulburn was appointed and became a devout but unexceptional headmaster. When Temple got there, the school was in a "trough of the wave", having lost much of Arnold's and

Tait's momentum. The roll had stood at around 500 on Tait's departure; when Goulburn left, it had fallen to 300, but Temple attributed the fall, in part at least, to the Crimean War, as with Kneller Hall. He was to write on 31 August 1860:

> Poor Goulburn in his third year had precisely the number that I have now in my third year. Then came the Crimean war, and Rugby was the first to feel it . . . I wonder whether, if another war were to carry off all the youth to military tutors etc., as the last did, Rugby would be the first to feel it again.[385]

His appointment to Rugby was announced on 12 November 1857. Temple initially caused surprise and comment when he arrived at the school on foot from the railway station carrying his own bag. He moved into the headmaster's house with his mother and sister Jennetta, known to the family as Netta, who took an active part in the management of the headmaster's residence. She became involved in the lives of some of the pupils, particularly when difficulties or tragedy struck, but was not immediately popular with the wives of some of the assistant masters in their small world.

Under Temple the school roll climbed back almost to 500. He introduced a wider curriculum with specialist teachers developing work initiated under Tait. By the time of Temple's departure there were eight masters teaching what were described as "modern" subjects, including, from 1864, chemistry, botany, geology, and physics; with English language and literature added in 1865. He managed to find classrooms for the teaching of the new subjects and pushed for a minimum of three new ones to be built. At first there was no laboratory or science lecture room and no studio, so the headmaster's hayloft was converted into two classrooms, another was rented within the town hall, and a kitchen was brought into use as a "botanical school". He had to tackle problems caused by the relative status of staff recruited to teach the modern subjects over against the traditional subjects and also dealt with a disparity of salary levels which some of his staff tried to maintain. He inherited a system whereby individual masters could, in much of the school, work as tutors to individual boys whose parents paid the master direct. The vagaries of popularity meant that some masters had overcrowded tutor-rooms, and others stood empty. Temple negotiated an agreement regarding a maximum number of boys. However, he permitted masters to exceed the limit on condition that the surplus fees of those who did so were to be paid into a common fund. In that way the problem was solved. Despite that clever move, Temple was willing for his staff to pursue their own course through the curriculum. A former assistant master at Rugby, F. E. Kitchener, wrote the section of the *Memoir* about the school with contributions from several former colleagues. In the chapter entitled "Dr Temple and the Masters", they acclaimed his ability and willingness to delegate. But, under his predecessor the boarding masters had achieved a level of independence from the headmaster's authority with which Temple needed to deal. He did so skilfully and without causing undue rancour or much opposition.[386] His ability to delegate, however, left Temple as the years passed. By the time he became Archbishop of Canterbury, his chaplains frequently complained that he did everything himself and left them in the dark with regard to what was happening. Certainly, Bishop Davidson felt that Temple was unwilling to involve even senior bishops in the leadership of the Church. Another decision of Temple's was to appoint himself as the school's chaplain, like Arnold before him, and as he had done at Kneller Hall. The school day included chapel attendance, although Holy Communion was not a compulsory service. Temple took great trouble over his confirmation classes, devoting a considerable portion of time in his busy life to their preparation and delivery. His years at Rugby were acknowledged to be a success, and the school had begun to develop an international reputation by the early sixties, as evidenced by "an exceptional influx of American boys into the school". The *Memoir* identified the publication of *Tom Brown's School Days* as a contributory factor to the interest from the USA, plus the effect, later, of the American Civil War of 1861–1865, which led parents to send their sons to England. Although neither of these factors was conclusive, Rugby benefitted more than many schools from them because of the growing reputation of Temple as a headmaster.

In 1903, the Bishop of Hereford, John Percival, himself one of Temple's successors as headmaster, wrote of his time as an assistant master at Temple's Rugby:

> It might, I think, in our day have been described as a nursery of the strenuous life. We lived under a chief whom we felt to have been the embodiment of strength, vigour, truth, duty, unselfishness, all tempered by a domestic simplicity and a filial devotion to his aged mother which gave a tone of peculiar beauty to the life.[387]

In 1864, Temple gave evidence to a Public Schools Commission, and was rightly seen as having a contribution to make to a Commission of Inquiry into "all school education above the National and British schools and below the universities". The latter had a distinguished membership and Temple was one of the more significant contributors. He attended eighty-two out of a total of 115 meetings, not all of which were directly relevant to his expertise. He also drew up a first draft of the report that was issued in the spring of 1868. This was a substantial volume, supported by twenty others of subordinate reports and evidence.

—

The controversy stirred up by *Essays and Reviews* (1860) has run through this study since Archbishop Sumner's time. Temple's essay, as has been noted, was contentious beyond its theological significance which, nevertheless, is interesting in its own right. It was among the less radical contributions to the volume, but it caused its author a great deal of personal trouble at Rugby and the controversy reignited when he became a bishop. It is appropriate to examine Temple's essay at this point in his biography, as it appeared during his time as headmaster of Rugby.

Each author was aware of his colleagues' lines of thought and cannot have been ignorant of what they were likely to say, despite their claims that each one wrote without any knowledge of the other authors' contributions. When Temple declared that he had not seen the other essays before the publication of the book, sensibly he did not claim to be surprised at what he read. He revealed that his essay was a reworked sermon, delivered originally in Rugby School chapel, then revised and preached again in Oxford, before another reworking and its final appearance in the famous volume. He also claimed to have spent no more than ten hours working on it, but it is a substantial piece of work of around 17,000 words. A sermonic tone is occasionally noticeable, although other parts have the flavour of a formal essay. The result is a document which varies in its readability. By later standards it is entirely uncontroversial, and even at the time only owed its notoriety to the more radical contributions of some of the other authors and to the prominence of Temple's career.

The title of his essay, "The Education of the World", indicated that what would follow had a wide sweep. His first observation concerned the impossibility of a "world of mere phenomena", because such a world would be a "dead machine". A mechanical understanding of creation cannot be, for "the human heart refuses to believe in a universe without purpose".[388] He spoke on the first page of the universe working in "cycles . . . many millions of years in length", a hypothesis which disturbed those who had a conservative approach to biblical chronology.

He recognized that "man is a spiritual as well as a material creature" and that both aspects of human experience must be considered in the education of mankind. Individuals have the capacity to learn and grow intellectually and spiritually throughout their lives. This led Temple to the common Victorian assumption that modern humanity is superior, in the sense of greater knowledge and spiritual maturity, than people of previous ages. Temple identified parallels between human achievement overall and the growth from child to mature adult of an individual. He claimed that a child who grew up in the nineteenth century had at the age of twelve the same "development of powers" as one aged fourteen in a previous generation. He went further and claimed that the fourteen-year-old of an earlier generation had the same powers as an adult from a much earlier time. At each generation there was an "imperceptible but unfailing increase" of progress of "temper", or "character", along with improvements in manners and thought. He conceived an analogy whereby creation could be compared to the development of an individual person.

> The present ever gathers into itself the results of the past, [and] transforms the human race into a colossal man, whose life reaches from the creation to the day of judgment. The successive generations of men are days in this man's life. The discoveries and inventions which characterize the different epochs of the world's

> history are his works. The creeds and doctrines, the opinions and principles of the successive ages, are his thoughts. The state of society at different times are his manners.[389]

From this Victorian complacency, Temple felt able to argue that mankind had gone through a process which he optimistically described in terms of "a childhood, a youth, and a manhood of the world". Each category had to have an appropriate education. Childhood was required to obey. Youth had to follow the example of those older and wiser and grow towards maturity. Manhood had to follow principles in order to develop understanding and conscience. Not surprisingly, he identified his own times with that mature manhood of the world.

His contention was that the period of childhood was concluded when Jesus Christ came to this world,[390] for he gave the finest example to all humanity. "Youth" in the history of the world corresponds to "the meeting point of the Law and the Gospel", so the period from the closing of the Old Testament period to the closing of the New Testament was the time of mankind's youth. What Temple called "the second stage", therefore, "in the education of man was the presence of our Lord upon earth". Temple's argument became less specific as he turned to the "manhood" of humanity. He emphasized the adherence to principles such as self-discipline and personal devotion to the Lord. The work of maturity is the application of these principles, including temperance, to the whole of life.

Temple traced what he believed to be the most important influences of history on the process by which Christianity was enabled to spread. He identified four: the influence of Rome, of Greece, of Asia, and of Judea. "Each of these contributed something to the growth of the future Church."

First, he considered the Roman hegemony meant that the rule of law facilitated travel and communications, so the existence of the Roman Empire made possible the peripatetic ministry of the early Christian apologists. Coincidentally, and in Temple's mind less serendipitously, it was the Roman system that fuelled the concept that the Church needed a human "head" or leader, which led eventually to the development of the papacy; the eventual collapse of the Roman Empire hastened the development of the medieval papacy.

Second, he turned to the Greek contribution, which Temple dismissed as taking no more than 200 years. This was "the cultivation of the reason and the taste. Its gift to mankind has been science and art. There was little in its temper of the spirit of reverence and it was not concerned with a future world. Its morality did not spring from the conscience."

Third, Judaism contributed to the spread of the Christian gospel in two ways: Judaism provided the diaspora which enabled the Christian gospel to be disseminated through the Roman Empire. Then he noted the "toughness" of the "Jewish race", which enabled it to outlive the contributions of the Greek and Asian insights.

Fourth, and more tentatively, was the contribution of "Asian" thought to the process of human maturing. This contribution was valid, although in terms of Temple's argument, the monarchs who once led "Assyrian, or Babylonian, or Persian armies across the world . . . had in reality no substance, no inherent strength", but he could not ignore the "Asian" category, because notable among its elements was Athanasius, "a thorough Asiatic in sentiment and in mode of arguing, [yet] . . . the bulwark of the doctrine of the Trinity."[391]

Temple summed up this section of his essay, "thus the Hebrews may be said to have disciplined the human conscience, Rome the human will, Greece the reason and taste, Asia the spiritual imagination."[392]

Then came a short but eloquent discourse, possibly part of the original sermon, on the nature of the Lord's divinity and the timing of the incarnation in human history. Believers were able to recognize the "greatness and beauty" of the example which Christ had set before them. The importance of the four Gospels was obvious, but the inquirer does not go to the New Testament to find creeds or liturgies; it was the early Church which gave later generations, including his own, not precepts but an example. This would not have alarmed his critics, but his next point would have done as he gave examples of specific scriptural decisions which have become "obsolete", a word he did not shrink from using.[393] The modern Christian who seeks to "copy the early Church is to do *as* she did, not *what* she did".

This included the involvement of the intellect in the process he was trying to describe. Part of that process had been the involvement of the "Church's whole energy . . . in the first six centuries of her existence in the creation of a theology". The movement towards maturity "is the last stage in the education of a human soul, and similar . . . has been the last stage of the education of the human race", thereby recalling the main thrust of his essay as "The Education of the World".

It was when Temple turned to the consideration of scientific study that his theological liberalism was most fully revealed. What he called "physical science" had enlarged the "philosophy" and knowledge of humanity beyond the limits of the early Church and the Fathers. He described God's creation as to be read "by the side" of God's revelation, and not as something to be feared intellectually or spiritually. The Bible he readily acknowledged as the "firm spot" on which Christendom stands, and "the investigation of what it teaches and what it does not teach, the determination of the limits of what we mean by inspiration, the determination of the degree of authority to be ascribed to the different books . . . must take the lead of all other studies." Tellingly, he continued, expanding the basis of this argument:

> He is guilty of high treason against the faith who fears the result of any investigation, whether philosophical, or scientific, or historical. And therefore nothing should be more welcome than the extension of knowledge of any and every kind.[394]

It was, however, the next sentence which linked him to the more radical essayists in *Essays and Reviews*:

> If geology proves to us that we must not interpret the first chapters of Genesis literally; if historical investigations show us that inspiration, however it may protect the doctrine, yet was not empowered to protect the narrative of the inspired writers from occasional inaccuracy; if careful criticism shall prove that there have been occasionally interpolations and forgeries in that Book . . . the results should still be welcome.

However, "even the mistakes of careful and reverent students are more valuable than truth held in unthinking acquiescence."

In the closing paragraphs of the essay, he asserted that a "careful criticism" of the Bible gave it a relevance which some thought such study had lost, as "a thing of the past". Temple knew that modern Christian thinkers were obliged to follow where their studies led. They might make mistakes which would be corrected by further study; there was nothing to fear. Such assertions, bland as they were, fuelled the objection at the time of the confirmation of his election as Bishop of Exeter, and the last-minute attempt to stop his consecration.

When the controversy over *Essays and Reviews* had begun, Temple told his Rugby colleagues, but not the pupils, about his contribution. When the publicity began, he sought to retain the confidence of the parents of his pupils by publishing a volume of his sermons delivered to the boys. The sermons set out fully his religious opinions, and by and large it was a successful move which enabled him to run his school in his customarily energetic manner.

—

A significant personal event which occurred during the time that Frederick Temple served as headmaster of Rugby was the death of his mother on 8 May 1866, aged seventy-nine. Several of the *Memoir* authors mention the closeness of the mother and son, and one of them, F. E. Kitchener, described a typical day in the life of the old lady:

> At Rugby Mrs Temple had lived chiefly in her bedroom in the daytime, unless she went out in her chair. In the afternoon the son and daughter had five-o'clock tea in her bedroom, and at that time Dr. Temple would be at the height of his laughter and fun. During dinner the mother came down to the drawing-room, and was ready to receive the guests on their leaving the dining-room ... Dr Temple would then go over to his mother in her chair by the fireside, and, leaning down to her, introduce each of us to her ... Before prayer-time she would, latterly, retire to her room.[395]

By the time of Mrs Temple's death, however, Frederick Temple was clearly well-established at the school, and his Rugby years were purposeful and harmonious for him and his household, particularly after the *Essays and Reviews* controversy had died away. However, as the years passed, a man with his established professional reputation and his skill at managing a great school was a candidate for ecclesiastical preferment. In July 1869, Gladstone offered him the deanery of Durham, which carried with it the position of Warden of the University. The Prime Minister long remembered being impressed on hearing Temple speak at Liverpool in 1865. Having won the general election of 1868, Gladstone was committed to the disestablishment of the Church of Ireland, a concept publicly supported by Temple.[396] He hinted that if Temple accepted the deanery, he was likely to receive further promotion before very long. Perhaps wisely, Temple declined; his brusqueness would not have helped him manage a cathedral chapter or the university. Even the emollient Sandford had to admit later that there were tensions between the energetic Bishop of Exeter and his "stay at home" chapter.[397] Such a consideration might not have occurred to Temple, but he did not want a deanery at that stage of his life. As he told E. W. Benson in a private letter, "no other deanery for me till I am well past sixty." The link with Durham University did not attract him, for he also told Benson that he did not relish another educational appointment whilst still at the height of his powers at Rugby.

By the autumn of the same year, four bishoprics became vacant: Bath and Wells, Manchester, Exeter, and Oxford. Temple was asked to accept one by the Prime Minister. Thirty years later, Archbishop Temple said in a speech at the Guildhall, Exeter:

> When the time came that I was honoured with the bishopric by the Government, and was asked to choose which of the [vacant] bishoprics I should prefer to accept, I preferred to go to Exeter because of my strong affection for the place and for the people.[398]

With his appointment came the customary congratulations. Among those who did enthuse was Archbishop Tait, who probably wanted to rekindle the good relationship which had been damaged in the row over *Essays and Reviews*. Benson wrote in a typically fulsome way but made an interesting allusion to Temple's character and manner, indicating that he thought the time had come for Temple to leave Rugby. He said, amidst his congratulations, "I don't like to see (as at Rugby, I do) the sharp edges of the sword coming through the sheath, and at Exeter the scabbard may be mended."[399] Notable among those sending good wishes was Bishop Harold Browne of Ely, later of Winchester, who had sent his sons to Temple's Rugby. He had hoped for some statement from Temple distancing himself from his fellow authors in *Essays and Reviews*. Browne wrote in the capacity of a friend and as someone with many friends in Temple's diocese. Temple was reluctant to take his advice, and when he did so later, it was a rather bungled affair. Another who wrote was Samuel Wilberforce, who had ordained Temple. He also advised him to disassociate himself from *Essays and Reviews*, and later he expressed doubts about Temple's suitability and was rebuked by him accordingly, having previously sent his congratulations. Jowett wrote, in a private note to Florence Nightingale, "I do not feel very glad at Dr. Temple's bishopric (though I perceive a general joy is diffused among liberals)." Jowett did, however, in the same letter acknowledge that Temple was "a very able and clear-headed man".[400] Gerald Wellesley, the Dean of Windsor, perceptively remarked about the essay at the time of Temple's appointment to Exeter: "It is difficult for a man to make explanations with a bishopric hanging over his head." Temple's reticence concerning *Essays and Reviews*, he made clear in a letter to Coleridge, was deliberate.[401] However, his essay was the trigger of a disturbance that followed his nomination as Bishop of Exeter. Notwithstanding the delight of his friends, others were appalled by the announcement of his appointment. An unlikely alliance formed between Dr Pusey and Lord Shaftesbury, both prominent in opposition, and they publicly invited others to join them.

The date for Temple's election by the chapter of Exeter Cathedral was 11 November 1869. This was the first hurdle, and although episcopal elections are a formality, there remained the possibility that the diocese might express discontent through the ballot.

> When the day of the election came, nineteen answered to their names in the Chapter House. Thirteen voted for the election; six against it; four were absent. Dr Temple was chosen by a majority of seven. It must not be forgotten that amongst the opposing minority were some of those who stood highest among the clergy

in the diocese for character and devotion. They knew not what they were doing, but they were true to the system in which they had been trained.[402]

But Temple's trouble was not yet over. The law requires that episcopal elections are demonstrated to be valid by a ceremony of confirmation. This took place in Bow Church in London on 8 December. There is no provision at the ceremony for raising questions of orthodoxy of belief; rather it is to establish the identity of the individual and the *bona fides* of the election. Even so, objections were voiced by two beneficed clergy from the Exeter diocese. A former colleague from the Education Office gave "testimony to his personal character", and, at short notice, Temple's older sister had to vouchsafe that her brother was not illegitimate. The protests were overruled, but are, perhaps, an indication of the desperation of his theological opponents.

Next in the process was the consecration service in Westminster Abbey on 21 December 1869. The service was conducted by Bishop Jackson, the newly appointed Bishop of London, because Archbishop Tait was unwell. Alongside Temple, a new Bishop of Bath and Wells and a new Bishop of the Falkland Islands were also to be consecrated. Before it took place, various friends, Browne among them, tried again to persuade Temple to renounce his association with the *Essays and Reviews* scholars, but he would not budge. Even on the day, poor Temple was not allowed to proceed in peace. The consecrating bishops gathered in the Jerusalem chamber at the abbey and Jackson, the senior bishop because of Tait's indisposition, had the unhappy task of informing them:

> That he had at the last moment received protests from several of the bishops of the province against the consecration of Dr. Temple ... Putting together all the protests, their meaning was that the archbishop would not be acting in accordance with the law if he were to consecrate ... His own opinion, which had been fortified by the advice of the highest legal authorities, was that the archbishop was bound to proceed, but he asked each of the bishops present to state his own view ... Each in turn gave his voice against the acceptance of the protests ... Thus the last

formal obstacle to the consecration was withdrawn. The long procession filed its way into the great shrine round which gather so many memories and association of Church and nation. In these Frederick Temple was henceforth to hold a place.[403]

Finally, Bishop Temple was enthroned in Exeter Cathedral on 29 December 1869. However, he entered the city of Exeter to streets lined with crowds, and the obvious enthusiasm helped disperse some of the suspicion with which his appointment had been greeted. The enthronement service was attended by the usual ecclesiastical and civic dignitaries and was conducted without interruption or protest. Temple preached a sermon that was appreciated by the congregation. Throughout his Exeter ministry he was a frequent preacher in the cathedral, as well as elsewhere in his large diocese, but it was six months before he moved into the Bishop's Palace because of repairs and improvements to the accommodation and to the chapel.

—

Temple's immediate predecessor in the Bishopric of Exeter was the pertinacious Henry Phillpotts (1778–1869), who had governed the diocese from 1830 and had died in harness a few months after his ninety-first birthday. Initially Phillpotts had set high standards for his clergy and his leadership had been incisive and strong-willed. Courageous and pugnacious, he became disputatious, and eventually feeble. His most notable controversy was that with G. C. Gorham, which demonstrated the old man's tough-mindedness. Phillpotts had maintained his energetic ministry into old age, but in his later years he had been largely confined to his home at Torquay, and not in Exeter. An air of neglect had taken hold of Church life in Devon and Cornwall, despite the efforts of his son William, the Archdeacon of Cornwall. Those who knew Frederick Temple, some of whom had predicted even before his Kneller Hall days that he would be made a bishop, knew that such a situation would be strenuously addressed.

Having weathered the protests at his appointment, Temple's woes concerning *Essays and Reviews* were not over, because he made a rare but "unfortunate blunder" (his own description). He expected the controversy to die away. He hoped that there would be no new editions of the volume; he believed that it "could not be regarded as a permanent work and had already taken the opportunity to tell the editor [sic] that in his judgement the time had come for discontinuing the publication altogether".[404] He had told "a friend or two", one of whom was Canon Cook, a former colleague from his days at the Education Office, that "no edition . . . would ever appear with the Bishop of Exeter's name in the list of writers". Whether this was because he believed his wishes regarding discontinuation had carried the day, or whether he expected his contribution to be withdrawn, is not clear from the *Memoirs of Archbishop Temple*. However, Cook reported this to Archdeacon Freeman, who wrote to Temple and asked if he could tell Convocation. At this point Temple made his blunder. Freeman's handwriting was, apparently, illegible and Temple said he misread "Convocation" as "conversation" and answered in the affirmative.

> Armed with this authority archdeacon Freeman made the corresponding statement in the Lower House of Convocation at the ensuing group of sessions in February. The announcement was regarded as a public renunciation of Dr. Temple's previous position, and a character was at once given to the act different from what had been intended.[405]

His fellow essayists, and also A. P. Stanley (Dean of Westminster from 1864), were alarmed and said so. Temple was obliged to produce a lengthy explanation of his position in the form of a speech in Convocation, regretting the necessity to speak in such a way whilst "new to the Episcopal office". He had realized, he said, that the liberty which Frederick Temple enjoyed as a private individual was not available to the Bishop of Exeter, who would "be required . . . to be more guarded in everything that he did", realizing that everything which a bishop published was judged in association with whatever happened to be published with it. He explained that he had told a lay friend that he had already decided not to republish his essay and clearly hoped that that would be enough. He had reached his decision without the slightest thought that Convocation would ever be involved. Towards the end of his statement, however, he was true to his liberal instincts and maintained that scholarly liberty and discussions about the inspiration of the Bible should not be curtailed, and "that the freest inquiry in a reverent spirit will . . . uphold the dignity and honour of the Word".[406]

The blunder, however, had the effect of ending the controversy surrounding his appointment, and he was able to settle down to the work of his new ministry and soon demonstrated that Gladstone had made a good choice in selecting him for a bishopric. His capacity for hard work and his practical good sense were apparent and so, within a short time, Temple began to overcome the distrust that was so evident in the earliest days. There was "a gradual infusion of a new spirit" into the Diocese of Exeter. He implemented a policy of visiting each rural deanery every year, and began with an early tour of the whole diocese; he was confident that, "if I once get among them I have little doubt of winning them." With characteristic energy he set out to visit as many parishes as he could to conduct confirmations, often in parishes which had not experienced them in living memory; but he would not confirm more than seventy candidates on any one occasion. His clergy and their parishioners, even in the remotest villages, found that the new bishop had the ability to communicate the faith "in strong but simple words". If the plough boys and their families appreciated him as a preacher, the farmers in the diocese responded to Temple as to one who knew from experience something of their way of life and the difficulties with which they had to deal. At the same time, as a former don and a headmaster, he was recognized as one who could hold his own intellectually, and scholarly clergy were encouraged by his presence in their often remote parishes. Sometimes his visits to parishes proved to be alarming for the clergyman. An anecdote from his later career also illustrates his sometimes grim sense of humour. After hearing a poor sermon, he enquired as to why the priest had no notes or script. The reply was that the man had once been complimented on an extempore sermon and so vowed never to use notes; to which the archbishop responded, "I, Frederick, by Divine Providence Lord Archbishop of Canterbury, Primate of All England and Metropolitan, do hereby dispense you from your vow."[407] Temple's humour was tested on another occasion when he suggested that an elderly incumbent should resign his parish. The man refused, on the grounds that he was going to marry again and that "the new wife would be as good as a curate".[408] Sadly, the author of the relevant *Memoir* did not record Temple's response, which would have been robust. Unfortunately, his brusque and sometimes rude manner became increasingly apparent as the years passed. He was fierce with clergy when he thought them lazy or incompetent, but although they sometimes feared him, they were not dealing with a bully like Phillpotts. A boy at Rugby had long before described him as "a beast, but a just beast".

By the time Frederick Temple was appointed Bishop of Exeter, ritualism had reached even remote and isolated parishes. Temple, with the advantage of encountering the Oxford Movement soon after its earliest phase when he was at Balliol, knew a good deal about the background and convictions of the Tractarians, and that ritualism was a later and somewhat distinct development from those early days. Archdeacon Sandford, who wrote the Exeter section of the *Memoirs* as well as editing the whole, was anxious to refute any allegation that Temple let matters "drift". Although that was an unlikely charge to be levelled at a man with Temple's temperament, Sandford was not entirely successful in his aim. He stated that Temple's policy was relatively simple: passing fashion he would overlook, but illegality must be disciplined. He was sure of his authority as the bishop and objected to any attempts to set it aside or ignore it. Later, he expressed it by his adherence to the bishop's right to veto prosecutions after the Public Worship Regulation Act was passed. When castigated in his London episcopate by a man named Cobham for not using his veto, his reply was a pleasing example of his brusque manner. "The Bishop of London", he wrote, "is much obliged by being informed of the view which Captain Cobham takes of the duty of a bishop." More tactfully, he assured the House of Lords that he would not tolerate the hearing of confessions in church and that he forbade the invocation of the saints and the worship of the Virgin Mary, as had been his Exeter policy. Temple believed that a diocesan bishop could expect obedience from his clergy, but was not always successful in securing it, as Sandford was compelled to admit:

> If the business was uncongenial, or the point to be decided difficult, action was not always prompt ... The law was made for a righteous man—but if anyone did not respond to generous treatment, sometimes he was let alone ... Ritualism was not to be hunted down, but individual law-breakers needed to be followed up; for the most part they were merely passed by, and some of them went on breaking the law still more. The policy was good, but the author of it was not in all respects the right man to carry it out.[409]

Although Temple's reluctance to grasp contentious matters increased as he aged, there may have initially been an undetected degree of subtlety behind the procrastination. Temple knew that he had no coercive authority and had a dislike of litigation. He was always appreciative of the ministry of dedicated clergy, even when he did not approve of their methods, and he may have felt it was sufficient to register his disapproval and not proceed with what the priest in question would have regarded as persecution. It is possible that he saw a willingness to warn, but not compel, as a way of avoiding circumstances which occurred after the passage of the Public Worship Regulation Act, when several hardworking parish clergy were imprisoned for contempt of court for refusing to desist from ritual practices.

One good example of Temple's practical approach was his dealings with a parish priest of strong Tractarian views, G. R. Prynne, Vicar of St Peter's, Plymouth, from 1848 until his death in 1903. Early in his incumbency Prynne had supported the work of Priscilla Sellon and her community of Sisters of Mercy. They had ministered together in a cholera outbreak in 1849, and Prynne had become the confessor to girls in Miss Sellon's orphanage, which had sparked a pamphlet war, but he had continued with the work. On Temple's appointment, he learned of Prynne's reputation, but the two established a good working relationship. It began when Prynne had the courage to call on his new bishop and tell him that he was one of the diocesan clergy who had opposed his appointment. Temple was not a man to resent such frankness, and although he disapproved of Prynne's churchmanship, he encouraged him in his work. In 1882, Temple celebrated the Eucharist in St Peter's, when the new church was consecrated. He gave specific approval to the singing, which was considered to be "advanced" at the time, of the Kyries, the Creed, the Sanctus and the Gloria in Excelsis, and expressed his regret that he was unable to "intone the proper parts of the service". He remarked in the same letter, "I am always desirous of conforming to the wishes of the clergy when I can do so without breach of law", but he continued with his conviction that Holy Communion must be conducted with the celebrant at the "north side, and not before the altar". Afterwards, he wrote again with a generous tribute to Prynne's ministry in Plymouth, a town where Nonconformity and Anglican evangelicalism predominated.

Temple had to deal with the issues around the beautification of churches as the practices of the ritualists expanded. This was derived in large part from the insights of the Cambridge Camden Society, which got its original inspiration from the Oxford Movement and from the widespread Victorian appreciation of "gothic" architecture. By the late 1860s, these strands had come together and helped create a new understanding of the importance of the aesthetic element of worship. In 1872, the Dean and Chapter of Exeter decided to erect a reredos behind the high altar of the cathedral, as part of their plan to restore the cathedral "to much of its original beauty, and adapting it, under the altered conditions of modern times, to enlarge uses worthy of a cathedral". It should be noted that this was before the Public Worship Act which came into force on 1 July 1875. Temple was keen for the work to go ahead, and willingly spoke at fundraising meetings, usually appealing to local sentiments. At Exeter College, Oxford, he spoke more generally, appealing to his audience's religious and historical sense. In all, £50,000 was raised and spent. The reredos was an important part of the project. Although such ornamentation was not likely to have appealed greatly to the bishop, he felt a strong need to maintain good relations with the cathedral chapter. All the restoration work was under the supervision of George Gilbert Scott, and the dean and chapter commissioned the design of the reredos from him. He came up with an elaborate scheme which is well described by Hinchliff:

> It consisted of three panels sculpted in bas-relief. The left-hand panel, as one faced the altar, showed the transfiguration with Jesus

raised above the disciples; the central panel was of the Ascension, depicting Jesus in an ogival frame, with the disciples gathered in a wider picture below; the right-hand panel showed the descent of the Spirit at Pentecost with, again, the disciples gathered in the lower half ... Above the pictorial panels there rose a towering canopy in Gothic style with a cross on the topmost pinnacle. It rose in line with the central pillar between the two arches, changing the whole appearance and perspective of the east end of the cathedral.[410]

It was made of alabaster and marble, studded with what the *Memoir* called "costly stones". Doctrinally, he said it "had no controversial significance", but he felt that the design "expressed the high-water mark of general Anglican feeling on such subjects at the time". But the chapter were not unanimous in their decision to build the reredos, and Archdeacon Phillpotts, who was also canon chancellor, objected to the plan and petitioned against it, believing it to be illegal. Characteristically and consistently with his opinion of episcopal authority, Temple decided to hear the case himself with Mr Justice Keating as his assessor. It was alleged that Temple had no sympathy with the archdeacon's stance, but a hearing began on 7 January 1874 in the Exeter Chapter House and lasted three days. Temple, having "read the opinion of my learned Assessor" accepted it and declared that the reredos was illegal, "and I do order and adjudge that the said Reredos and the Images thereon be removed."[411] However, he went on to invite the dean and chapter to apply to him for a faculty. There is more than a hint in the *Memoirs*, quoting a letter by Temple to Sandford, that he had not expected Keating's assessment to be so sweeping and that he wished the cathedral authorities would appeal, although he did not feel that he could offer advice to only one party of the dispute. The dean and chapter appealed to the Court of Arches, which reversed the judgement. Phillpotts and his friends did not accept the Court of Arches decision and appealed further to the Privy Council, which only upheld part of the Arches' ruling; consequently, the reredos was allowed to remain in place, largely on the grounds that it was there for decorative purposes and was not an object of "superstition". It was characteristic of Temple to be clear in his own mind that beautification was distinct from superstition; he had no doubt that the decorative statues on the reredos were not put there as idols to be worshipped.

In 1876, on 24 August, Temple married. He was almost fifty-five years old, and his bride was Beatrice Blanche Lascelles, more than twenty years his junior. She was probably born in 1845, and Temple was very conscious of the age difference, yet his feelings were profound. Temple's sister described her brother as "very happy ... so happy" in a letter of characteristic generosity to give the news to Benson, at that time still in his Lincoln canonry:

> I daresay the bishop will write himself, but I write to ask you and Mrs Benson to share my joy in his happiness, for he is engaged to be married ... I saw her at once and liked her very much; she is a true, sweet woman with a most pleasant voice and charming, simple manners. He has so lived for others all his life that to see him at last with happiness for himself fills one with thankfulness ... He does look so happy—his eyes shine like stars. God bless them both.[412]

In the short term, his sister had been anxious about leaving Temple, as she planned to go abroad for the winter. Her health had been failing for a number of years, although she had continued to run her brother's house and to act as his hostess. The marriage produced two sons; the younger, William, born in 1881, was to be appointed Archbishop of Canterbury in 1942, making the father and son unique in the history of the Church of England. From the fragmentary evidence quoted and recorded by Sandford, and from William Temple's biographer, it is clear that the gruff-natured Frederick Temple loved his sons and his wife dearly.

During his remaining years at Exeter, as in his later appointments, Temple continued to be a busy man; on more than one occasion, as he went out to his work after a meal, he complained that it was "all gobble and go". He continued to be committed to the cause of temperance. For Frederick Temple, it was a personal conviction, and also a preference. As a boy he had, he readily admitted, preferred water to beer: in a letter to his brother Johnnie from school he said that there was "good beer, though, to tell the truth, I like water better", although he had incurred scorn from his school fellows at Blundell's when he said so. As an undergraduate his poverty had combined with his personal preference. The *Memoirs* claimed that he reached his teetotal view during his years as headmaster of Rugby, but that the "practice was not entirely adopted until later years", although it is not easy to imagine that a man of Temple's strength of character could hold an opinion but not act upon it. Hardly more helpful is an observation in the *Memoirs* that he never adopted the "doctrines of the extreme school" of temperance campaigners. Sadly, he was sometimes fierce even with innocuous offers of hospitality. After one confirmation service in a remote parish, the aged incumbent invited the bishop to his home for a glass of port, only to receive the blunt refusal, "Thank you, I do not drink wine."

Total abstinence from alcohol was unusual, but it became a small part of the nation's developing social awareness, and by the middle of the century some parish clergy were committed to it. One relatively early move in his Exeter episcopate was to strengthen the cause of temperance within the diocese. He had been impressed by a report of the Lower House of Convocation of Canterbury in 1869, which had revealed startling details of the havoc often caused within family life by drunkenness, but he hardly needed a report to reinforce his commitment to temperance as a constant factor in his administration of clerical discipline. In 1872, when Temple delivered his primary *Charge* to the Diocese of Exeter, he spoke very plainly, describing intemperance as increasingly a "great sin". He had been dismayed when interviewing a priest in his library who had described himself "as that most degraded of all creatures, a drunken clergyman". When having to deal with clergy who had a drink problem his brusque and curt manner cut through any excuses or attempted explanations. In the 1880s, he chaired a joint committee of both Houses of Convocation which led to the Clergy Discipline Act of 1892. In the same year, he found himself on the receiving end of public hostility at a meeting called in protest against a Licensing Bill which was before Parliament. His speech was interrupted, violence broke out in the hall, and the police were called. Temple was struck when an objector threw a bag of flour. The local press believed that the perpetrators of the violence had obtained entry by having forged tickets. The following year, at Lambeth Palace, a meeting of the Church of England Temperance Society took place with the endeavour of putting new life into the movement. Temple sent apologies for his absence but supported the formation of branches in his parishes. When he moved to the Diocese of London, he continued with his commitment to the work, as he did in Canterbury diocese. Temple widened his support for temperance beyond the activities of the Church. He became an honorary member of the Independent Order of Rechabites, and Mrs Temple also joined it. Founded in 1835, this was one of the many "friendly societies", but its principal aim was the encouragement of total abstinence from alcohol. It was through that society that he signed a total abstinence pledge. After he left Exeter, Temple became President of the National Temperance League and also chaired the Church of England Temperance Society. He accepted that the society contained activists who were not committed to total abstinence, but who shared the opinion that the consumption of alcohol needed to be much reduced for the good of society.[413] Even in the last year of his life, at a time when his own powers were failing and when he was anxious about his wife's health, he delivered a speech at the annual meeting of the Church of England Temperance Society in Salisbury. His support for the temperance movement was unwavering, but not everyone thought he retained a proper sense of proportion. When he addressed the Church of England Temperance Society in 1892, he admitted that "a great many of my friends tell me over and over again that I press total abstinence a great deal too hard. But I feel that I am only doing what I am bound to do." He spoke on the subject in the House of Lords on a number of occasions; the last time was in 1900.

—

As Temple grew in experience at Exeter, it became clear that Bishop Phillpotts's conviction that the diocese was fundamentally unmanageable if its bishop wanted to visit parishes and get to know his clergy was well-founded. Land's End, as Temple told the House of Lords, is 140 miles from the see city of Exeter. Bishop Phillpotts's arrangement that the income of one of the Exeter canonries, £800 per annum, should be transferred to a new Cornish see, should that come about, was a start. Temple was not the man to delay action once his mind was made up, and he was fortunate that his conviction regarding his diocese came at a time when increasing the episcopate was seen to be necessary. In 1875, the House of Lords put forward an enabling Bill that would have provided for such an increase, and Temple had worked for it and spoke in its favour. The general Bill was unsuccessful, but while it was being moved efforts began to raise the necessary money to finance and endow a Cornish see. By the following year Temple was ready, and a specific Bill to create a separate see for Cornwall was moved in the Lords. The existence of a pre-Conquest Cornish bishopric provided an attractive precedent. A magnificent and timely gift of £40,000 was received. The donor was Lady Rolle, the widow of Lord John Rolle (died 1842). Rolle was the man who fell down the steps at the Queen's coronation, but, more importantly, he had been a liberal supporter of the Church in Devon, and had also financed a new sea wall for Exmouth. Lady Rolle's generosity made the scheme a possibility, and the Bill promoting it received the royal assent in 1876.

An additional and more practical consequence, apart from the reduction in his workload, was that it had financial implications for Temple, whose income was reduced even though Benson, the new bishop, regarded his income as insufficient. Archdeacon Sandford believed that the creation of the Diocese of Truro, despite Temple's recognition of the need for it, was a cause of sadness to him because it severed him from his Cornish roots, although he said many recognized that "a Cornishman gave back Cornwall to herself". A more pertinent observation of Sandford's was to state that "many will think that his [Temple's] greatest piece of work was the revival of the Cornish bishopric". Any regrets which Temple may have had were reduced by the appointment of Benson, his friend of many years and former colleague, as the first Bishop of Truro. They worked happily alongside each other in the west of England, and established a working relationship which, with their close friendship, continued after Benson's unexpected translation to Canterbury in 1883 and Temple's move to London.

Temple was selected by the heads of the Oxford colleges to give the Bampton Lectures of 1884. The eight lectures were delivered in Lent in the University Church of St Mary, and Temple chose as his subject "The Relations between Religion and Science". At Exeter, he was, at least in his early days, a member of the Devonshire Association for the Advancement of Science, Literature and the Arts. He joined within a year of his arrival and served as president of the association. In a presidential address, he had said that the study of science is open to those who were not themselves able to make a contribution because it is a less "individual" or specialized subject than literature and the arts, and he had made the point that "science and Christianity have been given by God's providence to the same nations".[414] Despite what he had written in *Essays and Reviews*, and having introduced some scientific studies to the Rugby School curriculum, he was not, as he declared, a "student of science". However, he was happy to return to the subject almost a quarter of a century later, so the Oxford invitation was welcome.

The lectures attracted no opposition: his views were no longer controversial, but Hinchliff, Temple's modern biographer, speculated that Temple used the lectures to offer the explanation that many had sought at the time of his episcopal consecration. This seems unlikely, however, for it provokes the question as to why he should have bothered, especially after something in excess of two years as a bishop. More likely is Hinchliff's next hypothesis that Temple's real motive was to show that an intelligent believer could accept scientific insights and that, by the same logic, a scientist could hold religious convictions. These possibilities mean that to understand Archbishop Temple's mind it is essential to examine his Bampton Lectures.

The first two lectures considered "The Origin and Nature of Scientific Belief" and "The Origin and Nature of Religious Belief". He began the first lecture with the observation that "among religious men we ought to expect to find the most patient, the most truth-seeking, the most courageous men of science". But he readily admitted that this was often not the case. He regretted that religion appears "to fear and condemn science", while science seems to "despise belief". He drew his listeners' attention to the fact that science recognized the "uniformity of Nature", whilst for believers uniformity is seen to be part of the "character which

God has impressed on His works", who "is greater than all He hath made". Later, in lecture four, he was to argue that "the doctrine of Evolution restores to the science of Nature the unity which we would expect in the creation of God"; that is to say, creation *by* God. However, he had begun his second lecture by asserting that belief in God, and in the character we recognize as his, is not made from observation of phenomena, but is perceived through what he called "the spiritual faculty". That claim led him on to consider "moral law", and the call of religion to believe in "something higher". Temple acknowledged that his argument was "long ago" set forward by Bishop Butler in England and Immanuel Kant in Germany. His own conclusion, at the close of the second lecture, was that

> religion demands the submission of a free conscience, and uses no compulsion but that imposed by its own inherent dignity. Science gives warnings, and if you are capable of understanding argument, you will be incapable of disbelieving the warnings.[415]

The third lecture was a consideration of the "Apparent Conflict between Science and Religion on Free-will". This was the title of the lecture and it can serve as the summary of his argument. The "apparent" conflict was the first collision between science and religion. He referred to Bishop Butler's hypothesis of "divine foreknowledge" and drew a significant distinction between Butler and a modern contrast, for "we" have to work with the concept of nature's "blind mechanical rule".

It was in the fourth lecture that he began to close in on the chief problem between science and religion for many Victorian believers. He dealt with the "Apparent Conflict between Religion and the Doctrine of Evolution", and Temple's opinion is reflected in his title in the choice of the adjective "apparent".

> Now it seems quite plain that this doctrine of Evolution is in no sense whatever antagonistic to the teaching of Religion, though it may be, and that we shall have to consider afterwards as to the teaching of Revelation. Why then should religious men independently of its relation to Revelation shrink from it, as very many unquestionably do? The reason is that whilst this doctrine

leaves the truth of the existence of God exactly where it was, it cuts away, or appears to cut away, some of the main arguments of that truth.[416]

Rather later in the same lecture, Temple drew together the two strands of the "apparent conflict". He said that "we could not overlook the beauty of Nature and of all created things as . . . coming in many cases out of that very survival of the fittest of which Darwin has spoken". However, such a perception is not inimical to accepting the reality of God and, further, Temple's final assertion in that lecture was to conclude that such an understanding of creation and of evolution leaves the argument for an intelligent creator "stronger than it was before".

Temple, in his fifth lecture, set about analysing the nature of revelation, which he very conventionally believed to lead to what he called "the completing of spiritual knowledge". It was a necessary preliminary for his substantial sixth lecture. This was devoted to "The apparent Collision between Religion and the Doctrine of Evolution" and carried forward the conclusions of the fourth lecture. It seems very conventional to the later reader, but that was not the case when it was delivered. Almost his opening statement told his hearers and readers where the Bishop of Exeter stood in regard to the issue:

> It cannot well be denied that the astronomers and geologists have made it exceedingly probable that this earth on which we live has been brought to its present condition by passing through a succession of changes from an original state of great heat and fluidity, perhaps even from a mixture mainly consisting of gasses . . . that it has shrunk as it has cooled.

And then, he soon added, "it certainly could have been [so] formed, and there is no reason for supposing that it was formed in any other way." From this point, Temple went on to talk about the processes by which plants and animals developed. This was something of a by-way in his argument, but it did enable him to proceed to his view that, in the sense of the aim and plan of God, the purpose "behind" evolution is a miracle.

Temple said Darwinism consists of "the transmission of characteristics from progenitor to progeny, and the introduction of minute variations in the progeny with each successive generation", and he asserted that the theory is "incomplete".[417] Turning to the biblical accounts of creation, he said that Genesis does not attempt to say by what processes creation occurred, nor "how much time it took to work out those processes". However, Genesis has fundamental truths to communicate which Temple listed: creation "out of nothing"; the spiritual source of all existence; the orderly and progressive nature of creation; how creation progressed from the inanimate to the animate with mankind as its "crown", said Temple, once again accepting the common Victorian opinion of humanity.

He concluded, "we cannot find that Science in teaching Evolution, has yet asserted anything that is inconsistent with Revelation, unless we assume that Revelation was intended not to teach spiritual truth only, but physical truth also." This was a theme which he pursued in the penultimate lecture, where he sought to relate scientific knowledge to "supernatural power". This, however, tended to go over what he had already covered in some detail, and set the ground for the final lecture, which was "The Conclusion of the Argument". That conclusion was well-summarized in a sentence which, in itself, shows how far theological thinking had progressed during the nineteenth century, when, only two years after the death of Charles Darwin, a bishop who was soon to be promoted to the important See of London and who would become Archbishop of Canterbury, was able to declare:

> It is distinctly the fault of religious, not scientific men, that there was once a great contest between the Bible and Astronomy, that there has since been a great contest between the Bible and Geology, that there is still a great contest between the Bible and Evolution. In no one of these cases was the Revelation contained in the Bible in danger, but only the interpretation commonly put upon the Bible.[418]

Temple had had his sixty-third birthday just a couple of months before he moved to London and had been Bishop of Exeter for fifteen years. During that time, he had overcome the distrust and suspicion with which he had been met in 1869 and had won the hearts of many church members in his diocese and beyond. His Exeter farewells were protracted and sincere because, Sandford said, he was "trusted and followed as few, if any, of his predecessors had been". It could not have been more different from the situation when he had been appointed, and Temple long remained in the affections of the people of the West Country. He became chair of the governors of his old school; he was made a Freeman of the City of Exeter in 1897 and of Tiverton in 1901.

Despite the regard of the people of his first diocese and many in the wider Church, Frederick Temple was not an obvious candidate for London. The urbane Davidson, Dean of Windsor at the time, believed that none of the possible candidates, Temple, Lightfoot of Durham, and Goodwin of Carlisle, were ideal, but all three possessed many of the "necessary qualifications". Archbishop Benson recorded that the prime minister, Gladstone, would only appoint a man approved by the primate, and that the choice eventually lay between Lightfoot and Temple. Among the reasons for not appointing Temple was the incipient problem of his gradually failing eyesight, but it did not prevent Gladstone from selecting him, and Temple tried not to allow it to impede his activities. He was enthroned in St Paul's Cathedral in April 1885. This time there were no objections, and the confirmation of his election had also been without incident. Temple's predecessor, John Jackson, was described as "firm rather than strong", but the *Memoirs* asserted that in Temple the diocese got someone with both qualities: "the man best fitted for the work was, in God's providence, selected to do it."

The *Memoirs* author of the London years was H. E. J. Bevan, Archdeacon of Middlesex and Rector of Chelsea. He could not avoid describing Temple as "angular" and reported that the bishop, "terribly earnest", came among his clergy as an unknown quantity "with his dignified, swart, powerful figure".[419] If his reputation for brusqueness had not gone before him, it soon caught up, when he wrote a letter to his rural deans. His idea was to invite the clergy of the various rural deaneries to elect their own rural deans to represent them, rather than have them arbitrarily appointed by the diocesan bishop. Uncontroversial now, this was a novelty at the time, and Temple could have expressed his requirement with greater tact. His letter "caused considerable dissatisfaction" and seemed likely to lead to a meeting in protest. In the end, nothing happened, and when Temple did meet the rural deans, rather later, he humbly but firmly stuck to his position and averted trouble. His new procedure was introduced on 1 June 1885. That early incident could not have helped Temple, who was initially regarded by many of his clergy "as cold and unsympathetic ... brusque and overbearing". Within a relatively short time he began to win their respect and affection. Henry Scott Holland, a residentiary canon of St Paul's from 1884, who always wrote fulsomely, was not a man who wore his heart on his sleeve, but Temple won his affection with his "straight-forward nature". Further, his "apparent grimness which took in the grown-ups" could be penetrated by children. Holland also thought that "austerity only impressed itself on the face as years went on, and that roughness and burliness which became so characteristic were not there at all to start with".[420] This opinion was strengthened by the Canterbury *Memoirs* author, Bishop G. F. Browne of Bristol, who stated, "When Dr. Temple was Bishop of London, there was an idea in many quarters that he was a man of hard, unsympathetic character." Browne continued with the predictable observation that that was not so, but "the fault of such misconception did not lie altogether with those who formed it. In doing the business of his diocese he appeared to be working from the head alone." However, he concluded, Temple's "heart gave his head more guidance than others could perceive".

The Bishop of London has always had a prominent role in the life of the Church of England. The same applies to the wider life of the nation, not least through the House of Lords but also as a result of the multifarious elements of London life and society. Previously, Temple had tended to root himself in his diocese, partly to establish his reputation as someone who was not a dangerous liberal, but in London he could not avoid a greater involvement, even though he continued to feel awkward in the Lords.

Throughout his life, Temple's strong moral sense informed his approach to pastoral issues, and he had a well-informed social conscience. Among the issues that had concerned him in his Exeter days was the tendency towards early marriage among rustics. However, he was a practical man and realized that moral issues could be best addressed through the spread of education. His concern for poverty was not confined to morality and his educational work; he was anxious to improve the relation of the Church to the poor in his diocese and spoke about it to ruridecanal chapters and at his diocesan conferences. His busy life restricted the time he had available for visits to parishes for confirmation services and other matters, but he persevered with both. Years later he told the Canterbury diocese that he intended to continue his long-established pattern of personally taking a third of the confirmation services. The bishop's commitment to the temperance movement, and his concern for poor people, were among the driving forces with which he continued in his new and more demanding diocese. Still with the poor in his mind he added to the land which Jackson had made available as a public park attached to Fulham Palace, his official residence. Later, in 1901 when he was Archbishop of Canterbury, he made a similar gift of part of the parkland adjacent to Lambeth Palace.

In his first year Temple decided not to hold a diocesan conference, which had been his long-standing practice in Exeter, but to devote his time to familiarizing himself with his new diocese. As an experienced diocesan bishop, Temple slipped easily into a routine of confirmations and parish visits in the geographically much smaller, but more populous, Diocese of London. He set about reorganizing the administration of the diocese. Other actions included introducing a scheme for lay readers, which was partly responsible for the wider development of lay ministries in the Church of England. Temple increased the number of suffragan bishops, although his relations with the suffragan who was in place on his arrival in London, William Walsham How, were initially difficult as Temple did not allow him the same degree of autonomy as had Jackson. Bishop Jackson had allowed him to limit his work to East London, whereas Temple was prepared to let him concentrate on that area but wished him also to operate across the diocese. Temple, as diocesan, expected to work in all parts of it, including the east. For Temple his new work was enhanced by the friendship of Benson, who was also comparatively new to his role, having been translated from Truro to Canterbury in 1883.

Temple's appointment as one of Archbishop Benson's five assessors for the lengthy trial of Bishop Edward King was noticed in the previous chapter. It is unclear as to the extent of Temple's contribution to the process and its outcome, although Sandford stated that "it was an open secret that Dr. Temple was the archbishop's chief advisor throughout the trial". However, this seems unlikely when Benson's fascination with liturgy is remembered, and it is recalled that Temple was no devotee of ritual minutiae, although tolerant of some aspects of ceremonial. Quite probably, Temple's most important contribution to the trial was his ability to get swiftly to the core of a problem, which combined with his robust common sense and straightforward manner of expression. Certainly, the trial made an impression upon him, and he regarded it as sufficiently important to speak of it at some length in his addresses to his ruridecanal conference in 1892. He reviewed the case and offered advice which was simple: that clergy should consult their diocesan before making liturgical changes in their churches, and they should then follow his ruling. He also directed that nothing should be added to the order of service in the Book of Common Prayer; this was a cautionary way of establishing boundaries for both sides. If these points seem rather naive of Temple, it exemplified his tendency to treat his clergy as he had the boys at Rugby, expecting obedience when he issued directives.

Temple's experience of the Oxford Movement as a young man, and the later changes in ceremonial, had little influence on his liturgical practice, and he always celebrated Holy Communion at the north end of the holy table. He was rough with a clergyman who tried to get him to follow local custom and face east: "it will not be the custom this morning", he declared. He was reluctant to issue directives against practices that may have been lawful, or not forbidden by law, however much complainants persevered, and however great his personal dislike of those practices. This was consistent with his belief that clergy would obey his instructions over ceremonial once he had expressed his decision. Occasionally it was claimed that Temple allowed ritualistic matters to "drift", but that was unjust and was probably strengthened by the distinction which he drew between "the complaint of the genuinely aggrieved parishioner and that of an outsider—especially in the form of a self-constituted public body or association".[421] This was a relevant distinction in that it eliminated cases where an "outsider" attended an act of worship looking for ritual irregularities about which he could then complain to the bishop with the hope of pursuing a clergyman through the courts. Temple's practice was disliked by the protestant Church Association which followed that practice, as had been the case, in part, with the Bishop of Lincoln, when it had struggled to find a parishioner to be the complainant. Rather, his policy was to allow conscientious clergy to get on with their ministry within parameters that were clear to him. He was characteristically fierce with disobedient clergy when directives had been issued but ignored. He would not tolerate the hearing of confessions in church, and always investigated reports of "the invocation of saints or the worship of the Virgin", he told the House of Lords.[422] He was fortunate that he arrived as Bishop of London after the scandal of the imprisonment of four clergy, two from his new diocese, for contempt of court following ritualistic offences.[423] Much of the dust had settled, and clergy enjoyed more liberty from the mid-1880s. Even so the Church Association, convinced that high churchmanship was some sort of papal plot, had not given up, despite the obloquy that the case against Bishop King generated against it.

In the early 1880s, the Dean and Chapter of St Paul's Cathedral decided to erect a reredos behind the high altar. It was designed by the renowned architect G. F. Bodley, whom the cathedral commissioned in 1883.

> Bodley promptly produced suggestions for a splendid and elaborate reredos in marbles of many colours. The central feature was to be a sculptured group of figures representing the crucifixion of the Saviour, set in a frame of wreathed and twisted columns, with pediment over and crowned with statuary. This towering erection, reaching to the clerestory, was truly calculated to provide an impressive termination to the choir, and one, moreover, which would strike an unmistakably religious note.[424]

It was a splendid object, but inevitably controversial; even the high church Canon Liddon had initial misgivings. The design was utterly objectionable to the Church Association which, once again on the warpath, led the opposition which sought to prevent its erection, or if unsuccessful, gain its later removal.

For Temple, there were obvious similarities with his experience at Exeter, where the dean and chapter had undertaken a similar project, so he was aware of the need to tread carefully. There was a significant difference, however, between the two cases which had nothing to do with design or aesthetics or theology, but rather with timing. The Exeter case had been in 1872, whereas the St Paul's reredos was planned from 1883 and completed in 1888. The Public Worship Regulation Act had been passed in 1874 and, as has been noted, the Act gave the diocesan bishop the authority to veto proposed prosecutions. Temple exercised his right, although (again) he did not much like the proposal, and the case against the dean and chapter fell at that first hurdle. The unfortunate Temple was pursued through the courts by the Church Association in efforts to compel him to set aside his veto, but they were ultimately unsuccessful when in July 1891 the House of Lords supported his actions. The reredos remained in place until it was damaged by a bomb in 1940; the central figure of the crucified Christ survived, and it was alleged to be the largest crucifix to appear in an Anglican church since the Reformation.

Temple was much interested in social issues and became involved in efforts to end a strike by dockworkers in London, which began on 14 August 1889. His actions were described by Scott Holland as a "blunder", and he put it down to a "touch" of the bishop's customary "aloofness". The strike was due to the pay of casual unskilled dockworkers being very low, to the extent that men often could not adequately feed themselves or their families. Consequently, they withdrew their labour in the hope of gaining more; the situation was then exacerbated when the skilled dockworkers came out on strike in sympathy. Within a relatively short while 80,000 men were involved, the Port of London was brought to a standstill, and there was a fear of unrest. Many dockers were Irish Roman Catholics, and Cardinal Manning feared that there would be bloodshed. In the *Memoirs*, the situation was described by Sydney Buxton, MP for Poplar. He was a man committed to social reform and sympathetic to the strikers. Although he did not claim it, Buxton was probably the one who saw that "some recognized authority was required from whence effective intervention could practically proceed."[425] He contacted the Lord Mayor of London (Sir James Whitehead), who was on holiday, but who returned as a result. A committee was established which included the Lord Mayor, Buxton, and several others. Among them were Cardinal Manning and Bishop Temple. Manning had a more sympathetic general manner than Temple and commanded considerable respect among the dockers. In the end, it was the cardinal who emerged with the greatest credit from an unsatisfactory situation, and his biographer relished that fact. The two senior clergy were significant members of the committee. Canon Mason, the Vicar of All Hallows, Barking, near the Tower of London, thought that Temple's willingness to serve had induced the Lord Mayor to convene the group. Temple, like the Lord Mayor, returned from holiday to take part. Holland gave a lively description of how Temple was induced to come back to London:

> A little knot of us met and decided that he must come back. It was getting late in the evening, and we could only discover vaguely that he was in Wales. Cyril Bickersteth [the secretary of the Christian Social Union] was determined to rush off to the nearest town to Wales and wait there till we wired to him where the bishop might be found. We were all holding him back by his coat-tails from this impossible adventure, when there came a rap at the door and a wire from Fulham, to say Dolgelly. Bickersteth flew from our hands, only to find that he had got no money at all, and to turn back to implore us to lend him the needful. We poured out what we could from our pockets and he vanished into the night towards Euston.[426]

Whether Bickersteth's mission was conclusive, or whether Temple had already decided to return, cannot be known, but soon he was back in London giving strength and direction to the Lord Mayor's committee, which soon met with the leaders of the striking dockworkers, Tillett and Burns. A compromise was reached under which new pay arrangements would come into force on 1 March 1890 and the leaders went off to secure the support of the strikers. However, second thoughts brought them back to the negotiations, and the date was brought back to 1 January. The leaders still equivocated, because they were unable to win over the men they represented. Temple concluded that they were unreliable and that the committee's efforts could not succeed. He decided that he had no chance of making a difference and returned to his family holiday in Wales. This was described by E. S. Purcell, Manning's biographer, in less than flattering terms. Temple was "indignant at what he considered the duplicity of the Leaders of the Strike, shook the dust from off his feet and left the Committee of Conciliation in the lurch." Undoubtedly Temple had made a mistake, as it left the field clear for Manning, who was genuinely interested in achieving a settlement and was trusted by both sides. He arranged to meet with a larger number of dockers than just the original representatives and achieved a settlement at a meeting from which Temple was the only absentee. The strike ended on 14 September and for this Manning was lauded, and Temple suffered adverse comparison.

Archbishop Benson, on holiday in Switzerland at the time of the strike, was among those who recognized that Temple had blundered. Benson said, "Cardinal Manning has done well for London. But why has my dear Bishop of London gone back and left it to him? Are the dockers Roman Catholics all?" But Benson had no liking for Manning and was recorded as declaring that those who knew Manning with "his resourceless brain, his character and knowledge of dramatic effect, will not be deceived. All others will."[427] The urbane Benson would not have understood that for Temple the situation was uncomplicated. He felt let down by the temporizing, as he saw it, of the strikers' leaders and was unwilling to waste further time and energy. In this was revealed some of the less satisfactory aspects of Temple's character, particularly his inflexibility, and his impatience with persons who were less decisive than himself or who had to consult rather than direct others to a goal he thought desirable.

The 1889 dock strike was the most high-profile example of Temple's engagement with social issues but was by no means unique. He protested against "sweated labour" although he was reluctant to be associated with specific societies, such as the Anti-Sweating League, because he believed that good should be done secretly.[428] In October 1889, he wrote to a leading proponent of the league stating his conviction that employers should always pay a man wages "on which he can live". His advocacy of secrecy was conspicuously different from his very public identity with the temperance movement.

Throughout his entire episcopal career, Frederick Temple was always dedicated to the education of the poor. His experience meant that he was one of the most knowledgeable men in the Church of England in that subject. It is recorded that during his service as a member of a Royal Commission on Education in 1888, he never missed a session. One outcome of the commission was an Education Bill in 1890, and Temple threw his weight and influence behind it in the House of Lords and elsewhere. He recognized that the Church did not have the resources to be the sole provider of elementary education, but he urged the strengthening of the Church's commitment whilst seeking to influence the provision by government. He was convinced that it was the only long-term solution to the problems of poverty, and close to the end of his life his final visitation *Charge* as archbishop was concerned with the Education Bill, which was before Parliament in 1902. He continued to hold the belief that there were four basic principles of elementary education. First, that religion was fundamental to the inculcation of morality; second, that Christian homes were essential to teach religion; third, the religious convictions of school teachers were vital if the teaching of Christianity was to be effectual; and fourth, that the religious training of the young was an indispensable part of the mission and work of the Church. When he was invited to sit on a Royal Commission on secondary education in 1894, he "contented himself" with appearing as a witness. From 1887 Temple concerned himself with university education whilst in London and supported proposals to develop a "teaching university" element in the University of London, once again giving evidence to a commission, and asserting that there was no need for a theological faculty although, should one be established, it should not have any credal ties. He was, however, convinced of the continued need for King's College, London, to remain distinctively Anglican.[429]

—

Temple was immersed in his work as Bishop of London when Benson died in Hawarden parish church. At the age of seventy-five, he expected to end his distinguished ministry in London. When the call to Canterbury came, it was clear that he would not serve for long. His friendship and close working relationship with Benson meant that he had a knowledge of the primacy which, combined with almost twenty years of experience as a diocesan bishop, gives credence to his observation that the work would bring no surprises.

London was sorry to lose the bishop whom so many had at first feared. *F. Londin*, as he had signed himself, abbreviating his official *Londinensis*, had won the affection of Londoners from all walks of life. The growth of this affection had become evident over the years. In 1891, the diocese had presented him with a crosier as a mark of their affection for their chief pastor. It was a gift from both clergy and laity. The inscription bore his name and recognized his ministry, and yet anticipated the future: "*et successoribus*". The presentation was made in Sion College, and Temple himself was much moved by the occasion, which was an echo of a similar event in Exeter in October 1877. On that occasion the gift, again for the use of Temple and his successors, was from the laity; then the clergy gave a portrait, but the presentations all demonstrate that Temple had won the hearts of those he was sent to lead and serve, after early initial anxiety. On both occasions the famously gruff Temple was deeply moved and had the courage to say so.

The diocesan farewells began with a public event in St Paul's Cathedral on 23 December 1896. It was followed by a great gathering in the Guildhall in the middle of January 1897, which was attended by an estimated 1,500 people. The original venue was to have been Church House, the building of which Temple had vigorously supported, but the choice of the larger Guildhall was necessary and more appropriate for it served to link the diocese with the whole of the capital city, and thus acknowledged the ministry of the bishop to the whole of London. It was fitting that those present included the Lord Mayor and the corporation as well as Temple's senior clerical colleagues.

His welcome to Canterbury was also enthusiastic. The mayor and corporation of the city gave a reception in the Canterbury Guildhall on the eve of his enthronement. It was similar, according to the relevant *Memoir* author, to that given to Benson fourteen years before, although there is no reference to the blowing of the ancient "burgmote" horn which, as was noticed, caused "irreverent laughter" on the earlier occasion. Temple acknowledged a local sensitivity in stating his belief that the Archbishop of Canterbury should have a residence in the city. Benson had thought so too, and hoped that it might one day become possible, and that he would live to see it. Temple set about making it a reality. His predecessor had enjoyed the country house at Addington, near Croydon, acquired by Howley's predecessor, Manners-Sutton, but Temple never used it, believing that the day was passed when Archbishops of Canterbury should appear as "country gentlemen". He persuaded the Ecclesiastical Commissioners to let him sell it, which happened in July 1898. Since the inauguration of the commissioners, the Archbishop of Canterbury no longer had unfettered access to funds to spend as Howley had done at Lambeth. It was arranged for the sale proceeds to be used, in part, for the purchase and alteration of a house in the cathedral precincts at Canterbury. "The Old Palace", as it had always been known (and still is), stands close to the west end of the cathedral. It occupied the site of the original archbishop's palace; the last archiepiscopal resident had been Matthew Parker (died 1575), who had repaired fire damage that had occurred in the time of Archbishop Cranmer. During the intervening centuries part of it had been let to tenants. Temple's architect, W. D. Caroe, set to work on the site, which was restricted both by its size and the discovery of archaeological ruins. He managed to provide what the new archbishop wanted and even, with a nice historical touch, preserved some of the ancient remains and also the entrance to the cathedral cloisters through which Thomas Becket had passed on the day of his murder. The work was almost finished by the end of 1900, and Temple was pleased with the result. Asked whether he thought future archbishops would want a house in Canterbury, he was not worried; he declared that he wanted "to make 'em live there". Temple's desire for a home in his new diocese was not a mere flight of fancy. It was the expression of his conviction that a bishop should live among his people whenever possible. By the last years of the Queen's reign, the diocesan work of bishops had been much developed, notwithstanding the development of the ministry of suffragan bishops. Tait had needed such help because of his poor health, and Temple because he was aged. In addition, the Archbishop of Canterbury was more limited than other diocesans in the time which he could devote to his local responsibilities. Temple saw the acquisition of the Old Palace as an obvious way to facilitate what he could do in the eastern part of Kent, not least somewhere to answer "the need of more constant meeting" between the archbishop and his clergy. It gave the diocese some sort of headquarters that all could appreciate. The archbishop could more conveniently share in the worship of the parishes and the cathedral. Also, although not acknowledged, it gave the old man somewhere comfortable to retreat after going about the diocese.

—

Temple's enthronement in Canterbury Cathedral took place on 8 January 1897, the archbishop having stayed the night before as a guest of Dean Farrar and his wife. The service was designed to be a memorable occasion. As such, the enthronement of Queen Victoria's last Archbishop of Canterbury marked a significant contrast with that of the archbishop who was in post when her reign began. Howley, it will be recalled, had been enthroned by proxy in his absence. Such a practice would have been unthinkable to Temple; just as the time had passed when archbishops might be seen as country gentlemen, so the time of absentee bishops had also passed. Simply, the episcopal office demanded more from its holder than had been the case when the Queen came to the throne. The *Memoir* of the primacy described the two-fold nature of the enthronement ceremony. Archbishop Temple was placed in Howley's throne in the quire, and then a procession of senior bishops and cathedral clergy accompanied him to the "marble" chair, known as St Augustine's throne, in which he was also placed by the Archbishop of York. Afterwards Dean Farrar, who had been appointed in 1895, made a speech in the cathedral library at the luncheon which followed the service and Temple found his words very moving. In his reply, Temple acknowledged his two immediate predecessors, Benson, his friend of more than four decades, and Tait, his former tutor.

The enthronement took place on a Friday, and Temple got to work immediately. The most immediate claim upon the attention of the new Archbishop of Canterbury, however, was not diocesan. One of the issues which demanded urgent attention when Temple became archbishop was the need to respond to the Papal Bull, *Apostolicae curae*, which declared Anglican orders invalid in both their form and the intention behind them. The Bull had been issued in September 1896 by Pope Leo XIII, who had succeeded Pius IX in 1878. In 1894, Benson had had to contend with the unofficial endeavours of Lord Halifax and Abbé Portal to bring Rome and Canterbury nearer. Benson's extreme caution was noticed above. The Vatican had also offered no encouragement to the enthusiasts. Indeed, the efforts of Halifax and his friend had reignited the hostility of Roman Catholics, not least in England. Cardinal Vaughan had succeeded Manning in 1892 as Archbishop of Westminster and was no friend of the Anglican Church. In a speech in Preston, he made "a full-scale attack on the Church of England [with] a denial of any possibility of reunion conceived on terms other than those of total submission". Later, commenting on his speech, he uncompromisingly rejected the validity of Anglican orders.[430]

By the time Temple succeeded to the primacy, the decision had already been made that a response to the Papal Bull was necessary. Responsibility had been devolved to three of the Church's most learned bishops. They were the eminent historian William Stubbs of Oxford, who was an assessor at Edward King's trial, Mandell Creighton of Peterborough, and John Wordsworth of Salisbury. Creighton had been the first to see that a response was needed and, coincidentally, was to follow Temple at London. He was a historian whose principal work was a five-volume history of the papacy. Wordsworth, the son of Archbishop Benson's old mentor at Lincoln, had the theological expertise which meant that he was among the most appropriate Anglicans to lead the response to *Apostolicae curae*. He had studied the nature of the English episcopal succession, when the Vatican Council of 1870 had led to the schism which produced the Old Catholic Churches. Anglican orders were recognized by the Old Catholic Churches and, in 1890, he had written a response for, as he described it, the "General Assembly of the Church of Holland". The three episcopal scholars were to submit their response to the two archbishops and worked together to do so. Wordsworth drafted the Latin version. The document was received by Benson on the day he died. Wordsworth recorded his "sad and sore heart" on receiving the draft back, unopened, after Benson's death. It was eventually forwarded to Temple and William

Maclagan, the Archbishop of York. Wordsworth was anxious that the new Archbishop of Canterbury might be preoccupied, but, with his customary energy, Temple began to work on the document. On 4 January 1897, Wordsworth spent four hours with him, so the delay was short. Temple, in his own words, "cut out all the thunder". He was a man who knew thunder when he saw it. Wordsworth generously said that Temple's emendations were the result of his determination "that every trace of bitterness should be eradicated from the draft... and this was due, not to policy, but to deep Christian feeling as to what our Lord would wish to be the temper of controversy". The *Responsio* was published over the names of Temple and Maclagan in Latin, English, French, and Greek. Inevitably, Cardinal Vaughan produced what he called a "Vindication", and some correspondence followed, but the publication of the *Responsio* effectively ended Temple's brief but important involvement in the matter, which, as Wordsworth wrote, was "a very troublesome and painful dispute", which brought about "the thinly veiled hostility which now characterizes our official relations" with the Roman Catholic Church. At the Lambeth Conference later in the year, the bishops of the Anglican Communion repeated a declaration from their 1888 meeting "that, under present conditions, it is useless to consider the question of Reunion with our brethren of the Roman Church".[431]

—

Plans for a fourth Lambeth Conference, to be held in the summer of 1897, had already been drawn up by Archbishop Benson when Temple became archbishop. There were good reasons for holding the Conference then, rather than waiting for a full decade from its predecessor. That year marked the sixtieth anniversary of Queen Victoria's accession to the throne. It was also the 1300th anniversary of St Augustine's mission from Rome and the establishment of Christianity in southern England. Benson, with his finely developed historical sense, had looked forward to the two anniversaries.

Just before the Conference began, the Queen's diamond jubilee was celebrated with a service of thanksgiving at St Paul's Cathedral on Sunday, 21 June 1897, at which Bishop Creighton preached. Temple was present with a large number of other bishops. Another event which marked the jubilee occurred on the Tuesday, when the Queen attended a reception outside St Paul's. This was the occasion when Temple, noticing a delay among the departing carriages, called for "Three Cheers" for Her Majesty to cover the hiatus; it was said that the Queen was greatly moved by such a spontaneous outpouring of affection. The monarch was present at an event for the Conference when the bishops attended a service at St George's Chapel, Windsor Castle, on 13 July. The bishops assembled outside the chapel for the Queen's arrival and bowed as her carriage drew up. She was met by Temple and Davidson, now Bishop of Winchester, who presented some of the visiting bishops, including the only two black bishops at the Conference.

The Conference was attended by 197 bishops. On Friday 2 July, they commemorated St Augustine's arrival with a visit to Ebbsfleet in Kent, which is traditionally recognized as the spot where he and his party of forty monks landed in 597. A service was held near the memorial cross on the site, and then the party, which included some guests, moved to the nearby Roman ruins known as Richborough Castle. There they were greeted by the mayor and corporation of the nearby town of Sandwich. Another outing for the bishops occurred when Temple and more than a hundred went by special train to Glastonbury on 3 August. It was a pilgrimage to another cradle of British Christianity and a place "intimately connected with the much earlier Christianity of the British races".[432]

Bishop Davidson was the episcopal secretary to the Conference and shared his uncomfortable role with Bishop Kennion of Bath and Wells. He made his usual complaint that Temple did not delegate or inform his colleagues of his plans. The Conference got properly under way with a Quiet Day for the bishops led by Edward King on 30 June. Such an event and with such a conductor reveals something of the extent to which the insights and principles of the Oxford Movement had penetrated Anglicanism. The programme for the Conference had been thoroughly prepared by Benson or, at least, under his direction and needed little adjustment. The agenda had been expanded from six subjects to twelve since 1888. The first on the list was "The Organization of the Anglican Communion", which "suggested the possibility of both a consultative body of the Anglican Communion and a court of reference". The Americans doubted the wisdom of such a body, and others were disappointed that it would have no legislative authority.[433] There was the fear that a sort of Anglican patriarchate might be established in the person of the Archbishop of Canterbury. This was a particular issue for the bishops from the United States of America because of their historically different relationship to the archbishop than Anglicans from the colonies.

Gradually the bishops worked their way through their inherited agenda, with Temple in the chair. Initially there was some apprehension as to the quality of his chairing. His age led some to doubt his ability to sustain the leadership of a large group of men, each of whom were, almost by definition, accustomed to setting their own stamp on proceedings. The second anxiety concerned his reputation for abruptness. There was a fear that he would be blunt and intolerant; the Americans were at first particularly concerned regarding this, but Temple won them over. He was gruff and occasionally very nearly rude, but afterwards there was general approval for the way in which he had worked as chairman. At the close of the Conference, Temple was the sole author of what they called an *encyclical*, which preceded the resolutions of the Conference. He had not consulted anyone before he wrote it and, remarkably, he had worked on it overnight and laid it before the Conference as a finished document. Unremarkably, it attracted disagreement; several declared that he was unjust in his criticism of some aspects of missionary work. Equally unremarkably, Temple refused to make any alterations, and the discussion got nowhere because Temple persevered in what certain bishops regarded as stubbornness. The following morning, however, he opened the proceedings by announcing that he did propose to modify the passages which had been criticized. One bishop tried volubly to thank him, but Temple cut him off: "you may thank me as much as you like, but you must do it in silence."

He managed the detail of meetings well and was fair in his dealings with his brethren; despite his age, he led the Conference with significant energy. One bishop recorded Temple's "genuine considerateness and ... frequent gaiety and lightness of touch for which many were not prepared". By the end Temple had won the confidence and loyalty of the assembled bishops. After the Conference he was presented with a significant tribute by the Americans. Initially their plan was to give him a mitre (which would probably have pleased Benson), but Davidson, when approached for advice, shrewdly suggested otherwise and a private Communion set was commissioned. Archbishop Temple was delighted. It was made of gold and was appropriately engraved:

> F. Cantuar
> Archbishop Primate Metropolitan
> Presiding over the
> Lambeth Conference of 1897
> In the spirit of power and of love and of a sound mind
> From his brothers in the American Episcopate
> An affectionate recognition of his wise leadership
> His justice his generosity his gracious hospitality.

—

An example of Frederick Temple's energetic personality was his first official visit to Scotland as Archbishop of Canterbury. His enthusiasm for the temperance movement led to an invitation to address the General Assembly of the Church of Scotland on the subject, which he did in May 1898. The Church of Scotland is, of course, a Presbyterian body, so it was remarkable that, at that time, an invitation should be issued to a senior cleric of a body with which it was not in communion. The engagement in Edinburgh began with the archbishop as the guest of honour at a breakfast on the morning after his arrival, attended by 250 invited guests, before he went to a meeting of a temperance committee to which he made a short speech. Afterwards he went to Holyrood Palace and then to the Church of Scotland Assembly Hall, where he gave his main speech. He was introduced to the Assembly

> as the most distinguished living representative of the famous Church of England, a minister of Christ who had ennobled a great and gracious career by his courageous and unwearied and impassioned defence of the greatest of all modern social reforms, the cause of temperance.[434]

As Temple was led to the floor of the house to give his address, he received a standing ovation. His speech was typical of the kind he had given many times and dwelt upon the themes of hopefulness that the movement would spread and prosper as it must, because it was an aspect of Christ's command that people should love one another. Temperance, he argued, was consistent with personal liberty, but needed the support of the legislature. On a practical level, he sought to encourage the clergy of the Church of Scotland in their work for the cause and finished by expressing his appreciation of the "extraordinary kindness" he had received on his visit. Yet another meeting followed his success at the General Assembly before Temple was released to catch a train to London that afternoon.

Temple made another demanding visit to Scotland in 1902, not long before his eightieth birthday, when he accepted an invitation to preach at the dedication of a new chapter house added to the cathedral of the Episcopalian Church in Perth. The bishop was G. H. Wilkinson, who had been appointed in 1893. Before his Scottish appointment, Wilkinson had succeeded Benson at Truro in 1883, and so had been Temple's episcopal "neighbour" until he moved to London. Temple attended an early celebration of Holy Communion on the day after his arrival, and undertook a full programme of speaking and visiting, which ended with a reception. He stood to shake hands with innumerable people, and his geniality combined with his commanding presence was said to have made a deep and lasting impression.

As has been recorded, Temple moved into the work of the archbishopric without any qualms or hesitation and with his lifelong sense of dedication unimpaired, but his energy was not at the level it was, and there was the permanent problem of his eyesight. F. A. Iremonger, in his biography of William Temple, recorded that the old archbishop preached in St Mary's, Oxford, in his last year, and his son waited for him at the foot of the pulpit steps to guide him back to his place, for the archbishop was "unable—as he had been for some years—to see things at ground level".[435] Nevertheless, he continued his diocesan work with gusto and set about his primatial duties in a similar manner. During the six years that Temple served as Archbishop of Canterbury, he conducted two Visitations and issued two *Charges* to his diocese. The first was in 1898 and, consistent with his nature, Temple tackled contentious issues in what he said to the assembled clergy. The title of the published *Charge* was "Disputes in the Church", and at least 4,000 copies were printed and sold. The first section dealt with "The doctrine of the Eucharist" and he made the stark observation that some believers "hold that there is no special gift . . . bestowed in the Sacrament", but that its value is, mainly, "in the effect produced on the soul of the receiver". Other sincere persons believe that the Sacrament unites "us to Christ in a special manner and degree . . . far beyond the natural working of our minds". Temple picked his way between the convictions he had identified. He regretted the fact that "a good many" had come to accept what he called the "Lutheran" view in the previous fifty years, but he ended by referring to the teaching of that most classic Anglican scholar, Richard Hooker. That section of the *Charge* was a skilful exposition of what he believed to be tolerated doctrine in the Church of England. The following day he ventured on to more controversial ground with a paper on "The Proper Objects of Worship and Prayers for the Dead". In this, he reiterated his well-known conviction that prayers for the dead were not permissible to Anglicans, except in private:

> In our private prayers there is nothing in the Church of England teaching to forbid our prayers for those whom we love, and who are gone before us, but in our public worship there is need of that kind of reverence which restrains the language and which perpetually acknowledges our ignorance—our ignorance both as to what is happening in the world of spirits, and our ignorance of how God will bring to a completion the work which He has begun in Christian souls.

Next time he turned his attention to "The Practice of Confession". Temple pointed out that "a confession voluntarily made under pressure of perplexity and trouble is a very different thing from confession as a regular custom enforced by heavy sanctions". This was the core of his argument, and he recognized that it "is impossible to lay down rigid rules in such a matter". The fourth section of his *Charge* was delivered in Maidstone and dealt with what he called "Uniformity in Ceremonial". Once again, he was predictable in what he said, emphasizing that "ceremonial is not in itself a matter of very great importance", even though "it probably causes more bitter controversy than anything else with which religion is concerned". His last, and shortest, section of the *Charge* was headed "The Power of the Bishops". This power, he observed, is in two forms, "one coercive, the other not". He said, perhaps ruefully, that the coercive is exercised largely through the courts, and although a bishop "can be the prosecutor if he thinks fit", that coercive power is "largely independent of him altogether; the non-coercive is exercised personally and in accordance with his own judgment". The latter is an appeal to priests' consciences and to their awareness of the "sacredness" of the promises made at ordination. He drew the last section to a close by reminding his hearers of the value of the Book of Common Prayer as a stabilizing influence over the previous 200 years. This would have sent a clear message to Anglo Catholics and to Evangelicals to the effect that there was a definitive liturgy for Anglicans. The final paragraphs were both restrained and yet crafted as a clarion call to the Church; he had correctly assumed that his words would be scrutinised by a much larger public than those who were present when he spoke.

This *Charge*, however, was not his last word on ritualism. He encouraged his fellow bishops to submit any cases to him if they felt unable to make their own rulings and was pleased when he was asked to decide. The following year he was asked to adjudicate on the legality of the liturgical use of incense and the carrying of lights in procession. Because "the cases selected affected both provinces, the two archbishops sat together at Lambeth, and heard counsel on both sides for several days." Temple composed the formal document and it was published with the agreement of the Archbishop of York. It explored the whole matter exhaustively from an historical perspective and declared that "there is no direction in the Book of Common Prayer either enjoining or authorizing either of these practices".[436] They ruled the use of incense to be forbidden in public worship. Temple personally objected to incense and wrote in his own hand to order a Folkestone incumbent to stop using it. Naturally, there was a vigorous protest against the archbishops' decision. Temple reiterated the grounds for the decision when the Duke of Newcastle and a number of other laymen presented him with a petition of protest with 14,000 signatures. When they had finished, "the archbishop pronounced the benediction." Then he terminated the interview in a "characteristically friendly and genial manner". He made a similar decision regarding the reservation of the blessed sacrament: "I am obliged to decide that the Church of England does not at present allow Reservation in any form, and that those who think it ought to be allowed, though perfectly justified in endeavouring to get the proper authorities to alter the law, are not justified in practising Reservation until the law has been altered." That decision was his own and did not involve Maclagan, as the question had not come from the Northern Province, and it is interesting that he thought there was a possibility that the law might one day be changed.

—

By the time of the celebrations of the sixtieth anniversary of her coronation, it was clear that Queen Victoria was beginning to fail. The reception outside St Paul's Cathedral, where Temple had called for "Three Cheers", had taken place with the monarch remaining in her carriage. The reason for that rather odd situation was that infirmity would have made it difficult for her to alight and return to the carriage in public view. However, it was not until the last months of 1900 that the Queen's health began to cause serious anxiety. Bishop Davidson learned by telegram that her family had been summoned to the Queen at Osborne House, and he decided to go to the Isle of Wight himself and stay at the home of Sir Arthur Bigge, who had sent the telegram. He was fortunate to catch a late ferry, but unfortunate that it was "a stormy night with some rain", so he had an unpleasant journey. Davidson met most members of the Queen's family over the next few days and was with her when she died on 22 January 1901. As part of the prayers he read the Queen's favourite hymn to her. Ironically, in view of her implacable opposition to the Oxford Movement, it was Newman's "Lead kindly light", written as he returned from his continental trip in 1833. Davidson left a lengthy memorandum in which he described the events. But it seems that no one thought that the Archbishop of Canterbury should be called to the death bed. Perhaps the Queen did not want him there, although Archbishop Howley had attended the dying King William IV more than sixty years before, and then hurried to inform the young Victoria that she had succeeded to the crown.

Claiming that the Church of England had closer ties to the sovereign than any other institution, Temple spoke at some length about the Queen in the House of Lords on 25 January. His remarks were a conventional tribute to the late monarch's concern for the Church and the nation. He lauded her influence on the lives of all her subjects and spoke of her devotion to God and to her people. He concluded with a declaration of loyalty to the new king. What he had said in the Lords set the tone for when he preached at St Paul's Cathedral on the following Sunday; there was no Bishop of London as Mandell Creighton had died shortly before the Queen. Temple preached in the same vein at St Botolph's, Aldgate, and at a men's service in Croydon at the end of February 1901. The Queen's funeral took place at Windsor on 1 February 1901. The *Memoirs* do not mention his involvement in the service, and in Bell's *Life of Davidson* there is also no mention of the archbishop's presence when her body was laid in the mausoleum at Frogmore on the fourth of that month, and Hinchliff concluded that he was not there.

But the Archbishop of Canterbury was indispensable to the coronation of King Edward VII. Initially this was planned for 26 June 1902, but it was delayed by the King's illness and took place on 9 August. The Privy Council appointed a Coronation Committee. Temple was asked to prepare an order of service, but Davidson was much involved in the preparation. He had a lot with which to deal: the King was convalescent after his appendicitis; the aged Dean of Westminster, G. G. Bradley, was already infirm and died later in the coronation year. Archbishop Temple was nearly eighty-one and was beginning to have difficulty with walking, and his problematic eyesight had become very poor indeed. Temple's health posed problems for the conduct of a ceremony in which the role of the Archbishop of Canterbury could not be delegated. Temple would have emphatically rejected any suggestion that would have diminished his involvement. Davidson knew that it was necessary to reduce the length of the service without robbing it of its historic importance or leaving out any essential elements. He knew that at any liturgical event the time taken by individuals to move from their seat in order to carry out a task, or offer a reading or a prayer, caused more delay and that reducing the content of the service could not achieve much. Davidson also recognized the need for rehearsals. It will be recalled that Howley had made the same observation, but only after the coronation of Queen Victoria. Lord Halifax wrote to Davidson that it was a pity that Stanley was no longer Dean of Westminster and Benson no longer Archbishop of Canterbury, for both "would have been interested in all the historical and religious traditions and associations and would have seen that all was as it should be. Now the present archbishop is useless, and the Dean of Westminster more useless still."

In the end, Temple's words were set out on large sheets, which they called "scrolls". The arrangement meant that he could read what he had to say. He managed to do so, and his voice still had its customary power. Temple later offered to pay for the "scrolls" and hoped they would be kept for possible future use. When he knelt before the King to pay homage, however, he found that he could not get back on his feet without help. Those nearby saw that the King helped the old man to get up. They heard the archbishop, deeply moved, thank him and say, "God bless you, Sir." The King was also moved by the incident. Sandford, who wrote this part of the *Memoir*, made the incident at the homage seem relatively straightforward, but the newspapers reported that Temple's inability to rise was more serious than the biographers suggested. The day after the coronation, Temple wrote to Davidson expressing heartfelt thanks for all that he had done; Mrs Temple wrote as well and confessed that she had experienced much anxiety over the service. In August, the King called the archbishop to Buckingham Palace and conferred on him the Chain of the Royal Victorian Order. The Order had been established in 1896 by the old queen, but Edward VII introduced the new insignia. Temple was among the first to receive the honour.

Although Frederick Temple's long life and ministry was drawing to its close, he continued to work. The subject of the government's new Education Bill was close to Temple's heart. It sought to establish a way of helping to regulate the relation between state schools and those of the voluntary bodies, of which the Church of England was the most significant. A complication lay in the anxiety of Nonconformist denominations whose schools had needs at least as great as the Church schools, and some of whose leaders were vociferous in asserting their position.

The Conservative government was seeking to create a single authority to coordinate the work of all schools, whether "national" or voluntary, with regard to maintenance of premises and payment of teachers. It wished, however, to retain the distinctive nature and character of Church schools as such, whilst showing tolerance to other denominational schools.[437] Temple spoke about the Bill at its second reading in the Lords on 4 December 1902. Its purposes, he said, were:

> First, the establishment of a uniform system, which should handle all the different branches of education on one thoroughly consistent plan; secondly, the remedying of a long-standing defect by the organisation of secondary education; and, thirdly the redressing of an injustice of which the Church had for some time had cause to complain, namely, that the burden put upon the supporters of Church schools was not fair.[438]

He continued to assert the need for properly organized secondary education and Balfour, for the government, ensured that provision for secondary schools was included in the proposed legislation.

As Temple's speech drew towards a close, he became unwell and slumped back into his seat. He managed to complete what he had to say, then he was helped from the House, and never returned. The ever helpful Davidson expressed the Church's support for the government in the rest of the debate, and ended "by delivering a sick-bed appeal from the archbishop to Churchmen to work the Bill in such a way that no hardship should be inflicted on nonconformists".[439] The Bill received the royal assent on 18 December.

Frederick Temple died at Lambeth on 22 December 1902. He was aged eighty-one. His burial in the cloister garth of Canterbury Cathedral took place on 27 December; the ashes of his son, Archbishop William Temple, were to be placed next to the grave in 1942. They lie not far from the Old Palace, the house which Frederick Temple had turned into the Canterbury home of the Archbishopric of Canterbury. His monument in Canterbury Cathedral is at the extreme east of the building and is a considerable distance from Benson's at the west end of the nave. It depicts the old archbishop, clad in a cope. The figure is cast in bronze and is more than life-sized. It is kneeling in prayer on a slab of Cornish granite; a nice tribute to the devotion of a man described as "granite on fire".

Conclusion

This chronicle of the six men who served as Archbishop of Canterbury during the long reign of Queen Victoria has traced the contribution which each made to the history of the Church of England and the emergence of the Anglican Communion. Their combined work left the Church stronger and more effectively able to face the turmoil of the twentieth century. The death of Archbishop Manners-Sutton, nine years before the Queen's accession, brought William Howley to the primacy. He personified our starting point for the study of Church history in the great Victorian sweep of English ecclesiastical life, but he would not have imagined himself to be a figure of transition. The demise of Frederick Temple in 1902, coming relatively soon after the death of the Queen, provides a similarly convenient endpoint. This book also traced how the archbishops led the Church of England to develop, not only within, but beyond its national boundaries and become the acknowledged leader of the worldwide Anglican Communion.

During the six decades of the reign, the episcopal and archiepiscopal leadership of the Church within England, and to a lesser extent Ireland and Wales, became more closely involved in the life of the parishes which constituted their dioceses. The ordinary clergy and the worshippers within the Church's parochial network adapted to the best of their ability to the demographic changes brought about by industrialization, population growth, and urban developments, just as those phenomena directly affected the way that bishops and archbishops were required to work. At the same time, the bishops, and especially the archbishops, continued to be involved in wider national life by virtue of their seats in the House of Lords. The Archbishops of Canterbury could not avoid the Lords, and none sought to do so, even though it was an arena in which some were clearly uneasy. As those developments gathered pace, the Church's missionary work across the Empire meant that the unique role of the Archbishop of Canterbury gained an international element which had not existed to any real extent before the reign.

This study has followed the men who, by virtue of holding the archiepiscopal office, had to steer the Church through the eventful decades when Queen Victoria occupied the throne. It is possible to discern a coherence, mostly unplanned, in their work which no one could have spotted at the time.

Archbishop Howley had an ordered mind and a quiet determination. Those qualities enabled the Church of England to start adapting its long-accepted position in the nation to a point where it could influence the social developments that the energetic nineteenth century both demanded and facilitated. His successor, John Bird Sumner, was a devout man whose scholarship was soon overtaken by the emergence of biblical criticism, and also by the discoveries which natural science made about the origins of the natural world. Nevertheless, his years as primate left the old-fashioned Evangelicalism, which he exemplified, beginning to adapt itself within a Church widening its horizons across the globe, broadening its self-perception and its appreciation of its heritage. This unsung achievement was important, but not part of a deliberate strategy. Indeed, it happened even though Sumner's personality shied away from the developing ecclesiastical and ecclesiological perception. During his primacy, the unlikely yet continued coexistence between his own churchmanship and the similarly dated, old "High and Dry" strand within the Church endured and was consolidated. It was an uneasy juxtaposition which somehow ensured the flexibility that was necessary for the Church eventually to allow the insights of Tractarianism to find their place within Anglicanism. Together, these strands made possible the gradual, but accelerating, expansion of Anglicanism as a distinct Communion across the world. Despite his personal limitations, Archbishop Sumner's contribution to the future of the Church of England is not to be underestimated, not only in terms of the growth of an Anglican ecclesiology, but also the emphasis on education and pastoral care.

The third of Queen Victoria's Archbishops of Canterbury, C. T. Longley, is properly recognized as the architect of the international self-expression of Anglican ecclesiology across and beyond the British Empire. It was his decision to call the first international conference of bishops "in communion with the See of Canterbury" at Lambeth in 1867. That initiative made his archiepiscopate uniquely significant. He set in train a series of consultations which is still ongoing at the time of writing. It was his greatest achievement, and it would earn him a place in the Anglican firmament, if it had been his only success. It is a matter of regret that, in the twenty-first century, the unity of the Anglican Church is facing sincere but contradictory challenges, and Longley's achievement at times threatens to unravel. Whatever the outcome of the current situation, Longley's ability in recognizing the need for the Conference and his courage to act reveals a man of considerable wisdom, who had a personality willing to venture into unknown ecclesiastical territory. His endeavour will always remain an important element of the history of the Church of England and its relation to the autonomous Churches in communion with the Archbishop of Canterbury. In England, in his first archiepiscopal role, he finally secured the revival of Convocation in the Province of York and thus completed a quiet revolution of Church government from which the Church of England still benefits, albeit in an adapted form.

Longley's statesmanship was carried forward by his successor, Archbishop Tait. In many respects, Tait's personal tragedies made him a sad figure, but he ruled the Church of England with skill, insight, and determination. His health was often poor, and his time was not easy. Historians of the Oxford Movement have generally, with truth, seen Tait as definitely unsympathetic, but he was a man of considerable sagacity and wider vision than was supposed by those who saw him as an opponent. Even though the Public Worship Regulation Act of 1874 was soon recognized to have been a blunder, not least by the man himself, it was nevertheless to prove a fortunate blunder in the longer term. He went to his grave probably fearing that the ritualist controversy would prove schismatic, but that fear was unfounded even though the quarrels had years to run. His work did much towards the eventual defusing of the ritualistic crisis within the Church of England and, unexpectedly, made it possible eventually to find a place in the comprehensive bosom of the Church for the sons and daughters of the Oxford Movement. He also carried forward Longley's insight by calling, although with a degree of reluctance, the second Lambeth Conference in 1878. His primacy was that of a great man, and the Queen herself understood something of his greatness. He enjoyed the Queen's friendship and appreciation and is the greatest of the Victorian archbishops.

Archbishop Tait's statesmanship made it possible for the ministry of his successor, Edward Benson, to be effectively that of the first modern Archbishop of Canterbury and leader of the Anglican Communion. Fortuitously, Benson's long study of Cyprian gave him a perspective of the role of a bishop in an international sense, which translated into the role of the Archbishop of Canterbury in ways denied to Longley and Tait (who, before him, had most nearly filled that role in the modern Church of England and beyond). His handling of the trial of Bishop Edward King, which at first seems to be a ham-fisted exercise in egocentricity, at last cleared the way for Tractarian insights and catholic liturgy to contribute to the development of Anglicanism, even if not quite in the way he had in mind. Calling Lambeth Conferences appealed to the mind of Benson, and in 1888 he led with skill and some humour. His sudden death was seen by many to be a calamity. It came just before the fourth Lambeth Conference, for which he had done much preparation.

The last Archbishop of Canterbury in the reign of Queen Victoria, the redoubtable Frederick Temple, was already an old man when he succeeded to the primacy. He, too, was a model of Anglican orthodoxy; the *Essays and Reviews* perturbations were lost in the past when he began his archiepiscopate, just as much of his best work was behind him. Nevertheless, his primacy was significant. He wisely adhered to Benson's plans for the 1897 Lambeth Conference, and earned the approbation of the assembled bishops. That was despite the anxiety of many before the Conference about his capacity to lead. Within the Church in England, Temple did not fear to exercise his episcopal (and archiepiscopal) veto when matters ritualistic threatened to become litigious, particularly as he left the Diocese of London for the primacy. Temple's time as archbishop was short, and perhaps his reputation was reduced by his emphasis on teetotalism, but that should not detract from his often-evident wisdom. He was, in part, a "caretaker" archbishop in preparation for the long archiepiscopate of Randall Davidson, but there are worse labels than that of one who "takes care".

When Queen Victoria died, the reign of King Edward VII began with the Church held in higher regard than had been the case in 1837. It was more involved across the land; the Archbishopric of Canterbury was respected in the House of Lords and had strengthened the international element of Anglicanism that had been but vestigial when Victoria's reign began. The modern Church owes much to Queen Victoria's Archbishops of Canterbury. Amid the great wealth of study of the Victorian Church of England, this book is the first to look biographically at the six Archbishops of Canterbury, whilst considering their work as spiritual and theological leaders with inescapable political involvement. Each could only be a man of his own time. Many of the historically important aspects of their lives and ministries, whilst clear to those who read more than a century afterwards, might surprise the men themselves. Such is the nature of Christian ministry. Fortunate are those of whom it is said that their work, and their good endeavours, live after them.

Bibliography

Church of England biographies. Second series Bishop Thomas Wilson, Bishop Heber, Hannah More, Bishop Blomfield, Joshua Watson, Rev. Dr. Scoresby, Rev. Legh Richmond, Archbishop Longley, Bishop Mackenzie (London: SPCK, n.d.).

Addleshaw, G. W. O., *The High Church Tradition: A Study in the Liturgical Thought of the Seventeenth Century* (London: Faber and Faber, 1941).

Ashwell, A. R. and Wilberforce, R. G., *Life of the Right Reverend Samuel Wilberforce: Lord Bishop of Oxford and afterwards of Winchester, with selections from his diaries and correspondence*, 3 vols (London: John Murray, 1880, 1881, 1882).

Beeson, T., *The Bishops* (London: SCM Press, 2002).

Beeson, T., *The Deans* (London: SCM Press, 2004).

Bell, A. S., *Sydney Smith: A Biography* (Oxford: Oxford University Press, 1980).

Bell, G. K. A., *Randall Davidson: Archbishop of Canterbury*, 2 vols (Oxford: Oxford University Press, 1935).

Benham, W., *Catharine and Craufurd Tait: wife and son of Archibald Campbell Archbishop of Canterbury / a memoir edited at the request of the Archbishop* (London: Macmillan, 1869).

Benson, A. C., *Life of Edward White Benson, sometime Archbishop of Canterbury*, 2 vols (London: Macmillan, 1899).

Benson, A. C., *The Trefoil: Wellington College, Lincoln and Truro* (London: John Murray, 1923).

Benson, A. C. and Esher, V., eds, *The Letters of Queen Victoria: A Selection of Her Majesty's Correspondence between the Years 1837 and 1861*, i: 1836–1843 (London: John Murray, 1907).

Benson, E. F., *As We Were: A Victorian Peep-Show* (Harmondsworth: Penguin, 1930).

Benson, E. W., "Cathedral Life and Cathedral Work", *Quarterly Review*, 130:259 (1871), 225–55.

Benson, E. W., *The Cathedral: Its Necessary Place in the Life and Work of the Church* (London: John Murray, 1878).

Benson, E. W., *Fishers of Men. Addressed to the diocese of Canterbury in his third Visitation* (London: Macmillan, 1893).

Benson, E. W., *Cyprian: his life, his times, his work* (London: Macmillan, 1897).

Best, G. F. A., *Temporal Pillars: Queen Anne's Bounty, the Ecclesiastical Commissioners and the Church of England* (Cambridge: Cambridge University Press, 1964).

Bolt, R., *As Good as God, as Clever as the Devil: The Impossible Life of Mary Benson* (London: Atlantic Books, 2011).

Carpenter, E., *Cantuar: The Archbishops in Their Office* (London: Cassell, 1971).

Chadwick, O., *The Victorian Church*, 2 vols (London: Black, 1966 and 1970).

Chadwick, O., *The Mind of the Oxford Movement: An Anthology* (London: A & C Black, 1960).

Church, M. C., *Life and Letters of Dean Church* (London: Macmillan, 1894).

Church, R. W., *The Oxford Movement: Twelve Years 1833–1845* (London: Macmillan, 1891).

Cockshut, A. O. J., *Anglican Attitudes: A Study of Victorian Religious Controversies* (London: Collins, 1959).

Collinson, P., Ramsay, N., and Sparks, M., *A History of Canterbury Cathedral* (Oxford: Oxford University Press, 1995).

Davidson, R. T., *The Lambeth Conferences of 1867, 1878, and 1888* (London: SPCK, 1896).

Davidson, R. T. and Benham, W., *Life of Archibald Campbell Tait, Archbishop of Canterbury*, 2 vols (London: Macmillan, 1891).

Desmond, A. and Moore, J., *Darwin* (New York: Warner Books, 1991).

Evans, G. R. and Wright, J. R., eds, *The Anglican Tradition: A Handbook of Sources* (London: SPCK, 1991).

Fowler, M., *Some Notable Archbishops of Canterbury* (London: SPCK, 1895).

Fraser, A., *The King and the Catholics: The Fight for Rights 1829* (London: Weidenfeld and Nicolson, 2018).
Garrard, James, *Archbishop Howley, 1828–1848* (London: Routledge, 2016).
Hammond, P. C., *The Parson and the Victorian Parish* (London: Hodder and Stoughton, 1977).
Harrison, Benjamin, *The Remembrance of a Departed Guide and Ruler: A Charge* (London: F. & J. Rivington, 1848).
Hennell, M. M., *Sons of the Prophets: Evangelical Leaders of the Victorian Church* (London: SPCK, 1979).
Hinchliff, P., *Frederick Temple, Archbishop of Canterbury: A Life* (Oxford: Oxford University Press, 1998).
Holland, H. S., *A Bundle of Memories* (London: Wells Gardner, Darton & Co., 1915).
Holland, S., *A Memoir of the Reverend Sydney Smith by his daughter, Lady Holland, with a selection of his letters*, edited by Mrs Austin (London: Longman, Brown, Green and Longmans, 1855).
Iremonger, F. A., *William Temple, Archbishop of Canterbury: His Life and Letters* (London: Oxford University Press, 1965).
Jennings, D. A., *The Revival of the Convocation of York, 1837–1861*, Borthwick Papers, 47 (York: St Anthony's Press, 1975).
Johnson, M. A., *Bustling Intermeddler?: The Life and Work of Charles James Blomfield* (Leominster: Gracewing, 2001).
Johnston, J. O., *Life and Letters of Henry Parry Liddon, D.D., D.C.L., LL.D. / with a concluding chapter by the Lord Bishop of Oxford* (London: Longmans, 1904).
Kelly, J. N. D., *Early Christian Doctrines* (London: A & C Black, 1960).
Ker, I. T., *John Henry Newman: A Biography* (Oxford: Oxford University Press, 1988).
Liddon, H. P., *Walter Kerr Hamilton, Bp. of Salisbury; a sketch, repr., with additions and corrections, from the Guardian* (London: Rivingtons, 1869).
Liddon, H. P., *Life of Edward Bouverie Pusey: Doctor of Divinity, Canon of Christ Church, Regius Professor of Hebrew in the University of Oxford*, 4 vols (London: Longmans & C., 1893, 1894, and 1897).

Lockhart, J. G., *Charles Lindley, Viscount Halifax*, Part 2 (London: G. Bles, The Centenary Press, 1936).

Longford, E., *Victoria R.I.* (London: World Books, 1964).

Marsh, P. T., *The Victorian Church in Decline: Archbishop Tait and the Church of England 1868–1882* (London: Routledge & Kegan Paul, 1969).

McCord, N. and Purdue, B., *British History 1815–1914* (Oxford: Oxford University Press, 2007).

Morley, J., *The Life of William Ewart Gladstone*, 3 vols (London: Macmillan, 1903).

Neill, S., *Anglicanism* (Harmondsworth: Penguin, 1960).

Newsome, D., *Godliness and Good Learning: Four Studies on a Victorian Ideal* (London: John Murray, 1961).

Newsome, D., *The Parting of Friends: A Study of the Wilberforces and Henry Manning* (London: John Murray, 1966).

Newton, J. A., "The Trial of Bishop King", *Ecclesiastical Law Journal* 5:25 (1999), 265–71.

Palmer, B., *High and Mitred: A Study of Prime Ministers as Bishop-Makers* (London: SPCK, 1992).

Palmer, W., *A Narrative of Events connected with the Publication of the Tracts for the Times* (London: Rivingtons, 1883).

Pawley, B. and M., *Rome and Canterbury through Four Centuries: A Study of the Relations between the Church of Rome and the Anglican Churches, 1530–1973* (London: Mowbray, 1974).

Phillpotts, H., *A Letter to the Archbishop of Canterbury* (London, 1850).

Podmore, C., *Aspects of Anglican Identity* (London: Church House Publishing, 2005).

Prestige, G. L., *St. Paul's in its Glory: A Candid History of the Cathedral 1831–1911* (London: SPCK, 1955).

Prothero, R. E., *The Life and Correspondence of Arthur Penrhyn Stanley: late Dean of Westminster*, 2 vols (London: John Murray, 1893).

Roberts, A., *Salisbury: Victorian Titan* (London: Weidenfeld & Nicolson, 1999).

Russell, A. J., *The Clerical Profession* (London: SPCK, 1980).

Russell, G. W. E., *Edward King, sixtieth bishop of Lincoln: A memoir* (London: Smith, Elder, 1912).

Sandford, E. G., ed., *Memoirs of Archbishop Temple by seven friends*, 2 vols (London: Macmillan, 1906).

Scotland, N., *The Life and Work of John Bird Sumner* (Leominster: Gracewing, 1995).

Sparks, M., "William Howley and His Books", *Chronicle of the Friends of Canterbury Cathedral* (2004), 35.

Stephens, W. R. W., *The Life and Letters of Walter Farquhar Hook, D.D., F.R.S.* (London: R. Bentley & Son, 1880).

Stephenson, A. M. G., *The First Lambeth Conference, 1867* (London: SPCK, 1967).

Stephenson, A. M. G., *Anglicanism and the Lambeth Conferences* (London: SPCK, 1978).

Stephenson, A. M. G., *The Victorian Archbishops of Canterbury* (Blewbury: Rocket Press, 1991).

Tatton-Brown, T., *Lambeth Palace: A History of the Archbishops of Canterbury and Their Houses* (London: SPCK, 2000).

Temple, F., "The Education of the World", in *Essays and Reviews* (London: John Parker and Son, 1860), 1–49.

Temple, F., *The relations between religion and science: eight lectures preached before the University of Oxford in the year 1884 on the foundation of the late Rev. John Bampton* (London: Macmillan, 1884).

Virgin, P., *Sydney Smith* (London: SPCK, 1994).

Williams, D., *Genesis and Exodus: A Portrait of the Benson Family* (London: H. Hamilton, 1979).

Woodruffe, C. E. and Danks, W., *Memorials of the cathedral & priory of Christ in Canterbury* (London: Chapman & Hall, 1912).

Wymer, N., *Dr. Arnold of Rugby* (London: Constable, 1953).

Yates, T. E., *Venn and Victorian Bishops Abroad: The Missionary Policies of Henry Venn and their Repercussions upon the Anglican Episcopate of the Colonial Period 1841–1872* (Uppsala: Swedish Institute of Missionary Research and London: SPCK, 1978).

Ziegler, P., *Melbourne: A Biography of William Lamb, 2nd Viscount Melbourne* (London: Faber and Faber, 2013).

Notes

1. A. C. Benson, *Life of Edward White Benson, sometime Archbishop of Canterbury* (London: Macmillan, 1899), vol. II, p. 12.
2. H. S. Holland, *A Bundle of Memories* (London: Wells Gardner, Darton & Co., 1915), pp. 235-6.
3. M. Arnold, "The Church of England", *Macmillan's Magazine* 33 (April 1876), pp. 481-94.
4. These figures obtained from N. McCord and B. Purdue, *British History 1815-1914* (Oxford: Oxford University Press, 2007), pp. 86, 227 and 488.
5. 24 Henry 8, c. 12 quoted in the *Report* of the Archbishops' Committee on Church and State, 1916, p. 225.
6. Quoted in B. Palmer, *High and Mitred: A Study of Prime Ministers as Bishop-Makers* (London: SPCK, 1992), p. 10.
7. Benson, *Life of Edward White Benson*, vol. II, p. 30.
8. E. Carpenter, *Cantuar: the Archbishops in Their Office* (London: Cassell, 1971), p. 299.
9. M. Fowler, *Some Notable Archbishops of Canterbury* (London: SPCK, 1895), pp. 143-4.
10. A. C. Benson and V. Esher (eds), *The Letters of Queen Victoria: A Selection of Her Majesty's Correspondence between the Years 1837 and 1861*, Vol. 1: 1836-1843 (London: John Murray, 1907), p. 22.
11. Quoted in E. Longford, *Victoria R.I.* (London: World Books, 1964), p. 79.
12. Quoted in Longford, *Victoria, R.I.*, p. 81.
13. Quoted in Longford, *Victoria, R.I.*, p. 81.
14. Longford, *Victoria, R.I.*, p. 82.
15. Quoted in O. Chadwick, *The Victorian Church*, vol. 1 (London: Black, 1966), p. 162.
16. See S. Holland, *A Memoir of the Reverend Sydney Smith by his daughter, Lady Holland, with a selection of his letters, edited by Mrs Austin* (London:

Longman, Brown, Green and Longmans, 1855), quoted in A. S. Bell, *Sydney Smith: A Biography* (Oxford: Oxford University Press, 1980), p. 5.

[17] B. Harrison, *The Remembrance of a Departed Guide and Ruler: A Charge* (London: F. & J. Rivington, 1848), pp. 41–2. Episcopal and archiepiscopal Charges have been frequently used and are identified in the notes to each chapter with the year of their delivery. However, this Charge delivered by Benjamin Harrison shortly after the death of Archbishop Howley is listed here because of its biographical nature.

[18] G. F. A. Best, *Temporal Pillars: Queen Anne's Bounty, the Ecclesiastical Commissioners and the Church of England* (Cambridge: Cambridge University Press, 1964), p. 166, n. 1.

[19] O. Chadwick, *The Mind of the Oxford Movement: An Anthology* (London: A & C Black, 1960), p. 71.

[20] Harrison, *Charge*, p. 46.

[21] Garrard, *Archbishop Howley*, p. 4.

[22] *Charge* 1832, p. 29.

[23] Garrard, *Archbishop Howley*, p. 4.

[24] Harrison, *Charge*, pp. 46–7.

[25] M. Sparks, "William Howley and His Books", *Chronicle of the Friends of Canterbury Cathedral* (2004), p. 35.

[26] Garrard, *Archbishop Howley*, p. 10.

[27] Fowler, *Notable Archbishops*, p. 213.

[28] *The Times*, 12 February 1848.

[29] *Charge* 1818, p. 7.

[30] Garrard, *Archbishop Howley*, p. 121.

[31] *Charge* 1814, pp. 5–6: see Garrard, *Archbishop Howley*, pp. 113–14.

[32] Garrard, *Archbishop Howley*, p. 14.

[33] *Charge* 1814, pp. 7–8: see Garrard, *Archbishop Howley*, pp. 113–14.

[34] P. Ziegler, *Melbourne: A Biography of William Lamb, 2nd Viscount Melbourne* (London: Faber and Faber, 2013), p. 74.

[35] Hansard 20 July 1820, para. 585.

[36] It became the Incorporated Church Building Society in 1828.

[37] M. A. Johnson, *Bustling Intermeddler?: The Life and Work of Charles James Blomfield* (Leominster: Gracewing, 2001), p. 120.

[38] Garrard, *Archbishop Howley*, p. 14.

NOTES 363

39 H. P. Liddon, *Life of Edward Bouverie Pusey: Doctor of Divinity, Canon of Christ Church, Regius Professor of Hebrew in the University of Oxford*, vol. II (London: Longmans & Co., 1894), p. 251.
40 Johnson, *Bustling Intermeddler?*, p. 125.
41 Liddon, *Life of Edward Bouverie Pusey*, vol. II, p. 252.
42 The text of the letter is in Garrard, *Archbishop Howley*, pp. 135–6. The italics are mine.
43 *Charge* 1840, p. 24: see Garrard, *Archbishop Howley*, p. 129.
44 Harrison, *Charge*, p. 59. The list of consecrations is to be found in Fowler, *Notable Archbishops*, pp. 213–14.
45 See A. M. G. Stephenson, *The First Lambeth Conference, 1867* (London: SPCK, 1967), pp. 40–1.
46 Canterbury Cathedral Archive, ref: CCA-SCc/SVSB/1/168/1.
47 Garrard, *Archbishop Howley*, p. 36.
48 Liddon, *Life of Edward Bouverie Pusey*, vol. II, p. 133.
49 Harrison, *Charge*, p. 23.
50 Harrison, *Charge*, pp. 23–4.
51 Chadwick, *Victorian Church*, vol. 1, p. 24.
52 See Garrard, *Archbishop Howley*, pp. 150–1, extract from the House of Lords debate, 7 October 1831.
53 Garrard, *Archbishop Howley*, p. 48.
54 Garrard, *Archbishop Howley*, p. 79.
55 W. Palmer, *A Narrative of Events connected with the publication of the Tracts for the Times* (London: Rivingtons, 1883), p. 105.
56 Quoted in Fowler, *Notable Archbishops*, p. 145.
57 Liddon, *Life of Edward Bouverie Pusey*, vol. I, p. 251.
58 Liddon, *Life of Edward Bouverie Pusey*, vol. I, pp. 428–9.
59 Best, *Temporal Pillars*, p. 297.
60 Quoted in P. Virgin, *Sydney Smith* (London: SPCK, 1994), p. 262.
61 Best, *Temporal Pillars*, p. 308.
62 Chadwick, *Victorian Church*, vol. 1, p. 127.
63 Chadwick, *Victorian Church*, vol. 1, p. 136 fn.
64 Johnson, *Bustling Intermeddler?*, p. 23.
65 T. Tatton-Brown, *Lambeth Palace: A History of the Archbishops of Canterbury and Their Houses* (London: SPCK, 2000), p. 87.
66 Harrison, *Charge*, p. 57.

[67] Best, *Temporal Pillars*, pp. 436–7.
[68] Harrison, *Charge*, p. 61.
[69] Palmer, *High & Mitred*, p. 29.
[70] D. Newsome, *The Parting of Friends: A Study of the Wilberforces and Henry Manning* (London: John Murray, 1966), p. 332.
[71] Queen Victoria's Journal, vol. 25, p. 38, see www.queenvictoriasjournals.org.
[72] *The Times*, 8 September 1862.
[73] Carpenter, *Cantuar*, p. 301.
[74] N. Scotland, *The Life and Work of John Bird Sumner* (Leominster: Gracewing, 1995).
[75] C. Podmore, *Aspects of Anglican Identity* (London: Church House Publishing, 2005), p. 8, quoting G. O. Trevelyan's *Life and Letters of Lord Macaulay*.
[76] Liddon, *Life of Edward Bouverie Pusey*, vol. I, p. 17, n. 2.
[77] *Charge* 1857, p. 6.
[78] A. Desmond and J. Moore, *Darwin* (New York: Warner Books, 1991), p. 48.
[79] Unacknowledged quotation in I. T. Ker, *John Henry Newman: A Biography* (Oxford: Oxford University Press, 1988), p. 22.
[80] Scotland, *John Bird Sumner*, p. 156.
[81] Chadwick, *Victorian Church*, vol. 1, p. 8.
[82] Archive DNB.
[83] Johnson, *Bustling Intermeddler?*, p. 50.
[84] McCord and Purdue, *British History 1815–1914*, p. 206.
[85] Quoted in Johnson, *Bustling Intermeddler?*, p. 51.
[86] Scotland, *John Bird Sumner*, p. 153.
[87] Chadwick, *The Victorian Church*, vol. 1, p. 97.
[88] R. W. Church, *The Oxford Movement: Twelve Years 1833–1845* (London: Macmillan, 1891), p. 251.
[89] *Charge* 1841, p. 30.
[90] Fowler, *Notable Archbishops*, p. 159.
[91] *Charge* 1838, p. 42.
[92] Scotland, *John Bird Sumner*, p. 156.
[93] *Charge* 1841, pp. 78–81.
[94] *The Times* obituary, 8 September 1862.
[95] Quoted in Scotland, *John Bird Sumner*, p. 58.
[96] *Charge* 1853, p. 4.
[97] Palmer, *High and Mitred*, p. 35.

[98] Chadwick, *Victorian Church*, vol. 1, p. 247, n. 3.
[99] Fowler, *Notable Archbishops*, pp. 157–8.
[100] A. R. Ashwell and R. G. Wilberforce, *Life of the Right Reverend Samuel Wilberforce: Lord Bishop of Oxford and afterwards of Winchester, with selections from his diaries and correspondence*, vol. I (London: John Murray, 1881), p. 435.
[101] O. Chadwick, *The Mind of the Oxford Movement: An Anthology* (London: A & C Black, 1960), p. 19.
[102] Carpenter, *Cantuar*, p. 301.
[103] Best, *Temporal Pillars*, pp. 242–3.
[104] Newsome, *Parting of Friends*, p. 332.
[105] Quoted in Newsome, *Parting of Friends*, p. 301. Newsome's italics.
[106] C. E. Woodruffe and W. Danks, *Memorials of the Cathedral & Priory of Christ in Canterbury* (London: Chapman & Hall, 1912), pp. 363–4.
[107] Quoted in Newsome, *Parting of Friends*, p. 358.
[108] *Charge*, 1853, pp. 5–6.
[109] *Charge*, 1853, p. 9.
[110] *Charge*, 1853, p. 43.
[111] *Charge*, 1853, p. 74.
[112] A. O. J. Cockshut, *Anglican Attitudes: A Study of Victorian Religious Controversies* (London: Collins, 1959), p. 50.
[113] H. Phillpotts, *A Letter to the Archbishop of Canterbury* (London, 1850), p. 5.
[114] Phillpotts, *Letter to the Archbishop of Canterbury*, p. 15.
[115] Phillpotts, *Letter to the Archbishop of Canterbury*, p. 52.
[116] B. and M. Pawley, *Rome and Canterbury through Four Centuries: A Study of the Relations between the Church of Rome and the Anglican Churches, 1530–1973* (London: Mowbray, 1974), p. 160.
[117] Pawley, *Rome and Canterbury*, p. 146.
[118] Fowler, *Notable Archbishops*, p. 163.
[119] Pawley, *Rome and Canterbury*, p. 165, n. 2.
[120] C. T. Longley, *Charge* 1853, p. 9.
[121] Fowler, *Notable Archbishops*, p. 163.
[122] *Charge* 1853, p. 31.
[123] *Charge* 1853, pp. 11–12.
[124] Ashwell and Wilberforce, *Life of Samuel Wilberforce*, vol. II, p. 138.
[125] Longford, *Victoria R.I.*, p. 241.

126 Ashwell and Wilberforce, *Life of Samuel Wilberforce*, vol. II, p. 161.
127 *Charge* 1853, p. 13.
128 Carpenter, *Cantuar*, p. 307.
129 Chadwick, *Victorian Church*, vol. 1, p. 322.
130 *Charge* 1853, p. 25.
131 Ashwell and Wilberforce, *Life of Samuel Wilberforce*, vol. II, p. 153.
132 M. M. Hennell, *Sons of the Prophets: Evangelical Leaders of the Victorian Church* (London: SPCK, 1979), p. 46.
133 T. E. Yates, *Venn and Victorian Bishops Abroad: The Missionary Policies of Henry Venn and their Repercussions upon the Anglican Episcopate of the Colonial Period 1841–1872* (Uppsala: Swedish Institute of Missionary Research and London: SPCK, 1978), p. 169.
134 Yates, *Venn and Victorian Bishops Abroad*, p. 123.
135 See A. M. G. Stephenson, *Anglicanism and the Lambeth Conferences* (London: SPCK, 1978), p. 19.
136 Quoted in Stephenson, *First Lambeth Conference*, p. 43.
137 Stephenson, *Anglicanism and the Lambeth Conferences*, p. 18.
138 Quoted in Podmore, *Aspects of Anglican Identity*, p. 32.
139 Newsome, *Parting of Friends*, p. 216.
140 Liddon, *Life of Edward Bouverie Pusey*, vol. III, p. 427.
141 See Chadwick, *Victorian Church*, vol. 1, p. 493.
142 Liddon, *Life of Edward Bouverie Pusey*, vol. III, p. 429.
143 Liddon, *Life of Edward Bouverie Pusey*, vol. III, p. 430.
144 Liddon, *Life of Edward Bouverie Pusey*, vol. III, p. 430.
145 Chadwick, *Victorian Church*, vol. 1, p. 495.
146 Ashwell and Wilberforce, *Life of Samuel Wilberforce*, vol. III, p. 62.
147 Fowler, *Notable Archbishops*, p. 168.
148 J. Morley, *The Life of William Ewart Gladstone*, 3 vols (London: Macmillan, 1903), vol. III, p. 96, n. 1.
149 Ashwell and Wilberforce, *Life of Samuel Wilberforce*, vol. III, p. 62.
150 A. M. G. Stephenson, *The Victorian Archbishops of Canterbury* (Blewbury: Rocket Press, 1991), p. 19.
151 *Church of England biographies, second series: Bishop Thomas Wilson, Bishop Heber, Hannah More, Bishop Blomfield, Joshua Watson, Rev. Dr. Scoresby, Rev. Legh Richmond, Archbishop Longley, Bishop Mackenzie* (London: SPCK, n.d.), p. 177.

NOTES

[152] *Church of England biographies, second series*, p. 181.
[153] Quoted in N. Wymer, *Dr. Arnold of Rugby* (London: Constable, 1953), p. 136.
[154] *Church of England biographies, second series*, pp. 181–2.
[155] *Church of England biographies, second series*, p. 184.
[156] T. V. Short's sermon at Longley's consecration, p. 9.
[157] *Church of England biographies, second series*, p. 184.
[158] *Charge* 1853, p. 30.
[159] A. J. Russell, *The Clerical Profession* (London: SPCK, 1980), p. 41.
[160] *Charge* 1838, p. 26.
[161] Stephenson, *Victorian Archbishops*, pp. 23–5.
[162] *Charge* 1838, p. 15.
[163] *Church of England biographies, second series*, pp. 186–7.
[164] O. Chadwick, *The Victorian Church*, vol. 2 (London: Black, 1970), p. 523.
[165] Stephenson, *Victorian Archbishops*, p. 26.
[166] *Church of England biographies, second series*, pp. 194–5.
[167] Ashwell and Wilberforce, *Life of Samuel Wilberforce*, vol. I, pp. 434–5.
[168] *Church of England biographies, second series*, p. 187.
[169] P. C. Hammond, *The Parson and the Victorian Parish* (London: Hodder and Stoughton, 1977), p. 35.
[170] W. R. W. Stephens, *The Life and Letters of Walter Farquhar Hook, D.D., F.R.S.* (London: R. Bentley & Son, 1880), p. 221.
[171] Stephens, *Life and Letters of Walter Farquhar Hook*, p. 320.
[172] *Charge* 1838, p. 10.
[173] *Charge* 1838, p. 13.
[174] Liddon, *Life of Edward Bouverie Pusey*, vol. II, p. 472.
[175] Stephens, *Life and Letters of Walter Farquhar Hook*, p. 399.
[176] Liddon, *Life of Edward Bouverie Pusey*, vol. III, pp. 133–4.
[177] Stephens, *Life and Letters of Walter Farquar Hook*, p. 402.
[178] *Charge* 1868, p. 20.
[179] Stephens, *Life and Letters of Walter Farquhar Hook*, p. 586.
[180] *Church of England biographies, second series*, p. 185.
[181] *Church of England biographies, second series*, p. 195.
[182] *Charge* 1868, pp. 15–16.
[183] *Charge* 1868, p. 26.
[184] *Charge* 1868, p. 47.
[185] Stephenson, *Victorian Archbishops*, p. 26.

[186] R. T. Davidson and W. Benham, *Life of Archibald Campbell Tait, Archbishop of Canterbury*, 2 vols (London: Macmillan, 1891), vol. I, pp. 206-7.
[187] Chadwick, *Victorian Church*, vol. 1, p. 315.
[188] D. A. Jennings, *The Revival of the Convocation of York, 1837-1861*, Borthwick Papers 47 (York: St Anthony's Press, 1975), p. 8.
[189] Jennings, *Revival of the Convocation of York*, p. 25.
[190] *Charge* 1853, p. 19.
[191] *Charge* 1853, p. 25.
[192] *Charge* 1853, p. 23.
[193] E. G. Sandford, ed., *Memoirs of Archbishop Temple by seven friends* (London: Macmillan, 1906), vol. I, p. 223.
[194] Stephenson, *First Lambeth Conference*, p. 107.
[195] Ashwell and Wilberforce, *Life of Samuel Wilberforce*, vol. III, pp. 3ff.
[196] Davidson and Benham, *Life of Tait*, vol. I, p. 282.
[197] H. P. Liddon, *Walter Kerr Hamilton, Bp. of Salisbury; a sketch*, repr., with additions and corrections, from the Guardian (London: Rivingtons, 1869), p. 87.
[198] Cockshut, *Anglican Attitudes*, p. 82. This book has a valuable chapter on the *Essays and Reviews* controversy.
[199] Quoted in G. R. Evans and J. R. Wright, eds, *The Anglican Tradition: A Handbook of Sources* (London: SPCK, 1991), p. 325, para. 322.
[200] Stephenson, *First Lambeth Conference*, p. 74.
[201] Quoted in Evans and Wright, *Anglican Tradition*, p. 325, para. 322.
[202] Stephenson, *First Lambeth Conference*, p. 241.
[203] Yates, *Venn and Victorian Bishops Abroad*, p. 169.
[204] S. Neill, *Anglicanism* (Harmondsworth: Penguin, 1960), p. 226.
[205] Hennell, *Sons of the Prophets*, p. 89.
[206] Stephenson, *First Lambeth Conference*, p. 91.
[207] Stephenson, *First Lambeth Conference*, p. 55.
[208] Podmore, *Aspects of Anglican Identity*, p. 37.
[209] R. T. Davidson, *The Lambeth Conferences of 1867, 1878, and 1888* (London: SPCK, 1896), p. 10.
[210] Davidson, *Lambeth Conferences*, p. 16.
[211] Davidson, *Lambeth Conferences*, p. 11.
[212] Ashwell and Wilberforce, *Life of Samuel Wilberforce*, vol. III, p. 230.
[213] Davidson, *Lambeth Conferences*, p. 12.

NOTES

[214] Quoted in Stephenson, *First Lambeth Conference*, p. 238.
[215] Stephenson, *First Lambeth Conference*, p. 237.
[216] R. E. Prothero, *The Life and Correspondence of Arthur Penrhyn Stanley: late dean of Westminster* (London: John Murray, 1893), vol. II, p. 198.
[217] Davidson, *Lambeth Conferences*, p. 19.
[218] Fowler, *Notable Archbishops*, p. 177.
[219] *Charge* 1868, pp. 2–3.
[220] *Charge* 1868, p. 7.
[221] *Charge* 1868, pp. 46–7.
[222] Carpenter, *Cantuar*, p. 333.
[223] Davidson and Benham, *Life of Tait*, vol. II, p. 375.
[224] *Church of England Biographies, second series*, p. 194.
[225] Davidson and Benham, *Life of Tait*, vol. I, p. 535.
[226] Carpenter, *Cantuar*, p. 351.
[227] Carpenter, *Cantuar*, p. 356.
[228] Davidson and Benham, *Life of Tait*, vol. I, p. 33.
[229] Chadwick, *Victorian Church*, vol. 2, p. 85.
[230] P. T. Marsh, *The Victorian Church in Decline: Archbishop Tait and the Church of England 1868–1882* (London: Routledge & Kegan Paul, 1969), p. 82.
[231] Davidson and Benham, *Life of Tait*, vol. I, p. 83.
[232] Davidson and Benham, *Life of Tait*, vol. I, p. 81.
[233] Davidson and Benham, *Life of Tait*, vol. I, pp. 81–2.
[234] Reminiscences of Dean Lake, in Davidson and Benham, *Life of Tait*, vol. I, p. 105.
[235] Davidson and Benham, *Life of Tait*, vol. I, p. 122.
[236] W. Benham, *Catharine and Craufurd Tait: wife and son of Archibald Campbell Archbishop of Canterbury / a memoir edited at the request of the Archbishop* (London: Macmillan, 1869), p. 10.
[237] Benham, *Catharine and Craufurd Tait*, p. 7.
[238] Davidson and Benham, *Life of Tait*, vol. I, pp. 116–17.
[239] Prothero, *Life and Correspondence of Stanley*, vol. I, p. 316.
[240] Benham, *Catharine and Craufurd Tait*, p. 11.
[241] Benham, *Catharine and Craufurd Tait*, p. 17.
[242] Davidson and Benham, *Life of Tait*, vol. I, p. 149.
[243] Davidson and Benham, *Life of Tait*, vol. I, p. 154.

244 Catherine Anna, born 15 March 1846; Mary Susan, born 20 June 1847; Craufurd born 22 June 1849.
245 Davidson and Benham, *Life of Tait*, vol. I, p. 178.
246 Benham, *Catharine and Craufurd Tait*, p. 31.
247 Marsh, *Victorian Church in Decline*, p. 83.
248 Davidson and Benham, *Life of Tait*, vol. I, p. 187.
249 Davidson and Benham, *Life of Tait*, vol. I, p. 189.
250 Davidson and Benham, *Life of Tait*, vol. I, p. 202, note.
251 Davidson and Benham, *Life of Tait*, vol. I, p. 194.
252 Davidson and Benham, *Life of Tait*, vol. I, p. 193.
253 Johnson, *Bustling Intermeddler?*, p. 147.
254 Johnson, *Bustling Intermeddler?*, p. 148.
255 Davidson and Benham, *Life of Tait*, vol. I, p. 255.
256 Davidson and Benham, *Life of Tait*, vol. I, p. 256.
257 Carpenter, *Cantuar*, p. 353.
258 Davidson and Benham, *Life of Tait*, vol. I, p. 213; quotation from diary, 30 August 1857.
259 Davidson and Benham, *Life of Tait*, vol. I, p. 260.
260 Davidson and Benham, *Life of Tait*, vol. I, p. 298.
261 Davidson and Benham, *Life of Tait*, vol. I, p. 214.
262 Davidson and Benham, *Life of Tait*, vol. I, p. 234.
263 Davidson and Benham, *Life of Tait*, vol. I, pp. 237–9.
264 Davidson and Benham, *Life of Tait*, vol. I, pp. 216–21, parentheses in original.
265 Davidson and Benham, *Life of Tait*, vol. I, p. 223.
266 Davidson and Benham, *Life of Tait*, vol. I, p. 225.
267 Marsh, *Victorian Church in Decline*, p. 17.
268 Davidson and Benham, *Life of Tait*, vol. I, p. 536.
269 Davidson and Benham, *Life of Tait*, vol. I, p. 538.
270 Marsh, *Victorian Church in Decline*, p. 9.
271 Davidson and Benham, *Life of Tait*, vol. II, pp. 42–3.
272 See *The Chronicle of Convocation 1869*, pp. 104–8, see Marsh, *Victorian Church in Decline*, p. 31, n. 44.
273 J. O. Johnston, *Life and Letters of Henry Parry Liddon, D.D., D.C.L., LL.D. / with a concluding chapter by the Lord Bishop of Oxford* (London: Longmans, 1904), p. 169.
274 Carpenter, *Cantuar*, p. 348.

[275] Davidson and Benham, *Life of Tait*, vol. II, p. 191.
[276] Davidson and Benham, *Life of Tait*, vol. II, pp. 225–6.
[277] Quoted in Stephenson, *Anglicanism and the Lambeth Conferences*, p. 49.
[278] Davidson, *Lambeth Conferences*, p. 24.
[279] Benham, *Catharine and Craufurd Tait*, p. 23.
[280] Davidson and Benham, *Life of Tait*, vol. II, p. 370.
[281] Davidson and Benham, *Life of Tait*, vol. II, p. 369.
[282] Davidson and Benham, *Life of Tait*, vol. II, p. 375.
[283] *The Second Lambeth Conference*, by the Bishop of Iowa; quoted in Davidson and Benham, *Life of Tait*, vol. II, p. 377.
[284] Davidson and Benham, *Life of Tait*, vol. II, pp. 396–8.
[285] Davidson and Benham, *Life of Tait*, vol. II, p. 397.
[286] Davidson and Benham, *Life of Tait*, vol. II, p. 394.
[287] Davidson and Benham, *Life of Tait*, vol. II, p. 396.
[288] Davidson and Benham, *Life of Tait*, vol. II, p. 411.
[289] M. C. Church, *Life and Letters of Dean Church* (London: Macmillan, 1894), p. 307.
[290] Benson, *Life of Edward White Benson*, vol. I, p. 2.
[291] A. C. Benson, *The Trefoil: Wellington College, Lincoln and Truro* (London: John Murray, 1923), p. 253.
[292] E. F. Benson, *As We Were: A Victorian Peep-Show* (Harmondsworth: Penguin, 1930), p. 59.
[293] Benson, *Life of Edward White Benson*, vol. I, p. 300.
[294] Benson, *Life of Edward White Benson*, vol. I, p. 116.
[295] Benson, *As We Were*, p. 65.
[296] Quoted in R. Bolt, *As Good as God, as Clever as the Devil: The Impossible Life of Mary Benson* (London: Atlantic Books, 2011), p. 217.
[297] Benson, *Life of Edward White Benson*, vol. I, p. 129.
[298] Benson, *As We Were*, p. 107.
[299] Sandford, *Memoirs of Archbishop Temple*, vol. II, p. 248.
[300] Benson, *As We Were*, p. 3.
[301] D. Williams, *Genesis and Exodus: A Portrait of the Benson Family* (London: H. Hamilton, 1979), p. 23.
[302] Benson, *Life of Edward White Benson*, vol. I, p. 173.
[303] Benson, *As We Were*, p. 68.

304 E. W. Benson, "Cathedral Life and Cathedral Work", *Quarterly Review*, 130:259 (1871), pp. 225-55. See also E. W. Benson, *The Cathedral: Its Necessary Place in the Life and Work of the Church* (London: John Murray, 1878).
305 Benson, *Life of Edward White Benson*, vol. I, p. 345.
306 Bolt, *As Good as God, as Clever as the Devil*, p. 119.
307 Benson, *As We Were*, p. 81.
308 Benson, *Life of Edward White Benson*, vol. I, p. 414.
309 A. C. Benson's *Prefatory Note* to E. W. Benson, *Cyprian: his life, his times, his work* (London: Macmillan, 1897), p. iv.
310 Benson, *As We Were*, p. 77.
311 Benson, *Life of Edward White Benson*, vol. II, p. 413.
312 J. N. D. Kelly, *Early Christian Doctrines* (London: A & C Black, 1960), p. 204.
313 Benson, *Cyprian*, p. 313.
314 Benson, *Cyprian*, p. 86.
315 Benson, *Life of Edward White Benson*, vol. I, p. 412.
316 Prothero, *Life and Correspondence of Stanley*, vol. II, p. 448.
317 Benson, *Life of Edward White Benson*, vol. I, p. 444. This was a diary entry in February 1878.
318 Benson, *Life of Edward White Benson*, vol. I, p. 431.
319 Benson, *Life of Edward White Benson*, vol. I, p. 531.
320 Henry Sidgwick, quoted in Benson, *Life of Edward White Benson*, vol. II, pp. 686-8.
321 Benson, *Life of Edward White Benson*, vol. I, p. 531.
322 Chadwick, *Victorian Church*, vol. 2, p. 299.
323 Benson, *Life of Edward White Benson*, vol. II, p. 665.
324 Benson, *Life of Edward White Benson*, vol. I, p. 448.
325 Chadwick, *Victorian Church*, vol. 2, pp. 389-90, n. 4.
326 T. Beeson, *The Deans* (London: SCM Press, 2004), p. 79.
327 Bolt, *As Good as God, As Clever as the Devil*, p. 152.
328 Palmer, *High & Mitred*, p. 88.
329 Benson, *Life of Edward White Benson*, vol. I, p. 547.
330 P. Collinson, N. Ramsay, and M. Sparks, *A History of Canterbury Cathedral* (Oxford: Oxford University Press, 1995), p. 276.
331 Benson, *Life of Edward White Benson*, vol. II, p. 65.
332 Benson, *Cyprian*, p. 42.
333 Benson, *Life of Edward White Benson*, vol. I, p. 526.

[334] Benson, *Life of Edward White Benson*, vol. II, p. 17.
[335] G. K. A. Bell, *Randall Davidson: Archbishop of Canterbury*, 2 vols (Oxford: Oxford University Press, 1935), vol. I, p. 63.
[336] Bell, *Randall Davidson*, vol. I, p. 65.
[337] Benson, *As We Were*, p. 98.
[338] Benson, *Life of Edward White Benson*, vol. II, p. 706.
[339] Bell, *Randall Davidson*, vol. I, p. 97.
[340] Benson, *As We Were*, pp. 216–17.
[341] Quoted in Benson, *Life of Edward White Benson*, vol. II, pp. 489–90.
[342] Benson, *Life of Edward White Benson*, vol. II, pp. 499–500.
[343] Benson, *Life of Edward White Benson*, vol. II, p. 168.
[344] G. W. E. Russell, *Edward King, sixtieth bishop of Lincoln: A Memoir* (London: Smith, Elder, 1912), p. 146, quoted without source.
[345] Benson, *Life of Edward White Benson*, vol. II, p. 324.
[346] Benson, *Life of Edward White Benson*, vol. II, p. 339.
[347] Russell, *Edward King*, pp. 147–8.
[348] Russell, *Edward King*, p. 165.
[349] J. A. Newton, "The Trial of Bishop King", *Ecclesiastical Law Journal* 5:25 (1999), pp. 265–71, here at p. 270.
[350] Church, *Life and Letters of Dean Church*, p. 349.
[351] G. W. O. Addleshaw, *The High Church Tradition: A Study in the Liturgical Thought of the Seventeenth Century* (London: Faber and Faber, 1941), p. 131.
[352] Davidson, *Lambeth Conferences*, p. 34.
[353] Listed by Davidson, *Lambeth Conferences*, p. 37.
[354] Benson, *Life of Edward White Benson*, vol. II, p. 213.
[355] Bell, *Randall Davidson*, vol. I, p. 120.
[356] Quoted in Stephenson, *Anglicanism and the Lambeth Conferences*, p. 78.
[357] Benson, *Life of Edward White Benson*, vol. II, p. 216.
[358] Pawley, *Rome and Canterbury*, p. 241.
[359] Benson, *Life of Edward White Benson*, vol. II, p. 584.
[360] Benson, *Life of Edward White Benson*, vol. II, p. 586.
[361] E. W. Benson, *Fishers of Men: Addressed to the Diocese of Canterbury in his Third Visitation* (London: Macmillan, 1893), p. 123.
[362] Benson, *Life of Edward White Benson*, vol. II, p. 584.
[363] Bell, *Randall Davidson*, vol. I, p. 230.

[364] J. G. Lockhart, *Charles Lindley, Viscount Halifax*, Part 2 (London: G. Bles, The Centenary Press, 1936), p. 47.
[365] Pawley, *Rome and Canterbury*, p. 245.
[366] Benson, *Cyprian*, p. 434.
[367] Lockhart, *Halifax*, vol. II, p. 55.
[368] Bell, *Randall Davidson*, vol. I, p. 233.
[369] *The Times*, 12 October 1896.
[370] Benson, *Life of Edward White Benson*, vol. II, p. 780.
[371] Quoted in Bolt, *As Good as God, as Clever as the Devil*, pp. 249–50.
[372] A. Roberts, *Salisbury: Victorian Titan* (London: Weidenfeld & Nicolson, 1999), p. 679.
[373] Quoted in Bell, *Randall Davidson*, vol. I, pp. 287–8.
[374] Quoted in Sandford, *Memoirs of Archbishop Temple*, vol. II, p. 45.
[375] Sandford, *Memoirs of Archbishop Temple*, vol. II, p. 245.
[376] Sandford, *Memoirs of Archbishop Temple*, vol. I, p. 87.
[377] Sandford, *Memoirs of Archbishop Temple*, vol. I, pp. 97–8.
[378] Sandford, *Memoirs of Archbishop Temple*, vol. I, p. 99.
[379] Sandford, *Memoirs of Archbishop Temple*, vol. I, p. 100.
[380] Sandford, *Memoirs of Archbishop Temple*, vol. I, p. 564.
[381] Sandford, *Memoirs of Archbishop Temple*, vol. II, p. 577.
[382] Sandford, *Memoirs of Archbishop Temple*, vol. II, p. 583.
[383] Sandford, *Memoirs of Archbishop Temple*, vol. II, p. 152.
[384] Sandford, *Memoirs of Archbishop Temple*, vol. II, p. 151.
[385] Sandford, *Memoirs of Archbishop Temple*, vol. II, p. 577, fn. 1.
[386] Hinchliff, *Frederick Temple*, p. 105.
[387] Sandford, *Memoirs of Archbishop Temple*, vol. I, p. 222.
[388] Frederick Temple, "The Education of the World", in *Essays and Reviews* (London: John Parker and Son, 1860), pp. 1–49, here at pp. 1–2; all references are to the ninth edition.
[389] Temple, "Education of the World", p. 3.
[390] Temple, "Education of the World", p. 20.
[391] Temple, "Education of the World", p. 19.
[392] Temple, "Education of the World", p. 19.
[393] Temple, "Education of the World", p. 41.
[394] Temple, "Education of the World", p. 47.
[395] Sandford, *Memoirs of Archbishop Temple*, vol. I, p. 232.

[396] Sandford, *Memoirs of Archbishop Temple*, vol. I, pp. 274–5.
[397] Sandford, *Memoirs of Archbishop Temple*, vol. I, pp. 353–4.
[398] Sandford, *Memoirs of Archbishop Temple*, vol. I, p. 275, see also footnote.
[399] Sandford, *Memoirs of Archbishop Temple*, vol. I, p. 276.
[400] Quoted in Hinchliff, *Frederick Temple*, p. 174.
[401] Sandford, *Memoirs of Archbishop Temple*, vol. I, p. 285.
[402] Sandford, *Memoirs of Archbishop Temple*, vol. I, p. 291.
[403] Sandford, *Memoirs of Archbishop Temple*, vol. I, p. 296. The protest had been addressed to Archbishop Tait on the assumption that he would be doing the consecration.
[404] Sandford, *Memoirs of Archbishop Temple*, vol. I, p. 301.
[405] Sandford, *Memoirs of Archbishop Temple*, vol. I, pp. 301–2.
[406] *Chronicle of Convocation*, quoted in Sandford, *Memoirs of Archbishop Temple*, vol. I, pp. 303–5.
[407] T. Beeson, *The Bishops* (London: SCM Press, 2002), p. 121.
[408] Sandford, *Memoirs of Archbishop Temple*, vol. I, p. 312.
[409] Sandford, *Memoirs of Archbishop Temple*, vol. I, pp. 591–2.
[410] Hinchliff, *Frederick Temple*, p. 154.
[411] Sandford, *Memoirs of Archbishop Temple*, vol. I, p. 530.
[412] Sandford, *Memoirs of Archbishop Temple*, vol. I, p. 519.
[413] Sandford, *Memoirs of Archbishop Temple*, vol. II, p. 222.
[414] *Transactions of Devonshire Association for the Advancement of Science, Literature and Arts*, vol. xxx. 28, quoted in Hinchliff, *Frederick Temple*, p. 178.
[415] F. Temple, *The relations between religion and science: eight lectures preached before the University of Oxford in the year 1884 on the foundation of the late Rev. John Bampton* (London: Macmillan, 1884), pp. 62–3.
[416] Temple, *Relations between religion and science*, pp. 107–8.
[417] Temple, *Relations between religion and science*, pp. 171, 172, 173.
[418] Temple, *Relations between religion and science*, p. 242.
[419] Sandford, *Memoirs of Frederick Temple*, vol. II, pp. 5–6.
[420] Holland, *Bundle of Memories*, pp. 160–1.
[421] Sandford, *Memoirs of Archbishop Temple*, vol. II, p. 102.
[422] Sandford, *Memoirs of Archbishop Temple*, vol. II, p. 104.
[423] Arthur Tooth of Hatcham, 1877; T. P. Dale of St Vedast's, Foster Lane in the City of London, 1880. The others were R. W. Enraght of Birmingham,

1880-1881, and S. F. Green of Manchester, 1881-1882. Later came Bell Cox of Liverpool in 1887.

424 G. L. Prestige, *St. Paul's in its Glory: A Candid History of the Cathedral 1831-1911* (London: SPCK, 1955), p. 211.
425 Sandford, *Memoirs of Archbishop Temple*, vol. II, p. 142.
426 Holland, *Bundle of Memories*, pp. 167-8.
427 Benson, *Life of Edward White Benson*, vol. II, p. 281.
428 Hinchliff, *Frederick Temple*, pp. 231-2.
429 Sandford, *Memoirs of Archbishop Temple*, vol. II, p. 79.
430 Pawley, *Rome and Canterbury*, p. 245.
431 Quoted in Stephenson, *Anglicanism and the Lambeth Conferences*, p. 106.
432 Sandford, *Memoirs of Archbishop Temple*, vol. II, p. 279.
433 Stephenson, *Anglicanism and the Lambeth Conferences*, p. 100.
434 Sandford, *Memoirs of Archbishop Temple*, vol. II, p. 283.
435 F. A. Iremonger, *William Temple, Archbishop of Canterbury: His Life and Letters* (London: Oxford University Press, 1965), p. 59.
436 Sandford, *Memoirs of Archbishop Temple*, vol. II, pp. 295-6.
437 Bell, *Randall Davidson*, vol. I, p. 373.
438 Sandford, *Memoirs of Archbishop Temple*, vol. II, p. 380.
439 Bell, *Randall Davidson*, vol. II, p. 380.

Index

Aberdeen, Lord (PM) 30, 73, 97, 115
Addington Palace (Croydon home of Archbishops of Canterbury) 60, 70, 120, 234, 263
Albert, Prince Consort 24, 94, 113, 234, 244, 245, 253
Alexander, M. S. (Bishop in Jerusalem) 44–45
Anglican Church 18, 41, 141, 167, 168, 231, 331, 338, 353,
Anglican Communion 3, 162, 166, 170, 173, 222, 228, 234, 278, 285, 340, 351
Appointment of Bishops Act, 1533. 10
Arches, Court of 65, 104–105, 123, 207, 319
Arches, Dean of 65, 123, 132, 134, 157, 161
Arnold, Matthew 1
Arnold, Thomas 1, 131, 187–189, 196, 245, 301
Association for the Relief of the Manufacturing Poor 37
Association of the Friends of the Church 59
Athanasian Creed (*Quicunque vult*) 216
Atlay, J. (Bishop of Hereford) 276
Augustine of Canterbury, Saint 339, 340
Augustine's (St), College of, Canterbury 118
Augustine (Bishop of Hippo, Saint) 61

Bagot, R. (Bishop of Oxford, then Bath and Wells) 60, 120–121, 184
Balliol College, Oxford 185, 295–296
Barclay, J. (Bishop in Jerusalem) 269
Baptism 87, 103, 106, 107, 115, 120, 281
Bath and Wells (Diocese of) 120, 122, 308, 340

Belli, A. C. (Precentor of St Paul's Cathedral) 33
Benham, W. (joint biographer of A. C. Tait) 231
Benson, E. W. (Archbishop of Canterbury) 1, 19, 45, 126, 162, 179, 234, 291, 292, 293, 308, 321, 326, 329, 333, 335, 336, 338, 339, 341–342, 348, 354; *also* Chapter 6 passim, pp. 237–289, *including*:
Canterbury appointment and enthronement 261, 262
Truro bishopric 248, 258
Truro Cathedral and Diocese 253, 258–259
Lincoln, canonry 246–247, 249
Wellington College, Headmaster 240, 244
Mary (Minnie, née Sidgwick, wife of EWB) 242, 243, 244, 247, 249
Martin. eldest son of EWB 141, 254
A. C. B. son and biographer of EWB 237, 240, 243, 245
E. F. B. (Fred), son of EWB and author 237, 238, 239, 243, 245, 250, 262, 266, 270, 287, 292
Ada, sister of EWB 242
Lis Escop (EWB's Truro residence) 254
visit to Rome, audience with the Pope 241
Ladies' Study Group (Lambeth Palace) 256
death 289
monument and grave in Canterbury Cathedral 289

Blomfield, C. J. (Bishop of London) 3, 24, 33, 41-4, 49, 50, 52-3, 65-67, 70, 75, 85, 91, 96, 105, 113, 196-197, 204, 207
Blundell's School, Tiverton 295, 326
Bodley, G. F. (architect) 330
Book of Common Prayer 18, 24, 44, 88, 89, 101-103, 114, 137, 157, 204, 208, 216, 273, 329, 345
British and Foreign Bible Society (BFBS) 8
British Critic, The 8
British Empire 2, 18, 141, 168, 171, 351
Brontë, Charlotte 137
Brontë, P. (Rector of Haworth) 137
Browne, E. H. (Bishop of Winchester) 234, 238, 261, 276, 309
Buckland, W. (Dean of Westminster) 51, 81
Bunsen, Chevalier (German statesman) 42
Burials Act, 1880 231
Burradon Colliery disaster 149
Butler, W. J. (later Dean of Lincoln) 176, 271

Calvinism 81, 184
Cambridge Camden Society 316
Canada, Church in 170, 172, 224
Caroe, W. D. (architect) 336
Caroline of Brunswick (consort of George IV) 27, 38
Carter, E. F. (Canon) 257
census figures 4, 91, 140
Chambers, R., *Vestiges of the Natural History of Creation* 82
Charles I, King 14
Charlotte, Queen Consort of George III 31
cholera (London outbreak, 1866) 5, 192, 200, 315
Church Association, the 121, 272-275, 277-278, 330-331
Church Building Society 8, 9, 40, 92, 150
Church in India 42, 228
Church Missionary Society (CMS) 41-42, 45, 118-119, 167, 169
Church of Scotland, General Assembly 342

Church Union, English 208, 272-273, 285
Church, R. W. (Dean of St Paul's) 89
Clapham Sect 7, 8, 78
Claughton, T. L. (Bishop of Rochester, later St Albans) 253
Clergy Discipline Act, 1892 319
Colenso, J. W. (Bishop of Natal) 45, 131, 162-165, 170-172, 174-175, 177, 266-269
Coleridge, S. T. 4
Colonial Bishoprics Fund (1841) 41, 118
Commons, House of 11, 15, 54, 55, 152, 213, 220
Confirmation, sacrament of 23, 32, 95, 127, 139, 145, 154, 198, 234, 301, 313, 319, 328
Convocation of York, (revival) 11, 150-154, 353
Convocation 111-117, 137, 150-152, 172, 197, 200, 202, 209, 215, 217-220, 224-225, 232-233, 263, 283, 312, 319
Conyingham, Marquis 22, 24
Corporation Act (1661) and Test Act (1673), & repeal of 14, 15, 47, 51
Council on Education, Committee of 296
Creighton, M. (Bishop of Peterborough later London) 338, 339, 347
Cumberland, Duke of 83
Cyprian (Bishop of Carthage, martyred in 258) 246, 249-250, 256-257, 263, 276, 280, 284, 287, 354

Darwin, Charles 50, 81, 82, 155, 324-325
Davidson, R. T. (later Archbishop of Canterbury) 166, 182, 195-196, 199, 224, 230, 234, 264-265, 274, 279, 280-281, 283, 286, 288, 291, 294, 301, 326, 347-349
Davies Gilbert 50
Deceased Wife's Sister Marriage Bill 80
Denison, G. A. (Vicar of East Brent, later Archdeacon of Taunton) 120-124, 202, 215, 233
Devonshire Association for the Advancement of Science 322

INDEX

Disraeli, B. (PM, Lord Beaconsfield) 12, 180, 181, 211, 213, 219, 221, 231, 244, 252, 261
Ditcher, J. (initiator of litigation) 123
Divorce Act 1857 80, 137, 199
Doane, J. W. (Bishop of New Jersey) 170
Dock Strike, London 1888 331, 333
Durham bishopric 24, 69

Ebbsfleet, Kent, landing place of Augustine of Canterbury 340
Ecclesiastical Commissioners, formerly Ecclesiastical Duties and Revenue Commission; later Church Commissioners 65, 70, 93, 96–97, 191, 196, 336
  Dean and Chapter Act 67
  Established Church Act 67
  Pluralities Act 67
  Estates Committee 191
Ecclesiastical Titles Act 111
Education Act (Forster Act, 1870) 257
Edward I, King 112, 151
Edward VII, King (and coronation) 347, 348, 355
Elizabeth I, Queen 51, 85
Ellicott, C. J. (Bishop of Gloucester) 181
Emancipation Act, Roman Catholic 14, 15, 39, 46–47, 51–54, 84, 109, 182, 212
English Church Union 208, 272, 284
Enthronement (Enthronisation, Inthronement) 48, 96, 99, 109, 197, 311, 335, 337
Episcopal appointments, pre-Reformation 10
Episcopal Church, Scotland 120, 165, 168
Episcopal Church in USA, see USA
Erastianism 11, 13, 17, 84, 87, 91, 98, 108, 117, 163, 203
Essays and Reviews 125, 154–159, 161–162, 171, 201–202, 241, 293, 302, 306–311, 354
Established Church Act, 1836 67, 132
Eton College 79, 80
Evangelical Alliance 121, 144

Evangelical Revival 6, 18, 134, 228
Exeter cathedral reredos controversy 316–317

Farrer, F. (Dean of Canterbury) 337
Farrer, W. J. 296
Forbes, A. P. (Bishop of Brechin) 145
Forster Education Act, 1870 257
Four Tutors, protesters against *Tracts for the Times* 186, 188
Frederic William IV, King of Prussia 42
Friends of the Church, Association of 59
Fund, Bishop of London's 197

General Elections
  1830 15, 54
  1868 181, 212, 308
  1874 218, 222
  1880 231
George I, King 12, 13 and 112
George III, King 31
George IV, King 15, 21, 23, 37, 38, 47, 53, 54, 84
Gladstone, W. E. (PM) 12, 31, 98, 129, 181, 193, 212–215, 218, 221, 231, 237, 244, 261, 288–289, 308, 326
Glasgow (University of) 184, 187
Glastonbury 340
Gobat, S. (Bishop in Jerusalem) 44
Gordon Riots, 1780 51
Gorham, G. C. 81, 87, 102–109, 113, 115, 120, 123–124, 204
Gray, R. (Bishop, later Archbishop of Capetown) 45, 162–164, 166, 171–176, 225, 267
Grey, Lord (PM) 15, 54, 55, 57

Hackney Phalanx 8, 9, 36, 37, 39, 40, 59, 69, 78, 97
Halifax, Viscount (Wood, C. L.) 256, 284–288, 338, 348
Hamilton, W. K. (Bishop of Salisbury) 157, 174, 217
Hampden, R. D. and controversies (later Bishop of Hereford) 60, 62–63, 71–74, 77, 94, 96, 98, 113, 138, 297

Harcourt, V. (Archbishop of York) 42, 65, 66, 71, 132
Harrison, Benjamin (Archdeacon, Chaplain to A.C. Tait) 26, 28–29, 42, 45, 53, 59, 63
Harrow School 130, 131, 162
Hawarden (country seat of W. E. Gladstone) 288
Hierarchy, Roman Catholic 109, 110, 111, 284
Henry VIII, King 10
Holland, General Assembly of Church of 338
Holland, H. S. (Canon of St Paul's and Oxford don) 1, 2, 327, 331, 332
Holmfirth reservoir disaster 148
Hone, W. (pamphleteer) 39
Hook, W. (Vicar of Leeds, later Dean of Chichester) 5, 9, 140–144, 146, 211
Hopkins, H. (Presiding Bishop PECUSA) 119, 169, 170, 175, 177
House of Laymen 263, 283
Howley, W., Archbishop of Canterbury 9, 15, 77, 83, 93, 94, 97, 98, 125, 137, 163, 262, 336, 346, 352; *also* Chapter 2 passim pp. 21-75, *including:*
Canterbury appointment 20, 47, 48, 49
Enthronement by proxy 48, 98
London bishopric 31
Queen Victoria, Accession 22
Regius Professor of Divinity and canonry, Oxford 27, 28
House of Lords 37, 52, 55–56
Howley's library, Canterbury Cathedral 29, 30
overseas dioceses 41, 42, 45, 46
death 75
monument in Canterbury 125–126

India, Church in 42, 176, 227, 228
Irish Church Temporalities Act, 1833 16
Irish Church Disestablishment 212–213, 214, 215, 223, 308

Jelf, R. W. (Principal King's College London) 87, 90
Jenkyns, R. (Master of Balliol College) 184, 295
Jerusalem Bishopric 42–44, 118, 269, 270
Jeune, F. (Master of Pembroke College, Oxford, later Bishop of Peterborough) 193
Jowett, B. (contributor to *Essays and Reviews*, later Master of Balliol College) 154, 155, 201, 297, 309,

Kay Shuttleworth, James 296
Keble, J. (Tractarian) 17, 58, 61–62, 64, 88, 112, 121–122, 129, 149
Kersfoot, J. B. (Bishop of Pittsburgh) 223
King, B. (Rector of St George's in the East, ritualism dispute) 205, 206
King, E. (Bishop of Lincoln and ritualism case) 139, 251, 271–274, 277–278, 329, 340
King's College, London 87, 334
Kneller Hall, near Twickenham 297–300

Lake, W. (Dean of Durham) 187, 189
Lambeth 'Quadrilateral' 281–282
Lambeth Conference 1867 45, 165–167, 170–179, 223, 353–353
Lambeth Conference 1878 167, 222–230
Lambeth Conference 1888 239, 270, 279–283, 354
Lambeth Conference 1897 239, 283, 339–342, 354
Lambeth Palace 31, 44–46, 69, 74, 96, 173, 213, 218, 226, 265, 283, 328
Lambeth Palace Library 59, 227, 277
Laud, W. (Archbishop of Canterbury) 168, 219
Lee, J. P. (headmaster, later Bishop of Manchester) 240, 241
Leeds Vicarage Act 144
Leeds Parish Church (St Peter) 145
Leeds, St Saviour's Church 143, 144–145, 146, 148, 154
Legge, E. (Dean of Windsor, later Bishop of Oxford) 30

INDEX

Leo XIII (Pope), Papal Bull (*Apostolicae curae*) and Responsio 287–288, 338–339
Leopold, King of Belgians 22
Lewis, J. T., (Bishop of Ontario) 171
Library of the Fathers 61
Liddell, H. G. (later Dean of Christ Church, Oxford) 193
Liddell, R. 207
Liddon, H. P. (Canon of St Paul's and Oxford don) 60, 80, 88, 155, 157, 199, 212, 216, 217, 241, 269, 276, 277, 330
Lightfoot, J. B. (school friend of E. W. Benson, Bishop of Durham) 240, 241, 247, 249, 253–254, 274, 283, 326
Lincoln Cathedral 273
Liverpool Diocese 91
Liverpool, Lord (PM) 30, 33, 38, 40
Lloyd, C. (Bishop of Oxford) 47
London Gazette 48
Longley, C. T., Archbishop of Canterbury 45, 69, 72, 93, 113, 119–120, 181, 201, 210, 212, 217, 223, 225, 229, 231, 279 352–353; *also* Chapter 4 passim pp. 127–180, *including*:
Canterbury appointment 127, 129, 150, 153, 163
enthronement in Canterbury 154
York archbishopric 150, 153
Durham bishopric 128, 149, 150
Ripon bishopric 69, 93, 112, 120, 128, 132, 133, 134, 136, 137, 145, 149, 169
Headmaster of Harrow School 130–131, 148, 162
Caroline (née Parnell, wife of C. T. L.) 131
death 180

Macrorie, W. K. (Bishop of Natal) 164, 166, 267, 268
Magee, W. C. (Bishop of Peterborough, later Archbishop of York) 211
Maltby, E. (Bishop of Durham) 24, 71, 73, 128, 148, 199

Manchester, Bishopric of 68, 240
Manners Sutton, C. (Archbishop of Canterbury) 9, 13, 21, 29, 31–32, 37, 41, 46–47, 54, 125, 351
Manning, H. E. (Anglican priest, later RC cardinal) 109, 122, 284, 331–333
Martin, F. (benefactor of E. W. Benson) 240, 241
Melbourne, Lord (PM) 12, 23, 38, 62, 63, 64, 66, 67, 70, 131, 132, 296
Merewether, J. (Dean of Hereford) 73
Milman, H. H. (Dean of St Paul's) 198
Monsell, H. (Superior, Clewer Sisterhood) 183
Moore, J. (Archbishop of Canterbury) 47, 168
Mozley, T. 48
Musgrave, T. (Archbishop of York) 71, 105, 113, 150–152

Napoleonic War 52
National Society for the Education of the Poor in the Principles of the Established Church 58, 36, 135, 257, 283
Newman, J. H. (Tractarian, later RC cardinal) 17, 43, 58–64, 81, 87, 89, 90, 130, 140, 143, 185–186, 187, 203, 296, 346
Nightingale, Florence 309
non-residence of clergy and pluralism 32, 33, 34, 36

O'Connell, D. 52
Old Catholics 229, 279
Old Palace, Canterbury, the 336
open-air preaching (ACT) 198
Ornaments rubric, *Book of Common Prayer* 147, 178, 206, 208
Osborne House, Isle of Wight 127, 197, 212, 234, 346
Oxford Movement 17, 18, 58, 59, 61, 62, 88, 89, 101, 110, 111, 134, 140, 185, 186, 314, 316, 340, 353

Palmerston, Viscount (PM) 127, 128, 129, 148, 150, 195, 196
Parnell, H. B. (Baron Congleton) 131
Parry, E. (Bishop of Dover) 215, 234, 263
Patriarchs
Antioch 270
Constantinople 270
Jerusalem 270
Peel, Sir R. (PM) 26, 39, 53, 54, 64, 65, 66, 128
Perceval, S. (PM) 28
Percival, J. (Bishop of Hereford) 301
Percy, H. (Bishop of Carlisle) 194
Phillpotts, H. (Bishop of Exeter) 71, 72, 81, 103–109, 113, 114, 125, 255, 311, 314, 320
Pitt, W., the Younger, PM 13, 27
Pius IX (Pope) 110
Pluralities Act, 1838 67
Ponsonby, H (Queen Victoria's Private Secretary) 265
Poole, A (curate) 209
Poor Law Amendment Act 85, 86
Portal, E. F. (RC priest; pen name F. Dablus) 285–287, 338
Privy Council 31, 32, 165, 296, 347
Privy Council, Judicial Committee of 104, 107, 115, 123, 153, 157, 164, 165, 177, 202, 207–288, 275, 278, 317
Prynne, G. R. (parish priest, St Peter's, Plymouth) 315
Public Schools Commission, 1864 302
Public Worship Regulation Act, 1874 219, 221, 231, 234, 271, 272, 277, 314, 315, 331, 353
Pusey, E. B. (Tractarian and Oxford don) 32, 42, 43, 60, 61, 63, 64, 88, 89, 90, 115, 124, 130, 142–145, 203, 212, 216–217, 230, 309

Quartely Review 125, 155, 246
Queen's Bench, Court of 73, 121, 123, 151, 274–275

Randolph, J. (Bishop of London) 30, 35
Read, E. de L. (litigation initiator) 272

Real Presence, and reservation of sacrament 120, 122, 148, 346
Reform Act 1832 (Representation of the People Act) 14, 16, 54, 57, 85, 112
Ridge, E. L. (chaplain to EWB and FT) 292
Ripon, Diocese & Cathedral 112, 132–137, 299
ritualism etc. 17, 18, 60, 62, 88–89, 101, 111, 120, 147, 172, 178, 183, 200, 202–204, 207, 208, 217–221, 223, 228, 251, 262, 270–274, 276, 278, 285, 314–315, 329–330, 345, 353–354
Rolle, Lady (benefactress of Diocese of Truro) 321
Roman Catholicism 110, 203, 204, 288
Rose, H. J. (parish priest) 59
rotten boroughs 15, 54–55
Royal Commission
on Ecclesiastical Courts 274
on Education 334
on Oxford University 192–194
on ritual 147, 217
Royal Victorian Order 349
Rugby School 1, 154, 184, 187–190, 201, 241, 243–244, 294, 299, 300–302, 322
Russell, Lord John (PM) 37, 57, 68, 71, 72, 73, 77, 94–95, 138, 192, 194
Ryder, H. (Bishop of Gloucester, later Coventry) 97

sacramental confession 18, 101–102, 145–146, 208–210, 230, 273, 284, 314, 330, 334, 345
Salisbury, Lord (PM) 291–4
Sandford, E. G. (editor of *Memoir* of F. Temple) 294, 296, 308, 314, 322, 329, 348
Seabury, S. (first bishop in USA) 168–169
Sellon, P. L. (founder of the Sisters of Mercy) 314
Selwyn, G. A. (Bishop of New Zealand, later Lichfield) 44–5, 175, 222, 223–225, 229

Shaftesbury, Lord (formerly Ashley) 42, 121, 127, 128, 137, 196, 198, 219–220, 309
Short, Thomas Vowler (Rector of Bloomsbury, later Bishop of St Asaph) 130, 133
Simeon, C. (Cambridge vicar and don) 5, 6, 78, 79, 93
Simeon Trustees 6
Sinclair, G. R. (first organist, Truro Cathedral) 260
Smith, Sidney (Canon of St Paul's) 7, 25, 33, 48, 66, 67, 103, 197
Society for Promoting Christian Knowledge (SPCK) 128, 141
Society for the Propagation of the Gospel (SPG) 41, 46, 57, 118–119, 152, 169–171, 173
Spens, A. (ecclesiastical lawyer) 220
Spurgeon, C. H. (Baptist preacher) 139
St James' Church, Picadilly 197
St James's Hall, London 212, 217
St Paul's Cathedral 198, 224, 254, 283, 326, 330–331, 339–340, 346
St Peter at Gowts, Lincoln 273
St Augustine of Canterbury anniversary celebrations 1897 339–340
Stanley, A. P. (Dean of Westminster) 156, 213
Stuart, E. (Vicar of St Mary Magdalene, Munster Square, London) 207
Stubbs, W. (Bishop of Chester, later Oxford) 274–277, 338
Sumner, J. B., Archbishop of Canterbury 5–6, 34, 69, 72, 74, 135, 154, 163, 167–8, 190, 203, 207, 257, 352; *also* Chapter 3 passim pp. 77–126, *including*:
Canterbury appointment 77, 94, 97–98
enthronement in Canterbury 77, 98, 99, 109
Chester bishopric 34, 83, 92, 93
Durham canonries 82
JBS as an author 81, 82–83, 86
schools work 91–93, 100, 116
Marianne (née Robertson, wife of JBS) 79, 83
Oxford Movement, opinion of 87, 89, 90
death 125
monument in Canterbury Cathedral 125–126
Sumner, R. C. (Bishop of Winchester, brother of JBS) 78, 98

Tait, A. C., Archbishop of Canterbury 13, 129, 149, 155, 157, 168, 174, 176, 179, 237, 254, 261, 264, 274, 278, 279, 280, 296, 299, 308, 310, 337, 353, 354; *also* Chapter 5, passim pp. 181–235, *including*:
Canterbury appointment 210–211
enthronement in Canterbury 197
London bishopric 196, 197, 200, 203, 205, 208
Rugby School Headmaster 189, 191
Carlisle deanery 190, 191, 192
Catherine (née Spooner, wife of ACT) and death 188, 189, 190, 195
Craufurd (only son of ACT) visit to USA, death 195, 225, 226
Edith (daughter of ACT, wife of R. T. Davidson) 231, 264, 291
Lucy (daughter of ACT, friend of Minnie Benson) 194–195, 243
family bereavements 195
Stonehouse (ACT's private residence) 210
Wade, Lady C. (sister of ACT) 183
health of ACT 182, 190, 195, 210, 215–216
reputation in House of Lords, and final speech 199, 200
death 234
memorial in Canterbury Cathedral 235
Temperance League, National 320
Temperance Society, Church of England 320

Temple. F., Archbishop of Canterbury 29, 154–155, 179, 201–202, 238, 241, 243, 244, 246, 253, 254, 259, 264, 276, 284, 354; *also* Chapter 7 passim pp. 291–350, including:
Canterbury appointment 335–337
Canterbury enthronement 337
London bishopric 326, 327–328, 330, 331–333, 335
Exeter bishopric, choice of appointments, controversy 307, 308, 310, 311, 327–328
Rugby School, Headmaster 299, 300, 308, 322
Lefkada, birthplace of FT (formerly Santa Maura) 294
Beatrice. B. (née Lascelles, wife of FT) 318
Dorcas (mother of FT) 294, 307
Janetta ('Netta' sister of FT) 300
William (younger son of FT, later Archbishop of Canterbury) 318, 343, 349
Old Palace, Canterbury (restoration as residence) 336
Essays and Reviews (FT's contribution, "The Education of the World") 302–307, 308, 309, 310–311, 312, 322, 354
Bampton Lectures, 1884 (FT on "science") 202, 322–325
Coronation of King Edward VII 347, 348
health and failing eyesight 343, 348–349
House of Lords, final speech 349
death and monument in Canterbury Cathedral 349–350
Thomson, W. (Archbishop of York) 129, 157, 161, 173, 211, 213, 218, 221, 229, 230, 279
Tracts for the Times 16, 17, 58, 59, 60, 62, 89, 185, 186
Tract 90 60, 87, 89, 90, 140, 155, 185, 186, 201, 203, 204

USA, Anglicanism in, and General Convention (PECUSA) 46, 118, 120, 141, 168–169, 223–234, 226, 228, 281, 341

Van Mildert, W. (Bishop of Durham) 9, 33, 46, 53, 56
Vatican Council, 1870 183, 223, 228, 229, 338
Vaughan, H. (Cardinal) 285, 286, 288, 338–339
Venn, H. 167–8
Venn, J. (Rector of Clapham) 8
Victoria, Queen,
baptism and confirmation 22, 23
accession 6, 23, 265, 339
coronation 23, 321, 346
marriage 24
death and funeral 346–347
Villiers, H. M. (Bishop of Carlisle) 194

Wade, J. (author: *The Extraordinary Black Book*) 35
Ward, W. G. (Tractarian disciple, later Roman Catholic) 185, 203, 296
Waterloo churches 9, 40
Watson, John. J. (Vicar of Hackney) 8
Watson, Joshua H. (philanthropist) 8, 9, 36, 40, 41
Wellesley, G. (Dean of Windsor) 235, 309
Wellington College 243–246, 249, 253, 258, 293
Wellington, Duke (PM) 14, 15, 46, 47, 52–54, 64, 83–84, 138
Wells Cathedral 121
Westcott, B. F. (school friend of EWB, later Bishop of Durham) 238–239, 240, 247, 249, 254
Westminster Abbey 39, 119, 170, 176, 177, 198, 248, 265, 268, 310
Whately, (Archbishop of Dublin) 58
Whitehouse, H. J. (Bishop of Illinois) 173
Wilberforce, H. (parish priest, later RC convert) 98–99, 109

Wilberforce, R. I. (Archdeacon, later RC convert) 109, 117, 150
Wilberforce, S. (Bishop of Oxford, later Winchester) 3, 72, 94–96, 115, 125, 129, 149, 154–155, 174, 181, 210, 224, 245, 297
Wilberforce, W. 78, 83
Wilkinson, G. H. (Bishop of Truro, later Perth) 343
William IV, King 14, 21, 23, 54, 63, 75, 149
Williams, R. (contributor to *Essays and Reviews*) 155–159, 161, 202
Wilson, H. B. (contributor to *Essays and Reviews*) 155–158, 161, 201, 202

Winchester College 25–26
Windsor (including St George's Chapel) 21–22, 79, 95, 248, 340, 347
Wiseman, N. (Cardinal) 110, 111
Wordsworth, Charles (Bishop of St Andrews) 172
Wordsworth, Christopher (Bishop of Lincoln) 131, 232, 246–247, 254
Wordsworth, J. (Bishop of Salisbury) 276, 338–339
Wordsworth, William 4
Wright, W. 35

York, Diocese 132, 133, 135

Lightning Source UK Ltd.
Milton Keynes UK
UKHW021140131219
355327UK00015B/1768/P